KU-447-267

MOON
MARKED
AND
TOUCHED
BY SUN

PLAYS BY
AFRICAN–AMERICAN
WOMEN

EDITED BY
SYDNÉ MAHONE

Theatre Communications Group

1994

Copyright © 1994 by Theatre Communications Group, Inc.
Introduction copyright © 1994 by Sydné Mahone

Moon Marked and Touched by Sun *is published by*
Theatre Communications Group, Inc., 355 Lexington Ave., New York, NY 10017.

All rights reserved. Except for brief passages quoted in newspaper,
magazine, radio or television reviews, no part of this book may be reproduced in any form or by any
means, electronic or mechanical, including photocopying
or recording, or by an information storage and retrieval system, without permission in writing from
the publisher.

Professionals and amateurs are hereby warned that this material,
being fully protected under the Copyright Laws of the United States of America
and all other countries of the Berne and Universal Copyright Conventions,
is subject to a royalty. All rights including, but not limited to, professional, amateur, recording,
motion picture, recitation, lecturing, public reading, radio and
television broadcasting, and the rights of translation into foreign languages are
expressly reserved. Particular emphasis is placed on the question of readings
and all uses of these plays by educational institutions, permission for which must be
secured from the authors' representatives.

Owing to limitations of space, all individual copyrights, authors'
representatives and contact information will be found at the end of the book,
which will serve as an extension of the copyright page.

The photographs in this book are reproduced by kind permission of the following: p. 145, Diana
Blok; p. 189, Joseph Schuyler; p. 215, Wendy Jane Workman; p. 242, T. Charles Erickson. All
uncredited photographs courtesy of the individual authors.

Moon marked and touched by sun : plays by African-American women /
edited by Sydné Mahone.—1st ed.
Contents: White chocolate for my father / by Laurie Carlos—Cage rhythm /
by Kia Corthron—X / by Thulani Davis—WOMBmanWARs / by Judith Alexa Jackson—The
dramatic circle / by Adrienne Kennedy—Sally's rape /
by Robbie McCauley—The death of the last Black man in the whole entire world /
by Suzan-Lori Parks—The mojo and the sayso / by Aishah Rahman—
Excerpts from The resurrection of the daughter: Liliane / by Ntozake Shange—Excerpts from Fires
in the mirror / by Anna Deavere Smith—
Live and in color! / by Danitra Vance.
ISBN 1-55936-065-8 (pbk.)
1. American drama—Afro-American authors. 2. American drama—Women authors.
3. Afro-American women—Drama. I. Mahone, Sydné.
PS628.N4M66   1994
812'.540809287—dc20   93-11831   CIP

Cover painting: Moon Masque (1971) by Lois Mailou Jones
Cover and book design by Cynthia Krupat
Composition by The Typeworks

First Edition, April 1994

My work is dedicated to my mother,
Mary Lou Mahone,
whose awesome love and laughter
move the whole world out of my way;
her mother, Ethel Romina Maxwell,
my father's mother, Josephine Hall Mahone,
and my great-grandmother, Mary Lou Elder,
my ancestral guides.
In praise of the divine MotherSpirit.

Acknowledgements

My family sustains my strength, courage and sense of purpose. For their love and support, I thank: my mother, Mary Lou Mahone; my father, Arthur Freeman Mahone; my sister, the eldest, Ardis Lynn; my brothers Bruce Michael, Malcolm Freeman, CerCi Anthony, Jonathan Jai and Timothy Todd; my niece and nephew, Jennifer Elaine and Sean Keir; all of our children; my uncles, Chester and LeRoy Sheard; my cousin, Karen Jelks; and the matriarchs, Gertrude Sarah Glass and Catherine Sheard.

I am eternally grateful to the following people: Lynda Gravatt, for honoring my spirit/work, reading the raw first drafts and inspiring me through her own artistry, brilliance, humor and love; Janiera Warren, for constant friendship and wise counsel; my mentors, Dr. Cheryl A. Wall, Avery Brooks and Dr. Elizabeth Comtois; my Crossroads Theatre Company family, beginning with Ricardo Khan for being the dream-keeper and nurturing my growth with his trust, Lee Kenneth Richardson for the encouragement to become a dramaturg, Ken Johnson for the hope in the midnight hours, Pamela Faith Jackson for unfaltering faith, and the staff for keeping our theatre alive; the sisters of Sangoma; Steven Samuels for bringing his respect, passion and fierce intelligence to the editorial process; the Theatre Communications Group staff, especially Gillian Richards and Linda MacColl for copy editing and proofreading with such care and concern; Dr. Daniel Margolin for getting me off my feet; and all my cherished friends who have blessed this book with their joy—especially Joan Wilk, Valeri Fekete, Erma Walker Holmes, Kali, Georgette Kelley, Barbara Seyda and Meredith Woods. I honor Audre Lorde and Lois Mailou Jones for vision and artistic mothering.

Lastly, I give my thanks to the playwrights for their pure genius, vision and power.

—Sydné Mahone

Contents

MOON MARKED AND
TOUCHED BY SUN

INTRODUCTION

by Sydné Mahone

Moon marked and touched by sun
my magic is unwritten
but when the sea turns back
it will leave my shape behind

—AUDRE LORDE, *from "A Woman Speaks"*

As mysterious and metamorphic as the ocean's markings upon the sand, the plays in this anthology make new markings and thus alter the shape and shoreline of the world dramatic canon. The tradition of African-American women playwrights can be traced back as far as the late nineteenth century; nevertheless, contemporary women playwrights remain on the edge, scrawling in the margins of today's mainstream theatre. But as the author, bell hooks, so eloquently asserts in *from margin to center*, the margin need not be defined as a place that holds markings of less value; rather, for African Americans, it is a "site of resistance" to racial and gender oppression, silence, despair and invisibility. I have come to view these writers as Seers perched on the rim of revelation.

Moon marked. . . . Is there such a thing as the female imagination? Who knows? I do know that the moon's phases make of us the "restless pounding oceans," as Audre Lorde writes later in the poem from which I take the title of this anthology. Magnetic and relentless, the playwrights' words are coursing through the inner terrain of the psyche like blood and mother's milk, making waves, turning the tides, constantly shifting the coastlines of consciousness; and here, reshaping dramatic form and narrative.

Moon marked. . . . Waiting, wading through the dark lunar phases, fixing the Third Eye on the tip of the crescent moon, hanging dreams and visions there like prayer flags or clean laundry, in preparation for the adornment of oneself, and for the proper greeting of the new day. In tune with the cycles of the moon—swelling, maturing, releasing, rebirthing, filling up with self. Burrowing into the darkness, digging among the bones, these artists—archaeologists of spirit and psyche—recompose the fractured self.

Touched by sun. . . . Womanwords and images are unleashed with the fury of tongues tipped with lightning. Sparks of truth illuminate the path towards transcendence of the gender-bent and race-wrung perspectives that would bar us from occupying the syntactical place of "subject" in our own narratives. These playwrights speak for the silent ones; they listen for the ancestral whisper as they carve new forms from the clay of intuitive impulse and recover lost wisdom from the meticulous manipulation of craft.

Touched by sun. . . . These playwrights venture beyond the linear, the cornered, the squared-off edge of dramatic convention to find the rounded edge of reinvention that turns one's gaze towards the morning of sacred memory, to the ubiquitous noonday sun of perfect presence, and on to the midnight of imagination.

The work of visionaries, these plays confront our pain and carry us beyond it to that simple turn of thought, that dramatic spiraling up which releases one from the prison of forgetfulness. Omissions are admitted, distortions are corrected and sometimes by the mere act of speech—naming—balance is restored.

Word weavers. Wor(l)d weavers. Literary quilters placing memories alongside imaginings; threading testimony through ritual; myth-making, uncoiling truth from skeins of make-believe. These diviners nestle with their dreams and nightmares in the bosom of night, knowing it to be the womb of light. Their plays live in that embrace of dark and light, where life reveals its magical and mystical meanings.

Each writer in some way has created a testament to Originality, defining theatre on her own terms. Borrowing from a wide range of styles and genres, they create a new matrix for the narrative of the ever-evolving human spirit. The emergent aesthetic is one that is luminous like moonbeams; cyclical, circular, spiraling in its progression; psychically fluent; incisive like teeth; poetic, revelatory, oracular and sacred. As they crack open the stories that reveal shrouded truths, they unearth the voices that have dwelled too long in the canyons of silence.

If we place these playwrights, along with all other playwrights, in a circle, then there is no margin. Each writer claims her space on the continuum of dramatists who play a dynamic role in the evolution of the artform, using it as a tool for the transformation of human consciousness. As is true for all dramatists, the full experience of their work lies in the magical space of the theatre—where the human instrument of the actor, the light, the sound, the spectacle and the language awaken the senses. The words of the texts in this volume are the maps, the mothered instructions for the ritual reawakening of the feminine spirit within us all.

The Social Context

When I consider the status of African-American women playwrights within the social context, my first thoughts wrap around the high-profile ascensions of black women in the larger American society. Call the roll on recent "first black woman" titleholders: Toni Morrison, winner of the 1993 Nobel Prize for literature; Dr. Joycelyn Elders, surgeon general; Illinois Democratic senator Carol Moseley Braun; Sharon Pratt Kelly, mayor of Washington, D.C.; Dr. Johnetta Cole, president of Spelman College; Queen Latifah, ruler of her own rap empire, Tommy Boy Records; Oprah Winfrey, the only African-American woman owner of a television studio, the wealthiest black woman of all (prime) time. And the list rolls on. As we entered the nineties, more than fifteen million strong, we made up eight-and-one-half percent of the American population, twelve-and-one-half percent of American women and fifty-two percent of African Americans.* No question: African-American women wield power in certain circles.

My second thoughts wrap around the various crises facing all women in America. Every day five women lose their lives in domestic violence, murdered by men they know. More women end up in hospitals because they have been raped and battered by men than women needing treatment for cancer and heart attack. Clearly, black women are among the victims

---

*These figures and those that follow are drawn from the following sources: for population and single mothers below the poverty line, "The Facts of the Matter," *Essence*, May 1990; for rape, abuse and hospitalization, "The Other Facts of Life," *Deals with the Devil and Other Reasons to Riot*, Pearl Cleage (Ballantine Books, New York, NY, 1993), "AIDS: In Living Color," Beth Richie, and "Teenage Pregnancy: A Case for National Action," Faye Wattleton, in *Black Women's Health Book*, edited by Evelyn C. White (Seal Press, Seattle, WA, 1990); for poverty among African Americans, "Facts & Figures—The Widening Wealth Gap," *Black Enterprise*, January 1992; for women in prison, "Bar None: The Health of Incarcerated Black Women," Sean Reynolds, in *Black Women's Health Book*, op. cit.; and for race/gender median income and family composition, "The State of Black America 1992," Playthell Benjamin, *Emerge*, March 1992.

and casualties of our losing battle against drugs and violence in our communities. The number one cause of death for us is AIDS; fifty-two percent
of the women with AIDS-related illness or diagnoses of HIV-positive are
black. The fragility of the black family translates into one in four black
children born to teen mothers. Fifty percent of all black households are
headed by single mothers, many of whom swell the ranks of the working
poor. One-quarter of all black families are living below the poverty level;
more than two-thirds of these families are headed by single mothers.
Forty-three percent of the women incarcerated in federal prisons are
African-American. Our median income is still below that of black men,
and of white women and men.

It's all true. In terms of economics and power, a few of us are at the
top, many of us are at the bottom and most of us are in the eye of the
storm. I place the African-American women playwrights represented here
in the thick of it all. They're clockin' it, bringin' it down front and unlocking our own code/conspiracy of silence.

The Theatre Industry

Like every other African-American woman—be she first or last—the playwright is living in a very hostile environment. The American theatre is
still, for the most part, a white patriarchal institution. Its hostility towards
African-American women writers and "others" has been expressed, not
through malevolence, but more dangerously through avoidance and neglect.

On the commercial theatre scene, the black woman playwright is rendered invisible. When was the last time you saw a play on Broadway written by an African-American woman? For me it was ten years ago, when
Whoopi Goldberg appeared in her one-woman show. An even more gall-
ing fact is that at the time of this writing there is not a single black play on
Broadway. Obviously, Broadway is not the only measure of success, but it
does reflect the largest capital investment in American theatre, conferring
star status upon its writers.

In the nonprofit professional theatre, African-American women writers are present, but a survey of plays produced delivers an alarming comment on the nature of that presence. The 1991-92 season preview of
American Theatre magazine included listings for more than 190 theatre
companies nationwide, a handful of which were African-American companies. Of the more than 1100 plays scheduled, nearly sixty were written
by African Americans, representing approximately five percent of the

total productions. About fifteen of those plays were written by African-American women—one-third of the black plays, and roughly one-and-one-half percent of the overall total.

Taken at face value, these figures suggest that the contributions of African-American women playwrights are insignificant. In contrast with this bleak quantitative summary, *Moon Marked and Touched by Sun*, a volume of contemporary, cutting-edge plays, invites a qualitative assessment in hopes of yielding a deeper understanding of the true value of black women playwrights.

Over the past nine years, in my work as a dramaturg at Crossroads Theatre Company and as a panelist for many playwriting awards, I have read hundreds of plays in search of "the extraordinary voice" in today's theatre. The playwrights in this volume represent some of the voices I find most compelling, thought-provoking and stylistically fresh. Defiantly poised on the vanguard, they sustain my hope for a dynamically evolving theatre as we move towards the year 2000 and beyond.

If these plays exemplify excellence and innovation in dramatic writing, then how do we account for their near absence in mainstream theatre? One could argue that their very extraordinary qualities justify their "outsider" status; to include them would somehow compromise or corrupt their integrity, thus diminishing their power to challenge the status quo. If this were the case, the pages of modern theatre history—from Bertolt Brecht to George C. Wolfe—would never have been written. So the question remains: Why are the plays of black women writers so rarely produced? The answer is a complex one involving the tangled web of economics, race and gender politics, and social conservatism—all of which have a direct impact upon the theatre as an industry and an artform.

The first point sounds like a cliché: America is a profit-driven, racist, sexist and homophobic society. Black women playwrights are not included in mainstream American theatre because their work in some way challenges or simply does not reflect the images and interests of the financially dominant culture, the white patriarchy. The black female playwright presents an alternative viewpoint and therefore is more likely to be embraced in those venues that serve alternative, progressive artistic agendas.

In most cultures, the traditional theatrical vocabulary includes character types—archetypes, stereotypes and prototypes. We have heroes and villains, foils and *raisonneurs.* Historically, male playwrights, both white and black, have molded the image of the black woman into the stereotypes of mammies, "ho's," bitches and loons. In this way, the American theatre has devalued and denied the human dignity of African-American women.

The very act of a black woman telling her story, speaking her truth, can be perceived as an act of resistance to oppression; the real power in her exercise of artistic freedom is the casting of her own image by her own hand. This process of self-definition inspires African-American women playwrights to render new characters that spring full-blown from the wordwomb, with new attitudes and new world views.

These playwrights thrive on artistic risk and aesthetic adventure. To the commercial and nonprofit producer alike, artistic risk represents an inflation of financial risk. In this period of extreme economic and political conservatism, such risk poses a threat to institutional survival, which often results in artistic anemia, a lack of dare, a "play-it-safe-till-the-storm-passes" mentality. In some cases, spectacular set-and-light shows feed the production machine, masking the lack of substance with form, and the laboratory is reduced to an assembly line. Those who keep doing what they've done before drain their resources in repetition and cut themselves off from the lifeblood of the theatre—the words of the playwrights whose daring visions open on new pathways of perception.

In the 1980s, many resident theatres pursued growth by taking a firm hold of the nonprofit corporate model for institutional organization. The critical process of making art for the advancement of culture was coopted by the bottom line. The market-driven, product-over-process approach began to lock theatres into rigid, formulaic methods of programming, and the aesthetic adventurer could not fit into a marketing equation for mass appeal.

When I came into the theatre fifteen years ago, it seemed that artists were packing agendas for social change the way people pack pistols today. Many artists who carried the spirit of revolution in the 1970s now find themselves in mid-life crisis, sitting in power at theatre institutions (within a nation and a world) suffering a similar identity crisis. For them, the battleground is in the meeting room where they struggle with the board of trustees to hold onto the artistic ground they gained ten years ago. They are now officially a part of the establishment, with all the rights, privileges and responsibilities of membership—credit cards, corporate accounts, faxes, modems, conferences, state-of-the-art technology, annual deficits and competition for a declining market. The social agenda for institutions has also been influenced by funding shifts: cuts in the arts and increases in education and outreach programs.

The revolutionary agendas of the seventies are now in the hands of the evolutionaries—the avant-garde artists, many of whom are women and artists of color.

Multiculturalism

The cultural diversity movement of the nineties has altered the economic climate in the arts by its significant increase in opportunities for women and artists of color. With increased opportunity comes increased competition. Theatre companies compete for funding and artists compete against each "other" for the multicultural "slot" in production schedules. Women and artists of color have greater access to the mainstream, but true entitlement is limited. Artists are not involved in setting national policies and strategies. The scent of paternalism and tokenism lingers in the air. In other words, women and artists of color are welcome to visit the mainstream, but it is not their "home." The current cultural diversity plan marks only the beginning of a much more complex process that will eventually have to address the residual racist and sexist conditioning that undermines the integrity of the diversity movement.

As currently administered by government, foundation and corporate funders, multiculturalism addresses the problem of demographic disparity; it also creates opportunities for artists and producers to address the equally pervasive problem of aesthetic inertia. In the 1991-92 season, there were seven planned productions of *Ain't Misbehavin'* in white-run theatres across the country. Clearly, jobs were created and the ethnic audience (the untapped market) was served. But what's wrong with this picture?

Ain't Misbehavin', a black musical with a small cast and a single set, is an economical, marketable choice. It also showcases the performance virtuosity of black talent, honoring our rich musical and dance heritage. People leave the theatre feeling good, and that is no small accomplishment. But the incidence of so many productions in one season reflects an absence of new ideas, a clinging to a portrait of black people created by others that romanticizes the past rather than engages living black artists who present new views of black life.

The many artists who create provocative new work are rarely given an opportunity for full production. Often these works are recognized for their potential but ultimately deemed "not ready" for the big leagues. Beyond the confines of the mainstage slot-system, the "other" artist languishes in the Sisyphus-syndrome of the developmental track; i.e., workshops and readings, presented on "the second stage." Because so few writers of color move beyond that purgatory phase, in effect it forms a ghetto of multi-culturalism within the theatre. In order to move beyond the sharecrop-ocracy model, the new faces, themes and styles call for an innovative rede-sign of the process for developing and producing new plays.

The model of development for August Wilson's plays—taking each play on a regional tour en route to Broadway—is an alternative process that produces excellence and completion. It calls for the kind of partner-ship that is rarely seen in nonprofit theatre, yet it holds great possibility for the cooperative enhancement of our artistic process. Uniquely, Wilson's circuit is formed by an elite group of the nation's white theatres; this model advances both the aesthetic and the cultural diversity agendas.

An encouraging "multicultural" factor in the increasing visibility of black women playwrights is the appointment of several African-American men to artistic directorships at prominent white companies. The key play-ers are: Kenneth Leon at Atlanta's Alliance Theatre; Tazewell Thompson, former artistic associate at Arena Stage in Washington, D.C., now artistic director at Syracuse Stage; Benny Sato Ambush, former artistic director of the Oakland Ensemble Theatre, currently associate artistic director at San Francisco's American Conservatory Theatre; and Tim Bond, artistic direc-tor of Seattle's Group Theatre, founded by Ruben Sierra, a company wholly devoted to multicultural programming. Their sole predecessors are Lloyd Richards, former artistic director of the Yale Repertory Theatre and dean of the Yale School of Drama, who retains his post as artistic director at the O'Neill Theatre Center in Connecticut, and Harold Scott, former artistic director of the Cincinnati Playhouse, who is currently the head of the directing program at Rutgers University's Mason Gross School of the Arts. Their most prominent colleague, George C. Wolfe, is the newly ap-pointed producer of the New York Shakespeare Festival at the Joseph Papp Public Theater; unparalleled in his mainstream achievement as an experimental playwright and director, he has the distinguished charge of continuing the Public Theater's legacy of producing cutting-edge plays as well as sustaining the classics.

These men, forming a new constellation of leadership in American theatre, consistently include African-American women in their artistic plans. Pearl Cleage and Cheryl West are two writers who have been rec-ognized by resident theatres as a result of their affiliation with these highly visible directors.

Whatever the course of the economic and political trends in American society, the resuscitation of imagination in American theatre will depend upon our collective ability to negotiate a balance of power, and a recognition of the interdependence of polarities—male/female, black/white, rich/poor. True diversity will empower and enfranchise each interest group as cultural allies.

The African-American Theatre

The African-American theatre as an institution is struggling for survival—as evidenced by the recent fiscal traumas of our flagship theatre, the Negro Ensemble Company. In the same way that government set-asides for small black businesses were withdrawn under Reaganomics, multicultural criteria replace the "social cause" funding once reserved for black institutions. In theory, the playing field is now leveled. In reality, black theatre institutions are competing with the old boys' network. A black-owned computer business can adapt to such changes because it does not rely solely upon the black market; it can pursue the white market to meet its profit goal. A black theatre cannot pursue a similar strategy without compromising its cultural purpose.

Facing the limiting reality of its overdependence upon corporate, foundation and government funding, black theatres are now challenged with diversifying their funding strategies. Unlike many white companies, they lack a strong individual donor group within the community, and most of them have no endowments or other assets. Consequently, their growth has hit a plateau.

Only a handful of professional black theatres has survived for more than ten years and maintained full, uninterrupted production schedules: Ricardo Khan's Crossroads Theatre Company in New Brunswick, New Jersey, the largest African-American company with its almost three-million-dollar budget; Lou Bellamy's Penumbra Theatre in St. Paul, Minnesota; Jomandi Productions in Atlanta, headed by co-artistic directors Marsha Jackson and Thomas W. Jones, II; and Ronald J. Himes' St. Louis Black Repertory Theatre. Woodie King, Jr., head of New York's New Federal Theatre, is the only institutional black producer who works in both nonprofit and commercial theatre. Other companies that keep the spirit of black theatre alive include the Lorraine Hansberry Theatre in San Francisco, the Oakland Ensemble Theatre, the Billie Holliday Theatre in Brooklyn, the Carpetbag Players in Tennessee, the North Carolina Black Repertory, Cleveland's Karamu House, and Bushfire and New Freedom Theatre in Philadelphia.

These theatres sustain the visibility of black playwrights and continue to introduce new writers to the field. Crossroads and the New Federal Theatre have led the field in premiering new plays by black women. Importantly, these two companies were the original producers of the last two milestone productions in black theatre history: Ntozake Shange's *for colored girls who have considered suicide/when the rainbow is enuf*, produced by New Federal Theatre; and George C. Wolfe's *The Colored Museum*, premiered at Crossroads Theatre Company. These breakthroughs underscore the importance of the ethnically specific theatre in any diversity plan.

The national economic and political conservatism also affects the aesthetics of black theatre. First, very few black theatres have aggressive new play development programs. Most producers have cautiously withdrawn from earlier, bolder programming choices in favor of traditional forms with black themes. Secondly, as is typical of the larger black community, a deadly silent homophobia prevails, isolating gay and lesbian playwrights who are also breaking new aesthetic ground. Although gay artists populate every area of the theatre, plays with homosexual themes rarely grace the stage, and invariably they come to tragic conclusions. A final reflection of conservatism is the proliferation of historical dramas and one-person biographies, which serve to recover many chapters of lost history and fill gaps in community education, but they have slight impact on the evolution of the artform.

In order to move from survival mode toward growth, we must examine our relationship to our own community, in all its diversity. As more black people move into the middle and upper classes, the theatre will have to rely on them to assert consumer power on behalf of our cultural institutions. Black-owned corporations and elite entertainers and athletes who tend to contribute to organizations that address more pressing social problems—poverty, hunger, housing and drug rehabilitation—must be courted the way we court all other corporations. Our representatives in Washington, D.C. need to be called upon to advocate for the arts. We must challenge the unspoken perception in the black community that theatre—and perhaps art in general—is a frill.

As black theatre has adapted to the marketplace, it has moved off-center from its African-rooted purpose. In its original context, the theatre was closer to the church than the circus. Unifying the community through rituals that honored or sought the favor of the ancestors who influenced daily life, its function was akin to that of the griot—the keeper of history, tradition, cultural values and imagination. We need to examine our assimilation and adaptation to a value system in which we disconnect our theatre from our community.

Many of the playwrights represented here innovate by returning to and reinventing African-engendered elements: signifyin', ancestral invocation, the incorporation of music and movement, use of the circle of time, the word as magic and storytelling as healing. They use these cultural charms to voice universal concerns as they advance the recovery of purpose in black theatre. Black women playwrights—like their sisters in every other sector of society—are turning the tide. And as they do, the masses of the African-American community will acknowledge the theatre, and the arts, as a spiritual necessity.

African-American Women Producers
Of the few African-American women producers, two have harnessed the entrepreneurial spirit and applied their artistic vision to the creation of new organizational models, expanding their theatre companies into multi-million-dollar cultural centers: Barbara Ann Teer, founder and chief executive of the National Black Theatre in Harlem; and Dr. Abena Joan Brown, president/producer of the ETA Creative Arts Foundation in Chicago. Ellen Stewart's La MaMa E.T.C. is one of the few avant-garde theatres in the world that has managed to survive on the "fringe," sustaining Stewart's prescient vision of global theatre. Marsha Jackson, co-artistic director of Jomandi Productions, is the only female producer with an ongoing artistic career as performer, director and writer. Other black women in artistic leadership positions include: Margaret Taylor Ford at Karamu House in Cleveland; Rosetta LeNoire, head of AMAS Repertory Theatre in New York; Sharon Walton of the Oakland Ensemble Theatre and Bhetty Waldron's Quest Theatre and Institute in Palm Beach.

Oddly, none of the African-American women artistic directors has a publicly expressed agenda for black women playwrights. Nevertheless, their leadership brings a wholistic approach to community enrichment. Their attainment of institutional security not only celebrates the living legacy of African-American culture, but provides artistic homesteads for generations to come.

Despite the valiant efforts of black women to form their own companies—Chameleon in Chicago, Black Women in Theatre in New York and Sangoma, The Women's Company at Crossroads, we have yet to create a viable, lasting workspace that is singularly devoted to the work of black women theatre artists. What would it take for African-American women to assume greater responsibility for the protection of our own interests? Clearly, the relative lack of black women in power is reflected in the minimal presence of black women playwrights in the field.

African-American Women Playwrights
Alice Childress was the first black woman to win the Obie award for best play with *Trouble in Mind* in 1956. Three years later, Lorraine Hansberry became the first black woman to receive a Broadway production and her play, *A Raisin in the Sun*, won the Drama Critics Circle award for best play of the year. Although these works were structurally influenced by European models, they changed the course of theatrical history by introducing the black experience as subject matter worthy of dramatic treatment and mainstream attention. These plays now stand as classics within the African-American canon; but at the time of their premieres, these writers were pioneers who took up a pen and, as Zora Neale Hurston wrote, "threw up a highway through the wilderness" for the passage of the many writers who would follow.

Hansberry's untimely death from cancer at the age of thirty-four left us with several unfinished plays that still beg the question: Where would she have taken the American theatre had she lived another twenty years? From her ancestral seat, she whispers to the ones who will hear, and walks with the ones who accept her call to continue the work.

The arc of stylistic innovation in African-American women's writing begins thirty years ago with Adrienne Kennedy, who won an Obie award in 1964 for her play *Funnyhouse of a Negro*. The preeminent matriarch of surrealism once said, "My plays are meant to be states of mind." A heady swirl of stark images drawn from dreams and nightmares, African and European iconography, history and imagination, fills her plays. Linear time gives way to psychological time in which memory collides with the present or an imagined time is delivered up in the urgency of now. A multi-layered, often fractured time/space reality hosts the recurrent themes of a black woman struggling through the crisis of identity. The blatant embrace of ambiguity, shifting levels of reality, specters and tentative grasps on sanity in her plays continue to challenge theatre artists.

As compared to her previous works, *The Dramatic Circle* may seem stylistically sedate in its use of linear time and unity of place. Nevertheless, the psychological trauma of a woman's experience of terrorism—a revolution rumbling through the subtext—still serves to bring new characters to the stage. The themes of internal and external terrorism have a profound resonance. A woman who can't catch her very life's breath fights the inner demons of intuition, dread and immobilizing fear. The landscape of the play is a metaphorical minefield.

Despite her obvious preoccupation with race and gender, Kennedy's plays have never been fully embraced by African-American theatres. Ironically, she is one of the most studied playwrights in the universities, where her work is most often produced, but she—like all the other writers in this anthology—stands among the many artistically homeless playwrights in America.

Ntozake Shange startled the theatre world in 1979 when her choreopoem, *for colored girls who have considered suicide/when the rainbow is enuf,* moved to Broadway. She did not call it a play and did not identify herself as a playwright. She claimed her space as a poet in the theatre. Categorizations aside, the power of her poetry voiced the silent rage and pain of black women with unparalleled complexity, poignancy, dignity and beauty. It gave us new words to invoke for strength; it freed us to speak out, to "not bite our tongues" and through it all to love ourselves.

for colored girls set off a heated national debate, polarizing black men and women. Shange introduced black feminist thought-in-action to theatre and brought a new level of intensity and engagement to the national discourse on race and gender. This theatrical event reclaimed black theatre's role as a catalyst for social change. Mainstream theatregoers ate it up and it continues to be produced all over the world—from European women in Paris performing the French translation to the recent Zulu translation performed in South Africa.

The Resurrection of the Daughter: Liliane marks a stylistic departure for Shange, but in reading the text, one must bear in mind that the excerpted scenes have been taken out of their root context, the novel. Although the novel is being adapted for the stage, it is unlikely that it will appear in this stripped-down form. The totality of *Liliane*—a series of poems, multiple narratives and dramatic scenes—is more accurately described as an evolution of the choreopoem. Liliane is a young visual artist who transcends the prison of the English language through her artistry. Her struggle to sort out her own personal history within the context of the history of racism and sexism takes us into the depths of the wounded psyche. Liliane is one daughter who will not be sacrificed to the demons of racism and patriarchy. Through psychoanalysis, she confronts the shadow realm of the self—the realm of dreams, intuition, eroticism, terror, rage, desire and death. She dares to journey through the labyrinth of her unconscious life and gains access to the hidden power of her own truth. The pursuit of self-knowledge is a death-defying dance of the spirit that initiates the healing and the resurrection of Liliane.

In *The Mojo and the Sayso*, Aishah Rahman uses the domestic drama as a launching pad for a highly imaginative flight into new dimensions of style. Her self-defined jazz aesthetic creates a dynamic synthesis of several genres, including allegory, farce, satire and myth, all of which culminate in this reinvention of the miracle play. The playwright's meditation on the blood mysteries resonates throughout the subtext while the text is riddled with the sometimes harmonic, sometimes dissonant poetics of Christian doctrine in collision with African-derived vodoun, the wisdom of jazz and the passion of political militancy.

The play opens on Acts Benjamin building a car in his living room; his wife, Awilda, lights candles to find her white gloves as she prepares to go to church. Rahman's realism becomes hyperrealism through the use of symbolism, poetically charged language and the daring use of ritual—both sacred and secular. Each character has a mojo, a mechanism for magic, that gives them the sayso, the power to move through moments of terror. The Benjamin family's attempt to cope with incomprehensible heartbreak becomes a lens through which we see the deadening effects of police brutality upon the victim's survivors; as they struggle against despair and absurdity, we recognize the sheer heroism of survival. In this play, the powerful and corrupt authority figures that prey upon the innocent meet with justice. Ritual purification enables confession, forgiveness, healing and transformation. Revelations signal the end and the beginning. As they reshape their responses to grief, the characters recover their ability to conjure, to dream and ultimately to live again.

Adrienne Kennedy, Ntozake Shange and Aishah Rahman have been partially accepted into the mainstream. They have garnered major awards; the subjects of countless critical essays, they are widely taught in black and white college theatre courses. Black theatre history of the 1960s and 1970s was written upon them and through them. As the first generation of stylistic rebels to reach maturity as playwrights, they have held the ground for black women playwrights, steady singin' "I Shall Not Be Moved," all the while movin' mountains.

Their presence in the academy should not be underestimated. It directly influenced the birth of a new generation of playwrights who undoubtedly gained inspiration and validation from the existence of African-American female models. The new generation is represented here by Kia Corthron and Suzan-Lori Parks, who emerged from the dramatic writing programs at two of the most prestigious universities in the country—Columbia and the Yale School of Drama, respectively. They are among the growing number of black playwrights who choose the rigorous path of academic professional training. One of the benefits of an Ivy League degree is that it almost guarantees access to the professional network already populated by fellow graduates. Both writers bring a technical maturity that belies their youth.

In *Cage Rhythm*, Kia Corthron draws our attention to the harsh realities of African-American women in prison serving life sentences. Although inspired by the need to sound the alarm on the injustices that make incarceration the fate of a disproportionate number of our women, she breaks down the politics and sociology into very poignant, fast-paced, emotionally taut scenes that turn on a dime. Two levels of reality—one physical and one spiritual—are rendered as absolute truth. The baldly naturalistic setting takes on the provocative power of metaphor. Humanity and hope radiate through the author's manipulation of the almost microscopic details of life that we "on the outside" take for granted: a phone; a photograph; a hairbrush; a piece of paper. Women help each other to survive. Lesbian love is dignified as one of the few remaining signs of human tenderness. Within this barren, hard-edged reality, one character's ability to live through astral projections offers the landscape of the mind as the only outpost of freedom. And the final questions that the playwright plants, subliminally, linger for days: How are you spending your life sentence? What are you living for?

In *The Death of the Last Black Man in the Whole Entire World*, Suzan-Lori Parks uses word wizardry to unravel the essential tension of the human experience. Her search for the key to identity takes us on a vicarious journey through an acrobatic use of language. The rhythm of syntax is used to upset the systems of thought that mangle and murder the human spirit. Rummaging among the ruins of words and history, she sparks race memory and prods the imagination to transcend the boundaries of language that define us solely in terms of race history.

Her work is distinguished not only by the alchemical effect of language, but also by the confident fusion of different genres—part comedy, part farce, part absurd/surreal, part classical Greek, part minstrel, part satire, part political, part mystery, part play of ideas, part this-don't-make-no-damn-sense. The astonishing part is the paradoxical way in which meaning pierces the perplexity. The ancestors speak through this writer.

Thulani Davis, author of the libretto *X*, is one of the few African-American women writers to venture into the musical theatre genre and the first to be embraced by the mainstream opera houses in America. I came to know her poetry in the late 1970s. Poets were collaborating with jazz musicians, putting words to music in ways that sharpened the fluency of both arts. It was an avant-garde, neo-Afro-bohemian atmosphere in which the poetry reading became a heightened theatrical event. Opera and jazz, on the surface, appear to be at opposite ends of the musical spectrum. *X* reflects one woman writer's use of lyrical language to leap across an aesthetic and cultural divide in the creation of a new, unified whole that is greater than the sum of its parts. Epic in scope and form, this libretto expands the existing canon of African-American musical biographies with its entirely sung text that honors one of our greatest heroes and cultural icons, Malcolm X.

The performance art posse in *Moon Marked and Touched by Sun* is composed of Robbie McCauley, Laurie Carlos, Judith Jackson, Danitra Vance and Anna Deavere Smith. Performance art, the catch-all phrase for unorthodoxy in solo performance, often incorporates media, installation art, dance and music to deconstruct logical, linear narratives. It often makes use of the performer's biography or employs the tools of agit-prop, and is therefore often dismissed as an egocentric, elitist excursion into obscurity. As a genre, it is the aesthetic frontier in theatre; the only rule is that there are no rules.

Embraced by the New York City downtown art theatre, these artists achieved some measure of acclaim in the 1980s. They hail from the ranks of actors, and their work relies upon a multi-disciplinary font of creativity; they write, direct and perform their own material. These professionally trained, card-carrying members of Actors' Equity paid their dues on the audition circuit, built a solid reputation as actors—some even won major awards—but reached a plateau and ultimately had to confront their disillusionment with the limited, often stereotypical roles available to them in the mostly male-authored plays that were being produced.

These women are products of both the Civil Rights Movement of the

1960s and the feminist movement of the 1970s. Even if they worked on the alternative, experimental theatre circuit, the white male power structure could not accommodate the liberation pedagogy that had transformed their conceptions of self. Though free to express themselves through the roles created by other writers, there was still a fundamental hierarchy—director and playwright over actor—that relegated them to the role of interpreter of someone else's vision. They lacked authority. Their stories and points of view were absent. Rather than die on the vine as actors, they took up the pen for artistic survival.

In *Sally's Rape*, as Robbie McCauley breaks through her own silence, the voices of her foremothers emerge to reveal the historical precedence for the use of rape as a tool of oppression. McCauley presents a fractured perspective that decodes cultural difference and deciphers the subtle and outrageous dynamics of race as entitlement to privilege and power. She breaks the fourth wall and engages the audience in dialogue—sometimes directed, sometimes leaving space open for impulse. In this dramatic reckoning with the personal, familial and collective past, she reclaims her power to speak, and generates a dialogue that asserts the possibility of a more conscious, liberating level of communication.

Laurie Carlos creates her own performance vocabulary with the language of stylized gesture and text-based improvisation. In *White Chocolate for My Father*, she is joined by an ensemble of performers in the exploration of the multi-generational devastation of rape; rooted in the uncomplicated language of a twelve-year-old girl, the multiple narratives function like jazz solos or duets. One family of women breaks the cycle of abuse through the simple but courageous decision to love each other. *White Chocolate* is a world in which the ancestral spirit continues to guide, protect and instruct the living. The play begs us to listen, to look for her signs and symbols.

Danitra Vance and Judith Jackson have made profound contributions to the genres of comedy and satire. Both Vance and Jackson elicit the roar of laughter that is synonymous with the roar of recognition, the roar of emotional release. If theatre can be a healing agent, Vance and Jackson bring the laughter cure.

In 1985, Vance was the first black woman to join the cast of television's *Saturday Night Live*, blazing the trail for other black comedians and performance artists to move from the comedy clubs and theatres into television and film. I think of her as the "comic strip-search" artist. Her comedic persona charms and disarms the audience without trivializing her subjects. She takes an iconoclastic approach to the creation of widely varied, specifically drawn characters, and takes the black folk style of "clownin'" to new heights. In strict observance of one rule of comedy, her humor is born of human tragedy turned on its head. The line between comedy and tragedy becomes a dangerous tightrope she walks, elevating the unheralded heroes among the anonymous, ordinary people whose real lives are often summed up in statistics. In *Live and In Color!*, the menagerie of zany characters forms a lens through which we can scrutinize societal illness and recognize the ridiculous and ennobling ways in which we attempt to heal ourselves.

Judith Jackson is a satirist who chronicles, deconstructs and reconstructs current events. She plays a host of characters—archetypes, stereotypes, spirits, celebrities and everyday people. Issues that affect the national consciousness and conscience figure prominently in her work. Though precision in characterization takes precedence over polemics, Jackson is not afraid to put forth her political point of view. Spinning off of news headlines and trends in pop culture, she uses mime, movement, music, mask and video to support her text. An Afro-centric feminist brand of spirituality and a razor-sharp wit mark out her unique territory.

At this moment in history, Anna Deavere Smith is one of the most celebrated theatre artists in America. In 1991, she arrived Off Broadway with her solo performance piece, *Fires in the Mirror*, and began a meteoric climb to celebrity status. Not since the debuts of George C. Wolfe and Ntozake Shange has an "experimental" play authored by an African American so astonished the theatre community and commanded national attention.

Fires in the Mirror is part of a series of theatre pieces developed by Smith entitled *On the Road: A Search for American Character*. Each piece is focused on a timely event that has sparked controversy within the community. She conducts interviews with a diverse group of women, men and young people who represent varied points of view on the subject. She then performs each character using their verbatim testimony from the interview process. Her goal, far beyond impersonation, is the embodiment of the spoken word which reveals the essence of human character. Her performance assembles a diverse group of characters in a way that is only possible within the contextual reality of her work in the theatre.

Anna Deavere Smith uses the power of the oral tradition and mask as mirror. Each character's "difference," finely etched in the particular rhythm and cadence of language and gesture, is the point of departure; but paradoxically, each monologue effectively removes the mask of difference in a miraculous revelation of sameness. Smith's interview process gains access to those places that exist beyond the superficial soundbites of news media coverage. Her dramatic adventure is a journey through the interior landscape of the heart and mind—that recognizable space in which vulnerability wrestles with pride. These confessional testimonies place not people but American society on trial. There are indictments, statements of defense and unanimous pleas of not guilty. The audience sits in judgment, hearing all sides of the argument, only to discover their own culpability and innocence. Anna Deavere Smith's unique, riveting dramatic form reclaims the power of the voice of a solo artist to become the voice of the people.

The Dramaturgical Orb

Although I find the distinctiveness of each play in this collection to be more compelling than the similarities among them, I am fascinated by their variations on two themes: the presence of a spiritual or psychic dimension and the presence of the political voice.

My dramaturgical point of view is rooted in an Afro-matricentric perspective derived from personal experience: my mother is the center of my world. Her dark beauty rivals the midnight sky; a deep well of love, she is a spirit-fixer. Through her womb, I am rooted in the continuum of life. The womb signifies possibility, conception, concept—the thought that precedes the deed. In this context, the MotherSpirit rises not in opposition to but in cooperation with divine male energy as a re-creative, balancing, healing force moving to ease human suffering. Clothed in compassion, the mother warrior speaks the truth to bring about change, a sudden change, a needed change.

In *Moon Marked and Touched by Sun*, the dramatic embrace and exploration of the spiritual dimension is a "sign of the times," an unorchestrated, spontaneous choric response to a world in crisis. The inner struggle against racism, sexism and homophobia has become a crisis of the soul. In a world spinning out of control, this turning inward—this use of subconscious, metaphysical tools—is a matter of life and death, a matter of survival and revival.

Herstory and history, invoked for the restoration of memory, become a source of power, catalysts in this revival of spiritual power. Contemporary warriors now arm themselves with this power. Note the embrace of the African concept of the Ancestor-as-Guide by African Americans and the parallel ascension of the Goddess among feminists the world over. In this final decade of the twentieth century, the invocation of spiritual power is not only an act of survival; ultimately, it is a call for collective transformation that begins with the process of self-definition. In design and purpose, this spiritual realism is a form of social activism, a politicizing force.

Spiritual realism uses the theatre to reveal the unseen through that which is seen. Metaphysical realities illuminate, transform or enable escape from physical realities. Spiritual forces direct the action of the protagonist towards an elevated, integrated consciousness. The text-performance transfers spiritual energy to the audience, galvanizing an irreversible and contagious change of mind or heart.

The presence of the political perspective varies in each play. In Judith Jackson's *WOMBmanWARs*, Anna Deavere Smith's *Fires in the Mirror* and Thulani Davis's *X*, the politics are placed in the foreground by virtue of the explicit text regarding a political event or figure. In *Cage Rhythm* by Kia Corthron, Aishah Rahman's *The Mojo and the Sayso*, Laurie Carlos's *White Chocolate, Sally's Rape* by Robbie McCauley and in Danitra Vance's *Live and In Color!*, the politics are situated in the middle ground; the focus of each play is on the characters' internal struggle to cope with a specific social circumstance shaped by the politics of race, gender and/or class. In *The Dramatic Circle* by Adrienne Kennedy, *The Death of the Last Black Man* by Suzan-Lori Parks and *Liliane* by Ntozake Shange, the political landscape is in the background as offstage event that functions as the antagonist. Because these forces are unseen, the focus of the dramatic inquiry or meditation remains centered on the protagonist's interior psychological struggle to make meaning out of chaos.

Regardless of the placement of the political narrative, there is an implicit subtextual awareness of a larger communal context that is directly affected by even the most idiosyncratic protagonist's intimate search for meaning. Personal politics diversify the discourse and add new perspective to the global preoccupation with identity and survival of the species.

The spiritual and political narratives converge, overtly or covertly, to reflect women's concerns as well as their resolve to sustain a sense of hope, often evidenced through a sense of humor, as we face the turning of the century. There are many echoes of concern for the fate of children, the family and extended family within the larger community. The escalation of violence sounds an alarm. Rape, racially motivated and gender-biased crimes, terrorism, poverty and political corruption all factor into this volume's composite sketch of contemporary society as viewed from the perspectives of African-American women dramatists.

The need to liberate the self from narrow, caging definitions placed on us by other people reflects the universal hunger for freedom. In many of these plays, language is the liberator. Speech—the speaking of truth—becomes a ritual of healing to make whole or unify the splintered psyche. This liberated, ritual use of language lifts the borders that separate the speaker from the hearer of the word. Articulation signifies the awakening of a new or remembered power. In the moment of epiphany, the deceit is decoded and change occurs.

At the heart of this dramaturgical paradigm is the circle, the spiral, the helix, which in many cases give clues to the structure and use of time. Whether time is compressed or extended, we move from beat to beat and scene to scene not by the clock on the wall but by the rhythm of revelation. In the same way that jazz musicians ritualized improvisation, these writers take the liberty to extend the solo or "take as many eights" as they need to reach the peak of understanding. I compare it to Ella Fitzgerald in scat-mode; full knowledge of the chord changes gives her the freedom to flirt with her favorite phrase or break out into a whole new song in the middle of the song (and it ain't about a medley). Or consider the rap artist's freedom found through sampling. Similarly, the circular use of time allows for rapid transit from one reality to another, for the past to become present, for exaggerated stillness or for several timeframes to come alive in a single moment.

Dramatic action is rarely encoded through physical behavior but more profoundly through the experience of mystery and revelation. There is a "rule" of western dramaturgy that says one comes to know a character by what they do, not by what they say. The sistren serving up the word in these texts revise that rule. The act of speaking and the precise words spoken become the keys that unlock the doors to the inner chamber(s) of character. In these plays, character objectives are intangible. They want things as complicated as meaning, as simple as even breathing; they want to know, to remember, to love, to be free, to live.

About the Interviews

During the summer of 1993, I had the privilege of conducting telephone interviews with each playwright to create an introduction for each work. With a few exceptions, I posed the same "twenty questions" to all of them. In editing the interviews, I selected the segments that held the most dynamic ideas and revealed the most information about the writers that could not be found from simply reading the plays.

In each interview, there is a section entitled "The Darkness and the Light." Just before I began the interview process, I read an article in the *New York Times* about the discovery of a halo of darkness surrounding the Milky Way. In the effort to codify "dark matter," scientists assert that darkness has a gravitational pull which bends light and functions as a lens, making things appear brighter and larger than they are. Inspired by these findings and their resonance with the title of the anthology, I developed these questions: What defines the darkness for you as an artist? What is the light of your vision towards which you are moving?

Although each interview is unique, I have included each author's comments on "The Darkness and the Light," as well as their "Definitions of Heroism."

WHITE

CHOCOLATE

FOR MY FATHER

LAURIE

CARLOS

White Chocolate is *White Chocolate for My Father*. It was written to let him understand something about the nature of our lives when he was not there. At some point, he blamed himself for not being able to be there, but I realized that there was no way anyone could have been there with my mother because she was the product of this cyclical rape and violence. By the time she was fourteen years old, she had been basically destroyed as a human being because of the beatings and the rapes.

I didn't want to blame anybody, I wanted to talk about how the violence that happened to my mother was the same violence that had happened to my grandmother, or that had come out of slavery; and that we had passed all that violence and shame on—the shame we all felt about our mouths being too big, our noses too flat.

If he had known I was molested at twelve years old, I don't know what he could've done, but I never could tell him. He found out in this piece.

I also wanted to talk about the fact that my grandmother's grandmother had no white men's children. She made a choice even as a slave. And my mother who always said we were the mistake, somehow felt helpless.

White Chocolate has a lot of personal things for me, but I was also clear that the story was one that everyone knew. "White Chocolate" was something that we had become in this process: we're still here, but we are unrecognizable to each other. We don't know what tribes we come from, who the father is, who the spirits are that we're looking at. For instance, in the play, the White Light Spirit (the last African family member before the Middle Passage, who never left the shore) becomes the junkie. It's the same spirit, but we don't know how to even value what we are from moment to moment.

Finding Voice

Because I have written *White Chocolate*, I can now speak about other things that are not autobiographical, and that are also not in my child's voice, which I had been unable to do for a while. The language is so simple because I had to say it in the language that I knew at the time, as the child in the moment. I couldn't write it from the point of view of re-flection back.

My sisters' voices in the travel sequences are voices that they had when they were twenty-five, twenty-six years old. I used those voices to let you know where they moved to, what happened to these girls. And the White Light Spirit's voice is just the voice that I heard from that spirit. I don't know what the value of what she says is. I only know that that was how she came to me.

White Chocolate finally allows me to move through the next moment in my voice. The child has finally spoken. Finally said what has been bothering her, what has motivated her, shaken her up, run her round the room. And now, with *White Chocolate*, I have given voice to my matriar-chal lineage. It is for those women who could not speak, for those women who were speaking for themselves but were never heard.

The Darkness and the Light

I'm not in the darkness in my work. I'm in a state of twilight or dawn. Be-cause I do know my little girl, my voice has changed. It changed physically because of the [taxi] accident [in the winter of 1992]. I found I didn't have a voice, but I had to speak as a grown person through that. In the past six months, it has brought my work into a state of dawning. There are things I didn't understand or know before, things I would not even approach or try to address before. Those things I can now address. I can stand in the middle of what it is I don't know about it, and I'm not afraid to tremble now because I understand the trembling is a part of how the work is made.

Artistic Challenges and Discoveries

I learned a lot about facing up to incredible fears. That thing where the mother, Mickey, ties the children up, that experience came back to me like a flash in the night. I had forgotten it. Having to go through it to write about it, I confronted a lot of fears, memories, and swallowed it.

The most compelling artistic challenge was making the very last line work within the context of the piece. "Do you love me, Lore?/Yes/Do you love me, Lore?/Yes. Yes." I had never told my sister how much I loved her but I risked everything to untie her that night, because the next night my mother tied both of us up, and the night after that, too, and the night after that. The risk I took was a risk my grandmother did not take for my mother while she was being raped all the time; which was also the risk my mother never took for me when she found out my stepfather had molested me. But I risked everything for my sister.

The Aesthetic

I have never been able to move within the boundaries of the Eurocentric play form. It doesn't tell my story because I'm always dealing with the present, the past and the future. Of course when you start to tell the story, it changes the face of history as we have known it.

I haven't named the aesthetic; it is not absolute. I don't write to tell an audience what to feel. I tell the stories in the movement—the inside dances that occur spontaneously, as in life—the music and the text. If I write a line, it doesn't necessarily have to be a line that is spoken; it can be a line that's moved, a line from which music is created. The gesture becomes the sentence. So much of who we are as women, as people, has to do with how we gesture to one another all the time, and particularly through emotional moments. Gesture becomes a sentence or a statement of fact. If I put on a script "four gestures," that doesn't mean I'm not saying anything; that means I have opened it up for something to be said physically. I have no way to define it right now. So in that way, my aesthetic is without definition, which is not a terrible thing. I can really let it start to define itself.

Distinctions between Women's and Men's Writing

I see an enormous difference even when black men are writing about us. Their definitions are still white men's patriarchal definitions of what is valuable, what is pain, what is love, what is masculinity, what is good, what is bad, what dictates a success or a failure. Black men writers are still trying to gain their manhood based on how white men view them. Even all of the movies about us are written from the perspective of how white men can sell the blues.

Women write from our perspectives. There are some black women who write just like white men. We've been sold such an irrational bill of goods about who we are and what our value is, not just as black people, but as women in the world. It's very difficult to get up every day and have to redefine yourself, give yourself legitimacy and declare your beauty.

Definitions of Heroism

Heroism is that ability to keep moving in the face of disaster; to keep breathing after you've seen Emmet Till's face in the newspaper; to keep breathing when your mother looks at you and sees herself and believes it to be the most hideous thing; to keep breathing after your brother, the slave master, puts a bag over your head and rapes you constantly. Those we know are acts of heroism.

ABOUT THE AUTHOR

Laurie Carlos, playwright, director and performer, has worked in the theatre for twenty-five years creating new works and new roles for the American stage. In addition to *White Chocolate*, her recent plays include *Monkey Dances, Persimmon Peel, Organdy Falsetto* and *Nonsectarian Conversations With The Dead*, which have been produced at Lincoln Center Outdoors in New York, Walker Art Center in Minneapolis, Jacob's Pillow in Massachusetts and the National Black Arts Festival in Atlanta. Carlos is currently working on the libretto for a new opera, *Pagan Violins*, composed by Lawrence Butch Morris. The opera, commissioned by Penumbra Theatre Company, is scheduled to be performed in 1996.

Carlos has toured with Jawole Willa Jo Zollar's Urban Bush Women throughout the United States and in Europe, and is a member of Thought Music, a performance group with Robbie McCauley and Jessica Hagedorn. The text of their collaboration, *Teenytown*, appeared in TCG's *Out from Under*, an anthology of works by women performance artists. Carlos received a Bessie award for her extensive and exceptional work in *Heat* with Urban Bush Women and Thought Music. She has also presented workshops and seminars for numerous colleges and arts institutions, including Yale University, City College of New York, SUNY Purchase and the Arizona Commission on the Arts.

A resident of New York City, Carlos received an Obie award for creating the role of Lady in Blue in Ntozake Shange's *for colored girls who have considered suicide/when the rainbow is enuf*, a Gregory Millard Fellowship from the New York Foundation for the Arts and a National Endowment for the Arts Inter-Arts Grant.

ABOUT THE WORK

White Chocolate, recently awarded a Bessie, was originally commissioned by Greta Gundersen for the 1989–90 Fringe Series at BACA Downtown. The play received further developmental support and production at Jacob's Pillow, Walker Art Center and Penumbra Theatre Company and the National Black Arts Festival in Atlanta, as well as at P.S. 122.

CHARACTERS

LORE, the oldest ⎫
TONY   ⎬   three sisters
TINY   ⎭
MICKEY, the sisters' mother
MAMA, Mickey's mother
EMILYN, Mama's paternal grandmother
DEOLA, Emilyn's great-grandmother—the White Light Spirit
RADIO, the Spirit of Red Light

AUTHOR'S NOTE

White Chocolate strives to create a contemporary American aesthetic grounded in, and drawing from, the experience of the black American diaspora. It seeks to tell the stories of an American black family.

    White Chocolate is a theatre piece exploring the life of an American black child in 1959 as she grows under the influences of an old African spirit and the radio. The story is told through the voice of a ten-year-old child, whose relationship with herself is influenced by elements over which she has no control. She learns about life, history and sociology from the images of the white light of her ancestry and the red light of the radio. The project uses old music and new music from both Africa and the Deep South to take you on this unique historical American journey.

    The contributions of the major collaborators lift the language of this text to greater accessibility: The music—accompanying choreography, singing and dialogue—provides a conduit for social understanding and historical development. The character Radio—Red Light—performs live onstage and is always present. The choreography creates and brings to life the connection with history and self-determination. The lighting design functions as both character and set, sustaining the images of the red light of the Radio and the white light of the child's ancestors.

WHITE CHOCOLATE
FOR MY FATHER

Three children, all girls, speak and move thru darkness and the influence of white and red light. These children are old and young. The voice of their mother tears in and around them—her body is beautiful, her voice screams and laughs as she dances and folds clothes. Mama, the children's maternal grandmother, comes and sits, changing hats and gloves. She speaks to herself, she moans out loud. Emilyn is Mama's paternal grandmother. She is the slave, she can't go away, she is the ghost, she carries the bag, she is the last before freedom. Deola is the White Light Spirit. She is the last African person before the passage, she never left the shore. Deola is the great-grandmother to the slave. She speaks to the little-girl one of the three—the oldest, the one who also listens to the red light of the Radio. The child who is caught between memory and music.

The Radio is on. We hear the static of the Radio and the red light seeps through the sound of "Itty Bitty Pretty One," an old song of rock and roll. The girl-child, in the memory of Mister Lee, sings off-key and in the passion of an inside dance.

LORE: Mister Lee Mister Lee, oh! Mister Lee, Mister Lee, Mister Lee, oh...! Radio, radio, there is a man in the radio who loves me! Yes a man in the radio who loves me! Radio. Radio. Someday Im gonna go all over the world. All over.

Red Light/Radio plays "When You Wish upon a Star." Lore sings and circles in the red light.

OPENING: EVERYONE KNOWS A DANCE!
This is a voyage of improvisational movement and sound.

TRIP NUMBER 1

*The Trips are vaudevilles, improvisations told in two voices,
Tiny's and Tony's. The actors should remember to keep up the
dispute.*

TONY: Third person past tense. That was some holiday, thought
Tony as she remembered her first trip to Italy, "I had the experience my life." It all began when Tony, her sister Tiny and
Ida, a friend, entered the airport in Rome. They had spent four
weeks vacationing in Italy and now it was time to move on.
They were scheduled to fly to Africa on Trans World Airlines
at ten o'clock that evening, and arrived at the airport at nine
o'clock with plenty of luggage and souvenirs. They found several baggage carts in the airport and loaded their bundles on.
Then they made their way thru the mass of people and arrived
happy and excited at the ticket counter to check in. They
thought they had arrived early because there was no one else
there, not even the ticket agent. The girls rejoiced in being the
first on line—that meant seats by the window for all. Thinking
they had time to spare, Tony and Ida decided to explore the
airport. They walked around, peering through shop windows,
anxious to buy more souvenirs, although they knew they could
not. This was their first trip to Europe, and they had already
overextended themselves financially. Now they had only
enough money left to buy a meal and catch a cab when they
reached Africa. In Africa they planned to stay with their
mommy, Mickey, who lived there. When Tony and Ida returned to the ticket counter a short time later, they were surprised to find there was still no one on line. They were puz-
zled: it was already twenty past nine o'clock, surely there
should be a line forming or at least a ticket agent on duty.
There was something wrong. Tony checked the tickets again;
they read plain as day "Departure time ten o'clock p.m."
Could it be that we arrived too early? asked Tiny. Maybe our
watches are wrong, said Ida. The girls checked their watches
against the clock in the airport, the time was the same. Then
what could the problem be? asked Ida. Could the flight have

been canceled without our knowledge? The three girls sat down anxiously awaiting a word, an announcement, something. Ten o'clock (departure time) came and went. By this time the girls were frantic! They didn't have enough money to check into a hotel, and they recalled when they bought the tickets the agent had said there would not be another flight to their destination until the sixth, which was three days away. What were they to do, sleep in the airport? And what about food? Three days in the airport with little food seemed like a horrible possibility.

Then Tony had an idea, she remembered there was a TWA office on the floor above. She told Tiny and Ida to wait downstairs while she went upstairs to talk to a representative. The TWA office was fairly large with a variety of travel posters on the walls. There were five desks in the office with an abundance of papers on them all. The office was empty except for one representative who was preparing to leave. Tony walked right up to the rep. and began to explain her dilemma. The man sat patiently listening to her story, then asked to see the tickets. After examining the tickets and checking the flight schedule, he turned to Tony and said "Oh, we made a mistake!" A mistake, she replied with a look of surprise and a lift of her eyebrows. Yes, a mistake, repeated the rep. Your tickets say departure time ten o'clock, but the actual departure time was nine o'clock. It seems that one of our agents put down the wrong time. Ooooooooh, replied Tony, folding her hands across her chest. That means it was your error and not ours. That's correct, said the rep. but don't worry, since it is our mistake TWA will pay in full for the remainder of your stay in Italy. Simply choose the hotel you wish to stay in while in Rome, and we will cover everything for the next three days, until there is another flight to your destination. With that the man proceeded to fill out a TWA financial voucher.

Five gestures.

Tony sat there disbelieving. Wait a minute, she said, do you mean all of the hotel's services were at their disposal? And they took full advantage of the privilege. It was a wonderful experience for a nineteen-year-old and two twenty-one-year-old girls traveling on a limited budget.

AMERICAN THEME AND READING
Five patriotic songs.

TONY: Whenever all of this is gone, over, the lights will come up strong. Every face will lean over and cry a silly moaning. Frame these thoughts simply with a question. Songs grow in swells of long lights.

MICKEY: Tough little puddin heads. They all dance. Yes sir. All my children dance. Whirl around and sing too. These children of mine all mistakes. All of them dance to the radio and to little songs they make up in the night. I work and they sing songs. Yes sir they sing old songs too. Just like you remember. New words sometime, cause they change the words on you. Go inside their heads and come out with mistakes. Their heads miss the lights.

Two gestures.

TINY: Why dont you ask your question?

LORE: I havent any question to ask sir.

TINY: Ask it! You scared?

TONY: Who are you?

EMILYN: Who are you?

LORE: Yes.

MICKEY: Tough little puddin heads. They all dance. Yes sir.

EMILYN *(She sings)*: Clap hands clap hands till daddy comes home daddy has money and mommy has none . . .

TINY: My daddy is gonna call me up, send kisses thru the phone. Kisses my daddys kisses.

Emilyn is caught by the rhythm of a drum sound away. The red light comes up.

RADIO: Jimmie Rodgers' "Kisses Sweeter than Wine" and "Love and Marriage."

Radio plays "Why Do Fools Fall in Love." The children sing "My Name is Jimmy Durante." They sing and move to their own places. The White Light Spirit comes up across the red light in drums and movement, in grace. Lore gets caught up in drums and other children dance to what they can hear.

LORE: You dont know him do you? They wont let us see no pictures.

DEOLA: Fill yourself up girl. Its this thing they call the classics.

LORE: Every time we think we are gonna see his picture they take everything away. Have you seen his picture. What does he look like? Is he like Jackie Wilson? Is he like George Johnson? I want to marry him.

DEOLA: I can fly. I learned how to in the hole. In the hole like a bird I flew. Ears first. I tore open my thighs when the back of my head was chewed away. My beautiful breast lost in the hole in the earth. Buried up to the neck. My hands became my head and the legs bleed. Their dogs eat my head.

TINY: We want him to send kisses thru the phone.

DEOLA: I am old and I fight the men. They have seen his picture and rewrite his name. They feed my nose to the dog. My thighs are torn by my own hands. The breath of dogs against my teeth.

MICKEY: All these mistakes are mine.

EMILYN: Cotton and flax dont need to be boiled. Spoons. Vinegar, alum. Getting closer to my joy. Nettle, black alder, tansy. Forget thunder and leaves. Every little neatly combed head is counted as profit for my father and his wife. We all been sold two times.

TINY: Third person. Past tense.

EMILYN: First person. Present tense. I have no white mans children. Raw wool or silk must be washed to take out the grease. I have no white mans children, sister has nine. Mama has us. Yes I am taken by the same man who is the father of my sisters children. Dyers all of us. We know the ways to get color. Red? Alkanet, barberry, cranberry. He can only take me like this. *(She places the bag over her head and loosens her dress)* Cant look at my face.

LORE, TONY AND TINY: Clap hands clap hands till daddy comes home daddy has money and mommy has none!

DEOLA: My father was tender & smiled at me and welcomed me with music his hands made music from air.

LORE: Who are you?

EMILYN: I am his sister.

The red lights take over. The children dance to the Radio.

RADIO: Sam Cooke, Dion, Ruth Brown. "Mama He Treats Your Daughter Mean," Frankie Limon.

MICKEY: We got out just in time. The truck was coming to evict us. Memphis was hard to live in, everything was high. Rent, meal, fatback, ribbon. We got out before they could get us. Mama would roll up newspaper to stick in the holes to keep the wind out. So eat those goddamn peas. Eat em and be glad there aint no Mr. Chissolm.

TINY: Who?

MICKEY: Yes!

MAMA: Sho as you born!

ALL: Sho as you born!

LORE: I come here with nothing. My mothers face my grand-mothers hips my fathers nose & pudgy hands, his heels.

MAMA: Your nose is too wide too big too flat. *(She repeats line four more times)*

You need to teach those girls to play piano. They need to learn to sew. That dancing wont get em nowhere.

This is a moving photograph.

MICKEY: I dream of Sweden and Paris in your eyes.

MAMA: Looking at your face I see what the race will come to.

TONY: The face moves over to cry in crowds.

MAMA: Your face lives like belching on ice cream.

TINY: This face is Sharon & Walter dreaming.

MICKEY: This face is always a photo & music.

MAMA: Your face is remembered & ruined.

MICKEY: My face is unimagined & forgotten.

EMILYN: Rain water, copper kettle or an iron pot can be used for darker colors. Ammonia, lime.

TONY (*Sings*):

> I got a girlfriend and her name is lore lore lip lip.
>
> She is my girlfriend and her name is lore lore lip lip.

MAMA: Only men would talk to me even in the church was them niggers in them cloth caps. I aint never want no nigger in a cloth cap, and old sports coat. These folks in New York dont care nothin bout a good-looking well-dressed cultured colored woman.

MICKEY: My great-grandmother was a white woman

EMILYN: looked just like a white woman

MICKEY: and she brought a good price.

EMILYN: First person. Present tense. Brings a good price.

MICKEY: We picked cotton till I was twelve and came to New York. Where I met your father & made my mistakes. Yes sir they can dance.

Mickey sings "Blueberry Hill"; the children do back-up.

MAMA: Chicken feet onions salt black pepper Do Re Mi Fa So La Tee Do & 947-7947 lx" 902? "91 ? 17 71-71Q4-v

TONY: And what does Ching Chow have to say today?

MAMA: Ching Chow say 16 whites horses does not secure future make.

TONY: Ching Chow say anything else?

MAMA: He say if I had hair like my sister I would never have to pay my rent!

LORE: You look at his hat, at his ear, and you dont see nothing.

LORE, TONY AND TINY: Clap hands clap hands till daddy comes home daddy has money and mama has none.

They create and play hand games—everyone spirit and slave.

TONY: Avenue C Friday 4:30.

TINY: For you 10¢ off a yard. You take 6 yards 11¢. Just for you!

LORE: I am closing! Sorry closed!

TINY: Before Shabbat Shabbat Shabbat.

TONY: Buy the best fish heads anyplace you could find better? Impossible.

LORE: Come over here rings, lace, shirts, I got for you towels.

TONY: One day your people will be free.

TINY: For you I give an extra half-pound.

TONY: Just for you.

LORE: Run before sundown catch them before sundown run catch them before sun—

TONY: Are you a smart girl you look like a smart girl.

LORE: So if you want a bargain? You got a bargain here. I got it for you.

TONY: We got colored work here.

LORE: Sorry. Sorry. We are closed. Closed at 4:30.

TONY: Amidst the clash of laughing and pennys-worth of swatches I was loved, patted and cherished. I was expected, planned for. Hands moved over my head and marked my growing with tears.

TINY: Memories for so many no longer here.

TONY: My back gave refuge to hugs too full for strangers.

TINY: Strong arms helped me ascend to giggles.

LORE: A half-size was put away till I got there. A licorice. A half-yard of white lace and velvet ribbon stored under the heaps till I got there.

TINY: Essex Street pickle man waiting to lift me by my head with two hands up so I could see my great-grandfather.

LORE, TONY AND TINY: Can you see? Can you see him?

TINY: Yes.

TONY: Up so he could guide me careful over the top of the pickle barrel to hold me awkward. Pickle juice so are up my arm.

LORE, TONY AND TINY: My laughter expected.

TINY: My joy welcomed on Essex Street.

LORE: Sometime I gave way to believing my being was justified. Known to be a valuable whimsy. I grew up in a love zone with a reputation for tough endings.

EMILYN: No white mans children. Put every one of those in the ground bloody with no hands.

MAMA: Second person. Present tense.

EMILYN: We make the best cloth in Legrange and all around. My mama know the roots for dyeing the cloth. She showed us the flowers for gold and red and death. No white mans children. The dogs chewed away my great-grandmothers lips she was still in Africa. We carry that picture in our heart when giving birth. Mama birth us with that in her & it helps us fetch a good price. *(She places bag over her head and sings and loosens her clothes)*

TONY: I need new shoes.

TINY: My ponytail & my tight skirt & my Aunt Anna & my new train & my castor oil & my dog Billy & my frankfurters & my boy bug & my playground & my daddy.

TONY: Lets Speak Chinese.

They make language.

Lets Speak Spanish.

They make language.

LORE: I think we might be Spanish.

TINY: I want to be Catholic. But I think we're Indian first.

MAMA: You aint nothin but some ignorant niggers?

TONY: Forever ever ever ever forever.

Ida digs them up over there. When they tear down the buildings. We put all the rats in our pockets and in Pitt Street Park we bury our friends. Tiny sings them away from the devil. Ida and me we kiss them.

TRIP NUMBER 2

Tony and Tiny execute five gestures then walk into the light and speak at will.

TONY: The day the girls were to leave started like the others. They awoke early to breakfast in bed, and discussed at length their plans for the day. They decided to pack early and preordered an elaborate dinner to celebrate their final day in Italy. They decided to take a long walk on that last day to get a final look at the country, and to say goodbye to some of their favorite monuments in Rome. At day's end, when their plans were completed, the girls prepared to leave. When they called downstairs for a bellboy to assist them with their luggage, the management sent one up right away. He loaded their luggage onto a cart and went ahead of them to deposit it all at the front desk, where they were to meet for the final pick-up. Tony, Tiny and Ida turned before leaving the room for one last look. They wanted to remember where everything was, and felt a pang of sadness at the thought of never seeing the room again. When they reached the front desk the bellboy was standing by. They tipped him, and thanked him and thanked him for his services. Then they turned to the clerk behind the desk to thank him for the hotel's hospitality. He smiled, shook his head and handed them the bill. What is this? asked Tony with a look of surprise. It's your bill Señorita. Oh no, I said in a confident tone, this is not our bill, it's the bill of TWA. TWA? said the man. Yes, TWA is to pay for our stay here. No, no, replied the clerk, TWA is required to pay only a portion of the bill. What do you mean only a portion of the bill? asked Ida in a less confident tone . . . I interrupted, Oh no sir, TWA is to pay all of the bill; with that I summoned Tiny and Ida, and the three girls turned and left the hotel. Outside the doorman hailed them a cab. As the cab was loading their luggage into the trunk, the manager ran from the hotel with the bill in his hand. Wait, wait, he insisted, you did not pay your bill! Tony turned toward him and again tried to explain that the bill was to be sent to TWA. The manager shook his head and said he had just called TWA. He said TWA had refused to pay such a large bill for such a short period of time. Well how much is the bill for in dollars? asked Tony. The manager did some quick calculations, then turned and said $1,600. American dollars. WHAT!! SHOUTED TONY. Sixteen hundred American dollars, why that's crazy! Crazy maybe, replied the manager, but that is the amount of your bill. By now the girls were frantic. Ida began to break out in hives, and Tiny began to cry. Tony tried to appear calm, as the palms of her hands started to sweat and her heartbeat accelerated. She knew they didn't have that kind of money, and the thought of scrubbing floors or making beds in a hotel where they had just been treated like royalty made her wish the ground would open and swallow them all. Again she tried to explain her position to the manager but by this time he did not want to listen, and threatened to call the police. Well then call them, shouted Tony, trying to appear confident in her position; I don't care, the bill is not our responsibility and we will not pay! With that she shoved Tiny and Ida into the cab, then jumped in herself; she screamed Airport!

Five gestures.

TINY: My refrigerator & my tight skirt & my love & my piano & my window.

LORE: Oatmeal & pinto beans.

TONY: New shoes new shoes new shoes . . .

MICKEY: 62¢ & 53¢ new shoes pinto beans, frankfurters.

LORE: Pinto beans!

MICKEY: 62¢ & 53¢ Eat those goddamn peas & be glad!

Movement.

LORE: Can I have those pictures I just want to see him. He might be my husband I have no pictures of my husband. Those pictures might be of his face. I have never seen them. You took the pictures of my husband, you have them. I want to see his face!

EMILYN: Who are you?

LORE: Yes.

MAMA: You eat what you can get. I begged food for my children. Some rice two potatoes and we would eat off that for days. My babies in my arms so tiny from hunger, I had no one to help me.

EMILYN: They give you any old somethin. You eat roots & chicken feet boiled up with onions I like that.

MICKEY: Where are the oranges?

TINY: Tony, she eats the oranges, she eats the bread, she eats the eggs.

MICKEY: 53¢ *(She ties a rope around Tony's hand. She counts her money)*

LORE: I cant do nothin, you know it too.

TONY: I have to pee Lore. My hands hurt. I wont do it again I swear, I wont eat the jelly.

LORE: She said if I let you loose I have to get tied up too.

TONY: I cant run & the devil is under my bed & he will get me again. I wont do it. Let me go for a little while. I have to pee Lore.

LORE: I cant do nothin you know it too.

TONY: I try to love you Lore.

The red lights come up.

RADIO: "Lordy, Lordy, Lordy Miss Claudy," Fats Domino. Then "Good Golly Miss Molly."

Lore dances a hard dance and sings with the Radio.

LORE: If you want to be in love with a boy you take his picture and put it under your pillow and you dont let your sisters see it ever. Your heart. If you really like his face take a picture of it, dont let your mother see it. Your heart. Make your own picture, and live with it. Keep your head out of holes.

Drums. Deola, in deep breath and movement, enters.

DEOLA: I faced the sea calling
    Oranyan ogun ma de o. I am calling you. My lips are gone.
My voice is coming up from this hole.

LORE: We are under attack.

DEOLA:
        Oranyan agun ma de o.
        Oranyan agun ma de o.

LORE: We are under attack. Come on your charger. My husbands pictures are hidden from us. We dont know his face. We dont know how he is dying. His enemies are digging holes for us, we are tied to keep us from eating and we cannot wet the bed again.

Deola and Lore take the ropes off Tony's hands and feet. Tony dances a hard dance.

TONY: I just want to go to the bathroom.
LORE: Please dont you go eating anything.
TONY: I do feel a little hungry. Just a few eggs. Some grapes, bread!

Tony pulls food out from hidden places and moves downstage to eat.

LORE: If you do it she is gonna tie me up too. Tony, Tony.
TONY: Those pictures of the dead boy are on the top shelf. I saw them. He is dead and his face looks like the rats. I kissed his face, his picture. The picture makes me hungry Lore. I have to eat everything.
LORE: He is dead then?
MAMA: Sho as you born.

Dancin to ragtime and that low-count Bessie Smith. Niggers all along the tracks wailin all night in that part of town for no-counts like they was. The swells were not picking cotton in the morning with me and my children. They had hair like my sister.

I will never marry no man that wears a cloth cap. Pick it children—we going away from this place. One dollar a hundred pounds. Pick! We gonna go where all the men wear suits and drink with the swells.

Mama sings the "Toreadors Song" from Bizet's Carmen. *Mickey sings the "Toreadors Song" from* Carmen Jones.

WHITE CHOCOLATE

Mickey and Lore move into a memory in which Her is Lore and She is Mickey. This is a night story.

HER: So there would be no *Sunrise Semester*. No Marty & Millie cartoons. You never knew who was on the couch or why. Who was this one asleep in the living room. Who was this in his shorts like he thought he was my daddy. From here he was short with a big ring on his finger.

SHE: Oh yes! That's a fabulous ring...

HER: That must be why she brought him home. Was he going to take us to Sweden?

SHE: Live for your dreams. Stand on the strength of your own convictions. When you...

HER: When she became a dancer she and Vernon Profit's mother were both making plans to go away. Vernon's mother I was told was going to Paris. So she would go to Sweden. People would ask when we were going? And if she had one like this we were going soon. When she worked in the pencil factory I could always get in the living room to watch the TV. Since she became a dancer and now a singer too, we had to stay in bed until the poets, songwriters, dancers and barmaids got off the couch, the floor, the big rose chair. Then in one of her voices she'd call us out to meet them.

SHE: His name is Otis. He writes songs. He writes music for the radio. He writes hits. He writes for...

HER: Then she said it. That name we hadn't mentioned since he said "all a nigger could do for him is tie his shoes."

SHE: He's famous!

HER: He's ugly!

She made me go with him to buy the things for breakfast. Eggs, bread, even orange juice and bacon from Abbey's. We rode the elevator down. He wore a suit. I said "yes" a lot and he knew! You had to give Abbey a note for bacon. He would take you to the back and give you the package there. In the back is where you would see the numbers from the place they had been before. And you knew he was being kind to you. Out loud. Otis asked for the bacon out loud in the front. Didn't he know anything? We got kosher salami with the store full of people. Lloyd Archibald crossed my path asking when we goin' to Sweden. S-H-I-T. Otis told me what he would do if I was his child. And for at least the fourth time I informed him that I was not. My father is the most handsome man in the world. And why she would want somebody like him with those pop eyes? "You are a smart girl."

SHE: You are a smart...

HER: He did not play the piano well, only a few changes like Joe Webb. But I had heard blind Calvin and his fingers moved all around. We talked anyway after all he owned all the elevators.

SHE: Billie Dawn, Eddy Jones, Laura Webb, Ricco! Teddy Vann & Champ!

HER: All the stores on Avenue D sold special. Mirch sold special! Toys at special prices. Mr. Max made shoes and he made special ugly shoes. Tony needed shoes every other month. Five dollars every time. Mr. Max could make you the same ugly shoes. The bakery was owned by a couple who had been married a long time. And the Chinese sold everything Chinese. Chinese...food. Chinese...laundry. Chinese...apples. Chinese checkers. Chinatown. Chinese

She and Her sing "Ching Chow."

SHE: Fabulous!

HER: I stood in the laundry waiting to pick up the sheets. This new man who was taking us to Sweden...

SHE: Where I go my children go. If you love me my children...

HER: This one had to have all the sheets ironed. He ran a booking agency. As soon as the lady came out I sang her my song. It was a wonderful day I told her. I told her see John O'Conner that's a boy in my class, he's in the third grade too. He asked me at the monkey bars to marry him. To be a bride with him. His father was a teacher at our school P.S. 188. And John's father and his sister were Irish. His mother was Irish too but she was dead so John and his sister came to school with their daddy. We gonna marry and have Chinese children. See he said I am pink and you are brown that makes yellow Chinese! So I told the lady I went to the Chinese restaurant and I sat down where the Chinese food lady could see me. And I thought about our pretty house with a place for everything. She came out from behind the counter and asked me what I wanted where was my note? "I want to see your children. Your children." She got her husband and I shook his hand. "I want to see your children." The children lived in the back I showed him where they were. They are cute I told John just like kittens. The fourth grade John was sent to a private Catholic school. His father said he would never come to 188 again. We laughed in celebration that day, I was happy, I was singing.

There are Chinese apples. Chinese checkers. Chinese children!

SHE: We are the same as ever. We are here. This is where we came to be free. Learn the difference between domestic champagne and French. Good clothes are good even second-hand. *(She sings "Hineh mah tov... ")* Me casa es su casa en la dia en la noche en toda. Won't let nobody turn me around turn me around...

HER: First she moved to Brooklyn and then to Zaire in 1971 she has not returned. She made both moves alone with her children. She has never been to Sweden. *(She sings the "Ching Chow" song)*

SHE: Fabulous, fabulous, brava, brava!

They applaud one another.

Lore moves from this memory into a play space with the sisters. Mickey is left dancing at the club. This is her work.

MICKEY: 62¢ and 53¢ new shoes pinto beans frankfurters. & we all picked. A hundred pounds a dollar. Rema was 11 & I was 9. Mr. Chissolm would call one of us in and use his fingers inside us. And I would cry and Rema would scream. Mama would make us go into him again & again. We picked cotton rather than have to stay home with him. One hundred pounds a dollar. My brother stayed in trouble. In Memphis they took a niggers life for any reason. And Mr. Chissolm beat Mama and they both beat us till they drew blood then his fingers. Tore me open with his thing. Tore Rema open from behind. She was too sick to work but she worked and she bled & we picked a hundred pounds of cotton & we slept in the same bed with Mama and Mr. Chissolm & I pulled lint out from between my legs & I picked cotton till we left Memphis till we boarded the train.

MAMA: Why dont you ask your questions?

EMILYN: I havent any question to ask sir.

TONY: Ask it! You scared?

MAMA: They all dance. Yes sir.

TINY: There are a lot of pictures on top of the closet Lore.

EMILYN: Coltsfoot herb, yellow, green, wool, alum

Dandelion plant magenta wool

Common plum bark, black, wool, coppers

petals cotton roots dye bedstraw flowering ash bark and leaves. The lace must be finished & my Jadge must be fed. He is the son of a colored man.

MAMA: Third person. Present tense.

EMILYN: Kin to Dinah Shore.

Third person. Present tense.

Sold.

The lace must be finished & my Jadge must be fed. He is the son of a colored man. A colored man soul.

MAMA: My father named me Niagra Fall Montreal Ford for the Falls, "The most beautiful thing he ever saw," my father Jadge Anderson Wilford Ford said. The war set the whole race free. All my fathers children was educated. We wore our middle blouses and white dresses with blue satin or velvet sashes. My sister Pink ran away at age 17. Never saw her again her nature made her crazy. We all played piano and could read. Daddy yella. Mama black, black.

EMILYN: Ask your questions sir.

MAMA: If we picked enough cotton we would get out of there by the first of November. I made dresses for my girls. Pete and me worked the fields till dark in Arkansas we were gettin back fast as we could flyin up the road. White man stopped us and made Pete lay on the side of the road. "I has small children sir

& they is alone by theyselves." That man hit me so many times for sayin anything about the children. Pete heard everything. That man didnt leave me alone till day and we crossed the bridge that morning. "Goin in the wrong direction," folks shouted from the trucks goin into the fields. Thats what happened to us for we could get out of Memphis.

EMILYN: Marry that girl Jadge. Bring us back to our selves so she dont ever have to have no white mans babies. Look that girl in the face and do right by her. Make no mistakes. (She takes the bag into her mouth and dances the dog dance)

MICKEY: I know you told me but what could you say?

MAMA: I got you here. Thats what.

MONKEY DANCES

A trip up North. Kick up your legs and get onboard. Everyone's crossing the line. Everyone picks up a gesture.

TINY: BORINQUE!

Borinque thru azure & rain storms in ruffles, closed in fingers. An unknown listener of love and clear light playing guitar, answering questions about the origins of roaches and tears. Borinque clean washed linoleum raised against too much steam heat. High-rise 10 to 4 rooms and rice and rice and rice grateful for meat. Unable to find mangos in season or blue water. Loving everything American. Working New York brooms and Long Island gardens. Loving Ricky Nelson & Topo Gigo, Joselito on the Sullivan show.

Calling Carmen! Carmen Morales Rodriguez Ortiz Aiyala Arroacho Perez Cruz Carmen Sanchez Dominques Pinero Rivera Santiago Sonja Clara Jose Manuelo Edgar Ellia Luz Anna Borinque. Crying pleanas in Pentecostal basements. Just good dancers. Villains cut in brilliante. Singers leaning gorgeous in Woolworth powder. The Lord lives in us all! Borinque marching on the head of disaster. Declaring summer by congas and cheering loud for the Yankees. Parking Desotos sideways on Columbia Street repairing nylons for the week. Borinque a world of pink rollers bringing stripes to florals orange to gold. Flirting loud on corners lined with garbage.

Smelling summer in the eyes of Borinque thru azure. Eyelids lined in tragic black pencil.

EMILYN: They all dance. Yes sir all my children dance.

Lore sits waiting while Tony eats everything. Tiny dances and sings "I Took My Son upon the Sea." The phone rings.

TINY: Hello. Are you gonna come to see us. Where are you? Kisses chocolate kisses daddy kisses.

TONY: Grow up all of us are gonna grow up. The way I want to marry is in a big yellow dress with pretzels and my hair in bobby pins new shoes & a lot of cake & beer ahhh. My nose will point down. Shit Lore. You say shit better than anyone. We beat Boo Boo so bad his mother got so mad. Well he threw gravel on my head from the roof. I taught him how to get up there then he threw that on me. Apples and ant legs. Legs. Shit Lore. You say shit the best.

A key is heard in a lock. Tiny hangs up.

MICKEY: I knew you would let her go. You always choose them over me now I have to tie you when I leave here. Both of you. None of you will help me. So I have to do this by myself.

TINY: She was crying so much Mommy, we had to dance. We wanted to play.

MICKEY: I am sitting outside the house waiting my turn. Waiting. Mama, why didnt you help me? Mama, why didnt you help me? Mama, why didnt you help me? *(She sings "Look Away Dixie Land")*

TONY: We are all together Lore see we are all in the same hole.

LORE: Who are you?

TINY: Yes.

LORE: My sister saw his picture then he is her husband. Emmet Till is her husband. And so my sisters husband is dead. But at least shes seen her husbands face.

TONY: Clap hands clap hands till daddy comes home daddy has money and mommy has none.

TINY: Who?

TONY: My nose is too big too wide too flat. *(She repeats line four more times)*

The red light consumes the stage as voices scream about Bobby Darin. Lore is caught. White Light Spirit circles her and sings the blues, a refrain.

TRIP NUMBER 3

TONY: All the way to the airport Tony tried to calm Tiny and Ida, who were hysterical. They began to fantasize all kinds of things, one of which included them all going to jail. The whole scene resembled a madhouse! When they reached the airport Tony presented the second TWA taxi voucher to the driver, he accepted it without hesitation. The three girls quickly made their way through the mass of people toward the TWA check-in counter. I told you, Tony began, trying to calm Tiny and Ida down, there would be nothing to worry about; pretty soon we will be on our way to Africa and this whole mess will be behind us. When they reached the TWA counter they presented their tickets and passports to the rep on duty. The lady accepted their credentials with a greeting and a smile. She proceeded to ask them about the seating and smoking arrangements they would prefer when she noticed the names on the passports. She made no outward sign to indicate recognition, but politely excused herself and went to the back. When she returned moments later she was accompanied by two men. The men were nicely dressed in business suits and ties. The girls noticed that one of the two men had their passports and tickets in his hand. The man smiled and quietly asked that we follow them to the rear of the airport. One minute, interrupted Tony, who are you and why do you have our things. Please, replied one of the men, we don't want to make a scene. A scene? said Tony, I'm very sorry but we will not follow you anywhere unless you identify yourselves. It was then that the two men presented their badges, and said "We are the Police." A huge lump began to develop in Tony's throat. Again she had visions of working in the hotel, or worse, going to jail. She looked toward Tiny and Ida, they were in a panic: she could tell by the blank, wide-eyed expression on their faces. The three girls walked silently behind the two men to the rear of the airport. There they went through a green door that led to a back room.

Five gestures.

In the back room stood the manager of the hotel along with two TWA executives. The girls walked in and silently seated themselves across the room from the men. They said nothing. It had been a long day and the girls began to feel weary. They were very tired of the ordeal and wanted an end to it all. Tony was the first to speak, What is going on? she asked. One of the TWA executives approached them with the voucher in his hand, he began to translate it from Italian into English. I don't recall the translation word for word but in essence it stated that TWA was responsible for fifty dollars a day in expenses. Fifty dollars a day, shouted Tony—now she was getting mad. Her feeling went from fear to anger at the audacity of the men. She began to say exactly what she felt, what the heck, they were all going to jail anyway. How dare you! she shouted. You son-of-a-bitches have put us through sheer hell today with this nonsense. She looked directly at the executive with the voucher in his hand, Your man assured us that TWA would pay for everything including telephone calls because of the three-day delay in our flight. He told us the voucher entitled us to full financial coverage, he said nothing about a fifty-dollar-a-day maximum. Why our suite came to more than fifty dollars a day, not including the meals and hotel services. Then she turned to the manager, If you knew our voucher was not enough to cover our daily charges, why did you allow us to charge everything to the voucher. Why is it you did not bring the fifty-dollar-a-day maximum to our attention? Why did you allow us to go on? It states clearly on the voucher that expenses shall not exceed fifty dollars a day, said the manager again. Where, asked Tony, show me. The manager took his finger and pointed to the sentence, Right here, he said. What the hell, she shouted, that's in Italian. We don't speak Italian, we are Americans and speak only English. Why isn't it also written in English? Look we only knew what the rep told us. We didn't know the actual nature of the voucher because we could not read the voucher; we had no way of confirming what it said, and we will not pay! With that she shouted, "Call the American consulate we want to talk to the American Ambassador about this matter." The men looked astonished and began to speak in Italian among themselves. After a time they excused themselves and all but one left the room. Tony, Tiny and Ida had no idea what to expect next. A short time later the second policeman returned to the room. He said nothing as he walked over to the girls and returned their passports and plane tickets. What's this? asked Tony. You can go now, said the officer. The girls looked at each other in disbelief. Does this mean we don't have to pay the bill? That's correct, replied the policeman, TWA will cover your debts. Why? said Tony with a surprised expression. It's the voucher, he said. The voucher? she replied. Yes, the voucher, he said, it states all limitations in Italian, and you don't speak or read Italian!

From now on if you happen to be in Italy, and for some reason are issued a TWA financial voucher, don't be surprised if the voucher is written not only in Italian and English, but also in Spanish, French, German, etc., etc.—thanks to TWA's ordeal with three lucky American girls.

Tiny and Tony, the sisters, walk off together. Emilyn, the slave, moves upstage as the stage turns red from the floor up.

LORE: I did not go on that trip to Europe or to Zaire. You see by now she, my mother wasnt talking to me at all. Well she had stopped talking to me years before, somehow she thought that I was capable of taking things away from her. See when I was twelve years old one of her boyfriends he came into my room and he . . . he. . . . *(She turns to the Radio and calls out)* Radio oh radio there is a man in the radio who loves me. *(She turns away from the Radio)* See he came into my room on Saturday morning. And I woke up his mouth was on my.... *(She again turns to the Radio)* Radio ahh radio radio...there is a man in the radio. In the radio oh. *(She turns away from the Radio)* And she blamed me for the whole thing said it my fault for.... Radio....I met my Mister Chissolm.

First person present tense.

Deola appears in red hot pants, white-blond wig and pumps: the junkie, the whore.

DEOLA: When this shit gets to 1979 Im gonna board a ship the fuck out of here. Niggers will be trying to get polite with these white dogs. I remember, I shoot this shit cause I remember I still feel the pain in my head. You gonna learn how to, live with them and talk like them and see the world like them. 1979 Im not doin none of this again. Where are your gods who will cry out for?

Mickey comes through with rope to tie the children up. She ties Lore and Tony together. Mickey hums "Look away, look away, look away Dixie Land."

LORE: Who are you?
TONY: Do you love me?
DEOLA: What wars do you remember?
LORE: Yes.

Red light climbs out from everywhere.

Yes.
TONY: Do you love me?

CAGE

RHYTHM

KIA

CORTHRON

When I write a play, I start with a political issue. I find out who the characters are, then I let them speak with each other so I can figure out what they are capable of. The last step is story.

In *Cage Rhythm,* the beginning was my feeling that no one was hearing the voices of women in prison. I started reading. While I was up in Connecticut, I visited a women's prison. When I came back to New York, I read more and contacted the Women's Prison Association in the East Village. This was a way of sifting through ideas to figure out what I was trying to say.

One of the big problems for women of color is that they tend to be sent to prison for drug abuse while white women go to rehabilitation centers. It's an illness that you should be treated for; you should not be punished for it.

Another issue was that often when men go to prison, the wives continue to visit them and the family unit is still together. But often the husbands or male lovers of women in prison don't come to see them. If the women don't have a close relative, they stand a chance of having their children taken away from them, so their family unit is split. Because of their connection with their children, I felt all of these issues needed to be addressed.

Artistic Challenges and Discoveries
This play differs from my previous plays because of the short, clipped scenes. In this piece, the most stimulating challenge was going directly to the heart of the scene, immediately hitting the climax, getting rid of the extraneous perspectives. There's something about the bare text that leaves the audience naked too; it puts them in the center of things perhaps because it makes an assumption with its sparseness that they know what's going on and they are part of this world.

The second challenge was related to the production. I didn't want the astral projection scenes directed in such a way that they were defined for the audience as dreams or as in Avery's imagination, because it's up to the audience—each individual's personal spirituality and what they believe.

The whole dramatic diagram is also very different. Previously my plays had a more typical growing action that led to a climax, but this piece is filled with many climaxes. It's a completely different heartbeat.

The Balancing Act
In general, I work at balancing the political with the specific. I don't write agitation-propaganda, which is not a judgment on it because I have no problem with that kind of material; e.g., posters urging workers to strike in Latin America. The most upsetting aspect of agit-prop is that people who control the media can best use it because they have the most access. The Persian Gulf War was all over the television, presented in a way to whip up the country into a pro-war frenzy.

I like to touch people on a more guttural level than simply with the words, so I have to find a balance. I don't like to go too far into the emotion because you can quickly lose the political point. And if people don't want to get the political point, they won't; so it's important that it be there but without being so heavy that people can easily dismiss it as agit-prop. It's a very delicate balance.

The Aesthetic
My style is somewhere between naturalism and experimental. And it is rhythmic; there's a certain rhythm that comes out of my subconscious that is necessary, even down to accented syllables, for the text to make sense.

Definitions of Heroism
Heroism is survival inside and outside of the prison. The times when Avery could make it through the whole day into the next outside of the prison and take care of her children were heroic accomplishments.

The Responsibility of the Theatre Artist
Theatre has a magic and an immediacy that can be used to tell people things that they are not hearing elsewhere. There is room for all kinds of theatre, but I am not a person who writes for the love of writing. I never have. I write because I feel there's something that needs to be said. It's my responsibility to put in my best effort to say it in the strongest way that will get the point across to the people.

Distinctions between Women's and Men's Writing
I think there is this split: Women can start with character, from a more inner place, and men can start with story, from an outer place. That's not to say one or the other is better—you have to get to character and story eventually—but there is a tendency for the starting point to be different.

The Darkness and the Light

There is an artistic place and a political place I'm moving toward which come together.

My work starts from a pinpoint, the smallest thing that touches me in some way. It's usually something negative in society that hits me in a way that I can't believe it, it's so ugly. I feel a sense of helplessness and I have to do something. The least I can do is try to make people think. I hope in my work, despite even a seemingly tragic ending, despite the fact that these ugly things exist, that there is some sense that it doesn't have to be this way. Something in the work suggests hope, possibility.

In *Cage Rhythm*, we know that Avery has the potential to be a good mother but society has put her into a situation where she can't even speak with her daughter. The tragedy is that societal mistake. If I had written it as an upbeat story, it would leave people thinking that there's no work to be done. I don't want the audience to leave feeling depressed; I hope that I've pushed them to a point where they were emotionally involved enough that they are thinking about these issues and the solutions.

It became clearer to me the more I knew about exactly which issues I wanted to point out; but originally, I went into the piece because I thought no one was hearing their voices at all. I didn't know precisely what I wanted to say, but I wanted somebody to hear.

ABOUT THE AUTHOR

Kia Corthron's *Come Down Burning*, which was workshopped at the Long Wharf Theatre with *Cage Rhythm*, was produced by the American Place Theatre in 1993. In 1992, Corthron received the Manhattan Theatre Club's first Van Lier Playwriting Fellowship and, under its commission, wrote *Catnap Allegiance*. The Circle Repertory Company Lab presented *Wake Up Lou Riser*, and her plays also have received readings at Playwrights Horizons, the Philadelphia Theatre Company and the Voice and Vision Retreat for Women Theatre Artists. Recently announced as the winner of the New Professional Theatre's Screenplay/Playwriting Festival, Corthron currently is at work on new pieces commissioned by Second Stage Theatre and the Goodman Theatre.

A member of the Dramatists Guild, Corthron received her MFA from Columbia University and lives in New York City.

ABOUT THE WORK

Cage Rhythm, written as a companion piece to *Come Down Burning*, was originally workshopped under the direction of Marya Mazor at Long Wharf Theatre in 1993. It subsequently received a reading, directed by Lynn Thomson, at the Philadelphia Theatre Company.

CHARACTERS

AVERY

T.J.

MONTANA

CORRECTIONAL OFFICERS (C.O.S)

JOY ANN

LEESY

ESPERANZA

MICKY

FAYE

OTHER INMATES

THREE CHILDREN, at least one is a girl

HOMELESS WOMAN

AUTHOR'S NOTE

Actors may double roles as individual productions demand. However, regardless of doubling, each inmate is intended to be a different woman; there should be, or appear to be, different C.O.s; and if one actor plays all four of the children (including Leesy), it is important that she appear to be a different child in each scene.

CAGE RHYTHM

Scene One

Cell. The two cots are necessarily bunked; the space is too narrow for any other furniture arrangement. The lower bunk is bare. There is a toilet and bureau, and a small window with a curtain. On the wall are a few photographs. Avery paces anxiously. She holds a short pencil in her hand. Eventually a Correctional Officer (C.O.) passes by.

AVERY *(Hesitation)*: Please?

C.O.: No! I ain't got no pencil I ain't got no paper, if I did I wouldn't give you none. You got money, go to the commissary.

AVERY: Not open 'til Wednesday.

C.O. shrugs.

I gotta write to my little girl, I need ta tell her somethin'.

C.O. starts to exit.

You can get it, you know you can get it.

C.O.: I said I won't! Lights out anyway, you ain't s'posed ta be engaged in any activity 'cept dreams.

Avery pulls out her pathetic pencil; shows C.O.

AVERY: Sharpen it?

C.O.: That ain't in my job description.

C.O. exits. Avery paces more. Then an idea: She takes out her cigarette lighter and begins burning around the pencil lead. From under her clothes she pulls out a roll of toilet paper, sets it on the floor and tests the pencil on it: It works. She sits on the floor to write the letter, rolling more toilet paper out as she needs it.

Scene Two

Avery's cell. Avery enters, discovers T.J., who stares out the window. There is now a blanket on the lower bunk, a hairbrush tossed on it.

C.O. *(Off)*: Ten o'clock lockup, ladies. Ten o'clock. Be in your cells and ready for the count. Good night.

T.J. *(Turns to Avery)*: Routine transfer. So they said, how stupid they think I am? They fucked up. The left hand never knows the right's business, I'm locked up, seg, three days and the admitting C.O. notices my empty cot, claims it for some new thing. No surprise my cellmate didn't pipe up, she and I starting to think the other smells too bad so she pounces her opportunity to keep her mouth shut. Don't worry, I'm hardly ever here. They like to keep me in segregation, seg's my second home. Or first. I'm T.J.

They stare at each other. T.J. turns back to the window.

You got a good view. The yard. And the street.

AVERY: Visitin' day you can see all the cars. *(She looks at the beds)*

T.J.: I took the lower cuz you looked set up there. One's as lumpy as the other. Okay?

Another woman walks by the cell.

WOMAN: Hey, Avery, come here. I got a present for ya. *(Avery doesn't look at her)* Come on, Avery, I made it special for ya. *(Pause. To T.J.)* She don't never want her presents. *(She aims her butt at Avery's face and makes a fart sound with her mouth. She exits laughing)*

AVERY *(Climbs up)*: I like the upper. Feels farther away.

T.J. *(Meaning the lower bunk)*: What happened to her?

AVERY: Parole. Yesterday. She wa'n't here long. *(Pause)* You here long?

T.J. looks at Avery; doesn't answer. Avery refers to photographs.

One rule: Don't touch the pictures.

Suddenly dark. A bit of light from the window.

You think that's good, wait'll the full moon. You can read in the dark. Hey. They forget our door?

T.J.: Used to be able to take it. Solitary confinement. Plenty enough experience in seg I've had, you'd think maybe I'd get used to it. Never, three days in the bin I almost knocked down Officer Robbins when she unlocked that door, free!

A C.O. appears. Clangs the door shut.

Scene Three

Avery holds a child's hand. They walk to the edge of a pond. Avery dips her feet in.

AVERY: Cool 'em off. Burnin' your shoe rubber the sidewalks all day, here's the relief. Wanna cool yours off?

Child shakes head.

Ain'tcha hot?

Child shakes head. Avery wades out into the water. Quiet awhile.

CHILD: Don't kick your feet, you'll scare the ducks.
AVERY: I won't.

Pause.

CHILD: You never talk like that before. *(Pause)* Yesterday you tole me I get in the pond you beat my butt.
AVERY *(Vague; confused)*: Did I? *(Pause)* That was yesterday.

Quiet.

CHILD: Can I have my gum now?

AVERY *(Looks around)*: Sure, where they sell it?

CHILD: In your *purse*.

Avery looks at her purse as if she has just discovered it.

AVERY: Oh. *(Rifles through and finds the gum. Holds it out to child)* You gotta come get it.

Child considers, then takes off shoes, wades over to Avery, takes a piece of gum. Avery takes a piece. They chomp big. Eventually child reaches into water, picks up a little shiny stone.

Oooh, that's a pretty one.

CHILD: I can have it?

AVERY: Uh huh. What for, show your teacher?

Child hands rock to Avery. She is surprised, and gives child a hug.

Scene Four

Yard. Avery leans against the fence, staring out. Montana sits near.

MONTANA: They practice it over and over. Strap 'em down, buckle 'em, pull down the switch. Lift it. Not enough? Again. Not quite? Again, again, they got classes and limited hands-on trainin', by the time they escort the real thing into the electro-cution room they oughta got the trick down solid. Still. Some-thin' always comes up, little monkey wrench I know someone scheduled for a fifteen-minute treatment at a minute past mid-night. They don't come collect his things 'til five to one.

AVERY: What do you care, they reduced you—death to life. Why?

MONTANA: Circumstantial proof. Not your concern though.

AVERY: Two years death row?

Montana nods.

And how long you behind bars, altogether?

MONTANA: Forever.

AVERY: How long?

MONTANA: How old are you?

AVERY: Thirty-three.

MONTANA: Longer.

AVERY *(Looks around, then pulls out a small wrapped parcel she smuggled)*: Here.

MONTANA *(Subtly takes and hides in her clothing)*: Thank ya, thank ya. What I owe? cigarettes?

AVERY: Got my shoppin' privileges temporarily revoked for cussin' out a C.O., every day a my life I cuss out a C.O. now suddenly one decides to write me up about it. Next time you go to the commissary, I 'preciate a chocolate bar. Almonds. Two! keepin' a few extra, sometime my kids come visit me I need somethin' to give 'em.

MONTANA: This ain't leave ya flat, will it? Felt like lotsa toothpaste in that piece a paper.

AVERY: Plenty a toothpaste I got, what I give ya just a sample from my king-size tube. Plus little bitta shampoo.

MONTANA: Hot diggity, need that, I'm always forgettin' to check off shampoo on my order list. Then deal with the turds behind the counter: "No buyin' less ya ordered it beforehand." Why I gotta be spendin' my forty cents a workday on hair shit no-how? shampoo s'posed ta be free, but the dole-out we get's for white women's hair. They's the minority here, and still got the advantage, anything guaranteed us made for them, we wanna wash our hair it's a luxury we gotta pay for.

AVERY: Never forget nothin' on my list, but what I check they never got half of, what's the difference. But where your blues come from? thought you had a "in" with the C.O.s.

MONTANA: I do, but they on their guard too, their smugglin's got limits.

AVERY: Funny taste you got in friends.

MONTANA: They oughta all be our best buddies, we employed 'em. This boondocks place beat out five others vyin' for where the prison be built, prison means jobs. Stable. Cuz never been one prison too many, they build it they always find enough a us to fill it. Quick. *(Pause)* Your new girl's in my beauty trainin'.

AVERY: Yeah?

MONTANA: Wonder 'bout her. She been to college, why she take beauty class? How much you make?

AVERY: Fitty-five cent. Half-day.

MONTANA: Fitty-five answerin' the airplane reservation phones like you. Sure she got that conversation skill, college, why you think she in shampoo and nails? There half-day only give her thirty.

Avery shrugs.

Ain't too friendly, I know that. She my student, I gesture nice, hand outstretched, "I'm Montana. I'm from Mississip'." She mumble somethin', her eyes don't meet mine.

AVERY: She just come to my cell week ago. Seem okay. *(She holds out her arm to the side, parallel to the ground)* Look at this, it's a line. You was born here *(Indicates shoulder)*, this is now *(Fingertips)*. When you came to jail?

Montana considers, then touches Avery's arm between the shoulder and elbow.

All this inside, *(She indicates the appropriate sections of her arm)* just this out?

MONTANA: You asked.

Pause.

AVERY: I'll show you a way out sometime.

MONTANA: Out, out, there ain't no work release, go to the men's prison you want work release.

AVERY *(Shakes her head)*: Somethin' else.

MONTANA: You get out?

Avery nods. Pause.

Next time you go, bring me back one a them word-find puzzle books, all these scrambled letters and ya look for the right words and circle 'em, *big print.* And a pencil.

Scene Five

Rec room. Avery sits on a couch, watching TV. Another woman plays solitaire at a card table nearby. T.J. enters, stares at Avery. Avery turns to T.J.

AVERY: Never seen you watch TV.

T.J.: Would've loaned you my brush if you'd asked, I do like to be asked though.

AVERY *(Turns to TV)*: Never seen you here at all, you usually spend your free hour alone in the library, solitary you hate when they give it to ya, but the resta your life you spend solitaryin' yourself.

T.J.: Also noticed my toothpaste supply diminished suddenly and severely, mysteriously, over one night. What else?

T.J. continues staring at Avery. Finally Avery turns to T.J.

AVERY: I didn't take it!

More staring, then T.J. exits.

WOMAN: Didn't want it too bad, did she?

Avery doesn't answer. T.J. reenters, looks at Avery.

AVERY: If you came to be around people once in a blue moon, you'd know the rules a the rec. You done made the decision to come means you stuck here for the hour, I coulda told you that if you'd asked, then ya wouldna had to get your little embarrassed ass turned 'round by the C.O. soon's you walked out the door.

T.J., pissed, flops down on the other end of the couch. On second thought, she gets up and drops her butt on the floor behind the couch so she and Avery can't see each other. Pause.

WOMAN *(Without looking up)*: You play Five Hundred?

For several seconds it appears the question will be ignored; then suddenly T.J. gets up and sits opposite the woman, who deals. As they play, Avery pulls the brush out of her clothes and holds it over the table as she begins to pluck out one bristle at a time. She doesn't look at T.J. or the woman. T.J. is concentrating on the game but eventually glances at Avery. T.J. jumps up and moves toward Avery, and Avery just as suddenly lets out a great scream/ moan, shaking her whole body in a very exaggerated fashion. This startles T.J. and keeps her from moving any closer.

WOMAN: Jesus! Nuts!

AVERY: Three more, three good ones. *(She brushes her hair three more strokes, each one long and luxurious. She hands the brush to T.J.)* That's somethin', that's somethin'. Not them damn little black combs they issue, pull your hair all day long you don't feel a thing, but that. First stroke a that this mornin' suddenly I remember what my scalp feels like.

Scene Six

The cell.

JOY ANN *(Off)*: Ole Black Joe was a merry ole soul and he played in the coal. *(Pause)* Ole Black Joe was a merry ole soul and he played in the coal.

Joy Ann will repeat this throughout the scene. She may say it twice, take a break, say it four times, long break, say it once. The number of repetitions should be irregular, but the rhythm itself always the monotonous same.
    Some stuff that T.J. bought at the commissary—box of cereal,

paperback books, etc.—is visible from under her bed.

Avery, sitting on her bunk, holds an icepack over a huge bruise on her leg. T.J., standing by the window, looks at Avery.

AVERY: Maybe I fell.

T.J. turns to the window.

She's a rich bitch, ain't she?

T.J. looks at Avery.

Right behind ya in commissary line, I saw all the stuff ya got. Notebook, pens, cold cereal so you ain't gotta eat the shit they serve.

T.J.: Helped yourself to that, I noticed.

AVERY: Top dollar you could get in here for a half day's sixty-five cents, and no one gets top dollar, now how you pay for Grape Nuts?

T.J.: If you budgeted, you could do it.

AVERY: Don't gimme that! you got a source.

T.J. *(Turns to the window. Pause)*: You got kids?

AVERY: *Why?*

T.J. *(Shrugs)*: Just wondered you had any kids. Any visitors. *(Pause)* Those little girls on your wall...*(Pause)* I guessed drugs put you in, that's the standard. But you get the clumsies too often, a scratch here, bruise there, you ain't too popular, that usually means kids.

AVERY: I was a good mother! *(Pause)* You sayin' I wa'n't?

T.J.: Not saying a thing, I don't know you.

AVERY: I'm a good mother, don't call me child abuse. Look.

Avery tries to climb down. T.J., noticing her struggle, helps her. Avery digs in her bedsheet and pulls out a crayon-colored Santa Claus which is taped to a homemade "sleigh"—a disposable Scotch-tape dispenser.

AVERY: A December thing, for my oldest. Leesy. I made it.

T.J. takes it.

You think I oughta color the sleigh?

T.J. shakes her head.

But it needs reindeer, right? I'll make some reindeer. *(She hides the sleigh back in the sheet)*
T.J.: Eighty-seven in the shade yesterday. Long wait 'til December.

T.J. turns to the window. A small hand mirror lies on the bureau. Avery gently touches it. T.J. turns around.

You can borrow it.

Avery does. Pulls out a small plastic comb and begins raking it through her hair.

AVERY: You got a wife?
T.J.: You know what I'm waiting for.
AVERY: Inside.
T.J.: Oh. No. Why? I have one on the out.
AVERY: Inside's where you need one. Lonely. *(Pause)* Maybe you ain't been in that long.
T.J.: Since twenty-four. I'm thirty-five.
AVERY: Whadju do? you don't look like drugs. Kill a white man?

Pause.

T.J.: Group I'm with, we do stuff. Hot plates and a clothes bin. Speakers. Rallies.
AVERY: So?
T.J.: Particular concern of mine: police brutality, racial.
AVERY: Gimme the meat.
T.J.: Weird tale, I'm waiting for the B when all the sudden this black man runs past fast. I'm staring after him, then I'm shoved. Twenty? thirty white cops? One black, the tail end. All

running his direction, guns waving, this cop stampede, one black man? Mobs scare me, something went through me. Tripped one.

AVERY: Into the tracks?

T.J. nods.

B train sliced him?

T.J. nods.

White cop murder, why ain't you death row?

T.J.: Manslaughter. Wanted him stopped, not dead, but forgot where I was, too close to the edge. Verdict should've been manslaughter, but... something else. Unfortunate for me, some kind of solidarity, invisible fraternity between cops and C.O.s, all come down to politics, why you think I spend half my time in seg?

AVERY: When you gettin' out? *(No answer)* She loyal to you?

T.J.: Doubt it. Eleven years? I wouldn't.

AVERY: Eleven years comin' to see ya is loyal, don't care what she doin' out there. My baby's father: gone. On the street pleadin' for a fix, he got the paddywagon long before me. I'd call, visit weekly and I make friends with other women doin' the same. And he so adorin' just don't let him out. Cuz let our man out watch him disappear off the face a our earth. On the other hand I don't know a woman in here whose boyfriend didn't dump her soon's he found out he wouldn't be gettin' convenient unlimited cootchie no more. They don't call to say goodbye. *(Pause)* I been in seven.

T.J.: Selling?

AVERY: Usin'.

T.J.: Seven for using?!

AVERY: They gettin' tougher. *(Pause)* I ain't seen 'em! all that time. My kids, Leesy four, Bina two when I'm took away, now eleven and nine, foster parents ain't required bring 'em more 'n fifty miles. I'm farther.

T.J. *(Turns to window)*: Too bad you're not white. White they send you to the rehab center. Black they send you to jail. *(Pause)* That's her.

Avery hobbles over to look.

AVERY: She pretty.

T.J. grabs the mirror from Avery, moves away and starts stroking her own hair.

I wa'n't finished.
T.J.: Why, you expecting somebody?

Avery shoves T.J. hard, knocks the mirror onto the floor. It breaks. They stare at it.

AVERY: You shouldna said it.

T.J. begins picking up the pieces. A moment, then Avery starts to help.

T.J.: Cut yourself.

Now Avery notices the blood on her hand.

C.O. *(Enters; opens cell door)*: Somebody here for ya. *(Sees blood)* Dammit!
AVERY: Nothin' big.
C.O. *(To T.J.)*: Get a rag.

T.J. runs off.

AVERY: Ain't nothin'.

C.O. has pulled out her handkerchief and is wrapping Avery's hand.

c.o.: You crazy?

AVERY: Accident! I didn't cut up.

c.o.: No, you wouldn't.

AVERY: That was two years ago, that was once. How'd I cut up? the cut's on my hand, not my wrist.

c.o.: No disaster, a nick.

AVERY: What I said.

T.J. returns with many paper towels and is ignored.

c.o.: I don't understand nunna you and don't wanna. I ain't never goin' to the city and my kids ain't never, last night you call me Country Bumpkin and snicker, all I got to say is thank God we're far enough out when your people come it's for a day visit and leave. *(To T.J.)* Come on.

T.J. exits with C.O.

Scene Seven

Avery sits at a picnic table. She is chowing down on a large pizza with all the works. A small brown paper bag also on the table. A homeless woman appears. She stares at Avery for several seconds. Avery belches big, keeps eating. Finally notices the woman. Stops.

HOMELESS WOMAN: Quarter? Or dime?

Avery looks at her meal. Considers.

AVERY: You like anchovies?

The woman nods. Avery picks up the paper bag, moves away from the table and gestures toward the pizza. The woman quickly sits, looks in box.

QUEEN MARGARET UNIVERSITY LIBRARY

HOMELESS WOMAN *(Surprised)*: You ate half a extra-large by your-self?

AVERY: You might wanna scrape off the red peppers. *(Belch)* I had Diet Dr. Pepper to save me.

The woman eats. Avery turns to leave. As she exits, she pulls from the paper bag a pint of ice cream and a plastic spoon.

Scene Eight

The showers.

C.O.: In there!

T.J. *(Entering with Avery and C.O.)*: Not now! Not now!

C.O.: Flat against the wall!

T.J.: *Why?*

T.J. and Avery's backs are against the wall. C.O. conducts a body-search.

C.O.: Whatcher girlfriend give ya?

T.J.: Nothing!

C.O.: Lie!

T.J. *(Showing)*: A bracelet! Nothing!

C.O. takes it.

You stared at us the whole time. You know.

C.O.: Strip. *(No response)* Strip!

T.J.: No!

C.O.: Goddammit—

T.J.: We don't have anything, you know we don't have anything—

C.O.: I know nothin', how much trouble you like to stay in? *(Pause)* You got a love thing with seg?

Avery begins to undress. T.J. stares at her.

T.J.: What are you doing? you weren't even there.

Avery continues undressing without pause.

It's a post-visit search, you didn't have any visitors, Avery.

Avery is naked.

C.O.: Couple a the women returned to the cells before we called the search, we gotta look at everybody.

C.O. and T.J. stare at each other.

(A soft plea) Do it, T.J. Or it's gonna be done to ya.

Pause. Then T.J. starts to take off her clothes.

T.J. *(As she undresses):* Sarah and I laughing, old times. For a second I forgot I was here. The zoo.

She is naked. C.O. feels in their mouths, behind their ears, through their hair, under their breasts, in their buttocks.

Scene Nine

Avery on her bunk. She stares at a letter in her hand. T.J. is trying to read a book.

JOY ANN *(Off):*
    Peaches in cream
    My nose itches
    Here comes someone with a hole in his britches.
    Peaches in cream
    My nose itches
    Here comes someone with a hole in his britches.

Over and over. The breaks between are shorter than in the earlier scene. Eventually T.J. emits a frustrated scream, throws the book across the room and slams her body down on her cot. Stillness for a few moments, then Joy Ann starts again.

T.J.: Fuck it. Fuck it! don't get involved, remember that time I asked her politely to please tone it down, she freaks, three-quarters of the floor freaks on her side against me and I know goddamn well she was driving them up the same wall. And who gets written up for inciting a riot? what riot? Who gets sent down? me, no more. Let her keep up the rhythm, she can rhyme her fuckin' brains out. *(Brief pause)* You ever been in seg?

AVERY: Once. Or twice.

T.J.: In seg they flush the toilet from the outside, you have no control they have it all. For a lark, they won't flush all day, especially if there's crap in the bowl, or they'll flush flush flush 'til it overflows. Get sent down for the fuckin' stupidest shit, once I refused a urine test. I'm not a junkie. You are and I've never heard 'em mention the subject to you.

AVERY: Please say "junkie" in the past tense, I been clean three years November. Narcotics Anonymous, Alcoholics Anonymous.

T.J.: Yeah. Trying to tell me inside the shit ain't readily available? tell someone else I sure ain't no bright-eyed rookie.

AVERY: Didn't say I can't said I don't. Who shoved the fiddle stick up your ass?

T.J. turns on the radio. Flips through several stations. Loud. An uproar protest from the other inmates. A C.O. enters, glares at T.J. T.J. clicks the music off. Joy Ann, apparently never interrupted, continues rhyming. C.O. exits. T.J. grabs book again, tries to read.

T.J. *(Eventually)*: When I leave I'll publish my memoirs and get the National Book Award, required reading, Criminology 101. They'll see women's prisons been getting the bad rap, appreciate we can wear our own clothes, with restrictions, plus radios in our room, curtains in the window. Pictures on the wall, cozy. Homey. *(Pause. Then drops book)* What's the difference? the library really stocks law books current enough to mean anything. You need that, better have a buddy in the men's prison.

AVERY: How come all your political friends ain't saved ya? Black power, always someone talkin' it and what it ever get us? Nothin'.

T.J.: Don't talk with your head empty. Listen: The FBI shot a hole clean through the Panthers and watched it crumble. The examples are numerous, here's just one: Geronimo Pratt, locked up in '68, far as I know still is. Engaged in typical Panther activity, Breakfast for Children, health clinics, but these weren't technically crimes so the feds made one up. Put him away for good. This is old news, you know it?

AVERY: Don't call me stupid.

T.J.: *Listen*: While Geronimo's awaiting trial, FBI polka-dotted his wife's body, bullets, stuffed it in a sleeping bag and gave it a fling. Not too easy: her belly's eight months' pregnant.

AVERY: So what? you guilty. You said so, ain't no FBI framin' you.

T.J.: I wasn't talking about me, not worried about me. I'm talking to you, trying to help you out, your politically slick self. Informing you for future reference, no the feds ain't framing me but they're still around and wherever they are you know what's next: corpses.

AVERY: One time my oldest Leesy pick up that needle, put it on her arm like Mommy. She don't push in 'fore I catch her, scare me to think about it now cuz I weren't afraid she hurt herself, instead afraid, mad she stealin' my stash, I slap her a lot, she only two. *(Pause)* I'm a bad mother. *(Pause)* I'm a bad mother?

T.J.: Yeah.

Avery looks at her.

Yeah, whadja think I'd say? "Don't sweat it, heroin's an underrated wellspring of vitamin C"?

AVERY: That was before, that don't happen now, I'm clean!

Avery and T.J. suddenly look to the window. Joy Ann gets quiet. T.J. moves to the window.

T.J.: What's today?

AVERY: Not visitin' day.

T.J.: What's that thing? Pinto? *(Pause)* Maggie? *(Turns back to Avery. Avery stares at her)* Parole?

AVERY: Why else you think she asked for protective custody? Friends a funny word here—find out you almost gone, they do everything get you in trouble, give ya couple extra months. Usually nothin' to do with they gonna miss ya so bad.

T.J. *(Stares out the window a few more moments. Suddenly)*: I'm not staying in jail forever! Even the jury stunned, sentence too harsh, I didn't do nothing but trip him, the rest is bad luck.

She and Avery look at each other.

What's that look—paranoid? Think I am? *wrong.* You know my preferential treatment, frequent invitations to private accommodations, the boom room, fuck. Made examples of them, Geronimo et al., and them guiltless, now what you think they plan on doing with me JOY ANN!

Joy Ann, who has gradually become very loud, stops rhyming.

You wanna pack of licorice sticks next commissary day? I'll get you a pack of red licorice sticks if you stop rhyming. You like the red strings, right? Red string licorice.

JOY ANN *(Pause)*: Six.

T.J.: What?

JOY ANN: Six packs.

T.J.: No!

JOY ANN:

    Peaches in cream
    No nose itches...

T.J.: I can't afford six packs you can't eat six packs.

JOY ANN *(Stops)*: I can. *(No response. Eventually she begins rhyming again)*

T.J.: Okay! six packs.

JOY ANN: Okay.

Long pause; T.J. seems relieved. Then Joy Ann begins again.

T.J.: Joy Ann!

JOY ANN: I gotta do it today, T.J., but if ya gimme the six packs I won't do it . . . mmmmm . . . mmmmm . . . Saturday.

T.J.: Forget it, Joy Ann.

JOY ANN:

Peaches in cream

T.J.: Fuck you, Joy Ann.

JOY ANN: Fuck you, T.J.

Joy Ann goes back to her rhyming. No other talking awhile, then T.J. starts searching under her bed.

T.J.: Fuck, fuck, where's my fuckin' potato chips? *(She comes out from under the bed)* Avery!

AVERY *(Holds up letter)*: Leesy's eleven, Bina's nine. Away from my kids seven years, jail. I gotta see 'em twice a year or they call me "negligent," a legal term. But the foster parents ain't required to bring 'em more 'n fifty miles, and don't. They adopted Bina away.

Long pause. Then T.J. goes under her bed, pulls out nail-care stuff, gets up with Avery on the upper bunk to tenderly file and paint Avery's fingernails.

T.J.: I hate those nail classes. And shampoo, the whole thing. This is nice though.

They begin to kiss.

Scene Ten

Yard.

MONTANA: You got a wife?

AVERY: Yeah. She don't wanna do the public weddin' though, two things: She's lez out there, got a real wife. She's lez out there, and pissed we only play gay on the inside, we get our papers, then back to men, nasty or nice, long as they men. She says we're hypocrites. She says we're stupid.

MONTANA: She says, she says, she must be the man a your pair, every word you repeat like gold.

AVERY *(Puzzles)* I don't know. Always can pick out the man and woman with everyone else, now I finally got one myself, don't know who's who. Neither of us is butch much. Neither of us is girl much. *(Pause)* She got sent down. *(Pause)* You was there.

MONTANA: TV fight. She don't give a damn, she not at all a soldier in the war 'twixt the stories and the game shows, a bloody strife. Finally somethin' gonna happen, finally that girl gonna find out by blood test who's the daddy. So wrong day for the other gang to have on *Wheel of Fortune* and give death stares to anyone come near the remote control. Yvette did. I heard two a Yvette's ribs crack. Her lips beat big, blue, bloody, right eye smashed closed. T.J. tryin' to intervene, break it up. T.J. lucky they just push her out the way. Finally they pull 'em off. Yvette's little finger twitch every few seconds, lemme know she weren't dead. Still when the ambulance come forty, fifty minutes later she handcuffed 'fore they carry her out.

AVERY: How come T.J. thrown in seg?

MONTANA: C.O.s gotta find someone. By popular vote she declared the riot rouser.

Avery stares at Montana.

Don't look at me, I don't vote.

Pause.

AVERY: How you appeal? Everyone 'round here know we gonna live out full sentence cuz you gotta have lawyer money not to, no one else 'round here got justice in the budget.

MONTANA: Civil rights guy. He do it for hardly no money, which is every penny we got. Local lynchin', everyone know who done it. They come into the restaurant I scrubbed floors for, I seen 'em every day. Rat poison in the soup du jour, seven dead. Probably all seven didn't kill that black boy but too bad, guess they died for the company they keep. The black cook assistant knew they'd go for him, so disappeared. Gotta find someone, I'm available, I'm pronounced not innocent. On appeal, they decide givin' death when they can't prove nothin's harsh. They gave life.

AVERY: You did it? *(No answer)* You want out?

MONTANA: You think I don't? Cuz I lived in hell so long you think now I call hell home? I want out. I want out!

AVERY: I know how. I go. *(Pause)* My mind.

MONTANA: Your imagination.

AVERY *(Shakes her head)*: My mind. I go.

MONTANA *(Pause)*: I know what you say, nothin' a that! No magic if that's what you say. That not kosher, not Christian.

AVERY: I'll show you the book.

Montana shakes her head, moves away.

'S easy.

Montana is gone. Avery goes under a tree, sits there. Relaxed. Eventually Montana reappears.

MONTANA: Avery?

Avery opens her eyes.

You here?

AVERY *(Nods)*: I like this tree. Didn't feel the need to leave. *(Pause)* Hope that thunderstorm comes tonight. Somethin' to see.

MONTANA: If ya leave, go to the beach. Where I'd go. *(Exits)*

Quiet a few moments.

C.O. *(Off)*: Lockup, ladies. Clear the yard.

Avery sits up, distressed. Briefly considers, then hides behind the tree.

C.O. *(Off)*: Lockup, ladies. Ladies. Lockup.

Scene Eleven

Avery escorted by a C.O. to the solitary room.

AVERY: What about my meetin's?
C.O.: What about 'em?
AVERY: A.A. N.A.
C.O.: Canceled. 'Til you outa the booby hatch.
AVERY: I'm s'posed to. Narcotics Anon, and A.A., haveta go.
C.O. *(Unlocking door)*: Not for the next four days.
AVERY: Three! *(Pause. Looks at C.O., confused)*
C.O.: Four.
AVERY: I gotta get let out just a hour: N.A. *(No answer)* I need it!
C.O. *(As she and Avery step just inside the door)*: Shoulda thoughta that when you was missin' behind that tree two hours after lockup.

The room is bare. The floor is wet in areas. T.J. is stooped in a corner. She is dirty, her hair is unruly. Spots of blood on her face and knuckles.

C.O.: Time's up.

A moment, then T.J. jumps up and rushes out of the room. She constantly bounces nervously.

T.J.: Knew it, I knew it was today. Counted the meals, I know how to calculate it, I know when three days are up. *(Suddenly the realization that Avery has come to replace her. She momentarily stops bouncing)*

C.O.: She's just keepin' it warm for ya, T.J. Ya know you'll be back.

T.J.: Won't be back.

C.O.: You can't behave yourself two minutes.

T.J.: Won't be back. *(Looks at cell, then at Avery)* I'll clean it for you.

C.O.: It's okay.

T.J. *(Starting to move)*: I'll get a rag—

C.O.: *It's okay.*

T.J. *(An attempt at confidentiality with Avery, but her nervousness makes the advice quite public)*: There, there's the dry part, there I slept, that corner, they flush from the outside, I told you, it's there, on the floor, there. I can't control the flush! sorry, it's dry over there that part. Sorry.

Avery touches the blood on T.J.'s face. T.J. rubs her hands.

Don't scrape the wall with your knuckles, takes days to heal, it's sore for days.

C.O. escorts T.J. out, locks the door behind.

Scene Twelve

Avery stands, her back leaning against a wall. She stares blankly into space for several seconds, then suddenly "comes back." She takes one step to move around in the cell, then grabs her belly and moans in pain. She reaches in her pants—blood on her fingertips.

AVERY *(Calling at the door)*: Hey. Hey. I got my period. I got my period, I ain't had one in seven months. Hey! I got my period I ain't got nothin'. You got a maxi-pad? And some aspirin? Please? Please? we're allowed a maxi-pad a day, right? Could I have my maxi-pad, and a little bitta aspirin? half one? Hey! Hey! this ain't about it bein' cold no more, I ain't complainin' no more, just a pad so I don't stain the cell. And a pill, or I might vomit this place, the pain's gonna have me vomit this place, please! I really got my period, need ta see it? *(Holds out her fingers)* Here. Need ta see it?

Scene Thirteen

There is a crash. Avery jumps. A child enters crying.

AVERY: Come 'ere.
CHILD *(Crying on Avery's lap)*: I didn't mean to.
AVERY: I know. Mommy knows.
CHILD *(Quieter. Surprised)*: You ain't mad?

Pause.

AVERY: Spell your name for me.
CHILD: C-A-S-E-Y.
AVERY:

> The pirate buried gold
> We looked everywhere
> But Casey knew they hid the gold
> Right in *there.*

On "there" Avery tickles child's belly. Child squeals.

CHILD: Do it again.
AVERY:

> The pirate buried gold
> We looked everywhere
> But Casey knew they hid the gold
> Right in *there.*

Tickles. Squeals.

CHILD: Do it again.
AVERY:

> The pirate buried gold

Child squeals. Stops.

The pirate buried gold

Child squeals. Can't stop.

Scene Fourteen

Rec room. T.J. is reading at the card table. Montana sits on the couch. She has a tattered 9 × 12 envelope, and takes photographs from it, laying them out on a coffee table in front of her.

MONTANA *(Not looking up)*: Nadine cut up.

The break in quiet startles T.J.

T.J.: I heard.
MONTANA: Wrists. Ain't deep though. Put her in seg overnight. *(Quiet awhile)* Useta cut up once in awhile. When I was younger, what's the point? *(Picks up a coffee mug; sips)* Whew! *(Puts it back down; obviously too hot)*
T.J.: They caught me with coffee in the rec room, they'd take away my commissary two months.
MONTANA: When you're old, been around for the last three wardens, they cut ya a little slack. *(Pause)* How come you in my shampoo and perm?

T.J., surprised, isn't sure how to answer.

I know the girls like to take my class, you ain't the type.
T.J.: How do you know?

Pause.

MONTANA: You Avery's wife?
T.J. *(Back to book)*: I don't owe you my business, Montana, just because you're old.

MONTANA: I know your business anyhow, T.J. *(Back to her photos. Quiet awhile)* You been in long?

T.J. looks at her, then back to book.

And got a lot ahead a ya. You know you can get out. Your woman got the secret.

T.J. looks at her.

T.J.: Avery?

Montana nods.

Avery doesn't get out.

MONTANA: Too devilish for me to play with, but I know the method: Ya leave your body. Your spirit lookin' for a body some other spirit left. You occupy long as you want, remember though, your vacant body's open for other wanderin' souls, and there's the catch: Some other spirit might decide it likes your body. Stays. Not too much jeopardy however—what spirit's gonna wanna set up permanent residence in a body in jail?

T.J.: What are you talking about?

MONTANA: Avery.

T.J. stares at her, then starts laughing.

She gets out.

T.J. stops laughing.

Always heard of it. I stay clear myself, sound too much like witchcraft to me. Still just cuz my religion says no don't forbid you.

Pause.

T.J.: What're you telling me for?

MONTANA: Just a neighborly suggestion.

Pause.

T.J.: You know my business? I know yours. From somewhere else.

MONTANA: Whatta you know? Male guards? Well ain't you got the inside scoop 'cept it ain't no secret. They jumped me. Got the best a me and everyone knew, my screams echoin' through the halls through the cells. First I hoped I have a baby, little ripple, scandal. Then afraid they see my belly swell beat it outa me, so I wanted my period instead. It came. Teased me, hid three months. And came. *(Pause)* No, you ain't the beauty type, nine years teachin' that damn curl course, you think it never cross my mind the back door through the tunnel lead to the escape: the roof?

T.J.: You know? And stay?!

MONTANA: How far you think you gonna get? this town. You don't belong. You think you the first to have a strategy? Plenty a breakouts. All of 'em foundouts. *(Pause)* You got the patience? Whatchu waitin' for? Think someone, accident, leave the door ajar? My eye on it a near-decade, never happen. *(Pause)* I know the combination.

Pause.

T.J.: The door? *Way out?*

MONTANA: I been around a long time, too many C.O. friends. They s'posed to turn the numbers not in inmates' presence, but lax 'round me.

T.J.: Tell me.

MONTANA *(Shakes her head. Then)*: Maybe. If I get the mood to. Wanna see some pictures?

T.J. shakes her head, back to book. Montana looks through pictures, periodically chuckling or cooing over them. Finally T.J., curious, goes to sit beside her.

T.J.: Family sent you?

MONTANA: Naw. Well. Long time ago.

T.J.: This your girl?

MONTANA: Ain't a girl no more. This her now. And little boys.

T.J.: Who's that?

MONTANA: My cousin Ernie. He was my brother, may as well been. That's my mother. And that ole dog. *(She picks up a photo, hands it to T.J.)*

T.J.: Your granddaughter?

MONTANA: Now how the hell that ole-time pitcher be a my grand-daughter?

T.J. *(Pause)*: You?

MONTANA: Looked good, didn't I? Well I had a hot date. Never cheated on my husband, never slept with nobody else after them vows. Cuz I never had the chance to, thrown in jail too quick in life, twenty-six. Lenny was the one, always had the big thing for me, went crazy once I married George. Too easy, that was Lenny's trouble, when they easy ya think somethin' ain't right. So after married I finally took a semilegal stroll with Lenny. To the carnival. *(Refers to the picture)* That day.

T.J.: This is you? When you first came in?

MONTANA: Just a month before all the trouble started, half-year later I was behind bars. Only picture I got a myself. (Pause) You a lifer too. Ain'tcha, T.J.? Guess what? That information, I didn't even had to rely on rumor, that information written all over your eyes, your walk. I know.

T.J.: You never been out?

She keeps looking at the photo and at Montana.

Not me.

Montana laughs.

They're not doing it to me. I'm not leaving here a grand-mother.

MONTANA: Maybe ya won't leave here at all.

T.J.: They're not taking it from me! All that, I got a life.

Montana starts to put her pictures back in the envelope. T.J. grabs Montana's arm.

Why'd you show me 'em?
MONTANA: Attackin' a ole lady, I scream, you be in solitary longer 'n Noah's cruise.

T.J. backs off. Montana takes the picture out of T.J.'s hand. She looks at it long. She doesn't smile. Suddenly T.J. snatches the photo back and rips it in two. They are both stunned.

Whadju do that for? *(Pause)* Whadju do that for! that was me.
T.J.: I'm sorry. I'm sorry.
MONTANA: That was me! That was me!
T.J.: I'm sorry.
MONTANA: That was my life, my life. That was me. That was it.

Montana grabs T.J.'s hand and pours the scalding coffee onto it. T.J. screams. Montana holds T.J.'s hand until the cup is empty, then T.J. runs off. Montana sets the two pieces of the photo together on the table. Sits. Gazes.

Scene Fifteen

T.J. and Avery in the cell. T.J.'s hand is bandaged.

T.J.: I'm gonna leave. One day. Not take it anymore: gone.
AVERY: I ever tell ya my little girl liked her restaurant lunch?
T.J.: Just wanted to let you know.
AVERY: Once in awhile I treat her. Diner, we chat: my coffee, her milk. *(Pause)* I be out five months, T.J. I had a lot left, I'd be with ya. But I just got five months. Which ain't plenty which means plenty to risk.
T.J.: I don't want you to! Like you to be with me, but you have stuff to lose. I don't.
AVERY: Lose your parole.
T.J.: A maybe. A fat "if" and that's a conjunction I'm tired of hearing. *(Pause)* Montana says you get out. *(Pause)* Dreams?

Avery shakes her head.

AVERY: Takes concentration, but not much practice. Show ya the book.

T.J., uneasy, shakes her head.

Yankees game, box seats. Subway, 5:30 rush, sardines. Central Park. I cool my feet in the pond.

T.J.: Wherever you want?

AVERY: Wherever there's a free body. You gotta find a body whose spirit's out meanderin' just like you. Can't force nobody's spirit out. *(Pause)* Believe me? *(T.J. doesn't answer)* Make your life easier. Seg. *(Pause)*

T.J.: I don't believe you, which is not to call you a liar. Wish I did.

Pause.

AVERY: Visitin' day, I help in the nursery. My first year, still crack nervous, and this little boy keep talkin' 'bout his daddy this his daddy that, I know he ain't got no daddy, get on my nerves. So he grab the playhouse, I take it away. He go to the train, I give it to the little girl. He grab the jumprope, I snatch it call him Sissyboy he start to cry. All the other kids is quiet, watchin'. His mama wanna kill me, and she got a lotta influence 'round here. I ain't a shit mother no more. One bad day, I get nursery-expelled and a reputation. I'm a good mother.

T.J.: I know.

AVERY: Do ya?

T.J. nods. Avery is pleased.

Leesy comin'!

T.J.: When?!

AVERY: Tomorrow, four. Scared!

T.J.: Foster parents bring her?

AVERY: Sure, but she the one asked. Begged, for the longest time, finally they grant it, see her mama. Meet her mama, she won't know me, she's eleven, ain't seen me since four. I'm shakin'.

T.J.: Normal, fine. Got all your stuff? candy bars?

AVERY *(Horror)*: I ate 'em!

T.J.: Not a tragedy, she probably gets too much anyway. Your sleigh?

AVERY *(Rips her bed apart)*: I can't find it! I had it right here under the sheets, that bitch Randy got it in for me, she done it, bet my life.

T.J. moves toward the bed.

T.J.: Stop.

Avery backs away from the bed. T.J. calmly feels under the bed; in a few moments pulls out the tape-dispenser sleigh. Santa has been torn. Avery moans.

You can make another before tomorrow. Here.

From under her bed, T.J. pulls stationery and a ballpoint pen that clicks four colors. Offers items to Avery, but Avery stares at pen.

Think Leesy like this pen?

Avery nods. Now she takes the pad and pen and begins doodling.

Better save the ink.

Avery puts the pen in her pocket.

AVERY: If you get out, then me, can I stay at your place? awhile? I ain't got a roof now, and here's the Catch-22: can't get my baby back no place to live, ain't eligible for housing assistance if I ain't got child custody.

T.J. nods. Pause.

T.J.: Why didn't you ever stay out there? In a free body?

AVERY: Be livin' somebody else's life. Somebody else's face in the mirror.

T.J.: Somebody Anybody else's life beats this one.

AVERY: Still not mine. *(Looks at T.J.)* Noticed somethin'. *(Pulls up her sleeve)* My track marks are gone.

Scene Sixteen

Visiting room. Avery sits on a couch, writing with the multicolored pen on T.J.'s pad. Leesy enters. She stares at Avery for several moments. Avery sees her, but fidgets and stares mostly at the floor.

LEESY: Are you my mother?

Avery nods. Quiet. Leesy looks around.

AVERY: Here.

She jumps up from the couch and motions for Leesy to sit on it. Leesy does, takes off her coat. Avery sits on a chair, turned slightly away from Leesy, and continues doodling.

LEESY: Can I turn on the TV?

Avery nods, doesn't look up. Leesy initially is confused, since the TV is so high on the wall, then she finds the remote control. Watches a few minutes.

You got any other kids?

Avery shakes her head.

I have a brother.

AVERY: Girls, I only had girls.

LEESY: He's a boy. He lives at my house. He's fifteen.

AVERY: Not me, only girls.

LEESY: He's not really my brother. Do I have a father?

Avery shakes her head. Long pause.

Do you like this program?
AVERY: I like the stories.
LEESY: I'll change it, what station you like?
AVERY: Ain't no stories on Saturday.

Pause. Leesy stares at the TV.

LEESY: My brother likes this movie. Watch, there's gonna be a fight at the party.

Avery is looking at the clock.

AVERY: 4:22. When you got here—4:15? 4:15, you said you was gonna be here four. *(Pause)* You said you gonna be here four, late now. I gotta go to work now, I got stuff to do. Sorry.

A hesitation, then Leesy gets up, puts on her coat. She pulls from her pocket a glass paperweight, gives it to Avery.

LEESY: I seen it in the store, I thought it was pretty for ya.

Avery takes it, puts it in her own pocket.

You think it's pretty?
AVERY: It's okay.

Pause.

LEESY: I like your ink pen.

Avery looks at it, puts it back in her own pocket.

Can I have a soda? Out the machine?
AVERY: No. No money.
LEESY: Please? Root beer?
AVERY: No money, I got no money. Ask your mother.

Pause.

LEESY: Okay.

AVERY: I got things I gotta do, I gotta answer the airplane reservations.

LEESY: Okay. *(Pause)* I have to go to the bathroom. Can I go to the bathroom in your room?

AVERY: Not my place! no!

Pause.

LEESY: Can I come another time?

AVERY: Next time, next time, yeah, next time we do stuff. I gotta go. Late.

Avery gets up to go. Leesy hesitantly gives her a hug; Avery pulls away sharply.

Okay, okay, next time we do stuff. Late now, go find your mother. Okay? *(She exits)*

Scene Seventeen

Phone room. Micky is on the phone. In line behind are T.J., then Esperanza, then Faye, then Montana.

ESPERANZA *(To T.J.)*: Did you sign that sheet?

T.J. shakes her head.

I signed that sheet. I was the first one signed that sheet this morning now look.

FAYE: I was third.

MICKY *(Into receiver)*: This clear bottle with a cartoon on it. Yeah. Smells sweet. Rich.

ESPERANZA: I was first on that sign-up sheet, I shoulda been first on the phone.

MICKY: Flowers.

ESPERANZA: Instead they change the rules at the last minute, I'm third to last.

T.J.: They always change the rules at the last minute.

ESPERANZA: Shoulda been first at two o'clock, I come by five to two, ready, see a line. What's this crap? I wanna know, I signed up first on the list this morning. "They threw that list out a hour ago," says someone like the news is old old now here I am, twenty-three 'til four o'clock closing time, still waiting. *(Pause)* Maybe not make it at all.

FAYE: *You?*

MICKY: Both combined, conditioning shampoo, but make sure it says it cuz one or the other—conditioner *or*—that don't do me no good.

ESPERANZA *(At Micky)*: And I gotta talk to my LAWYER I ain't interested in wasting time talk 'bout no damn SHAMPOO.

FAYE: Least her conversation got a point, she'll get her shampoo, whatcher lawyer getcha?

ESPERANZA: Outa here! I ain't stayin' twenty-five. Four times I ask for a restraining order—

FAYE: We know! we know!

ESPERANZA: And they don't grant it, that's evidence! Plus my broke arm, concussion, we got the records.

FAYE: What good it do you the first time? sittin' here, twenty-five to life.

ESPERANZA: Do me better next time around, she told me, just need to TALK TO HER! my LAWYER! *(The last aimed at Micky)*

MICKY: Hell with her! anything I can't stand is nobody's goddamn cat. And the people act like you like havin' their dumb animal jump on ya, nibble at ya.

Esperanza is looking at T.J. T.J., uncomfortable, begins glancing back and forth between clock and Esperanza.

T.J.: Five minutes?

ESPERANZA: Seven. Tops, time me.

T.J. *(Great hesitation)*: Okay.

Esperanza moves ahead of T.J.

FAYE: Hey!

ESPERANZA: I'll be quick, promise. And pay you back, next time I'm before you, we trade.

FAYE: Fuck that.

ESPERANZA: I gotta talk to my lawyer.

FAYE: And ain't that important. I got two baby boys, six. *(Pause)* I'd kick you for that if you wa'n't sick.

MICKY: Owners act like they's human bein's well their shit sure smells human but that's close as it gets.

T.J. is looking at Faye, who stares back.

T.J.: I have to use the phone!

FAYE: Speak to your sons? My twins is six, this all the mommy they get for the week. If they get it.

T.J.: I can't . . . I need this call.

FAYE: Yeah. So do my boys.

MICKY: They invite me to their house guess it be the first and last time, that feline come purrin' toward me she gonna have a whisker-face fulla coffee.

FAYE: Know when I see 'em? My birthday. Their birthday. Twice a year's it, how easy you think my mother can dish out a hundred bucks: bus fare to the boondocks?

MICKY: Ya see their couches all scratched to shit, then you say, Come over my place sometime, and they gonna mention, Can I bring Tabby? Hell no!

FAYE: Dollar five I gotta dump in for the first three minutes and a dollar five's all I got, all I can say's hi and 'bye, let me?

T.J. doesn't look at her.

MICKY: Shit, remember Aunt Grace, rashes, eyes all bulgy?

FAYE: I said I'll be quick.

T.J.: So will I. Try to.

MICKY: And Aunt Trude playin' ignorant, everytime: "You got a cold, Grace?"

FAYE: What's so fuckin' important, your *girlfriend*?

MICKY: And bringin' that fat lazy long-haired Sam, trouncin' around, sneaky and mean.

Faye shoves T.J.

FAYE: I was third.

MICKY: You see the story yesterday? Yeah. Amy kick the shit outa Leslie, or what?

ESPERANZA: Hey. Seventeen 'til.

MICKY: Amy. Amy! the one that's been pregnant for a year.

ESPERANZA: Seventeen 'til now, wasn't she s'posed to get off twenty-one 'til? Wasn't twenty-one 'til her fifteen limit?

MICKY: That *was* Amy. The blonde. When's the last time you watched? they changed her last week.

ESPERANZA *(To Micky)*: Seventeen 'til! You were s'posed to be off twenty-one 'til, your fifteen's over! You been on the phone nineteen minutes!

MICKY *(Takes the receiver from her ear, gives Esperanza a look, then back into receiver)*: I don't mind when they change 'em, but you think they at least replace a blonde with a blonde, brunette with the same.

ESPERANZA: Sixteen 'til!

MICKY *(Staring at Esperanza)*: No, I ain't seen that story in a year. Catch me up.

ESPERANZA: No! *(To others)* She's been on twenty minutes!

FAYE: What the fuck do I care? I ain't gonna make it nohow.

MICKY: Steven! Shit! ain't that the fourth almost rapist she killed? Or fifth?

ESPERANZA: I GOTTA SPEAK TO MY LAWYER!

MICKY: Her new husband be curious 'bout that closet fulla corpses, but at least relieved he married a virgin.

Esperanza turns to Faye.

ESPERANZA: You're her friend.

FAYE: So?

ESPERANZA: Talk to her! Please?

Montana groans.

I'll be fast, and *(To T.J.)* you be fast? Promise Faye her turn so Faye get Micky off? *(T.J. is silent)* We not gettin' on at all otherwise.

MONTANA *(To T.J.)*: No intervenin'. I say.

ESPERANZA *(To Faye)*: Talk to her, then five minutes me, five minutes her, *(T.J.)* five minutes you, we all get in. Please.

Faye considers, then walks up to speak privately with Micky. A few moments later, couple of giggles, then sounds of coins dropped into the phone and dialing. Micky steps away from the phone. Faye speaks.

FAYE: Mama! *(She glances at Esperanza; then she and Micky laugh hard)* No, Mama, just a joke. Where's my babies?

ESPERANZA: Get off!

FAYE: Tootsie rolls! don't let 'em eat all that junk, then not touch supper. Whatchu got on—chops and fries?

ESPERANZA: Faye!

Micky falls on the floor laughing.

Please.

FAYE: Put 'em on. *(To Esperanza)* I got fifteen minutes.

ESPERANZA: YOU DON'T!

T.J.: You told me you got money enough for three.

FAYE *(Into receiver)*: Hey! How's mama's baby? . . . You listenin' to Grammaw? . . . Huh? . . . Good boy! Good boy, your brother there? . . . Bring him here. . . . Don't fight. Don't fight over the phone, you can share it. . . . See, yaw can both hold it. How's Mommy's big boy? . . . You did? teacher like it? . . . Uh huh. . . . Lemme hear.

A very long silence. Esperanza meanwhile frantically looks between the clock and Faye.

ESPERANZA *(Finally, to Faye)*: What?

FAYE: He's readin' me his story, shut up. *(Pause)* Oh. . . . Oh, wait a minute, baby. *(She quickly pulls out more coins and drops them into the slot)* Okay, go ahead.

Esperanza screams and grabs the receiver.

Hey!

Faye grabs it back and smacks Esperanza's knuckles with it.

ESPERANZA: OW!

FAYE: You lost your goddamn mind? *(Into receiver)* I'm sorry, baby. Then what did the boy say to the rat?

Esperanza pulls down the receiver rest, cutting off the call. Faye screams.

MICKY: Fuck!

FAYE: You crazy?

T.J.: Just call again! just call again!

FAYE: The first minute's expensive, I ain't got enough goddamn money to start a new call.

ESPERANZA *(Taking receiver and dialing)*: You had enough to extend that one.

Faye yanks Esperanza away from the phone and punches her in the stomach.

T.J.: DON'T DO THAT TO HER!

FAYE: It was my fuckin' turn, bitch.

Esperanza tries to go after Faye but Micky grabs her by her hair from behind.

MICKY: No ya don't. *(She kicks Esperanza)* Nobody pulls the fuckin' dial tone.

ESPERANZA: I'm sorry! I'm sorry!

FAYE: Ain't it too late.

ESPERANZA *(Moving toward the phone)*: I just—

Micky and Faye pull her away.

Please lemme make my call!

MICKY: "Please lemme make my call."

ESPERANZA: I need my lawyer!

FAYE: You need your doctor.

They have Esperanza on the floor and are beating her. Esperanza is screaming. T.J. looks on, helpless. Turns to Montana. Montana shrugs, then drops coins into phone slot and dials.

T.J. *(Running into the fight)*: Stop it! *(Micky pushes her away)* STOP IT!

MONTANA *(Still holding receiver, to T.J.)*: When the C.O.s come, you know everyone here eligible for seg. Go.

T.J.: Everyone includes you.

MONTANA *(Shakes head)*: Retired, last time they locked me up I missed *Gunsmoke*. *(Into receiver)* It's Montana. *(Pause, then she laughs heartily)* I can't believe it's *you*.

T.J.: I'm getting the C.O.

FAYE: Don't.

T.J.: Then leave her alone, she's sick.

Faye and Micky are backing off, but Esperanza doesn't realize it and still struggles.

FAYE: Just don't bring no fuckin' pig.

T.J.: Let her be.

Faye kicks Esperanza. T.J. starts to exit.

FAYE: Don't go!

MONTANA *(Moving toward "fight")*: Dammit! Ain't heard her voice in ages, now still can't—

Esperanza inadvertently scratches Montana's arm: a long, bleeding wound. T.J. gasps. Micky and Faye jump back.

ESPERANZA: I didn't do it! I didn't do it!

MICKY: Ah . . .

ESPERANZA: Not on purpose! Accident, didn't see her.

MONTANA: Oh . . . Oh God. Oh God.

ESPERANZA: Don't worry. Don't worry, no blood to blood.

MONTANA: Oh . . . God.

ESPERANZA: Just my nails, you okay, don't worry. No open wounds on my hands, no contact, you all right. You can't get it unless open wound contact, I didn't hurt you, please don't say I hurt you. I don't hurt nobody, I'm careful, I don't touch nobody. Nobody touches me.

Scene Eighteen

Beauty class. T.J. combs white relaxer cream all through a woman's hair.

MONTANA *(To T.J.)*: You hate this shit. Don'tcha?

T.J.: Yes.

MONTANA *(To woman)*: T.J. think ya oughta keep your hair natural. Nappy.

WOMAN: And look at her head, you proud a that? They let me offa my floor for a perm up here, I come in, see you's my hairdresser, Lord! I think, I sure hope her stuff wa'n't on purpose.

MONTANA: And her hands. Manicures her specialty, but her nails bit down to the knuckle.

T.J. washes her hands.

WOMAN: Maybe she ain't got no woman, she ain't got no woman and there sure ain't no man, maybe she got no reason to be lookin' good. Course maybe she get a woman she do somethin' with that head YOW!

MONTANA: On fire?

Woman yell/moans.

Shouldna scratched.

WOMAN: All the goddamn hairdressers say that, I ain't had a perm in nine months, if my head itches I'm gonna scratch, if I scratch once it's my fault the lye burns AHHH!

MONTANA: Want it out?

WOMAN: Yeah! No!

MONTANA: She can wash it out if ya want, but then you gonna have all those little scalp scabs for nothin', all your old kinks back.

WOMAN: Don't worry, I can stand it. *(Pause)* HOW LONG?

MONTANA: You ain't started yet.

T.J. is reading a book.

Don't think T.J. even know her foundation skin tone. You liable to flunk out you don't apply what you learn in class to yourself.

T.J. gives Montana a look.

Forty-six sixteen thirty-three.

This is not what T.J. expected. They stare at each other. Woman screams.

Come 'ere, I'll take care a ya. *(Goes to woman)*

WOMAN: Ain't she gonna wash it out?

MONTANA *(Brings her to the sink)*: Her principles too opposed.

T.J. is gone.

WOMAN: It still gonna be straight, right?

MONTANA: We'll see.

WOMAN: It still gonna be straight?!

MONTANA *(Examining hair as she washes it)*: Whee, they gonna think you's a Chinese woman. From behind.

Scene Nineteen

T.J. in the cell collecting her things. Her bed is bare. Avery enters.

T.J.: Nine weeks segregation. You think it's a record, right? but Montana's still there. Don't ask me why, thought I was their whipping girl, guess she pissed 'em more, a betrayal thing. *(Pause)* Surprised to see me? I was here last night.

Pause.

AVERY: I been clean three years! one time I slip, you judgin' me? *(Pause)* Won't happen again, I don't need that stuff. Think I'm lyin'?

T.J. packs.

They movin' you?

T.J. nods.

'Nother floor?
T.J.: 'Nother prison.
JOY ANN *(Off)*: Avery! What's eight times three?
AVERY *(To Joy Ann)*: Twenty-four. *(To T.J.)* Never got to show you the secret. Way out. Easy, the book's in the library, wamme write the title down for ya?
T.J.: No. Cuz it's also gonna show me the way back in.
JOY ANN *(Off)*: Avery! What's eight times three?
AVERY *(To Joy Ann)*: Twenty-four. *(Avery takes the paperweight out of her pocket, shows it to T.J.)*
T.J.: Leesy?

Avery nods.

She like the pen?

Pause. Avery nods.

C.O. *(Enters)*: Come on, T.J.

Avery and T.J. look at each other.

Let's go.

T.J. exits. C.O. slams door behind. Quiet. Joy Ann walks by Avery's cell, peers in.

JOY ANN: Avery. What's eight times three?
AVERY: I gotta do stuff, Joy Ann. Back to your cell.
JOY ANN: Avery. It's my birthday.
AVERY: Happy birthday. How old?
JOY ANN: Guess.
AVERY: Mmmmm. . . . Twenty-four.
JOY ANN *(Laughs hard)*: Knew you'd fall for it! *Fifty*-four. *(Stops laughing. A sudden realization)* Nobody gave me a present. *(Her eyes are on the paperweight)*
AVERY: *No.*

Joy Ann seems hurt. Avery doesn't care.

JOY ANN: Touch it?

Avery reluctantly hands Joy Ann the paperweight. Joy Ann studies the glass from all angles, rolls it slowly over her face, smiles broadly. Sadly holds it out for Avery to reclaim.

AVERY *(Great hesitation)*: Happy birthday, Joy Ann.
JOY ANN *(Thrilled)*: Now I owe ya. I'll sing at your funeral. *(Exits)*

Scene Twenty

A little girl on a bike. Montana enters, eating out of a cup of French fries.

LITTLE GIRL: Don't just toss that thing when you're through, that's why the beach is so filthy. Take it with you to the boardwalk garbage can.
MONTANA: Okay.
LITTLE GIRL: You goin' swimmin'?

MONTANA: I don't know. Maybe.

LITTLE GIRL: My mother thinks the water's filthy and forbids me to swim it. Of course I do and dry off before I get home. The beach is filthy so watch out for glass if you take off your shoes.

MONTANA: I like Coney Island. Quieter than the other beaches.

LITTLE GIRL: That's cuz it's a garbage dump.

Pause.

MONTANA: You live around here?

LITTLE GIRL: That's none of your business. *(Stares at Montana, then giggles. Points)* Projects.

MONTANA: You remind me of my niece. A lot. When she was little.

Little girl shrugs.

(Mumbles) Her mama never gave her enough beatin's either.

LITTLE GIRL: There's a better parta the beach. Less carcinogens.

MONTANA: Far?

LITTLE GIRL: Naah. Wamme show ya?

MONTANA: Okay. What time is it though?

LITTLE GIRL *(Looks at her watch)*: Ten after.

MONTANA: Three?

Little girl nods.

I only got 'bout twenty minutes left.

LITTLE GIRL: Leave now, we just about have time for one good dip. That be enough?

MONTANA: Gonna have to be.

X

THE LIFE AND TIMES

OF MALCOLM X

THULANI

DAVIS

I started out writing a play, but realized that it would be too difficult to set
to music. So I called Anthony [Davis,
the opera's composer] and said, "I'm
going to write you a two-hour poem,
one long epic with different voices."

Stylistic Influences
The first thing that influenced the
style of *X* was Malcolm's voice. Having
listened to a lot of records and looked
at written material, I had to figure out
if there was a way to sing that would
sound like it was in his rhythm. When you write for music as I did, setting
the words first, the writer's rhythms dictate the rhythms that will be in the
music.

I started looking at Malcolm's rhythms. He spoke in very long sentences that would have been impossible to set to music. One of the require-
ments of working with music is that the lines have to be shorter and, with
a big orchestra underneath, you have to have a certain amount of repetition to make sure everybody gets everything. The sentences have to carry
concepts that are expressed very clearly in a few words. So I tried to trun-
cate his sentences and capture his rhythm, which itself was repetitive. He
came back to certain phrases like a jazz soloist, and then altered them
slightly on the repetition. If he said a line three times, the second and third
versions would be slightly altered in the way that we improvise in music.
That major influence gave the main character his voice.

[After] many different rehearsals with many different singers, [I can
say] most singers come to the work and "do" Martin Luther King, because
they don't know Malcolm's rhythms as well as we all know King. They
think in terms of our tradition of "preacher," and Malcolm is really quite
different. On a crude level, King was more melodic and Malcolm was
more percussive. Malcolm had more jazz rhythms and King was lyrical.
King did have a melody to his voice, but he would slowly work an idea to a
kind of crescendo that was very much in the preaching tradition of the
south. Malcolm was more staccato and he inserted humor, so he had a
more rapid-fire style. He improvised more. They both were improvisers,
but King used metaphors, whereas Malcolm used similes. He used vernacular language; King used biblical language. Martin strived for what they
call "elevated language," which was a transcendent language that lifted
you up with some of those very powerful images that we all know. The

Bible is like a second language, at least to the black southern audience. It used to be probably to most African Americans. Malcolm usually avoided all of that.

We were also interested in the sounds of the time periods covered in the piece, the 1920s to the mid-1960s. Those sounds in music would include blues, swing, bebop, jazz up to John Coltrane. In black poetry, that would take you from late Dunbar to Amiri Baraka. In the beginning, I set out to capture some of the flavor of the Garveyites' language of the late 1920s and early 1930s, using some of the actual language of that movement. Then I shifted to some echoes of Sterling Brown, who influenced the first act. He had a heavy, pounding rhythm and also a use of repetition with a blues quality to it. I put that in Louisa's aria about the Klan coming and terrorizing the family, "So many men/rushing in a black man's night" echoing "Not one, not ten," from Brown's poem "Old Lem," which says "They came by tens." In the latter part of the opera, I went back to the language of the period, black language about race and politics. Much of the poetry like Baraka's came from that language we were developing about race. So I tried to put it in that vernacular. From the 1940s, I used the flavor of Cab Calloway's lingo, ballrooms and dance halls.

Artistic Challenges and Discoveries

I discovered about my own work that this was probably the most highly controlled language I've ever written. I have never written a piece that was so stripped down, language-wise, and that became a style of its own. Probably I won't do it again, but it was interesting for me to look at totally stripping away the frills of language.

I dispensed with the conventions of naturalism. Opera, for the most part, is done in naturalism, even if it's fantastical and mythological. I looked at my relationship to Brecht and distancing qualities. I realized I was pulling into play a lot of things I'd been thinking about since I got interested in theatre at fourteen. Theatre about black people tends to be written with intense emotional content, even coming close to ritual intensity. To do this piece, we really had to strip that away. So I thought, what would happen if we tell a black story that primarily requires you to think about this character without being too attached to him? There's no personal side of Malcolm in this piece. You don't get to identify with him in terms of how he seems at home when he's alone. You have to think about the big picture. In doing this piece, I discovered other ways of looking at our story.

The Aesthetic

I'm primarily interested in character and internal journeys, although X stands as something of an exception to this rule. The single most identifying aspect of my work is that I'm interested in letting the content restructure the form. In whatever I do, I'm bringing together some of the developments of the last forty years in theatre and film in my work. I don't think I've ever worked on a well-made play, except for Shakespeare in high school. Brecht is the most traditional thing I've done.

Black theatre, overall, is pretty conservative. By now though, some of the new forms that arose in the seventies have become established forms. They don't surprise anyone particularly. A lot of new things are going on now which come out of that and will be new forms in the future. But storytelling has to change. I looked at Bill Gunn's work, Ntozake Shange's work and Adrienne Kennedy's work. These are black artists who influenced me a lot as I was coming along. They were more or less on the edge, rather than in the center. I read the mainstream black playwrights, but I felt that we needed to strip away some of the artifice of traditional plays. They sometimes don't feel real. We all know this is an illusion; it's not real life up there, so we could dispense with trying to recreate real life.

F/X of the Work

We wanted to bring a new music into the opera house; a music that is contemporary and comes out of our tradition as well as the European tradition.

We also wanted to show that you could take a story like Malcolm's and do this poem of it that has a larger life than the life of the individual. In terms of the libretto, one of the aims was to show how the history of a single individual becomes our history. We wanted to show how we appropriate that story and make it tell the story for all the voiceless people who are not on the TV. So in my libretto, whenever a story is told, the chorus appropriates the story, changes it and retells it, and that becomes the true version that people believe. In our process, we create our understanding and our history of America, and that's what we teach among ourselves. And that, in fact, is the truth for us. So there's a public or documented history and then there's our version. Those two things are on the stage at one time so that you see how they interact. For example, in the first act, this cop comes in and says that Malcolm's father was killed on the railroad tracks. The chorus tells us what that story really means. They believe that white supremacists threw him on the tracks. Then they say a white train cut him down. As the story transforms, you see that they are saying racism cut him down. It was no accident.

Definitions of Heroism

In X, heroism is the ability to transform the self; the ability to be alone and to say that I am going forward. He has this willingness; he's open to having a vision and pursuing it. We have a view of heroism that is built around individuals. Sometimes that may work against us because we become dependent upon new heroes. The power which Malcolm identified in his own story was the power of transformation. But then, even having made that change and having become this admirable image, he changed again. He wasn't afraid to even go against the esteem that people held him in to change again. So I'm offering a character who transformed himself and was willing to go against us if necessary to help us. He was saying to people, "If I could come from the bottom and make this change, anyone could." That, to me, is an African-American tradition. We have used the power of our stories to help others.

Distinctions between Women's and Men's Writing

Traditionally, black male writers in the culture have developed a kind of public voice. Women developed a private voice. Our literature has been very distinct, one from the other, along those lines. But I do think that those lines will blur. Some of the young black male writers, particularly some of the gay male writers, have learned a lot from women writers and have incorporated some of their colors and strands and voices into the work that's being done now. The twenty-five-year-olds are going to be distinct from their predecessors as male writers. I think after Lorraine Hansberry, black women took notes from Baraka and people like that who were changing structure and form. And because they were writing about a culture or a group of people who were sort of coming apart at the seams, they let the form come apart at the seams. A certain group of writers did not bother with trying to do the well-made play. Because we're habitually writing about people in crisis, women writers coming into the theatre struggle to create forms that can respond to that—whether it's Barbara Ann Teer doing ritual or it's Ntozake Shange abandoning traditional form and trying to just get to voicing the crisis.

We do write as though the personal is political, which I think was taboo in our tradition until after the sixties. Just as Lorraine Hansberry was able to write with such clarity about the dynamic even within the naturalistic—what George Wolfe calls the "Mama on the Couch" business—within *that* [tradition], she's still the best because she really did understand what those dynamics are between mother and son, mother and daughter, sister and brother, and the black male head of household who is absent for one reason or another. She understood those dynamics and I think she said it for all time, in a sense. A lot of people took her model and kept trying to write about that struggle. But in this work, in the eighties and nineties, black women have extended that family to other women that we know and treat as family, or should treat as family, and other sons, other men. We are really struggling to give expression to some of the things Lorraine was writing about, some of the things Ntozake's been writing about and some of the things Adrienne Kennedy's written about, which is some of the madness that inhabits us in this struggle. Lorraine made it very clear what it's like most of the time. Then Adrienne gave you some of the psychological underbelly of self-loathing and some of the madness within our family dynamic. Women in the nineties are pulling all those strands together to weave a more colorful cloth that puts those voices—the personal, the political, the psychological—in one space at one time.

I think black men will become more sensitive to intimate relationships, but I think black women will bring the knowledge we gain from experiencing people one at a time, so that we will not be drawn as much to the naturalistic model. It's not that we don't have any male role models; we do, but we've been struggling with opening up the form, to reshape theatre works to our voices, to give us enough room. I think we're all straining to get to an audience that watches movies at home, that is used to getting things quickly and used to a kind of vernacular, not studied language. When you're being trained for anything, you're being trained for the past. You're trained for theatre that used to exist. People have to take the good from their training and then abandon the things that don't work right now.

One of the things that happens in the traditional play is that no one ever gets to finish what they're saying because the conflict is there and somebody's going to interrupt them and say, "Well no, I'm gonna choke you right now for saying that." That happens in Lorraine. And what Ntozake did was to have one side totally say their say. In *Fires in the Mirror* and *Twilight*, Anna Deavere Smith does the next thing. And what happens in her work is that the conflict which is offstage is inside the body of every person in the audience. They sit through this mediating process where they hear all the voices and they must take all the voices inside themselves and let them wrestle inside the individual.

In *Oleanna,* David Mamet has made a conflict which he's stacked on one side, so the man's a victim and the woman's a cipher. There's no way anybody, male or female, could identify with the female in this piece. He's trying to have a dialogue about sexual harassment and the change that women are going through, and therefore the change that society is going through, but the woman never gets to say what she has to say. And that's what's wrong with theatre written by a lot of men.

We're at this interesting moment in which some black women are going to influence everybody's theatre by really investigating how to let us speak. How can we go about being heard?

The Darkness and the Light

I'm a great believer in some of the mysteries involved in doing art. I do believe, in some ways, we are receptacles for things that we don't create ourselves, necessarily. The darkness and the light both have an element of mystery which I prefer just to trust. In other words, the dark matter is not something that I will ever totally understand, but I allow it to pass through me; and the same is true of the light. I do occasionally move the dark matter into the light. It's a great pleasure for me personally, but I think those are the things that reach other people, those mysterious moments.

In terms of theatre, I agree with what George Wolfe said about what he was trying to do with *Jelly's Last Jam:* There is a lot that happens in the dark that never gets onstage. He was saying, particularly in musicals, the dark side is never there. Because the theatre is a dark box with light, you're struggling constantly to pull what's in the dark—which might be all the people there—into enough light for them to see this reflection of themselves. And you're not going to light up the whole room or everybody in it, but you might have a moment where a connection is made, when the darkness and the light are the same thing.

I don't know what the light is, but we tend to think about the darkness sucking things in. With theatre, you don't want all those human beings and their stories and openness to keep hiding in the dark. We tend to slink away into our private worlds, which is somehow like being in the darkness. If you get really sucked in there, you don't really connect to other people. And so the theatre is interesting to look at in terms of light and dark because it really does need both. You're using the dark to allow them to experience light. It's not permanent, it's fleeting. That is the same as spiritual revelation.

ABOUT THE AUTHOR

Thulani Davis's writings include journalism, fiction, poetry and works for the theatre. As a career journalist, she has covered politics and the arts for the *Village Voice, American Film,* the *New York Times Book Review,* the *Washington Post Book World, Mother Jones, Essence* and the *Nation.* She is the author of two volumes of poetry, *Playing the Changes* and *All the Renegade Ghosts Rise;* the novel *1959* (Grove Weidenfeld, 1992); and *Malcolm X, The Great Photographs* (Stewart, Tabori & Chang, 1993). Her adaptation of Brecht's *The Caucasian Chalk Circle* was produced by the New York Shakespeare Festival, under the direction of George C. Wolfe. Davis served as dramaturg on Anna Deavere Smith's *Fires in the Mirror.* She wrote the libretto for Anne LeBaron's opera *The E. & O. Line,* and is currently working on the libretto for a new opera by Anthony Davis, *The Amistad.* In 1985, she was co-producer and scriptwriter for *Fanfare for the Warriors,* an award-winning documentary on black composers. She has since written and narrated two video projects: *Why Howard Beach?,* and *Thulani,* a thirty-minute piece on her own work, which was selected for the Berlin Film Festival. Davis, who lives in Brooklyn, is the recipient of fellowships from the New York Foundation for the Arts and the New York State Council on the Arts, and of the Manhattan Borough President's Award in literature. She is also the recipient of a TCG National Theatre Artist Residency grant, under which she will be artist-in-residence at the New York Shakespeare Festival in 1994–95. In 1990, she was ordained a Buddhist priest.

ABOUT THE WORK

Work on *X* began with the support of a commission from The Kitchen in New York City. The opera was subsequently developed under the auspices of the American Music Theater Festival, Philadelphia, culminating in three performances of a workshop production devised and directed by Rhoda Levine and presented by AMTF at the Walnut Street Theatre in October 1985. The world premiere production of *X,* also directed by Rhoda Levine, was presented by New York City Opera and opened there on September 28, 1986.

CHARACTERS

MALCOLM

LOUISE LITTLE, his mother

ELLA, his half-sister

STREET

REGINALD, Malcolm's brother

ELIJAH

BETTY, Malcolm's wife

YOUNG MALCOLM, ten years old

YOUNG REGINALD, younger
than Malcolm

HILDA LITTLE, Louise's
oldest child

YVONNE LITTLE, Louise's
youngest child

POSTMAN

GARVEY PREACHER

GARVEYITES

POLICEMAN

SOCIAL WORKER

NEIGHBORS

POOL PLAYERS

DANCERS

SWEETHEART

BLONDE

POLICE OFFICERS

PRISONERS

WOMAN PREACHER

GARVEY SPEAKER

MUSLIMS

REPORTERS

FRUIT OF ISLAM

TWO OF MALCOLM'S
DAUGHTERS

PILGRIMS

MUEZZIN

MALCOLM'S ALLIES

ASSASSINS

TIME AND PLACE

ACT ONE (1931–1945)

SCENE 1 Lansing, Michigan
SCENE 2 Boston
SCENE 3 Prison

ACT TWO (1946–1963)

SCENE 1 Prison
SCENE 2 125th Street,
New York City
SCENE 3 125th Street,
New York City
SCENE 4 Muslim Mosque/
Velvet Drive, Phoenix

ACT THREE (1963–1965)

SCENE 1 Velvet Drive,
Phoenix
SCENE 2 Mecca
SCENE 3 New York City
SCENE 4 A Hotel in
New York City
SCENE 5 Audubon Ballroom,
Harlem

X

THE LIFE AND TIMES OF MALCOLM X

REPORTER: *And just what is the cost of freedom?*
MALCOLM X: *The cost of freedom is death.*

[*for El Hajj Malik El-Shabazz*]

ACT ONE
Scene 1

1931, Lansing, Michigan. The home of Reverend Earl Little
and his wife, Louise, and four of their children. It is a farm-
house with Depression-era furnishings. This evening there is a
meeting of the local following of Marcus Garvey's Universal
Improvement Association, led by Rev. Little, but he is late.
Mrs. Little has been uneasy all day. Members of the group go
on with the meeting; tensions are high because everyone is
concerned about two active white supremacist groups terrorizing blacks in the area. A visiting organizer is recruiting for
Garvey's Black Star Line, ships being fitted to take blacks back
to Africa.

The guest speaker leads the meeting as young Malcolm and
the other children watch. Louise, now very frightened that
Earl has not returned, slips into her memories of the terror
that has stalked their family. She forgets the others in the
room. Strange lights move in the distance. Shadows move near
the house and pass. A policeman arrives and announces that
there was an accident. Rev. Little was cut in half by a streetcar. The neighbors say a white mob attacked the man and left
him on the tracks. Louise becomes distraught, hysterical, sings
to herself and, after a time, becomes unreachable.

A social worker comes to the home and declares the children wards of the state. Malcolm tries to get his mother to help
him. Finally, Ella, Malcolm's older half-sister, arrives to take
him to her home in Boston.

LOUISE *(To children)*:

> Malcolm, Reginald,
> I hear you mumbling something.
> You know what your father says:
> Speak up and say your say,
> Mumble and the devil will play.
> Go see if your father comes.
> Go see if your father comes.
> Go see.

POSTMAN:

> Is the reverend back yet?

LOUISE:

> He'll be along. *(To children)* Go see.

GARVEY PREACHER:

> It's a mean time.

GARVEYITES:

> Yes, brother.

GARVEY PREACHER:

> Nothing left to call mine.

GARVEYITES:

> Yes, brother. Yes, brother.

WOMAN GARVEYITE:

> We didn't have much before the crash.

MEN:

> Now they're going to take the last.

GARVEYITES:

> Yes.

GARVEY PREACHER:

> We'll be heading out soon.
> Taking the Black Star home.

GARVEYITES:

> ‖: Takin' the Black Star home! :‖*
> We'll leave this white man's land,
> crushing us like the devil's hand.
> Garvey has shown us—Marcus!—
> Garvey has told us—

*Repeat marks, ‖:—:‖, indicate repetitions of a passage.

Garvey has shown us, home!
‖: No more "darkie," no more "Rastus." :‖
‖: No more "nigga" when we see Africa. :‖

MEN:
We'll be black men again.
‖: We'll be black men again. :‖

POSTMAN:
Hang his picture high,
Ethiop's prophet,
Marcus, man who says
"Africa for Africans."

GARVEY PREACHER:
Sign up now. Put your name where your heart is.
We have a zion across the the sea!

GARVEYITES:
‖: *"Africa for Africans."* :‖
‖: Yes, Africa's time has come. :‖
‖: Africa's time has come :‖
‖: like a thundrin' storm :‖

‖: We've been waiting for a prophet. :‖

LOUISE *(Thinking aloud, gazing out)*:
Earl should have been home by sunset.
His day ended hours ago.
When he left today
I tried not to fret or worry,
but when Earl is away
the air seems thin and fragile,
like it cannot carry the day.
My body quakes with fear
he will not return.
In these twilight hours
every shadow moves,
every light is a fire.

I remember so clearly
the terror of night riders,
horses coming closer,
riding down our lives.

When Malcolm came
the Klan came,
white hoods, thunder hooves,
hooting, howling, slashing,
galloping horsemen.

A boy born in terror,
marked by our fear.
Not four,
not ten,
so many men,
rushing in
a black man's night.

GARVEYITES:

Not four,
not ten,
so many men,
rushing in
a black man's night.

LOUISE:

When Yvonne came
the Klan came
silently, without sound,
burned our house to the ground.
||: Smoking, smoldering, burning. :||
||: Shots :||
fired by white men.
A girl born in terror,
marked by our fear.

GARVEYITES:

Riding closer, riding closer, white hoods.

LOUISE:

Not four,
not ten,
so many men,
rushing in
a black man's night.

I remember so clearly
the terror of night riders,
horses coming closer,
riding down our lives.

POLICEMAN *(Comes to door, does not enter, speaks to the room)*:
A man was on the tracks.
A streetcar ran him down.

Word passes among the group.

GARVEYITES:
‖: A man was on the tracks. :‖
‖: A streetcar ran him down. :‖

MEN:
Rev'rend Little is dead.

He says that Earl was on the tracks;
he says a streetcar ran him down.

A white train cut him down,
cut him down, cut him down.
Some white men cut him down.

They pushed him on the tracks.

LOUISE:
The air seems thin and fragile.
In these twilight hours,
every light is a fire.

MEN:
These devils hunt us down
like cursed dogs.
They want to kill us all
without a fight.
They killed his brothers too,
those devils dressed in white.

LOUISE:
Now mine tonight.
Now mine tonight.

MEN:

> Hung one high in Georgia,
> shot one dead up north,
> murdered one low in the night,
> and Earl tonight.
> Some white men cut him down.
> These devils hunt us down
> like cursed dogs.

LOUISE:

> The air seems thin and fragile.
> In these twilight hours,
> every light's a fire, fire.

She screams, runs. Returns. Collapses into a sitting stillness that cannot be broken by the confusion and hysteria of the others. The children keep trying to shake her out of it; she does not see them. Neighbors try to decide what to do about the children. One by one some turn to reach for a child. The children reach for each other. After a while a white social worker appears at the door. She intrudes directly into the living room.

SOCIAL WORKER:

> What is going on here?
> What is going on here?
> The father is dead.
> The mother is mad.
> The children are out of control.

> *(Directed at no one and everyone, apologetic, but determined)*
> No one's in charge.
> It's out of hand.
> These Negroes are living like strays.
> Make them wards of the state.
> Make them wards of the state.

NEIGHBORS:

> Brother, Sister.
> The father is dead.
> The mother is mad.

Social worker grabs the children, hands them over to one adult and then another. Malcolm keeps coming back to his mother.

YOUNG MALCOLM:
>Momma, help me.
>Momma, help me.
>I was good in school,
>the best in the class.
>They tell me to get some tools,
>I'll have to work with my hands.
>Momma, help me.
>Momma, help me.
>What do I do?
>The teachers tell me
>that what's wrong with you
>will never be right.
>Momma, help me.
>Momma, help me.
>Momma.

Malcolm sits staring at his mother. A neighbor tries to rouse him, but fails. Finally Ella, Malcolm's older half-sister, arrives and reaches out for him with the opening lines of her song.

Scene 2

About 1940, Boston. Malcolm comes to live with Ella in the Roxbury section. He is still very much of a country boy, an in-experienced adolescent discovering the lights and movement of a big city. But he is by no means giddy, he rarely laughs. He lights up most when someone mentions music—this is his passion. Otherwise he finds that to say nothing is his best defense against looking uncool or ignorant. Ella introduces him to "the hill," where middle-class blacks live, and the rest of the area where others who have come looking for work are moving about on the street.

Malcolm then meets up with Street, who schools him in the

after-hours life of the community. Street leads him to a ball-room, scene of black dances, the great big bands of the era and "the Life."

ELLA:

    Come with me, child. Come with me.
    Come with me, child. Come with me.
    Your sister Ella will care for you.
    You know me and I know you.
    Come with me, child.
    You're my special one,
    a child like me
    with darting eyes.
    I can remember
    the time you smiled.
    You told some tales,
    fantastic tales,
    of Arab lands and kings.
    Come closer my special one.
    You know that you are mine.

    Come child, come with me.
    The whole big city waits
    for you to see.
    My side of town
    they call "the hill,"
    it could be the "bottom,"
    the South Side or Harlem.
    It's always bustling and sprawling
    but it's still like a home.
    We call the streets
    by our very own names.
    We Negroes don't leave a place
    quite the same.

MEN ON THE STREET:

    We make a town dance
    with our sways and our glances.
    We're taking our chance

on some midnight romancing.
We make a town dance
with our sways and our glances.
‖: We're taking a chance, :‖
‖: taking a chance, taking a chance. :‖

ELLA:

Some men are bootblacks or doctors.
Some are lawyers or cobblers.
We're all kind of family,
almost next of kin.
We're just tryin' to make it
from where we've been.

*She lets him go off to walk past some of the sights. He wanders
into a pool room. People stand in the shadows watching a game.
Street speaks first to his opponent.*

STREET:

Shoot your shot.
Just forget your job,
play the dice that you got.
Shoot your shot.
Just forget your job,
play the chance that you got.

ELLA:

Some men are strivers
with dreams of their own;
and some are believers
who help a dream along;
and some speak of prophecy,
of Garvey, slavery,
of nations, visions and hope.
They make the street their church,
make a soapbox perch.

STREET:

Shoot the shot,
cut the talk,
admit your two bits are mine.

You'll be owin' me next week's pay
before you get out from behind.
Hey there! Take a look, it's a country boy
up from the farm.
I once had that look before
but now when their work is done,
‖: they all come to me. :‖
‖: They all come to see. :‖
‖: All come to me. :‖

PLAYERS:

‖: Sweet Street, sweet Street. :‖

ELLA:

Stay away from trouble,
the users and the foolish.
Never be careless.

STREET:

The "life" is a game
like this green felt table—
you die broke or win
if you're good and able.
Shoot your shot,
or gimme the dough.
You ain't got a lot
from the white man to blow.

Play the game,
don't fool with a job.
A job is a slave,
it will leave you robbed.
Doctors waitin' tables,
farmers carryin' loads.
They say they're in shippin',
or other fables.
They're just helpless losers,
liftin' totin' fools.
The white man takes
while the black man breaks.

Play the game
get into the "life."
Don't mess around
with the white man's strife.

(Spoken)
If you try and change things
they'll take your life.

PLAYERS:
‖: The white man takes :‖
‖: while the black man breaks. :‖

‖: Play the game, :‖
‖: get in the "life." :‖
‖: Don't mess around :‖
‖: with the white man's strife. :‖

‖: Play the game, :‖
‖: be smart like the Man. :‖
‖: Get in the "life." :‖
‖: Get your heaven while you can. :‖

Malcolm and Street shift to a ballroom. A shoeshine stand is at one side. Players congregate there, styling. They "signify" as if they are the sax section of the Ellington band.

STREET *(To be rapped)*:
But wait.
How about those clothes?
I mean your sartorial condition is curious.
Son, your future is dubious.
If you ever hope to be one of the cats
who has a chance to dance the dance
in this rude rat race,
you need a little dash
to get some cash.
To meet the girl of your dreams,
you've got to be clean.

(Sung)

> You need a zoot suit, a conk, and a pad.
> A hustler can't go 'round
> lookin' poor, lookin' sad.
> Work for no one but yourself,
> keep your feelings
> right on the shelf.

PLAYERS *(Joining in)*:

> Shoot the craps
> and make a big deal—
> but you gotta be cool
> or be someone's fool.
> ‖: If you want more, take it. :‖
> ‖: If you don't know, fake it. :‖
> ‖: Take more/Make more. :‖
> ‖: Play the game, :‖
> ‖: get in the "life." :‖

STREET:

> Play the game.
> Don't be afraid—
> make like you're shinin' shoes,
> sell them reefers and tips,
> and dates with fast gals.
> When you're in your suit
> stand real still/stay cool.
> Point your fingers to the floor,
> keep your feet wide apart,
> throw back your head,
> like you're not lookin' at all.

(Pause)

> Just stand real still,
> just stay real cool.
> The hustler gets them all.

During this sequence Malcolm picks up Sweetheart, leads her to the dance floor and back. He then spots a Blonde cruising him, grabs her as she comes close, twirls her and starts to exit. She has another idea in mind. Malcolm and Street come up with a plan to pull off a heist. They exit. While they are offstage the ensemble does a fantastic rendition of a crowded hot dance, in half-time.

STREET:

> Once in a while
> you dance the bop,
> show the lames
> you can Lindy Hop.
> Here's where it is,
> my side of town.

Players join in.

STREET AND PLAYERS:

> But they all come down—
> they're blonde or brown,
> they all come round
> my side of town.
> Let the ladies come to you.

PLAYERS:

> ‖: The player gets them all. :‖
> ‖: The hustler gets them all. :‖

STREET AND PLAYERS:

> You know what to do.
> ‖: Let them come to you. :‖

Street and Blonde enter with silver, furs and other valuables. A crowd gathers to buy the goods. Police Officers enter, billy clubs in hand.

OFFICERS:

> I see some nigras been
> on the wrong side of town,
> robbing leading citizens,
> instead of earning their own.

(To other officers, indicating Malcolm and Street)
Round up those hoods.
Put them away.
A white man's home
isn't safe anymore.
Niggers like you
break in the door.

MEN *(Mocking)*:
A white man's home
just isn't safe anymore,
‖: just isn't safe anymore. :‖

OFFICER:
Put them away.

(To the Blonde)
You're no common goods.
What are you doin' here?

WOMEN *(To the Blonde)*:
White women ought to know
where they belong.
They might be sold real low
and go wrong.

OFFICER *(To other officers, indicating the Blonde)*:
Take her too.
Take them all.

All exit.

Scene 3

Malcolm appears alone, handcuffed, under a glaring light. A chair sits stage center. He seems to be talking to interrogators who are maybe in the shadows, maybe not there at all.

MALCOLM:
I would not tell you
what I know.
You would not

hear my truth.
You want the story
but you don't want to know.
My truth is you've been on me
a very long time,
meaner than I can say.
As long as I've been living
you've had your foot on me,
always pressing.

My truth is white men
killed my old man,
drove my mother mad.
My truth is rough.
My truth could kill.
My truth is fury.

They always told me,
"You don't have a chance.
You're a nigger, after all.
You can jitterbug and prance,
but you'll never run the ball."
My truth told me,
quit before you start.
My truth told me,
stayin' alive is all you've got.

I've shined your shoes,
I've sold your dope,
hauled your bootleg,
played with hustler's hope.
But the crime is mine,
I will do your time,
so you can sleep.
I won't be out to get you
on the street at night
but I won't forget
any evil that's white.

My truth is a hammer
coming from the back.
It will beat you down
when you least expect.
I would not tell you
what I know.
You want the truth,
you want the truth,
but you don't want to know.

Lights out.

ACT TWO
Scene 1

1946–48. Malcolm broods angrily in jail, left alone by the others. Malcolm's brother Reginald comes to visit him and teach him about Elijah, the Messenger of Allah. Malcolm doubts everything Reginald says. Gradually he comes to a point of initial acceptance of this new idea. Reginald leaves Malcolm in jail as Elijah's voice is heard offstage. Malcolm spends time studying the Holy Koran and books on black history. He has to begin wearing glasses because of his habit of reading in poor light late at night. He becomes a serious and a more hopeful man. Malcolm X is born.

1952. The jail recedes as Malcolm hears, and eventually sees, Elijah. It is as though the word removed the bars. They come face to face. Elijah embraces Malcolm like a son and tells him he has much to learn. He tells him to obey the Law and to spread Allah's word. Malcolm is sent to start temples in the eastern states.

PRISONERS:
‖: In the devil's grip, :‖
‖: the black men mourn :‖
‖: the slaver's whip. :‖
‖: Black men, wake :‖

‖: from your living graves :‖
‖: before it's too late. :‖

Reginald comes to visit Malcolm. They sit opposite one another in the day room.

REGINALD:

It has been so long.

MALCOLM:

Longer than you can know.
You don't count time where I've been.

REGINALD:

You got my letter?
Read what I said?

MALCOLM:

I just can't understand.
What's the game?

REGINALD:

I've changed.
I've found a new way.
I'm clean,
Starting out new.
I met a man
who showed me the truth.

MALCOLM:

You talk in riddles
about truth and a man.
Don't try and kid me
when I need a plan.
They're riding me hard,
trying to make me break.
They're ready to nail me
if I make one mistake.

PRISONERS:

If he makes one mistake.

MALCOLM:

I thought you had a way.

REGINALD:

>Have you ever met a man
>who knows all things?

MALCOLM *(Incredulous)*:

>No, brother.

REGINALD:

>He knows who you are,
>where you've been.
>He knows your future.

MALCOLM:

>I can't understand.

REGINALD:

>Your past was stolen,
>taken from you,
>your children tortured,
>your women taken too.
>Black is your skin,
>the fate that's in your hands.

MALCOLM:

>Brother, I know no such man.
>Is he a god?
>I can't understand.

PRISONERS:

>I can't understand.

REGINALD:

>Black is your skin—

MALCOLM:

>I can't understand.

REGINALD:

>who once was king.

MALCOLM:

>Is he a god?

REGINALD:

>You're now a slave.

MALCOLM:

>I don't understand
>what you say.

REGINALD:

> Listen to me,
> the devil's got you in jail.
> The white man left you
> judged on a scale.
> This man taught me things:
> A nation we are,
> all of us.

PRISONERS:

> A nation we see.

MALCOLM:

> God does not know me,
> the hustlers or players.
> On the fast track I see
> only winners or losers.

REGINALD:

> This man taught me things.

MALCOLM:

> God knows the good ones—
> He betrays them.
> We're out there alone;
> God does not know me.

REGINALD:

> But God is a man.
> His name is Allah.

MALCOLM:

> We're out there alone.

REGINALD:

> He came to this land.

MALCOLM:

> God does not know me.

REGINALD:

> He told Elijah.

MALCOLM:

> We're out there alone.

REGINALD:

> He told a black man—

MALCOLM:
> Who is Elijah?

REGINALD:
> His own divine plan.

MALCOLM:
> How can God be man?
> Allah.
> What a strange sound.

Prisoners slowly transform into Muslim followers.

MEN:
> ‖: *Allahu-Akbar.* :‖

REGINALD:
> Elijah is the Messenger,
> the Messenger of Allah.

MALCOLM:
> Allah. Allah.

REGINALD:
> Say His name again and again.
> The rest will come in time.
> To say His name is to praise Him.
> *(Exits)*

MALCOLM:
> Allah.
> What does it mean
> to say His name?

MEN:
> ALLAH!

MALCOLM:
> Does He know I steal,
> lie and take dope?

MALCOLM AND MEN:
> Allah. Allah.

MALCOLM:
> To say His name
> is to praise Him.

Soon I will ask Him
how empty it feels
to be God of an empty man
like me.

ELIJAH (*Slowly appears in the back light*):

You are not empty—

CHORUS (MEN AND WOMEN):

Malcolm!

ELIJAH:

nor are you lost.

CHORUS (MEN AND WOMEN):

Malcolm!

ELIJAH:

You're Malcolm,
cold and just,
no fear of loss.

CHORUS (MEN AND WOMEN):

Malcolm!

ELIJAH:

You are not empty,
nor are you lost.

MALCOLM:

Allah. Allah.
From Africa like me.
A God black men will praise.
I can say His name.

CHORUS (MEN AND WOMEN):

Allah. Allah.

ELIJAH:

You are not empty,
but full enough to cry aloud.

CHORUS (MEN AND WOMEN):

Allah! Allah!

MALCOLM:

I hear the shudders of slavers—

ELIJAH:

Your rage He will claim.

CHORUS (MEN AND WOMEN):

      Allah!

MALCOLM:

      the sound that shakes the walls.

ELIJAH:

      Malcolm!

MALCOLM:

      It bangs against the cells,
      a name without fear.

ELIJAH:

      Who have you been?

MALCOLM:

      A power gathers I can hear.
      To say His name
      is to praise Him! Allah!

Malcolm leaves prison and comes to meet with Elijah.

ELIJAH:

      Malcolm,
      who have you been?
      Malcolm,
      from where do you come?
      Why are you so thirsty and worn?
      Who would you be?

MALCOLM:

      I came from a desert
      of pain and remorse,
      from slavery, exile,
      from jail's brute force.

ELIJAH:

      Who would you be?

MALCOLM:

      I would just be a man
      who knows right and wrong,
      who knows the past
      was stolen away.

ELIJAH:

>A life we see.
>
>A reason to be.
>
>But who will you be?

MALCOLM:

>My name means nothing.

ELIJAH:

>An "X" you must claim.

MALCOLM:

>My name means I was a slave.

ELIJAH:

>An "X" you must claim
>
>for what was lost—
>
>your African name,
>
>an ocean crossed.
>
>An "X" will stand
>
>until God returns
>
>to speak a name
>
>that will be yours.
>
>Come, Malcolm X,
>
>let me teach you.
>
>*Allahu-Akbar.*
>
>Allah is the greatest.
>
>Let me teach you.

CHORUS (MEN AND WOMEN):

>An "X" will stand
>
>for what was lost.
>
>An "X" will stand
>
>until God returns.
>
>*Allahu-Akbar.*

ELIJAH:

>*As Salaam-Alaikum.*
>
>Peace be unto you.

MALCOLM:

>*Wa-Alaikum-Salaam.*
>
>And unto you
>
>be peace.

ELIJAH:

> We join all others
> who love Allah.

CHORUS (MEN AND WOMEN):

> ‖: *Allahu-Akbar!* :‖

Elijah shows Malcolm how to pray in the manner of the Nation of Islam during the early 1950s, standing, as opposed to kneeling, facing east, palms out.

ELIJAH:

> We seek Freedom,
> Justice,
> Equality.
> But to know these things
> you must know history.
> And you must know
> Armageddon comes.
> I carry its word.

CHORUS (MEN AND WOMEN):

> ‖: Freedom, justice, freedom, :‖
> ‖: equality. :‖
> ‖: *Allahu-Akbar.* :‖
> ‖: *Allahu-Akbar.* :‖
>
> ‖: Freedom, justice, freedom. :‖
> ‖: Equality, freedom, justice. :‖
> ‖: Freedom, equality. :‖

MALCOLM:

> Dark is our history.
> A flame is our prophecy.
> Allah's Messenger
> carries His word.

ELIJAH:

> We have been blind,
> the white man's tool.
> For four hundred years,

we've been made his fools.
He laughs at us
who once were kings.
He has us beg
and call him boss,
then he gives us his God
to keep us downtrod.
We've sunk so low,
we can't let him go.

MALCOLM:

We've sunk so low,
we can't let him go.

MALCOLM AND ELIJAH:

Let our eyes see.
We can set our lives free.

MALCOLM:

I wanted to fight—

ELIJAH:

You did not know how.
It's your time now.
(Embraces him)
Spread His word!

ALL:

‖: *Allahu-Akbar.* :‖

Scene 2

1954–63. Malcolm begins his ministry, helping to found temples in Boston, Philadelphia, Springfield, Hartford, Atlanta
and New York.

The remaining scenes of this act span a considerable number of years in telescopic fashion. This is the time of the land-
mark Supreme Court decision, Brown v. Board of Education.
It is the era in which Rosa Parks refused to sit in the back of a
Montgomery, Alabama bus, thus sparking a long boycott organized by black working women, which integrated the buses

and brought to the public the name of Rev. Martin Luther King, Jr. The period closes at the time of the assassination of President John F. Kennedy.

Malcolm is seen on the corner of 125th Street and Seventh Avenue, in front of Micheaux's National Memorial African Bookstore, "The House of Common Sense, Home of Proper Propaganda." The front of the store is a tall montage of placards bearing black nationalist slogans from all over the globe and decades gone. "Repatriation Headquarters—Back to Africa movement, Register Here"; "Black Man's God." Portraits of African princes, ex-slaves, Americans such as W. E. B. Du Bois and Paul Robeson abound. It's like the secret attic of J. A. Rogers, author of *World's Great Men of Color* and one of Malcolm's teachers.

A woman street preacher is holding forth on a soapbox as Minister Malcolm approaches. She is dressed in long, sparkling African garb with a cloth wrapped around her head. She is trying to get people interested in her group, which promotes the adoption of African lifestyles. The general point is that blacks may return to their former greatness by returning to their former ways: religious practices resembling those of the Yoruba religion, communal living, polygamy, matriarchal family lines. She is followed by a Garvey speaker. Malcolm and several Muslims listen and wait for their moment to get the attention of the crowd. Later, as Malcolm takes to the soapbox, his comrades reach out for passersby and work up the crowds.

[RALLY #1]

WOMAN PREACHER:

We are an African people,
we must live as Africans here.
We are not from this place.
We've only been ruined by its ways.
Black men hide from the social worker,
afraid to claim their children,
'cause they ain't got a job.
Your ancestors didn't need money,

why, they dug gold out of the ground,
and grew their own food.
They had many wives.
Let's go back to our old ways,
find a land for our dreams.

GARVEY SPEAKER *(Interrupting; spoken)*:
We can go back, back to Mother Africa!

ALL:
Take us back.

GARVEY SPEAKER:
You were once kings of Mali,
Dahomey and Songhay.
Your prince now is Haile
Selassie I, [*"I" pronounced "eye"*]
the Lion of Judah.

MALCOLM:
Where are we now, brother?
Twenty million kings of Mali?

Crowd laughs and turns toward Malcolm, who strikes a formidable pose at the rear, smiling, head high, like a boxer waiting to climb in the ring. He moves forward a few feet, feeling the crowd is with him.

Where are we now, brother?
Twenty million sad and sorry?

Laughter in crowd.

MUSLIM:
Speak it, speak it!

MALCOLM:
I'm just trying to pull your coat, brother.

MUSLIM:
Let the man speak!

Malcolm moves to the front and takes over as the Garvey speaker relinquishes his spot.

MALCOLM:

  Yes, we had it once,
  now we got nothing to lose.
  When I was little
  they called me "nigger,"
  they called me "nigger" so much,
  I thought it was my name.

 Laughter in crowd.

  Now the chickens they sent out
  are coming home to roost.

 Laughter in crowd.

MALCOLM AND CROWD:
  Twenty million—
MALCOLM:
  kings of Mali,
MALCOLM AND CROWD:
  twenty million—
MALCOLM:
  so-called Negroes,
CROWD:
  asking the white man for mercy.
MALCOLM:
  Imagine that!

 Laughter in crowd.

  The white man tricked the Negro,
  used the Negro,
  made him a fool,
  till the Negro woke up!

  We have awakened!
  Allah is all-wise,
  the true and living God.

I come to say His praise.
I come to tell the history.
I come to tell the past,
of the black man's bondage.

MUSLIMS:

It may sound bitter,
may sound like hate,
but it's just the truth.

CROWD (Joining in):

‖: It may sound bitter, :‖
‖: may sound like hate, :‖
‖: but it's just the truth. :‖

MALCOLM:

We don't hate the white man—
his world is about to fall.
May sound like hate,
but it's just the truth.

Scene 3

Stage freezes for a second, then goes into motion. People who
were at the rally exit. One Muslim hands Malcolm a briefcase,
another hands him a suitcase. One picks up a paper, the other
grabs a bunch of leaflets to distribute. With everything in motion, they begin all over. While his fellow travelers continue to
"fish" in the crowd and hand out flyers, Malcolm speaks.
Sometimes he is preceded on the "rostrum" by another Muslim who warms up the crowd—in mime.

Malcolm always smiles when he speaks, not broadly, but he
is happy to do what he does and enjoys the audiences. He likes
to lead the crowd along a train of thought for a while and then
surprise them. He also likes to shock. He is physically reserved, not demonstrative, but a trace of the swagger of the
young Malcolm, once known as Big Red, is there in his bearing. Men and women like to be around him, find him charis-
matic.

One or two more people in the crowd appear to be Muslims

at each new rally until, finally, they are the majority. Once the group becomes largely Muslim, women stand or sit on one side, men on the other. This separation should not appear planned, but should just happen. Women who appear in Muslim attire in the beginning must be moving through and not linger in the street. One or two Muslims frequently return to Elijah to make reports on Malcolm's work.

Just before Rally #2 Elijah comes to advise Malcolm on his responsibilities.

ELIJAH:

> My son, I hear you speak—
> in you I see the Nation's
> power growing stronger.
> Your gift is a fire—
> once it is lit,
> it burns an unknown path.
> The more it breathes,
> the wilder it grows.
> Do not go alone, my son.
> When you speak,
> you speak for me.
> I am the eyes of the Nation;
> and I see what will be.

[RALLY #2]

PERSON IN THE CROWD:

> Say your piece, brother, teach.

MALCOLM:

> If we are going to be free,
> it will be done by you and me.
> And we won't turn the other cheek,
> we won't turn the other cheek
> to get our freedom.
> We are ready to die,
> to get our freedom.
> We will use any means—

whatever means necessary—
to stand for ourselves,
to live for ourselves,
to keep catchin' hell.

PERSON IN THE CROWD:
Teach, brother, teach.

Scene freezes for a second, then everyone moves. People at rally exit, perhaps leaving a policeman and a vendor.

[RALLY #3]

Muslims enter and set up rostrum. People gather as if for an expected speech at a given time; others are passersby who stop.

MUSLIMS:
All praises to Allah,
the All-Merciful, the All-Wise.

MALCOLM:
Allah does not teach us
to suffer more and more.
Allah does not teach us
to fight the white man's wars.
Allah does not teach us
to stay as slaves
after four hundred years.

(Spots a young man in the audience, singles him out)

‖: Jones is not your name, :‖
‖: it's a slave name. :‖
‖: Smith is not your name, :‖
(Crowd joins in.)
‖: it's a slave name. :‖

What are you gonna do with a slave name?
You need a good name,
you need a holy name,

a name that praises you and God—
a name like Malik, Amilcar.

ALL *(Crowd laughs, then whispers rhythmically)*:
‖: Toussaint, Toussaint, :‖
‖: Kenyatta, Kenyatta, Kenyatta. :‖

MALCOLM:
Lumumba, *(Broad smile)* Nkrumah, Ny-er-e.
(Short satisfied laugh)

ALL:
‖: Lumumba, Lumumba, :‖
‖: Nkrumah, Nkrumah, Nkrumah, :‖
‖: Nyere! :‖

Scene freezes, then everyone exits.

[RALLY #4]

*A large crowd gathers. Malcolm is now facing the audience at a
podium downstage center, with people onstage appearing to be at
the sides and front of the rally. He speaks directly to the audience.*

MALCOLM *(Spoken into microphone)*:
We're not askin' Massa to sit at a lunch counter.
We want *self*-determination.
We want to get our people off of dope,
off alcohol, off the welfare rolls.
We must *rebuild* the black family,
and our communities, ravaged by despair.
We need to look to our brothers in Africa
taking *back* their plundered countries,
tellin' Massa what time it is.
We need to work, we need jobs,
and *we* have to create them.
But we know if whites are forced
to give us their jobs,
there'll be war, *(Sung)* a bloody race war.

We want freedom, justice, equality.

ALL:

‖: Freedom, justice, equality. :‖

MALCOLM (*Spoken into microphone*):

Down south blacks sit in
and rednecks sic dogs on them, bomb their churches.
Now, who are the lawbreakers, who are the violent ones?
Muslims don't expect anybody
to give our people freedom.
We want to *stand up* against racism,
all black people together!

*After he finishes, Malcolm takes Betty, his wife and confidante, by
the arm as he moves to the next location.*

ALL:

‖: Freedom, justice, equality. :‖

Scene 4

*1963. Muslims gather at a mosque. Elijah comes in, greets Mal-
colm and then various people in audience, exits to position at the
rear.*

MALCOLM (*Spoken*):

As-Salaam-Alaikum.

MUSLIMS (*Spoken*):

Wa-Alaikum-Salaam.

MALCOLM (*Sung*):

We are a nation,
trapped inside a nation.
We are a nation,
dying to be born.

BETTY, ELIJAH, REGINALD:

We are a nation,
trapped inside a nation.

> We are a nation,
> dying to be born.

MALCOLM:

> We dream of our land,
> our own land.
> We dream of our home,
> a black zion.
> It is our will to be,
> our will to be free.
> A black zion.

ALL:

> We are a nation
> trapped inside a nation.
> We are a nation,
> dying to be born.

MALCOLM, BETTY, REGINALD:

> Chains took the lives of our young,
> took the blood of the old,
> and yet we go on,

ELIJAH:

> and still we are one.

MALCOLM AND ALL:

> We will only know peace—

MALCOLM AND REGINALD:

> in a land that is free.

MALCOLM:

> A black zion.

ALL:

> We are a nation,
> trapped inside a nation,
> dying to be born.

Muslims break into hurried organized activities, setting up stands to sell goods, running classes. Minister Malcolm X oversees the production of the Nation of Islam newspaper, Muhammad Speaks. *As he exits the mosque, he is greeted by the news reporters and TV cameras that frequently follow him. The Nation of Islam is the subject of much public attention and surveillance by police, whose presence should be obvious.*

As Malcolm is finishing a speech before a large gathering of Muslims, whispers of horror begin to fly through the crowd. A Muslim sent by Elijah brings a message to Malcolm. News is passed that President John F. Kennedy has been murdered in Dallas, Texas. Reporters first approach Elijah for comment and are rebuffed; they then press to the front of Malcolm's meeting to ask questions.

REPORTER *(Spoken)*: Mr. X, what do you make of the recent tragic events in Dallas—President Kennedy's assassination?

MALCOLM: America's climate of hate is coming back on itself. Not only are defenseless blacks killed, but now it has struck down the chief of state. That hate struck down Medgar Evers. That hate struck down Patrice Lumumba. In my view, it's a case of the chickens coming home to roost.

REPORTER *(Spoken, arrogantly)*: Thank you.

Flashbulbs go off in Malcolm's face. Reporters act astounded at what they've heard, huddle, exit. One or two Muslims quickly carry word to Elijah, who reacts angrily to news of Malcolm's remark. Malcolm exits with his men.

REPORTERS:

‖: The chickens come home to roost. :‖
‖: The chickens come home to roost. :‖

Velvet Drive, Phoenix.

ELIJAH *(To two of his men)*:

Now Malcolm disobeys the Messenger!
I do not know this Malcolm X!
I sent word to all the ministers:
Do not talk about the president,
do not talk about his death.
Do not make enemies for the Nation;

we have enemies enough.
Do not make enemies for black men;
black men have enemies enough!

Elijah orders the men out. Lights out.

ACT THREE
Scene 1

1963. Malcolm is called to see Elijah, who is incensed that
Malcolm has possibly jeopardized the situation of the Nation
of Islam by making his remark concerning Kennedy's assassination. He is also concerned that his chief spokesman may
have already become too powerful, within the Nation and outside as well. He is worried that perhaps he will no longer be
able to control his minister. Malcolm comes with his own mis-
givings about the Messenger's leadership. Muhammad cen-
sures Malcolm by silencing him for three months, even ex-
tending this to his teaching at Malcolm's own Mosque #7 in
Harlem.

Muslim community people are milling about and waiting
outside the Messenger's home. Many are Fruit of Islam (FOI),
Muhammad's army. An FBI agent can be seen, as well as one
or two reporters. As Malcolm passes through this crowd they
begin to mumble and whisper; their sounds become a kind of
drone.

ALL:

‖: Betrayal is on his lips. :‖
‖: Is it truth or lies? :‖

MUSLIMS:

Malcolm brings us down
with his talk.
He spreads poison.
He has a loose tongue.
The Nation is betrayed
by the Messenger.

Does he come to judge
or be judged?

Velvet Drive, Phoenix. Malcolm enters.

ELIJAH:

> *As-Salaam-Alaikum,* Brother Malcolm.

MALCOLM:

> *Wa-Alaikum-Salaam,* Mr. Muhammad.

ELIJAH:

> An uproar is all around us.
> It's a bad time
> for us all.
> You disobeyed.
> You have a loose tongue.

MALCOLM:

> It's a bad time.
> Have I not served,
> have I not served you?
> Spread Allah's teaching across the land?

ELIJAH:

> You disobeyed.
> Your fame helped us once,
> now it only does harm.
> ‖: Fame is a double-edged sword. :‖

MALCOLM:

> Look into my heart.
> I am here to serve,
> I am here to serve the Nation,
> the Messenger, the Law.
> I could still be in Hell,
> in the streets.
> For that I will believe.

ELIJAH:

> Is betrayal on your lips, my son?

MALCOLM:

> Betrayal flies around us.
> It haunts the air we breathe.

I hear things I cannot believe;
they say the Messenger
has his own law.

ELIJAH:

You speak so freely,
you speak to me of law.
Do you come to judge
or be judged?
They say you have grown too big
for the Nation.

MALCOLM:

This talk consumes our Nation.
We must stand up strong.
We must reach the people,
and bring change,
by whatever means.

ELIJAH:

Are you revolution,
whirling forward
without Allah's wisdom?
The white man has used you
to bring us down.
This is when your chickens
come home to roost.

MALCOLM:

I am a servant of the Nation,
and that is all.

ELIJAH:

They say you have grown too big
for the Nation.

MALCOLM:

Liars and betrayers cut me down—
it is not true.

ELIJAH:

You spoke against the Nation;
you spoke against my word.
Do you come to judge
or be judged?

MALCOLM:

> Liars and traitors cut me down.
> I'm a just man.

ELIJAH:

> You kick the dead
> while the country weeps!
> You will be silent!
> You will say nothing!

MALCOLM:

> I bow to your will.
> I will not speak.

Malcolm bows to Elijah, exits through crowd, which divides, with a small number falling out of the Muslim ranks to follow Malcolm. The rest pick up the mumbling chorus.

MUSLIMS/FOI:

> ‖: Betrayal is on his lips. :‖
> ‖: The chickens come home to roost. :‖

INTERLUDE

The Nation becomes divided, and although many Muslims come to follow Malcolm, he is in deep turmoil over the division and feels he must search alone for some answers. He feels betrayed by his mentor and many of his brothers in the movement. He tires of being constantly surrounded by other people—followers, reporters, people trying to warn him of various dangers ahead.

Behind him is the devastated landscape of Harlem, forbidding, isolating, a gray vacantness similar to the open spaces of his childhood, yet crowded with structures. He goes to his family and is consoled by Betty. Two of their young girls are present. She hands him an envelope, and urges him to go to make the *Hajj*, or pilgrimage to Mecca, of an orthodox Muslim, knowing that Allah somehow is with him and will help him.

BETTY *(At first addressing their daughters)*:
>When a man believes,
>you can see in his eyes,
>and know where he goes
>to hide his fears.
>When a man believes,
>do the stars die
>for a night,
>or does the city
>hide them
>in its glare—
>alone with his dreams
>in a light seldom seen.
>When his journey is done
>he will find us here
>in peace God will give.
>*(To Malcolm)*
>When a man believes,
>he'll find his God inside.
>He'll see it takes one step,
>and keep believing.

MALCOLM:
>Allah made me and left me here.
>Life is what He gave me,
>now I must ask His help
>to give a life back to God.
>*(Embraces them and exits)*

Scene 2

When Malcolm appears again he is making a pilgrimage to Mecca. He has abandoned his Western clothing for a simple white cloth, as all pilgrims must. Where he waits many other pilgrims pray, eat and sleep on rugs they have brought with them. Being unprepared, he has a space on the bare floor. At the first sign of dawn, a call to prayer is heard and the pilgrims rise to say their first prayers. Malcolm has not slept. The pilgrims face east and make the motions of ablutions and prayer.

PILGRIMS:

‖: *Bismillah hirrahman-irrahim.* :‖
[I begin with the name of Allah,
the Merciful, the Compassionate.]

MUEZZIN:

‖: *Ash-hadu an la ilaha* :‖
‖: *ill-Allah.* :‖
[I bear witness that there is
no God but Allah.]
‖: *Ash-hado anna* :‖
‖: *Muhammad-ar* :‖
‖: *Rasul-ullah.* :‖
[I bear witness that Muhammad is the messenger of
Allah.]

*Malcolm has made an attempt to follow the movements of those
around him, but he has never learned the orthodox prayer ritual
and now finds it is difficult to recreate what the pilgrims are doing. He gives up for a moment, watches them, speaks.*

MALCOLM:

I have come so far, among so many.
I have never been so alone.
No one knows who I am.
Perhaps the high court
will not believe I am true.
I am waiting for a message.
Mecca!

Here I hear so many tongues speak.
Allah is praised by all men.
I watch and I bow and pray,
I'm tied in a silence unknown, alone,
so alone.

My name is Shabazz,
El Hajj Malik El-Shabazz,
a name for one reborn.
El Hajj Malik El-Shabazz,

a name for one who has heard
the universe make but one sound.
It moves as one force,
a whirling desert storm.
Each of us a cloud of sand
flying round the silent eye.

I have seen both black and white men
all bow and pray before God.
El Hajj Malik El-Shabazz
has found a new way.
Praise!
‖: I bow and pray. :‖
‖: Praise! :‖
‖: New born today. :‖
‖: Praise Allah! :‖

At the closing of the song he returns to making the motions of prayer, stubbornly trying at least to approximate them. After all, this will be how he must live the rest of his life. Finally, he succeeds in getting his knees to really bend, his head to touch the floor.

PILGRIMS:
    ‖: *Bismillah hirrahman-irrahim.* :‖

Scene 3

1964–65. Just before Malcolm returns from his sojourn in the Near East and Africa a riot breaks out in Harlem. It starts when a white police officer accuses a black youth of stealing. One or two people on the street try to get into the matter. A scuffle ensues and the young boy tries to escape. He is shot by the policeman. People attack the policeman, seriously injuring him, and rioting breaks out in the area. As sirens are heard, people scatter.

Malcolm returns a deeply changed man, but outwardly he appears the same. He is greeted by reporters who wish to question him about the rioting. He is warned of death threats against him.

Some of Malcolm's allies are wearing dashikis and other African garb popular in the mid-sixties. One or two wear traditional Muslim garb, such as Malcolm would have seen in Cairo or Jedda. As before, he is constantly observed.

Malcolm is not concerned with the fear so evident all around him. Still, he takes some precautions for his safety.

REPORTERS:
‖: Mr. X—, Mr. X— :‖
‖: Malcolm X—, Malcolm X— :‖

MALCOLM:
The name is Shabazz.
El Hajj Malik El-Shabazz.
What do you want to know
that you've not been told?
(Indicating blacks around them)
We have explained ourselves
so many times.

You always ask
what you already know.
You wonder why
there is revolt—
A violent land
breeds violent men.
The slaver breeds a rebel,
not a slave.
Can't you see at all?
Do your eyes tell you lies?

It has begun
and I am no more its cause
than anyone here.

I do not stand alone
against your foolish blows.

MALCOLM'S ALLIES:

‖: It has begun, a rising tide. :‖
‖: There is no time to wonder why. :‖

MALCOLM:

Men pursue me
every step I take,
and yet they don't see
the brothers behind them.

ALLIES:

‖: Brothers behind them. :‖

MALCOLM:

Men of fifty nations
lead their people on.
We throw off the tyranny of states,
the slaver's greedy hand.

A tide rises at your back
and sweeps you in its path.
Can you see at all?
Do your eyes tell you lies?

Malcolm starts to exit with friends.

REPORTERS:

‖: Is he not the one? :‖
Is he not the one
‖: who sent the youth :‖
into our streets?
‖: Is he not the one? :‖
Is he not the one
who called us devils,
who preached black hate?
‖: Mr. X—, Mr. X— :‖

Malcolm turns his back and exits.

Scene 4

Malcolm has formed a new group, the Organization of Afro-American Unity. He plans to go to the United Nations with the grievances of black Americans. He proceeds to a hotel room where he meets with his close allies to tell them of his plans.

MALCOLM:
> I have learned so much in Africa.
> We're a part of something so big,
> a movement spanning the globe.
>
> *(Spoken)*
> I met with freedom fighters from
> Mozambique, Angola, Zambia, Zimbabwe,
> even from South Africa.
> This is no race revolt,
> it is the end of colonialism,
> it is revolution
> among African peoples.
> It is time for our new organization,
> the Organization of Afro-American Unity,
> to bring these ideas to our people,
> *all* our people—African-Americans.
> Once our people have seen
> how the master plays,
> offers us crumbs, small reforms;
> once blacks have seen
> our fight is human rights,
> our action will begin.
> We must first teach.
> We must teach by going to the U.N.
> to show the denial of our human rights.
> We must teach that we have
> a right to self-defense,
> that political self-determination
> comes from ballots or bullets.

(Sung)
We must aim well
for freedom.

They exit.

REPORTERS:

America is a house of glass,
anyone can see the violence inside.
Bricks fly to the walls.
The roof shatters.

ELIJAH AND FRUIT OF ISLAM:

The Nation is a house of cards,
men like Malcolm push too hard.
Men like Malcolm light the match,
‖: cards teeter and fall. :‖
The house collapses.

*Sound of explosion. Reginald, Malcolm and others enter hotel
room.*

REGINALD:

Who set the bomb,
destroyed your home?
Men are hunting you down.
Where will you go?

MALCOLM:

We've been hunted before—

REGINALD:

We've been hunted before—

MALCOLM:

by men who hid in darkness.
There is nowhere to hide.

ALLIES:

Nowhere to hide.

MALCOLM:

We do not know
which mask evil wears.

These men don't wear white hoods,
but hide on the street in suits.

ALLIES:

Who set the bomb,
destroyed your home?
Men are hunting you down.
Where will you go?

TWO WOMEN:

Where will you go?

ALLIES:

Have you heard the news?
Bricks and glass fly in Harlem.
Have you heard the word?
Your life is marked,
say the streets.

‖: First a car bomb, :‖
‖: then a fire bomb. :‖
‖: They'll get you, :‖
‖: hunt you down. :‖
‖: They'll keep coming. :‖
‖: Some say it's police. :‖
‖: Some say it's hired hands. :‖
‖: Some say FBI. :‖

‖: First a car bomb, :‖
‖: then a fire bomb. :‖
‖: They'll get you, :‖
‖: hunt you down. :‖
‖: They'll keep coming. :‖

MALCOLM:

They can call me names,
call me trouble.
They can kill Malcolm X,
but blacks will stand up
because we have rights.
We want our freedom
at any cost.

(Moving away from the others)
They do not know
El Hajj Malik El-Shabazz
is a man of peace,
a man already free.
Allah has set me free.
(Goes to make prayer)

Scene 5

The stage is in motion once again as members of the movement begin to rearrange the scene to set up the Audubon Ballroom.

The scene is a meeting of the Organization of Afro-American Unity, February 21, 1965. Chairs are set up for the meeting, the arrangement mirroring the Garvey meeting in Act I. A crowd slowly assembles—men, women, children of various backgrounds. Cops gather outside the ballroom, where they will remain. Malcolm's assassins gain entrance to the meeting, followed by reporters.

A member of the OAAU warms up the audience as Malcolm tries to free himself from people stopping him to speak as he approaches. He enters after everyone is seated and listening to the first speaker. This other speaker quickly wraps it up and sits. Malcolm goes to the podium.

MALCOLM:
   As-Salaam-Alaikum.

A scuffle stirs up in the back; those causing it are part of the assassins' group. Two men in the front row with handguns and a third behind them with a sawed-off shotgun, rise and shoot Malcolm.
   Lights out.

WOMBmanWARs

JUDITH

ALEXA

JACKSON

WOMBmanWARs was inspired by what I perceived as the "high-tech lynching" of Anita Hill after checking out the twenty-one or so odd hours of primetime woman-bashing.

My first response to the hearings was reactionary. I needed to find a way to answer back, to create the voice that we were unable to hear because Anita Hill was not getting the same kind of news coverage as Clarence Thomas. Writing the play released the frustration about what I was witness-ing and disagreeing with, but understanding that there was a lot of manip-ulation of what was not there at all.

I didn't experience the hearings as just a woman thing that had hap-pened; it was a male/woman thing. And everybody participated in it—the viewers, the media, the witnesses, Anita Hill herself, Clarence Thomas and the judiciary panel. It demonstrated the gender socialization that all of our spirits suffer from. The character in the play who carries us through many time zones and dimensions is Anima/Animus. She is the male/fe-male that exists in us. If the premise is that we all have some woman in us and we all have some man in us, then the Anita Hill-Clarence Thomas event couldn't have been about woman-bashing; it was self-bashing.

I wanted to demonstrate that there are wars that go on within women. Our wars start in our wombs. All women have wombs, even as fetuses. We are inside the womb with our own womb. *WOMBmanWARs* are wars that women have with themselves in just trying to be whole in this world.

In this country, where a lot of our sociopolitical problems are predi-cated on racism, it was fascinating to witness sexism and racism become interchangeable. It was about whatever was needed at the moment to win the fight. So we saw modern warriorism from the point of view of the pa-triarch, and we saw women trying to fight that war using patriarchal tools.

The Expansion of the Play

I had to explore the Senate committee's projection of Anita Hill's fantasiz-ing that she was harassed. On a personal level, I knew that when I rejected certain people who wanted to love me, I'd often been accused of leading them on in some way. I remember having an attempted date-rape when I was in college. Of course, in those days we didn't call it date-rape. (I don't know if we should call it "date-rape" in these days. We should call it "somebody attempted to rape me; I just happen to know the person." I don't know why we have to differentiate, because rape is rape.) I was strong and big enough, just determined enough I guess, not to have it happen, but I still let it go on a little further than I wanted it to. I kept waiting for it to end on its own. Well, years later, when I saw this person again and he was trying to remind me of who he was—I had really forgotten until a flash came in my head. I said, "Oh yeah, you're the one who tried to rape me." His nonplussed reaction was, "I don't think so. You probably fantasized it. And hey, I'm an attorney. You can't just throw things like that around." I couldn't believe I was actually hearing the exact same justifications that were used against Anita during the hearings. Since I could remember and he could not, the obvious conclusion was that I had fantasized it.

Then Desiree Washington and Mike Tyson had their media-propelled confrontation. Men and women don't speak the same language. Somewhere we lost the ability to hear each other. Even if Mike Tyson goes to his death saying that he did not rape Desiree Washington, and she goes to hers saying that he did, they were very clear that what they thought happened to them happened. Mike Tyson's whole defense was that Desiree had not clearly communicated her desire *not* to be sexually assaulted.

I realized that some people wanted us, all the women, and black women in particular, to be forgiving. They wanted us to say, "Mistakes happen. Miscommunication. She probably misled him. She helped in this, she didn't make it clear; and it's not right that he should be punished this way because she knows he only reads up to this level, and she was asking him to read a book that had a big word in it, and that word was 'no.'" He thought that was not fair because nobody explained that word to him. Whose fault is that? And who was miseducated? We all were miseducated.

She was treated the same way as Anita Hill—trashed. It didn't really matter what your background was or how far you had really gone in life to achieve or set yourself up as someone who should be regarded highly; if you cross the line of accusing a male person of a thing that would cost him money, take time away from work or have him incarcerated, then the men seem to come together over this issue, as if to say, "Whoa, we might have a war between ourselves as black and white, but we don't have a war between us when it comes to women."

Then I saw that the women were easily persuaded and willing to forfeit their civil rights in the case of Clarence Thomas. Just a week before those same people were questioning his record and asking, "What would he do for us?" As soon as he said he had been high-tech lynched, I saw that women were leaving the "Jezebels," as they were, out on the limb, re-tracting their statements and joining forces to say that these women could have handled it differently.

Two very skilled, knowledgeable black people were battling each other instead of a group of people standing up there saying, "I don't mind if you choose a black or a white judge, it has to be a judge who under-stands my rights and will protect those rights." That should have been the bigger issue over which we should have come together, but we got loud about other things. There were big issues happening at that time that should have overridden this debauchery.

Sex takes priority in this country in the news. Mia and Woody. A con-gressman found in some sex exploits. Priests who are sleeping around and getting excommunicated. We always get sidetracked from really big issues; for example, the Haitian refugees being unable to find refuge in this coun-try. In South Africa, they still don't have one person/one vote. And we don't know what happened to Winnie. Nobody mentions her anymore. We get soap opera kind of news—it keeps changing faces and colors, but it's always sex.

Herstory
The word "Jezebel" was bounced around quite a bit. To understand where we are today, I wanted to have an anthropological understanding of the original Jezebel. Who was she? How did her name come to be synony-mous with witchcraft, hussydom and whoredomness? During the matriar-chal time period, she was one of the last devotees of the goddess Astarte. Jezebel, who was the queen of Sidonia, insisted on worshipping this god-dess despite the threat of being beheaded by a new-age guru. Jezebel had to be put down because she spoke up against a new world order.

The Aesthetic
I define my aesthetic as political satire and movement theatre. I use the story format and the West African idea of telling a story in a circle, giving you bits and pieces but not in a linear order. In western culture, stories are told from A to Z. What I like about the West African storytellers is that they don't necessarily tell you where the beginning is and where the end is, but by the time they are finished, you have the whole picture.

Definitions of Heroism
The concept of the hero is based in patriarchal training. A hero is someone who is above the others. It is also based on religious concepts that said that there had to be someone to overcome a thing; and if that person could

prove that they could overcome something, then other people should follow them, adopt their religion and become controlled again.

The work (that I like) that I've seen from women, seems community-
oriented. The underlying point of view is that each individual is respected
for the thing that they can do; and that thing is exactly what this community needs. If we're going to talk about romantic ideals, the hero is the person who understands the concept of community and sacrifices themselves
and their ego for the better good of the larger whole. But I do have a problem with the concept of a person who is outstanding, who leads the way
and takes on the whole because they are trying to "be a hero."

It's not that I don't have people that I admire—and I must say that I
do admire Anita Hill in many ways. That she spoke up about what had
happened to her was not the part that I found so admirable. It was that
Anita Hill, right before our very eyes, in that time period, seemed to come
to the realization that it didn't matter if these people believed her or not;
she began to believe herself. She had been scheduled to come back after
several witnesses, but she refused. She had made her statement, and the
heroism in her was that she was a hero to her inner self. She saved the
child in herself. It's not that you have to go out and "slay the dragon," or
for her to come home and say, "Well we nipped that little confirmation in
the bud." The important thing was that at first she was trembling to say
these words that seemed to still bring back bad images, but by the end of it
we saw another kind of body language, another tilt in her head—there
was clarity. It seemed to me that she became aware that this was absurd,
that this was farcical and that she was even being misused in a way, but
still you saw her understanding that she had spoken up for her self. And
that was very heroic.

Her heroism instigated the Year of the Woman, not the women running around saying we need more congresswomen and more senators. It's
probably that a lot of people sat there and recognized that, "There's a few
things I'd like to identify in myself too. Whether I tell anybody else about
it or not, I need to discuss things with myself. I need to get in there and
say to my self, 'I am sorry I let that happen. I was unaware at that point. I
am aware now. You do not have to worry about *that* again.'"

The Responsibility of the Theatre Artist
Do I have one? No more so than a plumber has a responsibility to fix pipes
correctly, or a musician to play music. But I would like to say this: People
of my generation were raised by subliminal feminists. We have become

overt feminists because we were raised by the sacrifices of the subliminal feminists. This world is changing and it cannot be changing just because we jumped up and decided to be different. Our mothers were planting seeds in our heads.

There's a point in my play where the mother character, Sapphire, speaks about her daughter Danisha, and how she was afraid that when Danisha was born she was going to have to break her spirit. She really didn't want the responsibility of raising this girl child. I think a lot of people in my mother's generation stopped breaking the spirit.

I have a responsibility to be responsible to my mother's sacrifices. I owe it to all the women of her generation who were my teachers; and other people who went before and wrote plays, books, and painted, did sculpture, created music; and to those mothers who helped them to say you can do this thing. It's very important to teach the children, and not just teach them how to read, write and do arithmetic, but how to believe in themselves.

"What defines the darkness for you as an artist?"
Melanin.

"And the light?"
The light is the knowledge of your self. In East Indian culture, they have what they call *ghee*, a pure, milky, sweet substance that they boil. When you pour a cupful of the *ghee* into the larger pot, it becomes one with this larger pot. It becomes indiscriminate. To me, this is when that light becomes apparent, when you see your personal universe within the universality of the whole.

Dark and light exist for each other and without one there is not the other. Infinity requires that you know both the darkness and the light.

Remember: *familiar, family*, it goes on and on to *country;* I think one of the original words extends to *county, community, kinship*, to *cunt*— before cunt became a bad word; before Jezebel became a bad word. When you go back to the place where cunt meant the beginning of kinship, it's this dark tunnel you come through from a place where obviously you were not before, and you are born. You come through this tunnel into a light, so you become familiar with your whole. If you become familiar then you don't have to differentiate; you don't have to worry if one is there or not. You become familiar with the idea that you never left the light, never left the dark. *I* was always, and *it* was always, and *we* were always present.

ABOUT THE AUTHOR

Judith Alexa Jackson is a writer and performance artist whose one-woman performance plays have toured throughout the United States, Western Europe and Africa. Jackson mixes masks, dance, mime, film, video and live and recorded sound to create works that address a wide range of social, political and environmental issues from racism, homelessness and gender battles to nuclear disarmament and deforestation. She has performed her previous solo works, including *N*gg*r Cafe*, *Huhbebah's House* and *Origin of the Biscuit*, at such theatres as P.S. 122, the Kitchen and La MaMa E.T.C. in New York City, Crossroads Theatre Company in New Brunswick and the Painted Bride Art Center in Philadelphia.

Jackson has written teleplays for *The Cosby Show*, *A Different World*, *Pee Wee's Playhouse*, *Laverne and Shirley* and for an Emmy-winning PBS special, *Doing What the Crowd Does—Saying No to Peer Pressure*. Her stand-up act has been included in comedy specials for MTV and HBO, and she has appeared at cabaret and comedy venues such as B. Smith's, Green Street Upstairs, the Village Gate, the Comic Strip and the Harlem Cultural Council at Lincoln Center's Alice Tully Hall.

Her work in music-theatre has included contributing to the libretto for Julius Hemphill's *Long Tongues: A Saxophone Opera*, which Jackson directed at the Apollo Theater. She is currently working with Brazilian percussionist Nana Vasconcelos on *Pygmies in the Rain Forest*, scheduled to open in the spring of 1993 at Dance Theater Workshop, and she is collaborating with Craig Harris on a musical satire about the horrors of the Middle Passage.

In addition to serving a mime apprenticeship with Marcel Marceau, Jackson received a degree in playwriting from the University of Michigan and studied literature at the Sorbonne. She has conducted numerous workshops at U.S. and international universities and was selected in 1992 to participate in the Visiting Artists Program at Harvard University. A resident of New York City, she has received grants and fellowships from the New York State Council on the Arts, the New York Foundation for the Arts, the National Endowment for the Arts and the Rockefeller Foundation.

ABOUT THE WORK

WOMBmanWARs was commissioned by the Institute of Contemporary Art in Boston and premiered there in March, 1992. It received further production and development at La MaMa E.T.C., P.S. 122, the New York Shakespeare Festival, Ujima Theatre Company and Hallwalls in Buffalo, the North Carolina Arts Festival and Just Us Theater Company in Atlanta.

CHARACTERS

GORILLA

SAPPHIRE, mother/wife

DANNY, father/man

DANISHA, daughter/girl child

ANIMA/ANIMUS, fetus/spirit child

REVEREND

HILDA, feminist/activist

MS. INDY ANNA, beauty contestant

DESIREE WASHINGTON

MIKE TYSON

WITNESS I

REPUBLICAN SENATOR

DEMOCRATIC SENATOR

WITNESS II

SENATOR OUT-TO-LUNCH

MAMA THOMAS

REPORTER

GOOD CHRISTIAN WOMAN

ANITA ANIMA ANIMUS

AUTHOR'S NOTE

While one can imagine an ensemble production of *WOMBmanWARs*, a solo performance affords the actor the opportunity to explore her own anima/animus and to present evidence of that dichotomy by portraying both the male and female characters in the play.

Set: The rigorous speed at which the environment and characters change mandates a minimalist set design maximum, lighting and mimed props. Aligned vertically upstage center are three straight-back wooden chairs which symbolically represent the Senate Judiciary Committee. Upstage left of those chairs and diagonally facing center sits the witness chair. Positioned downstage right, with its back to the audience, is a kitchen chair.

Audio/visual: Integral to the set design are the audio/visual components. Not just there for amplification, the electronic media must pervade the performance space and evoke the mediated experience had by all who watched the confirmation proceedings. As was apparent during the hearings, microphones on stands are in abundance and are strategically placed about the stage for the convenient use by the performer. There are two television monitors, mounted on six-foot pedestals and positioned downstage right and left, and a large screen upstage center. Appropriate lenses and projectors are requisite for video and slide images to fill entire screen. One video camera on a tripod is visible upstage right. There are three scenes in the play which require the onstage presence and skills of a video camera person. She/he should be dressed in casual black street clothes and adept at artful manipulation of a video camera.

Props: one short stool; eyeglasses for Witness II, Mama Thomas and Senator; hairband for Danisha; folding fan for Good Christian Woman; pliers for Danny; Ankh for Anima/Animus and pamphlets for Hilda. All other props are mimed.

Costume: Performer wears unisex outfit with pockets for props and a belt from which a brightly colored dish towel hangs. The towel is used throughout the scenes, and its functions are as diverse as the characters.

Masks: one oversized paper maché headmask representing the "white male establishment" and one rubber headmask representing a gorilla.

SPECIAL THANKS

Bib-ba-da-boop. Boom Bang! Ya kno' wat I'm sayin'. Deep thanks from my kink-ee-yess dread. For strokin' my soul and weeding my mind, t'il a memory on paper recalled post-nappy times. Boom! Jillian Levine/ICA Theater; Boom! Meryl Vladimer and Ellen Stewart/La MaMa; Boom Buffalo! Ujima Theatre Company and Hallwalls; Boom! George C. Wolfe/ New York Shakespeare Festival and triple Boom, Boom! brilliant buddies for correction; Ricki Roer for perception; and director Paul McIsaac for perfection. Boom y'all and explosive love—to Linda, Lillian and Winston just 'cause they kinfolks.

WOMBmanWARs

[. . . *with love to Alice Virginia Welch Jackson 1930–1992*
. . . who nurtures my spirit still . . .]

Screen: If possible, project onto screen the actual video footage of the portion of the Senate Judiciary Committee hearings transcribed below. In lieu of video, project onto screen a collage of slides depicting the hearings—news stories, in media or print, of Judge Clarence Thomas, his wife, Anita Hill, President Bush and the Senate Judiciary Committee—while prerecorded voices read the transcript below. The objective here is to remind the audience through visual and audio means of the United States Senate Judiciary Committee's insensitive handling of the harassment charge brought against the Supreme Court nominee.

Audio and visual on.

HATCH: "Did you ever say to Professor Hill in words or substance, and this is embarrassing for me to say in public . . . but it has to be done. Did you ever say in words or substance something like 'There is a pubic hair in my Coke'?"

THOMAS: "No Senator."

HATCH: "Did you ever refer to your private parts in conversation with Professor Hill?"

THOMAS: "Absolutely not! Senator."

HATCH: "Did you ever brag to Professor Hill about your sexual prowess?"

THOMAS: "No Senator."

HATCH: "Did you ever use the term Long . . . Dong . . . Silver in conversation with Professor Hill?"

THOMAS: "No Senator."

HATCH: "Did you ever have lunch with Professor Hill in which you talked about sex or pressured her to go out with you?"

THOMAS: "Absolutely not. I've had no such discussions, nor have I ever pressured or asked her to go out with me, uh, beyond her work, uh, environment."

HATCH: "Did you ever tell Professor Hill that she should see pornographic films?"

THOMAS: "Absolutely not."

HATCH: "Did you ever talk about pornography with Professor Hill?"

THOMAS: "I did not discuss any pornographic material or pornographic preferences or pornographic films with Professor Hill."

HATCH: "So, you never even talked about or described pornographic material with her."

THOMAS: "Absolutely not. What I have told you is precisely what I told the FBI on September 25th, when they shocked me with the allegations made by Anita Hill."

Audio and visual out.

DREAMTIME

Gorilla sits in silhouette while video projection is on. Lights fade up gradually to full as monologue begins. Actor performs monologue with her back to the audience and gorilla mask on the back of her head, which faces the audience.

GORILLA: Was summa cum laude at Harvard. On the Dean's List at Yale. Taught law three years at Oxford. And was a Fulbright Fellow twice. My clothes are all designer. Elizabeth Arden does my nails. My face is by Borghese. My scent is politically correct. My hair was bought at Macy's. My wit is informed by the media. I avoid identifiable deviants; never socialize with liberals; and only speak Black English when it's absolutely necessary. While simultaneously cultivating a taste for arias by Mozart, I have successfully suppressed any urge to explore Hip Hop, Be Bop, or rap. I am amused by Afrocentricity, but invest enthusiastically in ethnic art. It is the least I can do for affirmative action. I subscribe to the *Wall Street Journal*, own stock in the *Washington Post*, and the *New York Times* is delivered on Saturdays to my rather large home in a treelined neighborhood that votes conservatively. What personal life I expose is created by my publicist. Granted I do not recognize myself on occasion. I do not know who I am. But surely you must see me. My mirror reflects the American dream. I am America the beautiful. Believe me. No *Gorilla* could have achieved all of this. So why do I get the impression that your perception of me has still not changed?

(Mannerisms become increasingly apelike) You sittin' there staring at me like you've just seen a walkin', talkin' ape. Some kind of an overgrown jungle bunny in a monkey suit. Do I have my head on backwards? I graduated summa cum laude. OK? So I ain't tryin' to hear dat see. Homey don't play dat. *(Gets up and begins to move downstage menacingly)* I don't want to have to go dere. What are you looking at? What does it take for you to see me. Don't let me have to go dere. Don't let me have to act like no nigger! I ain't tryin' to play dat see.

Blackout.

THE KITCHEN

SAPPHIRE *(Rushing in with bags of groceries)*: Is it on? *(Puts groceries on counter and goes into living room)* I told you not to touch it. I was only gone for a minute Danny.

LIVING ROOM
Danny straddling chair downstage right; remote control in hand.

DANNY: Hey, take it easy baby. Ain't nothing else on but Clarence. *(He clicks remote control)* Clarence. *(Click)* Clarence. *(Click, click, click)* Clarence. Bring me a beer babe.

Sapphire goes into kitchen, takes beer out of grocery bag and returns to living room.

SAPPHIRE: What did I miss?

DANNY *(Taking the beer)*: Nothing but her opening act. *(He opens can and gulps down contents)*

SAPPHIRE *(Studies the TV)*: Act? That's no act. That woman is telling the truth. I believe her.

DANNY: What...you some kind of a feminist now? Hey, I got something for your feminist. *(He takes empty can and crushes it against forehead)* What's for dinner? *(Playfully slam dunks beer can into garbage pail)*

THE KITCHEN

SAPPHIRE *(Puts away food in kitchen)*: Lamb chops. And what's wrong with being feminine?

DANNY *(Follows Sapphire into kitchen)*: I ain't got no complaints with feminines. *(He grabs her butt playfully and squeezes)* I'm talking about Feminists. La Feminista. You know what they say. *(Gets another beer from fridge)* Some of my best friends are feminist.... But I don't want my daughter to grow up and marry one. *(Laughs as he opens beer and chugs it back)*

SAPPHIRE: Where is that girl? *(Calls upstairs)* Danisha! Danisha! Mommy needs help with these groceries.

DANNY: She's not up there. I sent her outside. She was making too much noise.

SAPPHIRE *(Mildly alarmed)*: Outside? Where? I didn't see her when I drove up. *(Peers out kitchen window)*

LIVING ROOM

DANNY *(Returns to living room)*: She'll be all right. Shhh. Here come the judge. Now we'll see what's really what. *(Straddles chair, watches TV, chugs beer)*

THE KITCHEN

SAPPHIRE *(Opening door and calling out)*: Danisha...Danisha!

A YARD

DANISHA *(To playmate)*: I can see your ol' tepee from here Jerome.

I don't have to go inside if I don't want to. My mommy said I don't have to do anything I don't want to do and I don't want to so I don't have to my mommy said.

NO! Jerome, read my lips. *(She rolls her eyes with much attitude)* I. DO. NOT. WANT. TO. GO. INSIDE. YOUR. HOME-MADE. TEPEE!

Anyway your mommy didn't give you permission to use her blankets to make no tepee. Did not. Not. Not. Not Not Not NOT. *(Dances in circle and sings personal chant)* Go Danisha. Go Danisha. Go Danisha. I know you Jerome since you was a baby. Now you a boy and probably got somethin' in there that's gonna scare me.

What you say? You got cake inside. CAKE!!!? *(She licks her lips)* What kind of cake? *(She tries to look inside)* Chocolate marshmallow M&M sprinkles and peanut butter on top? Yeah! I want to see THAT! *(She begins to go in, then changes her mind)* You go inside and bring it out here so I can see it! *(She laughs and does dance/chant again)* GO DANISHA. GO DANISHA. GO DANISHA.

You crying? You not crying. You pretend crying. Why are you crying? I don't want to go inside Jerome. Stop crying. Jerome stop crying. *(Pause)* All right...if I go in, I can leave whenever I want to. Right? Ain't nothing in there gonna scare me. Right. It's just a tepee. Right...and cake. *(She steps inside warily)*

LIVING ROOM

SAPPHIRE *(Outside on porch)*: Danisha!!! Danisha!!! *(Takes one last look and goes into house)* Danny you'd better go look for her. I don't see her out back. *(Wipes hands nervously on dish towel)*

DANNY: She'll be all right honey. I told her we'd go to Toys 'R' Us later if she didn't get into any trouble. You making Stove Top or potatoes?

THE KITCHEN

SAPPHIRE *(Sits and begins peeling potatoes; shares with audience)*: Danisha is not my first child. The first I miscarried. Reaching for something too far over my head. My water broke. Heard it before I felt it. Then I dropped him. A boy. I don't think Danny ever forgave me for that.

Sapphire freezes in the action of peeling a potato. Anima/Animus emerges as a spirit from *Sapphire and stands.*

THE WOMB

ANIMA/ANIMUS *(To audience)*: That's my mother.
  (She poses as Danny crushing the beer can) That's my father. *(Poses as Sapphire wiping hands nervously on dish towel)* That's my mother. *(Poses as Danny straddling a chair)* That's my father. *(Now stands masculine)* That's my mother. *(Now stands feminine)* That's my father. *(She moves to center stage)* And I'm the child she thinks she lost.
  Why did I mess up? Everything was going just fine. I was all set. Cells were developing well. Had all my fingers and toes. All I had left to do was to file away information into my medulla oblongata. The medulla oblongata. The fate-knot. That knotty ball of muscular tissue between the left and right sides of your soul. Ties together the threads of your life. Keeps track of your history that's still to come.
  When my parents tied the knot, they bound their life threads as one and I was created as equal halves of them both. I am my mother. I am my father. I am the map carved from the roads built by their two lives. I am Anima/Animus.
  Anima you don't hear so much about these days. Can't even find it in the dictionary. It means female soul, from the roots an, "heavenly," and ma, "mother," recalling a time when all souls emanated from the Heavenly Mother. When all souls were male and female. When all souls were Anima/Animus.
  Well, that's how it was long ago. But, somewhere in the middle of Herstory, history intervened. Where once both sides were considered equal—the woman side became the sequel. Don't soundbites simplify things? I'm using soundbites because attention spans are so short in the twentieth century.

To make a long story commercial length, Anima got pushed off the page when some all-knowing know-it-all declared that souls needed redeeming. A savior came along in the body of a man and all praises be folks started believing he was a savior for men only. So the male half was redeemed and walked around all pumped up. I'm bad. I'm bad. The female half shrunk down like an out-of-date coupon. Unredeemable. Centuries went by as the world awaited the coming of a female savior. And let me tell you now. No one's coming. Save your Self.

I can still remember that stuff because I live here in dream-time where most of you only sleep. What I can't remember is why souls ever had to be redeemed in the first place. *(Crosses into kitchen and submerges into Sapphire)* I'm waiting for them to call up another child.

THE KITCHEN

SAPPHIRE: Ever since the miscarriage it's been like I've had a hard day that's lasted for a very long time. I want another child. I don't think he trusts me to have a boy. *(She puts potatoes on to boil)*

THE TEPEE

DANISHA: I only got one thing to say about your tepee Jerome. Where is the CAKE!? Why you got to always trick me? *(She suddenly dodges Jerome)*

Don't touch me Jerome. You've got mud on your hands. I promised my father I won't get ruint. *(Dodges him again)* You got mud on your hands. He don't like me when I'm all messed up. YOU'VE GOT MUD ON YOUR HANDS!

THE WOMB

ANIMA/ANIMUS *(To audience)*: I was sitting in the womb-tomb; place of birth and rebirth. Practicing my hieroglyphic alphabet when I realized I'd forgotten my melanin. That would never do. Without my melanin I looked like . . . well have you seen Michael Jackson lately? Well, you've seen my parents. Dark as Egyptian clay. My father would suspect foul play.

I'd have spent life on earth in therapy. I saw no other way. I jumped out of the womb-tomb; place of birth and re-birth. There would have been no anima/animus in my world. Only animosity.

LIVING ROOM

DANNY *(Watching TV)*: That's right. My man is right. You hear that Sapphire? Homey just accused the Senate Judiciary panel of conducting a high-tech lynching.

I hadn't thought of that. He's a smart one that Clarence. High-tech lynching. That's exactly what they're doing. My homeboy is calling it like he sees it.

SAPPHIRE *(Doing dishes)*: Your homeboy? Last week you were calling him an Uncle Tom.

DANNY: Aaahhh! Woman! You don't understand nothing.

THE TEPEE

DANISHA: N-O. No you can't look up my dress. Do you speak American? N-O. African? N-O. Spanish? French? Greece? N-O. N-O. N-O!!!

I'll use sign language if you're deaf! My fist upside your head is a sign that I mean business. Now move out my way Je-rome, I want to go home. *(She turns to leave. Jerome lifts up her skirt)* OOOOh. I'm telling.

Phone rings.

HOTEL ROOM

MS. INDY ANNA *(With phone in hand)*: Hello. Hold on. Desiree . . . it's for you.

DESIREE: What time is it? *(Puts on robe)*

MS. INDY ANNA: One o'clock in the morning.

DESIREE: Who is it?

MS. INDY ANNA: Sounds like a little boy.

DESIREE *(Taking the phone)*: Hello. . . . Yes, this is Desiree Washington. *(Covering receiver)* My God! It's Mike. My God! Tyson. What should I do?

MS. INDY ANNA *(Snatching receiver)*: Hang up.

DESIREE *(Snatching receiver back)*: Oh, girl please. Hello Mike. *(Pause)* I was in bed. Asleep. Dreaming about winning the contest tomorrow of course. *(Pause)* Just a minute, please.

   (Covers receiver) Girl, he has a LIMOUSINE! And he wants to take me out. Show me sights I have never seen before. What should I do?

MS. INDY ANNA *(Snatching phone again)*: Hang up!!

DESIREE *(Snatching phone back again)*: Girl, why don't we go?

MS. INDY ANNA: We?

DESIREE: Yes, we could start the morning off with a bang. We'll take the camera.

MS. INDY ANNA: Give me the phone Desiree. . . . We've got important things to do tomorrow. Now hang up.

They struggle back and forth with the phone.

DESIREE *(Securing the phone from Ms. Indy Anna; speaks sweetly)*: Mike, please hold one second.

Ms. Indy Anna snatches phone once more; they struggle back and forth again.

MS. INDY ANNA: Hang up.

DESIREE: No! *(Pulls phone back adamantly)* Now back off Indy Anna. I'm going.

MS. INDY ANNA *(Releases phone finally)*: Oh, it's like that girlfriend. Okay—well when I win the crown tomorrow, that's *Miss* Indy Anna to you. Good night! *(She exits)*

DESIREE *(Composes herself)*: Hello Mike. You were saying?

WEIGHT ROOM

MIKE TYSON *(Lifting weights lasciviously; speaks in high-pitched voice)*: Girl. I want you to come over.

LIVING ROOM

SAPPHIRE *(Watching TV)*: I understand this . . . that man don't mean black folks no good if he's sexually harassing young black women on the job.

DANNY: Sapphire. . . . If I've told you once I've told you a thousand times . . . don't go sticking your cute little nose in where it ain't got no business. You don't know what went on. She probably liked all that talk at first. Probably had a crush on him.

SAPPHIRE: It's in the eyes. He's got lying eyes.

DANNY: What chew talkin' 'bout?

SAPPHIRE: His eyes are all over the place. And look at the beads of perspiration rolling off his forehead. That's guilt water.

DANNY: Sometimes it's so hard to be married to you Sapphire. Come sit down right here. I want you to see it from my perspective.

Those balls of sweat pouring off of my man's head don't come from guilt. That's rage. Rage Sapphire.

A black man's RAGE! That's 400-years-of-being-treated-like-a-slave RAGE! That's I-don't-have-a-job-! RAGE. That's I-can't-feed-my-family RAGE. That's What-does-it-take-to-get-through-to-you-people-? I-went-to-Yale-dammit RAGE!!!

SAPPHIRE: Looks a lot like "I-got-caught" RAGE, to me.

DANNY: Sometimes, Sapphire, your naiveté astounds me. I guess you never heard of a woman scorned.

SAPPHIRE *(Exits abruptly into kitchen)*: That's it. I've got dishes or something to do. But I won't have *this* conversation with you.

THE KITCHEN

DANNY: Oh yes we will have *this* conversation *(Follows her)* If there's one thing I know, that's women. That woman is lying. She prob'ly bought the tape herself. Can you see a man like

Clarence Thomas in a porno shop? *(Gets another beer from fridge)* She's prob'ly mad about him marrying that white woman. You know how you sista's are. *(Opens beer and chugs)*

SAPPHIRE: Calm down honey...you're getting those beads of wet rage on your own forehead.

DANNY *(Gets another beer)*: Damn straight I'm mad. Can't let the oppressor...how'd my man put it..."high-tech lynch" us. Black folks got to learn to stick together.

SAPPHIRE *(Attending to lamb chops baking in oven)*: Correct me if I'm wrong, but ain't Anita Hill black?

A CHURCH

REVEREND *(Speaks into hand mike to congregation)*: Bow your heads tonight. Bow your heads low. Bow down with the weight we all carry when one of our neighbors is in trouble.

Look to your left and then to your right. See thy neighbor. Shake thy neighbor's hand. Love thy neighbor. And hope that thou shalt never find ye selves behaving unneighborly.

Let us get down on our knees and pray...for our neighbor who's gone astray...who is lost and can't find the way...on this, the final day...before the lowly trial...of our brother from the Nile...who's been hurting for a while...his dirty laundry all up in a pile...for the wide world to see...falsely accused by She...the dirty filthy liar...who has put herself for hire...and who will burn in hell's hot fire....Let us pray that neighbors like Jezebel be banished but for good...'cause with neighbors like Jezebel there goes the neighborhood. Let us pray. Let us pray for Iron Mike. Let us pray that he never becomes Iron Bar Mike.

THE WOMB

ANIMA/ANIMUS *(To audience)*: Ooops! Sorry about that aberration. Sometimes when I'm trying to key back into what's happening on earth I lose my place in the book of life. Can you blame me? It's always the same old story.

Like that preacher talking about Jezebel. I didn't know if he meant Anita Hill, Desiree Washington, Betty Davis or the original Jezebel herself.

I knew her you know . . . way back when she was the Queen of Sidonia. I was her maidservant. She was married to King Ahab who had seventy sons. No, not all by Jezebel . . . let's get real.

In those days the King could have babies with anybody he wanted. In fact, it was his sovereign duty to impregnate empty wombs.

There was a new age coming and with every new age comes a new religious order—and a new Big Willie in charge. This one called himself Yahweh after the lava that spit fire as it rolled down the mountainside into town. Talking 'bout "yah get outta my weh."

When Yahweh took over anybody still worshipping the Goddess Astarte was considered a radical. Jezebel was a radical. She remained a loyal devotee to the Goddess Astarte. She believed if she stopped worshipping Astarte, people would forget the Goddess. *(To audience)* By the way, have you ever heard of Astarte? *(Pause)* Jezebel was right.

King Ahab was always getting into trouble because of Jezebel. To please the townspeople he habitually banished his wife to her quarters. She'd be up there behind those stone walls lighting candles, burning sage, chanting and waving her Ankh. Y'all never heard of the Ankh either?

Way back before the cross was in style, everybody carried an Ankh. Looks like a capital "T," which represented men, with an egg-shaped circle, which represented women, on top. It meant man and woman mutually supported each other.

Yahweh came into power, and people were snatching the circles right off the tops of their Ankhs and converting on the spot. Anybody caught with the circle still on top would have their heads cut off, stuck on poles and paraded through town. Blood dripping and everything.

This sounds like a crass way to embarrass families and put their business in the streets, but we didn't have Barbara Walters or *60 Minutes* in those days.

Jezebel forgave them, for they knew not what they did, and went right on burning, chanting and waving. She became a closet Ankh carrier. But the townspeople knew she still had that circle on top . . . 'cause she always looked so happy—transcendent—while they marched around repenting their sins. Her name was accompanied by the words witch, whore, vixen, hellcat, she-devil, shrew, virago, and bitch so often that people took to just saying Jezebel for short 'cause they knew the rest would be implied.

Alas, one day the townspeople rushed the castle and caught Jezebel worshipping Astarte and waving her Ankh like there was no tomorrow. And for her there wasn't. They beheaded her on the spot. Her husband and all his seventy sons too.

Jezebel's teenage daughter Athaliah was the only one spared and allowed to rule for seven years. Then they found her hidden Ankh.

She was killed too and that's the last I ever heard of Goddess worship in those parts . . . or the Ankh.

THE CAPITOL

Hilda is about seventy and walks with a pronounced limp. She passes pamphlets throughout audience.

HILDA: Please take one . . . Miss . . . Miss please take one. We, the women of WOMB, W-O-M-B. Women to Overcome Men's Beliefs, are absolutely appalled at the insensitivity of the all-male Senate Judiciary Committee.

We of WOMB have joined forces with VITAL . . . V-I-T-A-L. Voices Invoking Total Attainment of Liberty, to create this pamphlet VITALWOMBMEN.

Please, take one . . . this pamphlet can save your lives. L-I-V-E-S. Living In A Vortex Can Envelop Self.

Don't let my age or this limp fool ya. Hilda ain't just out here passing the time of day. I've been marching since before you were born. Shoot, I've been an advocate for the rights of women since before I was born. That's right. Don't get me started. My mother was a suffragette. Pregnant with me when she marched for the woman's right to vote back in the early 1900s. So you see Hilda knows what she's talking about. It's in my blood.

Please Miss...take one. We must present a consolidated FRONT. F-R-O-N-T. Feminists Reeling Over Negligent Treatment.

It's your right to be informed. Miss take one. Don't continue to be without laws that protect your rights to the laws that already protect your rights to the laws that protect your rights. Until such time that these laws are recognized be LAWLESS. L-A-W-L-E-S-S. Let All Women Live Equally in a Shared Society.

(She notices a pack of jogging politicians and runs with them) Mr. President!...Please take one and pass it on to all of your "Women of the Year" nominees. Where is Hillary? Hillary? What are you doing in the back. Move up. Take the lead... and remember H-I-L-L-A-R-Y. Homemakers Invoking Libertine Limitations Are...Are...Really Yucky.

Please women...don't wait for Prince Charming to open your eyes. AWAKE NOW. A-W-A-K-E. ARISE WOMEN AND KICK ET.

The Camera Person (CP) enters with a camera mounted on a tripod. The television monitors, stage right and left, give a clear view of whatever the camera sees. The CP keeps the camera focused on the performer who, while seated in the witness chair stage left, will perform all speaking characters in the scene. At the discretion of the CP, closeup shots of Witness I's hands, teeth and eyes are alternately imposed on the established medium-close shot which encompasses the character, the microphone and the chair. All other characters portrayed in this scene will have closeups of their faces only.

TV monitors on.

THE SENATE
After standing in front of witness chair with raised hand as if being sworn in, Witness I sits and speaks into the microphone.

WITNESS 1: Is this on? *(She taps on mike)*

Slide of Senate Judiciary Committee fills the screen.

Yes, I knew Anita Hill. The uppity wench.

Slide of Anita Hill.

She was arrogant, opinionated, hard-nosed, ambitious, self-assured . . .

Slide of Haitian voodoun priestess.

. . . and if I may offer an uncorroborated opinion . . . she was a woman scorned.

Slide of The Exorcist *book cover.*

REPUBLICAN SENATOR *(Into mike)*: Yes. Could you elaborate on that unsubstantiated opinion?

WITNESS 1: Be happy to. I didn't know Anita Hill well, mind you. Through simple observation I concluded she had a jones for the man.

Slide of Thomas.

REPUBLICAN SENATOR: Jones?

WITNESS 1: Exactly. A deep need to be more than just professional with that big black strappin' buck of a mandingo . . . *(She fans herself)*

Slide of Long Dong Silver videocassette box.

DEMOCRATIC SENATOR *(Putting on eyeglasses and then removing them repeatedly as he speaks into mike)*: There is nothing in Miss Hill's statement that impressed me that way.

Slide of Mrs. Thomas on cover of People *magazine.*

WITNESS I: Well that's you. You didn't know her like I did.

DEMOCRATIC SENATOR *(Glasses on again; off again)*: But you just stated that you did not know her well.

Slide of Witness I in dominatrix costume.

WITNESS I: Yeah... well, I know a woman in love and I know a woman scorned! Any more questions Democrats?

DEMOCRATIC SENATOR *(Removing glasses and waving them emphatically)*: But to allow you to continue this way is unconscionable!

Slide of Republican Senators Spector, Simpson and Hatch.

WITNESS I: I have a right to my unconscious opinions. Don't I Republicans?

REPUBLICAN SENATOR: Please continue.

WITNESS I: She wanted and believed she should have direct access to my man... uh... Mr. Thomas. I was his political eyes and ears. I shared his confidences and I knew a great deal about his personal life as well. But, we never socialized, mind you.

Slide of Thomas with President Bush.

What I found most suspicious was the manner in which she spoke of the chairman. Always in highly admirable terms. Highly admirable. It seemed unnatural. I swear she wanted to be his love slave.

Slide of Capitol building.

Witness II stands with hand raised to be sworn in; she wears glasses and sits primly on edge of seat and speaks into microphone.

WITNESS II: Yes. I knew Anita Hill. No. I've never known Anita to make false allegations against anyone. We have been out-of-touch for some time, however. No fault of mine. I did write her once. *(Noticeable chill in her voice)* She never responded. Never, ever wrote back. Every day I would go to the mailbox. Nothing. Empty. Nada. Zippo. *(Agitated pause)* I can't say what she might be capable of doing. I don't EVEN know Miss Thing.

TV monitors off. CP leaves camera upstage and exits.
   Video projection of Anita Hill testifying before Judiciary Committee plays in slow motion and without sound as Senator Out-to-Lunch speaks.

SENATOR OUT-TO-LUNCH *(Wears large mask representing "white male establishment")*: Please turn with me, Professor, to page 94 in the transcript of your testimony.
   About halfway down the page, you will see the item in question. This morning I asked you if you intended to have lunch today. You answered, and I quote, "No, I won't be having lunch today."
   Do you see that on your copy Professor? "No, I won't be having lunch today"? Is that a fair reading of your statement?
   I'd like now to come to a consensus, an agreement, if you will, on the definition of lunch.
   If there are no objections, I'd like to submit as evidence the definition of lunch as stated in Webster's Unabridged Dictionary. And I quote, "a light repast taken between breakfast and dinner; usually around noon." Would you agree, Professor, that that is a fair representation of the word "lunch"?
   I want you to think before you answer this next question Professor. Is it fair to surmise that the sandwich I saw you eating at noon today was your lunch? Did you not state on page 94 of the transcript that you would not be having lunch. But, yet, as soon as our collective backs were turned you had lunch. LIAR. LIAR. PANTS. ON. FIRE. How can you expect us to believe anything you have to say about the honorable judge is beyond me. You . . . you . . . you Lunch EATER.

Video projection out.

THE WOMB

ANIMA/ANIMUS: Did I ever tell you the story of how I came not to be? Well, I'm sitting inside the womb/tomb, daydreaming about the Ituri Forest... *(She snaps her fingers)*

THE FOREST
The music of any indigenous forest people plays softly in background.

ANIMA/ANIMUS: My memory of the Ituri Forest is particularly strong. We played amid the trees as they made breath for us. The tree that gave me my name, whispered stories of the wind, protected me with bough and limb, healed me with her leaves and sap and fed me with her flowers.

   In early-morning dew she painted me with the secrets of the world until I was a dark groundnut stew. And then I went and forgot my melanin. Crushed my mother's heart broke my father's spirit. Oh, if they could only know the effort I made to return. I bowed to mother earth and crawled through the cave of harmony to peek the light that blinds one so that she might see...

She snaps her fingers again. Music out.

THE WOMB

ANIMA/ANIMUS: What I'm trying to say is... I went back to the Tree of Life, begged my bag of brown gold and dived back into the birth capsule. Moved my father to sing and my mother to dance with his song. Then I prepared for takeoff. All went fine... I was replanted in no time.

   Came out nine months later... a glorious girl. Danisha. I thought they'd be pleased. Instead, they leave half of me in dreamtime 'cause they can't see me whole.

TEPEE

DANISHA: Get outta my way Jerome. I'm going home now. *(She dashes out of tepee and runs gleefully around stage)* Jerome can't catch me. Jerome can't catch me. Go Danisha. Go Danisha. Go-ooooo! *(She exits offstage)*

THE PORCH

SAPPHIRE *(From offstage)*: Danisha! Danisha! *(Enters carrying short stool)* Danisha! *(She places stool downstage center and speaks to one female audience member as if they were old friends)* Hey girl. Hot enough for you? *(She sits on stool)*

    You see the kids around? Well, when you've got girls...you have to worry. So much going on nowadays.

    People snatching kids off the street. Bodies mangled in ditches....Girl...can't get a minute's peace....You must count your blessings every day that you've got a boy child. It's a man's world. And TV trying to make us believe things have changed. Especially the soaps.

    I don't care what those soap operas say...women don't want girl children no more than men do. You know what soap operas are for...to sell soap. Sponsors have to be into whatever is in at the moment.

    In the seventies right after Roe versus Wade, everybody and her momma's sista on soaps were having abortions. Nowadays, with the pressure from the pro-lifers...you know who I'm talking about. The ones who would kill *you* before they'd let you kill a fetus. Thanks to those fools you'd be hard-pressed to find one storyline that doesn't have a pregnant actress in it.

    I've been keeping count too. Did you know for every girl born on the soaps, there are four boys? Matter of fact, Erica Kane, *All My Children?* was the only character who had a girl child in the 1980s. And then the child went nuts. Started burning fires and speaking in tongues. Had to ship her off to live with her father...who was now on another soap with his new wife...and expecting a boy child.

I could understand it if we were still living in the ice ages. Back when boys were expected to pick up the ice...or keep the family name going.

But with automation, seems like nobody's lifting anything heavy...and with the hyphenated name thing...either side could keep the family line.

So, I don't care what the soap operas say....Women don't want girl children no more than men do.

I know it sounds like I don't love Danisha. Probably sounds like I don't love myself. I do love Danisha...I do love my child. When Danisha was born...

THE GARAGE

DANNY *(With pliers, he repairs stool; to male audience member)*: ...was born I was the happiest man on earth. She curled up around my thumb and I knew right then nothing would ever be the same again. I became a man that day. Before that, I thought being a man meant getting some.

JAIL CELL

MIKE TYSON: She should have knowed what I was after when I invited her up to my room. Everyone knows I'm a hound dog looking for someplace to bury my bone.

THE GARAGE

DANNY: But one look at my baby girl changed all that. I could cup her whole seven pounds in my hands like that. It was my job to protect her.

Man, I'd stand there, holding her, thinking about my first car. A Ford Mustang. I kept that baby pretty. Bought her everything she needed. Didn't let nobody touch her. Didn't have a scratch on her for six whole months. Then somebody banged her up and I just about had a nervous breakdown. My first car, man.

I wasn't gonna let nobody hurt Danisha like that. Nobody's gonna mess with her paint job.

Don't laugh man. I know I ain't no poet. Sometimes I wish I was so I could say what I'm trying to say.

(He sits on stool and leans toward audience member) Mind if I tell you something kinda personal? And don't let me catch you telling nobody what I'm about to say. *(Pause)* Sometimes I see you out there playing catch with Jerome and I get jealous man. *(Pause)* Jealous. *(Pause)* Seems like a man's not fully round 'til he's had a son.

I'm going to tell you something I'd never admit to Sapphire. I wanted a boy. Still do sometimes. *(Pause)*

Danisha tries hard though, bless her little tomboy heart. You know she's named after me. Danisha. Little Danny. Climbing trees. Playing ball. Jumping fences. But she'll grow out of all that. Be a lady. I'll see to it. *(He carries stool offstage left)*

A CHURCH

REVEREND *(Speaks into hand-mike)*: I'm not saying we should cast aspersions on the hussy. Mike Tyson's accuser deserves the same consideration as David Duke in the eyes of the Lord.

All I'm saying is every time a black man tries to get ahead he is brought down by a black woman. Black man takes two steps forward...who pulls him three steps back? Black woman. Black man reaches for a star. Who snatches his hand down? Black woman. Black man have a dream. Who wakes him up? Black woman! You know it's true. I got proof.

Adam Clayton Powell. Congressman from Harlem, USA until who brought him down? Black woman. Marion Barry. Mayor of Washington, D.C. until who told on him? Black woman. Clarence Thomas a United States Supreme Court Justice by the skin of his teeth. All brought down by who? A BLACK WOMAN.

And now look who she's after. Our young brother Mike Tyson. World-champion boxer. Warrior in the ring. Hard as a rock butt-kicker and millionaire to boot. *(He wipes his brow)*

Black women have got to stop stomping on the black man's dreams. Stop holding the black man down. Stop putting the black man on the back burner. What a black man needs is somebody to help him stand up. Somebody who will help him shake that monkey off his back. Get off me monkey. Offa my back. There's a war going on out there . . . and black men have got the heaviest casualties.

We not saying, the black man is perfect. You got problems? Don't run to the enemy. Don't call 911. Keep it in the family. Come to the church . . . that's what you do. That's where we can begin to sort things out. Pray for him black woman but don't bring the black man down. Raise him up. Raise him up.

PIN POINT, GA
Mama Thomas uses a chair as walker and moves downstage center.

MAMA THOMAS: I raised my son the best I could. Many people ask me why I was not at the hearings. I neva was much of a traveler. *(Sits in chair)*

Ya'll know I'm from Pin Point, Georgia. You eva seen the point of a pin? Well, we just a bit bigga than that. Thanks to my son it's on the map now though.

(Puts on glasses) My son left here over twenty years ago. Even before he went, there was miles between us. I don't know much about the world he live in. Feel foreign to me even if it is still called America. I'm glad his dreams are coming . . . happy for his success.

For the life of me, neva did I think he'd be no Supreme Court Justice. Not sure I even knew what one was before now. Down this way, any talk of justice was white folks' business. *(She laughs until she coughs)* We like to say that down here. Gets the whites all riled up.

All my life I was busy working with my hands. That's how they come to look this way. Hard. Knuckles knotted. I swear I could smooth out rough-cut wood by just running my palms over it a few times. *(She laughs)* These hands have done work I don't think hands was eva intended to do.

And they's done some praying of course. I prayed for my son. I prayed for someone to help guide his mind. Could see he was a smart boy . . . always had his nose in a book.

I neva thought I was no smart woman. Leastwise, nobody ever said I was. But, I kinda like to think my genes is in 'im somewhere.

He had a good mind my son. The nuns soon come and took care of his mind. *(Puts glasses away)*

I'm glad he been able to live the American dream . . . sure 'nuf family blood been spilt 'long the way . . . glad to see some one of us reaping what the rest of us done sowed. What the rest of us done sowed.

The actor suddenly falls with chair to the floor and is immediately transformed into Danisha.

A YARD

DANISHA *(In a heap on the ground)*: Ooooh, Jerome! Look what you made me did. *(She stands and examines herself)* Huh? Huh? My dress is tornt! I'm ruint. Where you think you going Jerome? You better run fast 'cause when I catch you . . . *(She lifts chair over her head in threatening manner)*

NEWS ROOM
CP enters and sets up camera and tripod downstage right.

Slides of Tom Brokaw, Peter Jennings, Dan Rather and other national and local news personalities are projected as Reporter and CP set up.

REPORTER *(Addresses CP as she positions chair for broadcast)*: How much time do we have?
CAMERA PERSON: Thirty seconds before we air. Here's your script. *(Hands her the script and positions camera facing chair for broadcast)* You need makeup.

Monitors on. The TV monitors project a medium-close frontal im-age of Reporter.

REPORTER *(Applies makeup)*: I need a new hair weave.

CAMERA PERSON: Five. Four. Three. Two.

Slides of print-media headlines about Hill and Thomas published during the 1991 hearing begin as news is reported.

REPORTER *(Speaks into mike)*: October 12th, 1991: THOMAS'S ACCUSER TELLS OF OBSCENE TALK AND LAS-CIVIOUS ADVANCES!

other news: former assistant secretary of state admits *(She yawns)* guilt in iran/contra scam.

JUDGE PREFERS DEATH BY ASSASSIN'S BULLET OVER LYNCHING!!

other news: all charges dropped against oliver north. *(Looks bored)*

TALK OF BIG BREASTS AND GIANT MEMBERS!!!

other news: slave practices discovered in oil-rich kuwait.

LONG DONG DOGGETT EXPECTED TO MAKE APPEARANCE AT HEARINGS!!!!

other news: haitian president ousted. haitian boat people re-fused refuge in the states.

PUBIC HAIRS FOUND IN COKE!!!!!

ex-head honcho of kkk gains in the polls.

ANITA IS LYING!!!!!!!

l.a.p.d. caught on video beating unarmed black man. *(Re-porter appeals to TV audience)* Can't we all just get along?

THOMAS WILL NOT DIGNIFY!

And that's the way it was October 12th, 1991. Now stay tuned for our "MAN ON THE STREET" interviews right af-ter these words from our sponsors. *(She smiles professionally into camera)*

CAMERA PERSON: Cut! *(Focuses camera on audience)*

Audience members can now be seen projected onto screen and TV monitors.

REPORTER *(Stands near monitor stage left and speaks into mike)*: Although street reactions to the hearings were mixed, we've selected to air only the views which reflect those like our own.

Closeup young white man.

"Clarence Thomas didn't do anything wrong that any American male hasn't done." Don Whitiker, machinist, middle America.

Closeup young white woman.

"She's making a mountain out of a moehill. Moe Hill...get it?" Priscellia Whitehead, owns Laundromat, middle America.

Closeup any black woman.

"I hadn't been a Thomas supporter until now. She's making it up. She wants to do a movie or something." Rhonda Jenkins, secretary. Northeast.

Closeup older white woman.

"A lotta people don't like that he got a white wife you know? My daughter married a black man." Effy Lamb, retired waitress, Way Down South.

Closeup older white man.

"I feel certain she did not fabricate all this...but that still should not disqualify the Judge. It's not like he's been raping women or beating children." Bob Dunhill, trucker, Northwest.

Closeup young black man.

"As a black man this has been painful for me to watch. I feel for them both. But especially Thomas, because I was accused of this once myself." John Franklin, a legal assistant from Harlem.

CP turns camera away from audience and toward Reporter.

Our last interviewee wanted to remain anonymous. *(Speaks into camera and holds blue dot in front of face)* "There's a high level of anger among black men, be they low-income or professional, that black women will betray them; that black women are given preference over them to use them. Black men feel that white men are using this black woman to get another black man." *(Reporter removes blue dot; speaks into camera)* Dr. Alvin Poussaint, psychiatrist and consultant for *The Cosby Show.* CUT!

Monitors off.

CP returns camera and tripod upstage and exits.

THE LIVING ROOM

SAPPHIRE *(Brings in dinner tray)*: Let's eat dinner in front of the TV tonight. *(Sits next to Danny)*

DANNY: Looks good baby. You know I love your cooking. *(Kisses her absently; then really sees his wife and kisses her again)* I love you Sapphire.

SAPPHIRE: Let's say grace first. To the children, the ancestors and the deities. Bless this food. *(She takes a bite of potatoes)* Oh, my goodness. Where is Danisha?

DANNY *(Mouth full of lamb, he looks at watch)*: That's right. She should have been home by now. Somebody better go get her. *(He looks in direction of Sapphire)*

SAPPHIRE *(With eyes on TV, she eats resolutely)*: Danny! You've been sitting in front of this TV all day. You need a break.

DANNY: Baby, I've got to watch this thing. This is history in the making. A black man is facing political assassination. Where are we? Third World?

SAPPHIRE: I'd like to catch a few minutes of the hearings. I'm dead tired. I've done the shopping, the cooking, the cleaning and do I have to remind you that I was the one who went to work today?

DANNY *(Stands up, annoyed)*: Wait a minute. Wait a damn minute. You going to throw that in my face? You got a job and I don't?

SAPPHIRE: I don't want to fight Danny.

DANNY: I asked to be laid off? I don't want to work?

SAPPHIRE: I'm sorry I mentioned it. Would you just go get your daughter please?

DANNY: Oh...you got a job, so you the boss now huh? You in charge. *(He paces)* This the kind of thing make a man lose his appetite. *(He takes another bite of lamb chop and speaks with his mouth full)* I want to understand. I'm a man who needs to understand. What is it? You on PMS? Is that it?

SAPPHIRE *(Cutting both meat and her eyes ominously)*: Yeah, that's it. P. M. S.

DANNY *(Away toward door)*: All right. I'll go get her. *(Exits out kitchen door)*

A YARD
Danisha is whipping Jerome's butt.

DANISHA: I told you not to play with me. I told you to stop. Why you didn't stop? If I'm going to get in trouble, then let it be some trouble worth getting into.

Danny enters. He is shocked at the sight of his daughter fighting.

DANNY: DANISHA!

DANISHA *(Surprised to see her father; straightens up)*: Daddy? *(Jerome runs away)* Where you going? That was Jerome. Daddy he tore my dress. I was just peeping in his TEPEE but I didn't want to look in but Jerome he started crying so I went in to eat some cake and he pushed me DOWNOWNOWN. *(She begins to cry)*

Danny grabs Danisha's hand and pulls her roughly toward home.

SAPPHIRE *(As Danny and Danisha enter)*: What's wrong Danisha? What happened Danny?

DANISHA *(Standing between parents crying)*: Auuuuuuwwww. *(Pauses for breath)* AWRRRRUUUWWW.

DANNY: No need to do all that crying. You commit the crime, you do the time.

SAPPHIRE: What crime? What happened to your dress?

DANNY: You can see what happened to it. It's tornt up.

DANISHA: Mommy, Daddy, listen to me.

DANNY: That's not no dress. That's money she tore up. Might as well have given her my wallet full of money and said tear this up when you go outside. Look at her. You getting a spanking today.

DANISHA: AWWWWRRRRAAIIWWGGYH!! But, Jerome, *(Gasps for the next word)* He ... AWWWWWRRRAAGGHH ... he pushed me dowwwwnnnnn.

SAPPHIRE *(Putting arms around Danisha's shoulders)*: What did Jerome do baby?

DANNY *(Pulling Danisha toward him)*: Don't baby her Sapphire. She was out there fighting some boy and now she going to suffer the consequences.

DANISHA *(Talking fast)*: I didn't want to go into his tepee, but he said he had cake and I could leave when I wanted. But he tried to look up my dress I said no and he pushed me down my dress got ripped and I beat him up uppppp uuppp.

SAPPHIRE: I think she was defending herself Danny.

DANNY: That's what I'm here for.

SAPPHIRE: Jerome was bothering her.

DANNY: That's what boys do.

DANISHA *(With fear)*: AWWWWRRRGGHHUUGGY!

SAPPHIRE *(Cries sympathetically)*: AWWRRGGYYUUHGGYWWR!

DANNY *(Cries argumentatively)*: AWWWRRGGYYUHHEENNYY!

> *The actor changes physical and emotional attitude to fit each of the three characters in rapid succession as each does successive rounds of expressive crying until dizzying climax is reached.*
> *Danny is first to break out of crying circle.*

DANNY: No. Enough talk. Time for action. Now get on up to your room Danisha. *(He adjusts his belt threateningly)* I'll be up in awhile. Might as well throw that dress away.

As she exits, Danisha casts a doleful eye at Sapphire.

SAPPHIRE: I can fix the dress Danny.

DANNY *(Agitated)*: You should have seen her Sapphire. Hands all wild. Legs kicking. Like she was fighting for her life. It was ugly. Ugly. I hate to see little girls fight.

SAPPHIRE: Seems like the boy was in the wrong some.

DANNY: That's his parents' problem. The rule here is no fighting.

SAPPHIRE: But she was fighting back, honey.

DANNY: NO FIGHTING AT ALL!!!

A CHURCH

GOOD CHRISTIAN WOMAN *(Dancing and fanning herself as if the spirit got her)*: Teach Preacher. Teach. Indeed she did know. Some kind of Beauty Queen. Had no bizness being there that time of night. She knew what was what. Paper says there weren't nary a sign of struggle. Teach Preacher. No bruises of any kind. She knew what she was doing. Teach Preacher. Indeed she knew. Never did put up a fight. And now she cry raped. Beauty Queen my good Christian foot. *(Stomps good foot for emphasis)*

DANISHA'S ROOM

SAPPHIRE *(Peeping into Danisha's room)*: Danisha? Are you awake. *(She enters and sits on edge of bed)* I guess it's just as well you are asleep. I don't think I came in here to talk to you as much as myself. Today is the last day.

Couldn't sleep. I was up watching *Sophie's Choice*. Didn't pay too much attention 'til one of the Nazis asked Sophie to choose which one of her children should live. The boy or the girl.

I saw Sophie standing there, holding both of her children close . . . trying to choose who would be cremated. How could she choose? How could any mother choose? I saw her mind working. He might be a warrior. He might change the world. It was a man's world to change. I knew her choice before she ever opened her mouth. I would have made the same choice. Death for the girl.

And that's when it hit me Danisha. I have never chosen you. I have never chosen life for you.

Today is the last day. When you were born, and they told me you were a girl, I was so unhappy I actually cried.

My heart knew it would be my job to break you. To break your spirit before you were grown and some stranger came along and did it. I had to do to you what my mother did to me and her mother to her. To protect you from your dreams.

But no more, my darling precious daughter. I don't know how. I don't even know why. I only know today is the last day. The last day. The last day I stand back and watch your spirit cry. *(She tucks covers around Danisha)* I choose you. I choose you. *(She hugs Danisha and rocks with her gently)*

Fade to black.

Videotaped portions of the hearings which best reflect the excerpted material below, edited together and projected onto screen, would be ideal. The objective is to expose, via audio and visual means, the manipulative interpretation of the hearings by the media. When possible, use the actual voices of Anita Hill and Clarence Thomas. The Reporter's statements are prerecorded and played through house speakers.

Audio and visual on.

THOMAS: "I never asked to be nominated. It was an honor. Little did I know the price; but it is too high."

REPORTER: But the testimony from Thomas's principal accuser, Anita Hill, was also riveting.

HILL: "After a brief discussion of work, he would turn the conversation to a discussion of sexual matters. His conversations were very vivid. He spoke about acts that he had seen in pornographic films involving such matters as women having sex with animals and films showing group sex or rape scenes. He talked about pornographic materials depicting individuals with large penises or large breasts, involved in various sex acts. On several occasions, Thomas told me graphically of his own sexual prowess."

REPORTER: Her description became even more explicit.

HILL: "One of the oddest episodes I remember was an occasion in which Thomas was drinking a Coke in his office. He got up from the table at which we were working, went over to the desk to get the Coke, looked at the can and asked, 'Who has put pubic hair on my Coke?'

"On other occasions he referred to the size of his own penis as being larger than normal and he also spoke of pleasures he had given to women with *(Pause)* oral sex."

REPORTER: In the afternoon Senator Arlen Spector *gently* began to try to discredit the testimony of Anita Hill.

SPECTOR: "Professor Hill, do you know a man by the name of John Doggett?"

HILL: "Pardon me?"

SPECTOR: "A man by the name of John Doggett?"

HILL: "John Doggett?"

SPECTOR: "John Doggett the Third?"

HILL: "Yes. I . . . I . . . have met him."

SPECTOR: "Is Mr. Doggett accurate when he quotes you as saying, quote, 'I'm very disappointed in you. You shouldn't lead women on, then let them down,' close quote."

HILL: "No . . . he is not."

REPORTER: Doggett is expected to testify. Several hours after Hill's departure, Thomas returned with a slashing attack on the committee.

THOMAS: "This is a circus. A national disgrace. And from my standpoint as a black American, as far as I'm concerned, it's a high-tech lynching for uppity blacks who in any way deign to think for themselves."

REPORTER: But, when all is said and done, the chances of his confirmation as a Supreme Court Justice hinge on who is believed *(Reverberation)* believed . . . believed. Thomas or his *Accuser.*

Audio and visual out. CP enters and takes position behind camera.

TV monitors on.

The actor enters, now fully costumed as Anita Hill. With her back to the audience, she stands in front of the witness chair, which has been positioned to face the screen center stage. As she raises her hand to be sworn in, CP captures her image on camera, and that image is projected onto both monitors and the screen. She sits in the chair, back to the audience, and speaks into the microphone.

INSIDE MANLAND

ANITA ANIMA/ANIMUS: It was shortly after my swearing-in that I began to hear voices inside me prompting me to "Drop them. Drop them Anita and speak your name before we all perish with you into the marshy grave of Mammie's candied yams, Lucy's confiscated bones, Fannie Lou's sick and tired, and Sojourner's truth. Drop them Anita," cried these voices from as far away as wombs in the female fetus. But an obtuse thud from the outside penetrated the ocean of comfort I felt in their chorus. It was urgent to return my consciousness to manland. The natives there seemed agitated. They pointed red-taped fingers at me and chanted what at first seemed a toe-tapping mantra:
  "Blackwitchmustdie.
  Blackwitchmustdie.
  Blackwitchmustdie.
  Black witch must die.
  Black. Witch. Must. Die."
Who was this black witch that made fires burn in the back of their throats? Then I saw the totem pole. There at the bottom sat me. At the bottom with the others. Only two up from Sapphire and one up from Welfare Queen. Me. At the bottom with the others. Straining against the weight of their disbelief. Backs bent. Holding the natives of manland up. "Drop them now Anita," sang the ocean within me. "And speak your name."
  (Performer speaks in the voice of Astarte) ASTARTE!
  "Speak your name."
  (In voice of Jezebel) JEZEBEL!
  "Speak your name."

(In voice of Desiree) DESIREE!

"Speak your name."

(In voice of Sapphire) SAPPHIRE!

"Speak your name."

(In voice of Danny) DANNY!

"Speak your name."

(In voice of Danisha) DANISHA!

SPEAK YOUR NAME. ANITA ANIMA/ANIMUS!

(Turns and speaks directly into camera) My name is Anita F. Hill. I believe my Self. I *believe* me. *(Lights fade as she chants in Danisha's voice)* Go Anita. Go Anita. Go Anita.

Fade to black.

THE

DRAMATIC

CIRCLE

ADRIENNE

KENNEDY

My idea of heroism is definitely taken from the Greek plays that I read in the mid-1950s when I was about twenty-two, twenty-three. *Antigone. Electra.* Of course, I also was very taken with Tennesee Williams, because he was so popular then. Laura. I studied those three characters very closely to see what made a dramatic heroine.

For me, a heroic woman is trying to create a mode in life that will sustain her. Heroism is trying to decipher life through work. My characters, starting with Sarah [*Funnyhouse of a Negro*], are doing this through writing; or, they want to be writers. they are also trying to explore in this work the history of race, which for me is the predominant question of my existence.

The women in my family have been heroic in the same way: They sustained themselves through work. My grandmother and my great-aunt were servants. My mother was a teacher. My aunt was a teacher. And they excelled at their work. I came to feel, from watching them, that you can be heroic by doing hard work. That's what I try to give my characters, starting with Sarah—Clara, Suzanne Alexander, all of them. They work very hard. This gives them the fortitude and the energy to face life.

Artistic Challenges and Discoveries

I lived in London for almost three years and I actually went through those experiences. Every time I go to London, I go back and look at that house. It's a house on Old Brompton Road. My son and I lived in that house once for three weeks while we were waiting for my husband to come from Africa.

The hardest thing was to decide when to set it. What year am I going to place these things in? Very often, I'm all at sea about that: what part to make your imagination, what to take from reality, and how to put those two things together.

And amazingly—it sounds so simple—but amazingly I ended up setting it in the time period that it actually happened. I learned that if I can get a story or a play or parts of it in the right year, something unlocks in my imagination that gives it a greater power.

I learned a lot from writing *The Ohio State Murders* because that was the very first time I put something in the exact time that it had happened, and then added my imagination to the story and the subtext. So I did that in *The Dramatic Circle*. That was the exact year that I was there. Three weeks in the winter. And I was waiting. All the other parts are my imagination.

I've discovered over the years that very often I'm trying to make up things when real things are far more powerful; they're begging to be used. The obvious is the answer very often.

The Darkness and the Light

I never thought about it in this way, but it's the same two themes [that inform my idea of heroism]. There's no doubt that I see life as tragic. I can talk about sunny days, but I definitely see life as trying to constantly wrestle with this tragedy and trying to not let it overcome you. I do feel oppressed by white American society. I'm very easily overwhelmed by numbers, or the fact that there are, say, more American whites than there are African Americans. A lot of my energy comes out of that feeling of oppression, and from trying to break through being overdefined by another group of people.

I just feel intensely—and it's really powerful—it's two-fold: White society defines blacks in terms of cliches (I always felt that I'm being defined in terms of a cliche by white society); and secondly, I always felt, when I was growing up even, I was *smothered* by my parents and their friends—their expectations of me were smothering my individuality. So my wanting to be a writer is very much tied to my struggle for my own individuality. And that's why I don't belong to any groups; I don't belong to any clubs. I was worried that you were going to use Audre Lorde's vision to define me as a writer because I've never been in an anthology that had a quote from another writer. That's how intense it is. I don't belong to anything. And I'm very leery of any kind of political affiliation. So my wanting to be a writer is very much parallel to the struggle for individuality.

In relation to the creative process, there are certain questions, and I don't really know what they are, but ever since I was a kid, these questions [have been] nagging at me all the time. These questions are very much in the dark, and I don't try to articulate them. Through reading, thinking and looking at other people's art, whether it's movies or paintings, and sometimes teaching, I try to very specifically write down little paragraphs about these questions. And that's very much still in the dark. I try to let these little paragraphs grow as much as they can on their own without trying to force them. And then I try to let the paragraphs on these questions grow into some illumination that surprises me. That's how I crystallize the things that are in the dark.

My work and my family are the light. I've learned over the years that there are four women who fascinated me—again, as a very young person—my mother, my aunt, my grandmother and my great-aunt. I was always studying them, how they spoke. I think, in many ways, I'm always trying to recreate those women as a part of my main characters. I'm always trying to recreate a synthesis of those women to make a statement, and of course to add myself.

I was taught, and I believe in it fiercely, to really value life. There are many things that I love. I love literature, I love flowers, I love my children. And so those things that I love somehow are spreading the light. They keep me in a light, I feel.

I also have a lot of desire to be recognized. Even as a kid in school, I wanted recognition. I felt that I had a message—not necessarily like a minister or a preacher—but I had a message for the world. I always was writing stories.

I think I'm exactly like my parents—both my parents—in that my mother was a very dedicated teacher and my father was a social worker. I think I'm just imitating them.

When I'm writing, if I'm really tired or something, one of the things that's sustaining me is the feeling that I'm writing my letter to the world. For that instant, [even] if I'm sitting in my living room, I'm taking stage center.

ABOUT THE AUTHOR

Adrienne Kennedy began to write and have her plays produced in the 1960s. She has been commissioned to write plays for Jerome Robbins, the New York Shakespeare Festival, the Royal Court's Theatre Upstairs and the Juilliard School of Drama. Kennedy has been a visiting lecturer at many universities, including Yale, Princeton, Brown, the University of California at Berkeley, Stanford and Harvard. She is the recipient of two Rockefeller Foundation grants and a Guggenheim Fellowship. Her 1964 Obie award-winning play, *Funnyhouse of a Negro*, was broadcast by the BBC and Radio Denmark, and has been translated into several languages. Her one-act plays and her first novel, *Deadly Triplets*, have been published by the University of Minnesota Press and her memoir, *People Who Led to My Plays*, is available from TCG.

ABOUT THE WORK

The Dramatic Circle, a radio play commissioned by WNYC, New York City, and first broadcast on January 12, 1992, is a dramatization of the events in the author's monologue, *The Film Club.*

CHARACTERS

ALICE ALEXANDER, narrator, a writer and college teacher
SUZANNE ALEXANDER, her sister-in-law, a writer
DAVID ALEXANDER, a writer and college teacher, Suzanne's husband
DR. FREUDENBERGER, an English doctor
THE DRAMATIC CIRCLE, Dr. Freudenberger's patients
THE AMBASSADOR
VOICE ON RADIO

TIME

1961

PLACE

London

THE DRAMATIC CIRCLE

ALICE ALEXANDER: London, 1961. We were staying in Old Brompton Road waiting for David to come from Ghana.

Sound of clock striking.

Suzanne had been delirious the night before, sleepwalking, speaking lines from the historical letters of Napoleon and Josephine. Her breathlessness had become worse.

SUZANNE ALEXANDER: "I can only write you a word at five o'clock in the morning. I have beaten the Russians and taken two cannons and their baggage train and six thousand prisoners. It was raining and we were in mud up to our knees...I was worried, the road..."

Sound of footsteps under.

ALICE ALEXANDER: In the past my brother had written me when he had been traveling with Frantz Fanon, the famous psychiatrist and revolutionary from Martinique. He'd written about the psychiatric cases they had encountered in Algeria. I realized now some of the symptoms of Fanon's patients were like Suzanne's symptoms. She had always missed David when he traveled to do research.

His first trip to Russia had been the summer she found a worn paperback of Napoleon's letters when he was away in battle. I had never seen her as sad as she was that summer that David traveled to Russia and then to France to meet Fanon. David and Suzanne had always traveled together, but now his research on Fanon, the trips the research required, were trips he forbade her to take. He said there was danger surrounding Fanon.

SUZANNE ALEXANDER: "I would like as much to see you, to live quietly, I could do other things but fight, but duty comes before all else. All my life I have sacrificed everything, tranquillity, my own desire, my happiness, my destiny." *(Sigh)*

ALICE ALEXANDER: Often he sent me notes on Fanon's observations, some on Gao.

DAVID ALEXANDER: Even the sky is constantly changing. Some days ago we saw a sunset that turned the robe of heaven a bright violet. Today it is a very hard red that the eye encounters. At Tessalit we cross the French military camps. We must work fast, time passes, the enemy is still stubborn, he does not believe in military defeat but I have never felt victory so possible, so within reach. We only need to march and charge. We have mobilized furious cohorts, loving combat, eager to work. We have Africa with us.

Music.

ALICE ALEXANDER: I decided Suzanne had to see a doctor. I found out from a chemist near the South Kensington underground station that National Health was right down the road from us. There were several doctors there. The chemist said, "Dr. Freudenberger is the one I recommend. I think you would find him most sympathetic. I believe he actually went to school in America for a while. He's very insightful. I'm sure he could help your sister-in-law."

Rain falling.

We went the next afternoon. It was raining heavily. Suzanne's breathlessness was worse. We sat in the outer office. Then Suzanne was called.

DR. FREUDENBERGER: Mrs. Alexander? Mrs. Alexander, yes. Would you—would you just—would you just come in for a moment?

ALICE ALEXANDER: Freudenberger came to the doorway, he was a dark-haired man, very tall, dressed in a suit. He smiled. Suzanne went inside.

DR. FREUDENBERGER: Mrs. Alexander. Mrs. Alexander, I've examined you and can find no reason in your heart or blood for your breathlessness. I recommend rest, especially since you're expecting a child. Have you been in London long? It says on this form that you're American.

SUZANNE ALEXANDER: I am from Washington, D.C., but my husband and I have been living in West Africa for the last two years.

DR. FREUDENBERGER: And why are you in London?

SUZANNE ALEXANDER: We are waiting for David. He is a writer and professor. He's still traveling. For many months he's been doing research, trying to find the source of Frantz Fanon's illness.

DR. FREUDENBERGER: Oh yes, I know his book, *Black Skin, White Masks.*

SUZANNE ALEXANDER: Yes.

DR. FREUDENBERGER: Are you friends of Fanon's?

SUZANNE ALEXANDER: David has traveled with him in Blida. He's writing Fanon's biography. Fanon is in Washington, very ill.

DR. FREUDENBERGER: You came here ahead of your husband?

SUZANNE ALEXANDER: Yes, the doctor in Accra insisted I start my journey home if I want to have the baby in Washington. My sister-in-law is with me.

DR. FREUDENBERGER: Oh, she came to join you?

SUZANNE ALEXANDER: Yes.

DR. FREUDENBERGER: I see here that you're living in Old Brompton Road.

SUZANNE ALEXANDER: We live on the top floor at Number Nine, in rooms with a green marble fireplace. It overlooks Bolton Gardens. We have not heard from my husband in two weeks.

DR. FREUDENBERGER: You are worried.

SUZANNE ALEXANDER: Every day we go to the American Embassy for word.

DR. FREUDENBERGER: That's the cause of your breathlessness.

SUZANNE ALEXANDER: He was to have arrived last week. We called Accra. They say the last they heard was that he went up country.

DR. FREUDENBERGER: Here, Mrs. Alexander, take this drink. It'll help. It's just valerian.

African music.

SUZANNE ALEXANDER: You see, in Blida with Fanon, David saw soldiers who were prisoners. Their disorders took various forms, states of agitation, rages, lamentations. I'm afraid David will be imprisoned. He has enemies. He insists West Africa has not yet achieved independence.

DR. FREUDENBERGER: You work together?

SUZANNE ALEXANDER: We write poems and essays, and we've been teaching at the University of Legon in Ghana. I want you to meet my sister-in-law, Alice. Alice! Alice!

ALICE ALEXANDER: Suzanne called me into the office.

SUZANNE ALEXANDER: Dr. Freudenberger, this is David's sister, Alice Alexander.

DR. FREUDENBERGER: Hello.

ALICE ALEXANDER: How do you do?

SUZANNE ALEXANDER: She came from Washington to be with me.

DR. FREUDENBERGER: Mrs. Alexander, I'd like to talk to your sister-in-law alone for a moment.

SUZANNE ALEXANDER: I'll wait outside.

DR. FREUDENBERGER: Good, good. . . . I'm worried about Mrs. Alexander's health.

ALICE ALEXANDER: Yes, yes. I am very worried too. We're a close family. I forced her to come to you because she seemed almost delirious last night. When I awoke she was sleepwalking. Since we've been in London she has inexplicable dreams of historical characters and speaks as the characters in her sleepwalking. I have written down what she said last night for you to read.

DR. FREUDENBERGER: Oh, thank you.

ALICE ALEXANDER: This is how she began as she walked down the hallway. "When I returned from Martinique to France at the close of 1790 . . ."

SUZANNE ALEXANDER (*Overlapping*): "When I returned from Martinique to France at the close of 1790, I leaped from one revolution in the new world only to encounter it in the old. A November journey across the French countryside to Paris brought me to a capital where violence and terror soon were to dominate the scene. A Paris mob burst into the Bastille with the bloody head of a governor. The next night Napoleon's secret plans for a French attack on Egypt were completed. The campaign would undercut British sea power. I was to accompany my husband as far as Toulon and later join him in Egypt. My husband's fleet of ships of war was spectacular."

Breathlessness. Sound of ocean.

DR. FREUDENBERGER: And she does this nightly?

ALICE ALEXANDER: Almost each night since we've not been able to reach David. The characters are in different stages but the themes of separation, violence and love are always present.

DR. FREUDENBERGER: She is greatly distressed. Are you able to stay with her until Professor Alexander arrives?

ALICE ALEXANDER: Yes. We were to meet here and return to Washington together.

DR. FREUDENBERGER: This sleepwalking and her troubled nerves are not good for her baby. Let me get her. Mrs. Alexander? Mrs. Alexander.

SUZANNE ALEXANDER: Oh, yes.

DR. FREUDENBERGER: Your sister-in-law and I have had a good talk. I was thinking, since you're both here waiting for Professor Alexander, perhaps you'd welcome a little diversion. I'd like to invite you both to my home. My wife and I have a dramatic circle. We're currently reading Bram Stoker's *Dracula*. Readings will distract you both while you're waiting for Professor Alexander. Suzanne, you could read the role of Lucy, and Alice, you might read Mina. My house is in the Little Boltons.

ALICE ALEXANDER: Very well. Thank you, we are lonely. We know no one here. We're to see a West African writer, but he's in Paris. We will be happy to come to your dramatic circle.

DR. FREUDENBERGER: Lovely. Please come this evening, you're nearby. My wife, Heike, is a translator. She makes tea. We have sherry.

ALICE ALEXANDER: Thank you.

SUZANNE ALEXANDER: Thank you. Goodbye, Dr. Freudenberger.

ALICE ALEXANDER: Goodbye, Dr. Freudenberger.

DR. FREUDENBERGER: Oh no, please, please. I'm Sebastian.

Overlapping goodbyes.

ALICE ALEXANDER: As we left I heard Dr. Freudenberger reading the paper I'd given him.

DR. FREUDENBERGER: "My life was transformed. Violence flared savagely when mobs appeared and the courtyards of the Tuileries ran with the blood of Swiss Guards. Danger struck everywhere."

Music—Wagner chorus. Dramatic circle greetings.

ALICE ALEXANDER: We arrived at eight for the reading of *Dracula.* Dr. Freudenberger's parlor was small and dark with water-stained gold-and-white wallpaper. His tall wife, Heike, poured tea. Dr. Freudenberger sat behind a large desk, we read from crimson books. He had a giant handwritten script. We later discovered that all the participants were his patients. We read sitting in a circle.

Music and voices in background.

DR. FREUDENBERGER: Ladies and gentlemen, please, everyone. We have two new actors tonight. They're both from America. I've invited them here to join us while they're here in England. In fact, both are writers themselves. Mrs. Alexander, Suzanne, writes essays and plays and Miss Alexander, Alice, writes po-etry. So, let us begin.

Dracula, Chapter 15, Dr. Stewart's diary continued: "For a while sheer anger mastered me, it was as if he had, during her life, struck Lucy on the face. I smote the table hard and rose up as I said to him, 'Dr. Helsing, are you mad?' He raised his head and looked at me. And somehow the tenderness of his face calmed me at once. 'Would that I were. My madness were easy to bear compared with truth like this. Oh, my friend, why think you did I go so far round? Why take so long to tell you so simple a thing? Was it because I hate you and have hated you all my life? Was it because I wished to give you pain? Was it that I wanted now so late revenge for that time when you saved my life from a fearful death?'"

WOMAN *(Reading)*: "'Oh, no. Forgive me,' said I. He went on."

WOMAN *(Reading)*: "We found the child awake."

DR. FREUDENBERGER: "It had had a sleep and taken some food and altogether was going on well. Dr. Vincent took the bandage from its throat and showed us the punctures. There was no mistaking the similarity to those which had been on Lucy's throat. They were smaller and the edges looked fresher, that was all. We asked Vincent to what he attributed them and he replied that it must have been a bite of some animal, perhaps a rat, but for his own part he was inclined to think that it was one of the bats which are so numerous on the northern heights of London. 'Out of so many harmless ones,' he said, 'there may be some wild specimen from the south of a more malignant species. Some sailor may have brought one home and it managed to escape or even from the zoological gardens a young one may have got loose, or one he bred there from a vampire. These things do occur, you know. Only ten days ago a wolf got out, and was, I believe, traced up in this direction. For a week after the children were playing nothing but Red Ridinghood on the heath. And in every alley on the place until this bloofer lady scare came along. Since then it has been quite a gala time with them. Even this poor little mite when he woke up today asked the nurse if he might go away.'"

Music. Voices.

ALICE ALEXANDER: After reading *Dracula* we had tea and sherry and listened to music. Dr. Freudenberger pulled his chair next to the divan.

Piano music—Chopin.

DR. FREUDENBERGER: Tell me about your teaching in Ghana.

SUZANNE ALEXANDER: Oh, we teach Césaire, the plays of Wole Soyinka, Chinua Achebe and Richard Wright and many other writers.

DR. FREUDENBERGER: And do you write plays?

SUZANNE ALEXANDER: My most recent play is *She Talks to Beethoven*, a play set in Ghana about a time two years ago when David disappeared.

DR. FREUDENBERGER: He has disappeared before?

SUZANNE ALEXANDER: There were threats against his life and he disappeared to protect me from danger.

DR. FREUDENBERGER: He must love you a great deal.

SUZANNE ALEXANDER: We went to school together as children. We won the state reading contest together.

ALICE ALEXANDER: After tea we read *Dracula* again. Then we started to say good night. Sebastian was once more at Suzanne's side.

DR. FREUDENBERGER: How do you spend your days in London?

ALICE ALEXANDER: Well, we walk all over, in Primrose Hill, Regent's Park, along Charing Cross Road. After we leave American Express we take tours of Trafalgar Square. Yesterday we went to Windsor in the rain.

SUZANNE ALEXANDER: Victoria grieved for Albert there.

ALICE ALEXANDER: In the evenings we return on the tour bus to Old Brompton Road and sit by the gas fire and write David.

SUZANNE ALEXANDER: Where is he? Where's my husband?

DR. FREUDENBERGER: Suzanne, you must rest. I'll walk you both home, you're just along the road. Perhaps I can help you. I know someone at the American Embassy, I'll ring there tomorrow. Also, another patient's daughter has lived in Ghana for years. I'll talk to her, but, Suzanne, you must not think of returning to Ghana. It might kill the baby. I forbid it.

SUZANNE ALEXANDER: I understand.

DR. FREUDENBERGER: I'll go with you to talk to the American ambassador tomorrow.

Music.

SUZANNE ALEXANDER *(Absently)*: In our garden in Legon, David read me the love poems of Léopold Senghor, then he'd tell me of the incidents in Fanon's life that he'd written about that day. His notebooks covered Fanon's entire life but always it was Blida that haunted him. He told me, "In Blida with Fanon, I saw soldiers . . . "

African music.

DAVID ALEXANDER *(His voice is heard)*: Generally speaking they had a noise phobia and a thirst for peace and affection. Their disorders took various forms, as states of agitated rage, immobility and many attempted suicides, tears, lamentations and appeals for mercy.

SUZANNE ALEXANDER: . . . appeals for mercy. *(Breathlessness)*

DR. FREUDENBERGER: Suzanne. I'll help you up the stairs. Here, let me carry you.

Footsteps.

ALICE ALEXANDER: Here. Here's her room. Thank you, Doctor.

DR. FREUDENBERGER: Not at all.

ALICE ALEXANDER: Good night.

DR. FREUDENBERGER: Good night.

ALICE ALEXANDER: Suzanne, are you all right?

SUZANNE ALEXANDER: Yes. . . . Alice?

ALICE ALEXANDER: Yes.

SUZANNE ALEXANDER: I feel like I've seen Sebastian somewhere before.

ALICE ALEXANDER: Where?

SUZANNE ALEXANDER: I don't know.

ALICE ALEXANDER: Before she let me leave her she began to relive those hours two years ago when she sat in the cottage in Legon and listened to the radio all day for word of David.

SUZANNE ALEXANDER: I can't forget.

ALICE ALEXANDER: As I walked down the hall to my room I heard her.

African music.

SUZANNE ALEXANDER: "Has David Alexander been murdered?"

VOICE ON RADIO *(Partly unintelligible)*: . . . again, David Alexander is still missing.

SUZANNE ALEXANDER: Still missing.

Music.

ALICE ALEXANDER: I too was agitated but finally fell asleep. But just after midnight Suzanne awakened me and stood over me.

SUZANNE ALEXANDER: I want you to come with me and look down into the garden.

ALICE ALEXANDER: What do you see?

SUZANNE ALEXANDER: It's shadowy but I think it's him.

ALICE ALEXANDER: What?

SUZANNE ALEXANDER: Over there in the corner of the garden, underneath the plane tree.

ALICE ALEXANDER: I can't see anything.

SUZANNE ALEXANDER: A figure sitting on a bench. I think it's Dr. Freudenberger.

ALICE ALEXANDER: I see nothing but a shadow.

SUZANNE ALEXANDER: No, it's Dr. Freudenberger, but his hair is white.

ALICE ALEXANDER: I see a shadow.

SUZANNE ALEXANDER: I see him.

ALICE ALEXANDER: I see only the shadow of the hedge. You've got to rest. I'll make you some chamomile tea. Please, rest. I'm worried about you and the baby.

Clock striking.

I had seen a figure and it had looked like Dr. Freudenberger and his hair had been white. I wanted to think about it and I didn't want Suzanne further upset. Why would Sebastian be in our garden? What was the cause of his changed appearance? Suzanne's mind was not at rest. In the morning she was still agitated and it was raining heavily.

Sound of rain.

SUZANNE ALEXANDER: "I cannot pass a day without loving you. I cannot even dream . . ."

ALICE ALEXANDER: I was awakened by the sound of Suzanne's

voice reading aloud. She hadn't walked in her sleep that night but now was awake, reading a love letter Napoleon had written Josephine. Reading it and rereading these historical letters seemed to give her strength at a time when . . . there were no letters from David.

SUZANNE AND DAVID ALEXANDER *(Together)*: "Every moment takes me further from you and at every moment I find it harder to bear the separation. You are the ceaseless object of my thoughts. My imagination exhausts itself in wondering what you are doing. If I think of you as sad my heart is torn and my misery increases. Write to me and write at length. Accept a thousand kisses of my love, as tender as they are true. I cannot pass a day without loving you. I cannot even drink a cup of tea without cursing the Army which keeps me apart from the soul of my existence. If I leave you with the speed of the torrential waters of the Rhône, it is only that I may return to you sooner."

ALICE ALEXANDER: I waited a moment before I went to her doorway.

SUZANNE ALEXANDER: How did you sleep?

ALICE ALEXANDER: Well. And you?

SUZANNE ALEXANDER: Well, but I'm concerned about what Sebastian was doing in the garden last night. His hair appeared white.

ALICE ALEXANDER: Now I'm convinced that was not Sebastian but a passerby. It would make no sense. Dr. Freudenberger is a charming friend trying to help us. We're both overwrought. I'm convinced it was someone who resembled him.

SUZANNE ALEXANDER: Perhaps this morning the ambassador will have word of David.

ALICE ALEXANDER: Suzanne was anxious that morning and on the bus to American Express I could not stop her from talking repeatedly about the time David had disappeared in Ghana and how she had news only from her radio.

VOICE ON RADIO: Mr. Alexander is still missing. He traveled with Fanon in Blida. His wife is recovering from an unspecified illness. Alexander was by her side in hospital when he suddenly vanished two nights ago.

SUZANNE ALEXANDER: Vanished.

ALICE ALEXANDER: She relived those moments. I worried about her. The writer we were to meet lived in Chalcot Square. We had gone to see him, but his wife said he was in Paris. We read that Sylvia Plath lived nearby. One night we saw *Billy Liar* at a theatre on Shaftesbury Avenue.

Music. Voices.

The next night Dr. Freudenberger sat behind his desk as we read. His nervous German wife, Heike, sat aside studying *Steppenwolf.*

Dramatic circle voices. Music.

Dr. Freudenberger hadn't been able to come to the embassy that day. Neither Suzanne nor I mentioned the figure in the garden. Sebastian read the part of Van Helsing.

DR. FREUDENBERGER: "Is it possible that love is all subjective or all objective?"

VOICES *(Reading together)*: "She yet no life taken . . . "

DR. FREUDENBERGER: "Though that is of time and to act now would be to take danger from her forever, but then we may have to warn Arthur, and how should we tell him of this? If you who saw the wounds on Lucy's throat and saw the wounds so similar on the child in the hospital. If you who saw the coffin empty last night and full today with a woman who has not changed only to be more rose and more beautiful in a whole week after she died, if you know of this and know of the white figure last night that brought the child to the churchyard, and yet of your own senses that you did not believe, how then can I expect Arthur, who knew none of those things, to believe? He doubted me when I took him from her kiss when she was dying."

ALICE ALEXANDER: Sebastian read one last passage about Lucy.

DR. FREUDENBERGER: "There lay Lucy seemingly just as we had seen her that night before her funeral. She was, if possible, more radiantly beautiful than ever and I could not believe that she was dead."

WOMAN'S VOICE: "Dead."

DR. FREUDENBERGER *(Others read along)*: "Her lips were redder than before, and on the cheeks was a delicate bloom."

Sound of rain.

ALICE ALEXANDER: Sometimes I wondered if Sebastian thought Suzanne was going to die. Had he told us the truth about her breathlessness? I continued writing my brother letters even though he was missing.
"Dear David,
   In the rain we take the 30 bus down Old Brompton Road past South Kensington Station, take another bus at Hyde Park Corner to American Express in hope of a letter from you. We went to Windsor Castle again. Paintings of the sad figure of Victoria seem to comfort Suzanne."

Dog barking. Footsteps.

The next night, in the garden, Sebastian seemed to have somewhat changed his appearance. That night his white hair was gone. He limped from one end of the garden to the other, not as the young man he was, but as an old man with a severe ailment. As he limped I felt he knew we were watching although he never looked up.

Piano music—Chopin.

The ambassador says tomorrow there may be word of David.

Music. Dramatic circle voices.

The next reading I still did not mention to Sebastian the figure in the garden, but I did tell him of Suzanne's sleepwalking and her words from her historical letters. He had me recite to him all that I could remember.
   "I move against a tragic background but it's clear I not only have a rendezvous with you but one with destiny. Wars have

always colored my existence. I was born during the Seven Years' War, and was imprisoned during the French Revolution. Now we are married, my whole life is overshadowed by war. Cannons sound."

Neither of us ever mentioned the garden but I was convinced the figure was Sebastian even though I insisted to Suzanne that it was not.... New patients joined our dramatic circle, a man from Budapest, a Trinidadian painter.

Music. Dramatic circle voices.

The ambassador said we must keep our bags packed, and although he could give us no concrete word, he had learned of some events but could not yet share them. Soon. Suzanne could not stop talking about David's previous disappearance.

At our dramatic circle, we read Stoker as a group.

DRAMATIC CIRCLE *(Reading together)*: "All at once, the wolves began to howl as though the moonlight had had some peculiar effect on them. The horses jumped about, reared and looked helplessly round with eyes that rolled in a way painful to see. But the living ring of terror encompassed them on every side."

DR. FREUDENBERGER: Suzanne, I would like you to recount the sequences of Lucy's life.

SUZANNE ALEXANDER: Lucy sleepwalks to the suicide seat on the last cliff. *(She reads breathlessly)*

DRAMATIC CIRCLE: Yes.

SUZANNE ALEXANDER: Dracula drinks her blood for the first time. She receives a blood transfusion. The wolf, Berker, escapes from the zoo, breaks a window providing a passage to Lucy again. Lucy dies.

DRAMATIC CIRCLE *(After each sentence)*: Yes.

SUZANNE ALEXANDER: She is buried in a churchyard near Hampstead Heath. *(Sobbing)*

Rain.

ALICE ALEXANDER: The passage made me cry too. We broke the circle then and said good night.... We continued going to the embassy each morning. The ambassador said we would be leaving London soon. We sailed to Greenwich on the Thames. One afternoon we saw a Bergman movie. Sebastian came again in the middle of the night. That time, just as he left through the gate he seemed to look up at our window. . . . I wrote David.

"On the Thames to Greenwich Suzanne recites one of your favorite Diop poems. She carries notebooks of your records of slave ships. Slave quarters, slaves crouching below the stern of the ship. My husband, she told a stranger . . . "

African music.

SUZANNE ALEXANDER: My husband gives lectures on the slave ships that crossed the Atlantic.

ALICE ALEXANDER: We reach Greenwich and see the place where Elizabeth I was born. Suzanne recites Diop as we cross the park up to the observatory.

SUZANNE ALEXANDER: "Way back then, with their civilizing edicts, with their holy water splashed on domesticated brows, the vultures in the shadows of their claws were setting up the bloody monument of the guardian era. Way back then laughter gasped its last."

Telephone rings.

ALICE ALEXANDER: Finally the ambassador said there was word. We went to Grosvenor Square.

AMBASSADOR: Mrs. Alexander, sit down please. May I get you some coffee?

SUZANNE ALEXANDER: No. No, thank you. Have you heard from David?

ALICE ALEXANDER: Yes, what's the news?

AMBASSADOR: You'll see him tomorrow morning. I spoke to Alexander a few hours ago. He is fine.

ALICE ALEXANDER: Thank God.

SUZANNE ALEXANDER: Are you sure he's all right?

AMBASSADOR: Yes. Last week we knew a few details but I didn't want to talk to you until I was sure of your husband's, and your brother's, freedom.

SUZANNE ALEXANDER: Freedom?

ALICE ALEXANDER: Freedom? He's been imprisoned?

AMBASSADOR: Yes. But please assure yourself, he is fine now. Let me explain. We have finally heard from our sources that there was a doctor in Algeria who had once tried to kill Fanon, a man named Sottan. And this same Sottan is behind a plot against your husband. We have also learned that this Sottan had you and your husband followed through the villages. There may have been a man who was your gardener at the cottage behind the Ambassador Hotel. And earlier there may have been a man with the ship's orchestra when you were on the *Queen Elizabeth.*

ALICE ALEXANDER: But is he all right?

SUZANNE ALEXANDER: How long was David detained?

ALICE ALEXANDER: How long was my brother in prison?

AMBASSADOR: I don't know. I'm afraid you should know that there has been a rumor that there may have been an attempt to poison him with a drug called filicin. There were rumors that he became violently ill after having an aperitif with a Swiss journalist and was hospitalized. It was at that time we made our connection. But I talked to David this morning and he sounds fine. And he will arrive at Gatwick in the morning at 8:10. I want to assure you, he sounded fine. You will all leave Heathrow at 2:35 in the afternoon, Pan American, he asks that you be ready. And one final note: In the morning there will be an article in the *Herald Tribune* that Frantz Fanon has died in a hospital in Washington, D.C. I'm terribly sorry.

SUZANNE ALEXANDER: No, no.

Crying. Piano music.

ALICE ALEXANDER: We hardly felt like going to the dramatic circle, but we went. We knew Sebastian would be disappointed. Instead of scenes, he had us read a litany of dramatic events. He seemed to have a purpose in doing this.

DR. FREUDENBERGER: "Jonathan Harker, arriving at Klausenberg, stays the night, leaves by coach for Castle Dracula."

WOMAN'S VOICE: "Realizes he is a prisoner."

DR. FREUDENBERGER: "Watches Dracula crawl, facedown, over the castle wall."

WOMAN'S VOICE: "Enters the forbidden room."

WOMAN'S VOICE: "Dracula makes Harker write three misleading letters to England."

DR. FREUDENBERGER: "Harker discovers his personal effects are gone. Dracula leaves the castle dressed in Harker's clothes and returns with a child for the three vampire women."

WOMAN'S VOICE: "The bereft mother is killed by wolves."

DR. FREUDENBERGER: "Harker climbs along the castle wall to the cellar, where he finds Dracula in a box."

ALICE ALEXANDER: Then he read the last section.

DR. FREUDENBERGER: "When I looked again, the driver was climbing into the calèche and the wolves had disappeared. This was all so strange and uncanny that a dreadful fear came upon me and I was afraid to speak or move. The time seemed interminable as we swept on our way now in almost complete darkness."

ALICE ALEXANDER: He reached out and held Suzanne's hand, staring at her. We returned to our rooms for the last night at Old Brompton Road and finished packing. Even though the ambassador had said David sounded fine, of course we were very fearful. Three weeks ago we had arrived in London happy and everything had changed. I forced Suzanne to go to sleep and then I went out into the garden and waited for Sebastian's arrival. He came a little before midnight. I ran toward him.

Footsteps.

Sebastian, why have you walked in the garden at night, limping, hair white, almost as an apparition?

DR. FREUDENBERGER: I wanted to appear as an apparition.

ALICE ALEXANDER: But why?

DR. FREUDENBERGER: To prepare Suzanne's mind for the darkness I knew she must face. The moment I met Suzanne I fell in love with her. As a matter of fact, I'd seen both of you before you came to my office, in a restaurant next to the South Kensington underground station. It was a Sunday. I was struck by Suzanne's fragile beauty. I followed you along the road. I had a premonition that David, like Jonathan Harker, was going through bad times and she, like Lucy, would become the victim of an unfair, tragic plot. I'd hoped that my dramatic circle would help her and you on this difficult journey.

ALICE ALEXANDER: So, David will be changed.

DR. FREUDENBERGER: Yes. But he will recover.

ALICE ALEXANDER: Sebastian kissed me and disappeared before I could even thank him. We never saw our friend again. As the ambassador had told us, in the *Herald Tribune* was the article on Fanon's death. . . . We arrived at Gatwick early and waited in the hall behind a glass partition for visitors from Africa. Suzanne had worn David's favorite dress, white silk with a kinte cloth sash. I hardly recognized David, he had changed so. He limped like an old man and his black hair had turned white. Suzanne ran toward him.

Sounds of terminal.

SUZANNE ALEXANDER: David!

ALICE ALEXANDER: It was hard to tell at first if he even recognized her. Finally he smiled, they kissed and embraced.

DAVID ALEXANDER: I wanted to see Frantz before he died to tell him of things I had discovered. We'll have to continue to live by his words.

"But the war goes on and we will have to bind up for years to come the many, sometimes ineffaceable, wounds that the colonialists have inflicted on our people."

Voices in terminal.

ALICE ALEXANDER: We helped David through the terminal. In months to come he would recover. The book on Fanon would be powerful, but for now he was lost in Blida.

Voices increase. African music.

SALLY'S

RAPE

ROBBIE

McCAULEY

I had a dream in which I heard Sally's voice. The line that came to me in the dream was, "I don't wanna do it." It was an interesting dream because the atmosphere was there of the town that I lived in in Georgia, and the smells were there. I was very close to the time of slavery when I lived in the South because we heard the stories, so I associated those smells that were in the dream with those stories. It was a wonderful kind of connection, the dream.

Stylistic Influences

I'm influenced by black classical music, or jazz, in that it has a clear theme and narrative, but it is also random and impulsive. It was the music that I came to knowledge in when I was a teenager. In the late 1950s, early '60s, what was then called modern jazz—the music of Charlie Parker, John Coltrane—was popular among the teenagers that I grew up with. It's the ability to sing the hard things and make them beautiful. That's what I gravitated towards in the music at that time. The blues is also a part of that. Living in the South, the blues was just all around me. Again, it's singing the hard things beautifully. I work with music through the passion that I have for it and the ability to hear it deep down. People tend to think of music as something written; however, when one is creating, one is not thinking of what is written. It helps me as a writer to think of it in the same way that I imagine a musician's passion connected to the form.

Artistic Challenges and Discoveries

Dialogue is an act. One of the comments I'm sensitive to is, "You're talking about it, but what are you doing?" In *Sally's Rape*, it released me physically to write it. From that personal dialogue, on to the dialogue between me and Jeannie Hutchins, on to the dialogues with the audiences, I found that just the nerve, the boldness to speak about the charged issues of race relations can be something right there. It is an act. It is not before or after the act. Saying the words, allowing dialogue, making dialogue happen is an act, a useful act in the moment.

This is not new, but it is something that we tend to gloss over too much. We carry in our bodies unspoken sadness and anger and resentment. It is bigger and harder to carry it than to release it. And when we release it, we find out more information about it; we help our ability to move with it. You don't get rid of it, but you're able to handle it, take it with you, and to transform.

The Aesthetic

I define my aesthetic as "content as aesthetic." The way I shape work is to listen to what is going on; and of course, "listen" is a big word. I'm looking, I'm smelling, I'm tasting, I'm touching, and I value that. This is what most artists do, but I continually sensitize myself to find in it those elements that I can personalize and put in my work.

What I'm concerned with in narrative is that the stories are known. We share the story that is known. Whether people know it or not, it is as I call it, part of their collective memory. Personal stories are the same. My listeners also know my personal story because my personal story is all of our story. This is just my part in it.

The thematic thread in my work is the connection of things that have been torn apart. I don't try to make connections. I'm trying to find the connections that are there. For instance, I know about differences between races. I know about commonness between races, between men and women, and so forth. The commonness is easier to speak than the differences. I'm most interested in speaking those differences. In a strange way, speaking the differences makes the connection happen. And I'm not talking about "we shall all hug and overcome everything." It's simply that it helps us to see where we are on this whole earth—and out of that, many things can happen.

Definitions of Heroism

For me, the particular story of Sally is not the rape. It is her understanding it. This comes from the fragments that I picked up about her that I do when I'm on the auction block. She asks the white man how much was the house that she wanted to buy, and then she worked for money to buy the house so that none of us ever had to do what she had to do. How many mothers does that cover? That's historic. That's heroic.

Distinctions between Women's and Men's Writing

I recently heard the writer Deena Metzger say that women can pay attention to the things that are immediate. To me, the immediate or so-called small things are the big things, the things that we are ignoring in our development. Sally says, "It wasn't nothin' to it," when the men came down to rape them. That's a loaded statement because it means that it was done constantly and people called it other things. They didn't call it rape. Now we know that rape has to do with power.

I'm going against the myth of the romance of the slave master and the overseers with the slave women, even Thomas Jefferson. I'm going against the myth because it was a power thing, so we call it rape. Sometimes it was actual, brutal rape; sometimes it might have been romantic. It doesn't matter. It was a rape in the sense that we know what rape is now. It's the everyday rape that happens in those power situations; and so it's "ha ha," a small thing. When I started *Sally's Rape*, of course, Bosnia wasn't in the picture. But now that's being talked about—rape as a part of domination.

This attention to small things has to do with our connection to our bodies. If you bleed every month for a large part of your life, then you are in touch with reality, with the moon, in a way that men don't have to be. The little things that we do are a part of us and are connected with the whole. I remember when I was pregnant, I said, "Oh, this is what women feel like! *This* is it!" Of course, I cried, fell down. I suddenly felt like millions of women in the world.

The Darkness and the Light

I'm constantly reversing the images of dark and light. *Sally's Rape* might be considered a dark image, but I go to it, and there is the light. There's a line that Jeannie says in the piece, right before she says, "I wanted to be Billie Holiday." She says, "I'm going through the dark places into the light." That came out onto the page out of nowhere. I was thinking, I'm writing really corny stuff here; and when she read it, it sounded really good. So that's my feeling about darkness and light.

I personally have dealt a lot in my life with depression and what is called darkness. In terms of artistic imagery, as many artists understand, the dark images are where one finds the light. Artistically and politically, I'm much more fascinated with what is difficult in beauty. When people think of the light, they think of being bright and at ease. I wish I could do that. But inside that darkness, that's what I am; I am at ease. I'm drawn to it. And here I'm using dark in the way that it's usually used, but I don't see it that way. I think it's because I'm an actor, my energy comes out of going to places that are difficult emotionally. When actors see pain, they run to it. What is personal about it is all of my baggage and heart stuff, but I've learned to find the light in that stuff. It's a hard thing to admit.

It's not like I'm trying to come out the other side. I'm trying to live in a place where that is usually what is going on—like I love to come back to New York City.

The light comes with simply exercising my mind, my sensibility, going to places full of energy and information. Pain is full of information. It exercises my mind to deal with that information. Again, it goes back to the body, the release. What you know is something you can carry with you rather than be burdened by.

So much of this has to do with sexuality. Black women particularly struggle to deal with the image of the saint and the whore, or the church lady and the slut. It's part of the puritanism of America, but it is also part of our own issues with sexism, how we are perceived as women. The issues are also economic as well as social. There are places in extreme, places in between, there are places all around, but we get stuck in the inside of sexual images and in the way we internalize what we're supposed to do and what we're not supposed to do. Part of my struggle is around those issues of having been raped and silent about it. I know that information, I've dealt with it and I can carry it with me. But in *Sally's Rape*, I found out more information about the tightness between my thighs.

In the piece, I say "There's a tension between her thighs. When it lets go, she screams with terror." So there's no good sex in there. Knowing that, the discovery of that power is something you can take with you as information, and let go. Whatever you wanna do with what you let go is your business.

ABOUT THE AUTHOR

Writer/performer Robbie McCauley was born in Norfolk, Virginia, but spent most of her childhood in Georgia and Washington, D.C. She came to New York in the mid-sixties and became involved in experimental and black theatre, working at La MaMa, Caffe Cino, the Negro Ensemble Company and the Public Theater. In 1979, she began developing her own performance theatre work with composer Ed Montgomery. She has also collaborated with Fred Holland (*What I like About Us*), Jowole Willa Jo Zollar of Urban Bush Women, and Jessica Hagedorn and Laurie Carlos (*Teenytown* and *Persimmon Peel*). Since 1990, McCauley has been developing a series of works with local actors in Buffalo, N.Y., Jackson, Miss., Boston and Los Angeles, creating personal and theatrical dialogues, with music and storytelling, about charged political events.

ABOUT THE WORK

Sally's Rape was first presented as a work-in-progress at P.S. 122 in New York City in December 1989. The piece subsequently played at BACA Downtown in Brooklyn and at The Kitchen and City College's Davis Center in Manhattan. It has been seen at numerous venues around the country, including the Boston Women's Festival and the American Festival Project in Louisville, and toured the Southwest in the fall of 1993. *Sally's Rape*, which was co-winner of the 1992 Obie Award for Best Play, is featured in two videos: Maria Beatty's *Sphinxes Without Secrets* and *Conjure Women* by Demetria Royals.

PLAYERS

ROBBIE, the one who plays the people in her and who tells all she wants to tell. She is an actor who sings and dances. She is black.

JEANNIE, the one who plays the roles she's given and who sometimes erupts. She is a dancer who sings and acts. She is white.

AUDIENCE, those who are there, who witness and talk back.

AUTHOR'S NOTE

Some of the scripted dialogue in this piece came out of my conversations over tea with Jeannie Hutchins. Some of it emerged from improvisations during our performances. So the actors—the parts of themselves that connected with the subjects of the piece—became the characters.

The improvisational dialogue in Parts IV and VIII may change somewhat if other actors play the characters. It would be best if these changes grew out of work between the actors and director on the subject of the piece.

The stage directions are just a guide to suggest the ease with which events between the actors, and between the actors and audience, can happen.

The music for the song "Grandma Sally," which is reproduced following the text of the piece, was composed by and for a performer with some minimal knowledge of how piano notes and chords are played. The piano playing is essential to the piece. If the actor playing "Robbie" cannot read music, she should consult with a musician. If she cannot manage the playing, the music may be recorded and played while she mimes playing the piano and sings.

My thanks to Ed Montgomery for transcribing the music for "Grandma Sally," and to Esther Kaplan for transcribing one of the November 1991 performances of *Sally's Rape* at the Kitchen in New York City.

SALLY'S RAPE

A bench up right. A piano up left. A large, sturdy square table up center and two chairs. All are set at angles. Rocks are lying about the space. General lighting. Audience enters, sits.

Prologue: Talking About What It Is About

Robbie and Jeannie enter with cups of tea on saucers. They walk to a space down left in conversation between themselves, aware of Audience. Easy talk.

ROBBIE: Somebody said it was about cups.

JEANNIE: Somebody else said it was about language.

ROBBIE: What do you think it's about?

JEANNIE: Well, that one person said it was about you and me. And I know it's not about me, but it's about you and I'm in it.

ROBBIE: It's my story, and you're in it because I put you in it.

JEANNIE: Fair enough.

ROBBIE: It *is* about cups.

JEANNIE: It's about getting culture.

ROBBIE: Cup says culture.

JEANNIE: Comportment.

ROBBIE: Commonality. Well actually, where I come from, cups and saucers were like.... We had to learn about these things. I mean we went from jars to cups and saucers...nothing in between. I once went to a class in tea pouring.... It was Japanese, but it was about containment...proper...deportment.

JEANNIE: Doing the...proper...

ROBBIE AND JEANNIE: ...right...thing.

ROBBIE: Like my Aunt Nell said: If you do the wrong thing, you could get your ass killed, so it was more like a matter of life and death.

JEANNIE: You know, we had cups and saucers. I even think we had six that matched. But mostly we used mugs.

ROBBIE: Mugs?

JEANNIE: Because they hold a little more, and they have a bigger bottom, so they don't tip. The only disadvantage of a mug is after you use a spoon you have to just kind of put it on the table, and it leaves a little mark.

ROBBIE: I think sometimes we did this for the sake of itself. Cups and saucers. Charm school. White gloves.

JEANNIE: But that's South, too. I mean, that's southern stuff. The one girl that was like that I knew . . . she had gone to charm school, she was being groomed to be a Southern Belle. She had monogrammed sweaters. She went to charm school one summer in junior high, and she learned to walk like this . . . *(Does the walk)* with a book on her head. And we all tried.

ROBBIE: We didn't worry about books on our heads. We already had this *up* thing. I guess that was the African in us before I even knew it. But we *(Walking, Jeannie following)* had to contain our hips. To keep tucked up. Slightly seductive but not too much . . . *(At the bench)* and when you sit . . . you know this part.

JEANNIE: Yeah, you touch the front of the seat with the back of the calf, and then you descend without bending at the waist.

They sit together; Jeannie crosses her legs.

ROBBIE: Now you can—no! *(Hits Jeannie's knee away)* Don't do that. *(Jeannie corrects)* Now you can drink your tea. *(They sip simultaneously)* My Aunt Nell would have *died* if she saw you—

JEANNIE: —cross my legs like that.

ROBBIE: That's it. Put your feet just so, or slightly cross at the ankle.

JEANNIE: Why was that?

1. Confessing About Family and Religion and Work in Progress

ROBBIE: Almost everybody in my mother's family was half white. But that wasn't nothing but some rape. These confessions are like a mourning for the lost connections.

Robbie starts singing and Jeannie joins in.

ROBBIE AND JEANNIE:

> "I'm going there to meet my mother
> I'm going there no more to roam
> I'm just a-going over Jordan
> I'm just a-going over home . . . "

Robbie continues humming like in church.

JEANNIE: That was the only thing that would make it worth going to church for me, to sing those songs. But I didn't really have a religion, so that's why I invented one. When I was about seven, I invented a religion, and it was all about rocks, and trees and leaves, and nature and so forth, everything that I knew. And I tried to convert my best friend, Eileen, who was Catholic. It ended up just being mine.

ROBBIE: I envy that. To have a religion that you find where you are was something I couldn't even conceive of until Africa. Before that, of course, it was the big white god up there. . . . If oppression is at the core, if there must be one at the top and others on the bottom . . . the struggle will always be . . . *(Gesture of pushing and straining)* You know, I mean, the way I dealt with religion was to be a Marxist . . .

JEANNIE AND ROBBIE: . . . another . . . big white god . . .

JEANNIE: What was it your Aunt Nell said when you said you were a Marxist?

ROBBIE: "Well, at least you're *sumpthin'*." If this . . . *(Same gesture)* kind of struggle, if oppression, is at the core, then this work will never end. It's a work in progress . . .

JEANNIE: Well, if you can dialogue, you can get rid of some of that.

ROBBIE: Well, *if* you can weed it out. *If* it's about something else, then—

JEANNIE: *Then* it's a work in progress . . .

ROBBIE: . . . a dialogue . . .

JEANNIE: Otherwise, there is no progress.

ROBBIE AND JEANNIE *(To Audience, alternating the lines between them)*: And we can't have a dialogue by ourselves. So you're in it. Don't worry I won't jump in your face or down your throat.

We'll feed you. *(They pass out cookies and apples, improvising about "fishes and loaves" and about how food eases tension, may help you talk)* We'll use hand signals, lead like camp directors, divide you into groups. One . . . *(One of them points out sections of the Audience)* Two . . . Three. Well, it doesn't matter what section you're in, it just matters who you are, and you can change your opinion as time goes on.

Group One will be the agreeable ones. When we signal like this, *(Two fingers up)* you say "That's right!," "Yes indeed" or "I'm telling you." Any short sentence of agreement. Let's practice. *(They lead responses with Group One)* Good . . . !

Group Two will be the bass line. You just go "uh huh," "umm humm," or "yeah, yeah." Here's your signal . . . *(One finger pointed out)* Let's try it. *(Group Two practices with sounds)* Very nice.

(Talking fast) Group Three is the dialogue group, people who have something to add, to disagree with, who like to talk.

ROBBIE: Don't worry, I'm in control. Your signal is two hands out flat like this. . . . Dialogue?

JEANNIE: Let's practice with something from the context of the piece. Lights!

Lights on Robbie and Jeannie in two house aisles. Stage black.

2. Stating the Context

ROBBIE: I believe white is a condition that anyone can take in. It causes one to feel superior in order to be okay.

They signal to Groups. Groups respond. In this improvisation with the Audience, when Robbie feels someone makes a strong point, agreeable to her or not, she impulsively stomps her feet.
Stage lights up. Aisle lights off. Jeannie moves among rocks.

(Walking in 6/8 time) It's about my great-great-grandmother Sally who was a young woman with children when official slavery ended. And she's in me. She was house but *field*.

My Aunt Jessie who died at the age of ninety-three—

JEANNIE: Ninety-six.

ROBBIE: She always put her age back. She said we was bad off in Harris County 'cause the white folks wasn't doing too good, and we were brought up to believe that, that our well-being depended on white people being well-off. You know how families can raise you with counterrevolutionary ideas in order to survive.

They call for Audience response. Robbie waves off dialogue.

We don't hafta discuss *that.*

Jeannie moves among the rocks. Robbie continues in 6/8 rhythm.

It wasn't *fine* like the gone-with-the-wind-type house-nigger mythology. Sally did the housework and the cooking, and she tended to Mistress when some really fine white folks come to visit. They say that day might not a been really rich white folks anyhow. They say Sally had them chillun by the master like that was supposed to a been something. They say Massa was mean and nasty. You know how white folks gets when they ain't doin' good. Word was freedom was coming, everybody know what happen on that day freedom come when we follow Uncle Buck—I believe that was his name—

JEANNIE: Yeah, Uncle Buck.

ROBBIE: —up to the Massa porch. *(Sudden anger)* But back up in *heah* 'fore freedom they say po' citter white folks was buying us ignorant! No telling what woulda happen! *(She pauses)*

3. Trying to Transform

ROBBIE *(Upset, she moves over left)*: I I I become others inside me, standing at the bus stop with my socks rolled down screaming things I shoulda said, "Just because people are crazy don't mean they can't think straight!" Hollering periodically at white men "YOU RAPED ME! GODDAMN MOTHER-FUKA! YOU RAPED ME!" *(Reaching out, gathering air)* Sometimes I'll gather and push away the wall of vibrations that make walls between us . . . *(Throws air to Jeannie)* Black

JEANNIE *(Catching, molding the bunch of air)*: Black

ROBBIE: Women

JEANNIE: Women

ROBBIE: Get

JEANNIE: Get

ROBBIE AND JEANNIE: Bitter.

JEANNIE: Black women get bitter. Scared somebody gonna look at them run and search for the wind, look at them go to the bottom of the pain and sadness, looking for breezes. You know how black folks gets when they ain't doing good.

ROBBIE: It's a journey of chains.

JEANNIE: I latched on, crawled in like a spider clinging to the walls, looking for light in tunnels of despair. I wanted to go deeper, darker, never to remember the empty days. I wanted to be . . . Billie Holiday.

ROBBIE: I wanted to be Rosa Luxemburg!

JEANNIE: Rosa Luxemburg?

ROBBIE: Poland.

JEANNIE: That's so idealistic.

ROBBIE *(Aside)*: So was Billie Holiday.

JEANNIE *(Responding to aside)*: I didn't have to know that to want to be her.

ROBBIE *(Does dance kicks)*: Poland. She liked Poland. Communism wasn't even a word back then. The main deity in Poland is a Black Madonna. In Eastern Europe women were more revered, more venerated.

JEANNIE: Do you have proof? Who told you that?

ROBBIE: A woman from Eastern Europe.

JEANNIE: Well, a woman from Turkey told me there was no racism in Turkey.

ROBBIE: Well, from her point of view, there probably wasn't.

JEANNIE: Why are you so understanding, so generous toward people in another part of the world?

ROBBIE: I was listening to a woman who had pride in her ancestors and that turned me on.

JEANNIE: That's very nice.

ROBBIE: Socialism goes way back. Way back women gathered in groups to pick. And Africa. Let's do 1964.

Light change: a pool of light center. They stand in it. Other areas dim.

ROBBIE: In 1964 at the library job a U.S. history major who'd graduated from Smith College said—

JEANNIE: I never knew white men did anything with colored women on plantations.

ROBBIE: I said, "It was rape." Her eyes turned red. She choked on her sandwich and quit the job.

JEANNIE *(Pointing at each Audience group in turn)*: Was the Smith College graduate denying...? lying...? or dumb? *(Audience response)* Yeah she was dumb. I keep telling you that.

They cross past each other. Light change.

ROBBIE: Why do I feel like crying...because she went to Smith College....I think of the dumb educated bourgeois thing in me...

JEANNIE: You have this thing that an Ivy League education could prevent her dumbness about that, and there's nothing that can prevent that.

ROBBIE: Right, I do have a thing that an Ivy League education oughta prevent that. I mean, look, okay. I wanted to go to Barnard, and they didn't let me in...a rejection letter...

JEANNIE: And you're bitter.

ROBBIE: Bitterness about Barnard I admit. But when I'm sitting around my grandmother's breakfast table, and she's telling me something that this woman who went to Smith College didn't know, a U.S. history major—

JEANNIE *(Overlap)*: Well, aren't you more fortunate then, that you learned so much more through your grandmother?

ROBBIE: The point is that Smith College, all those colleges, are places that people should go to learn things that help the world. All right? And if she went there and studied U.S. history and comes out sounding dumb about what went on during slavery time, I don't understand. I can't give her no credit for just being dumb. I mean my grandmother would also teach us that.... You know, we lived in a neighborhood back then down south that had black people and white people, back when they had signs that said *white* and *colored* to separate bathrooms and stuff. Well, back then there were white people who lived down the street from us because that was where they had to live. And we played together till we were about ten. After ten back then we couldn't speak to each other. Even back then my grandmother taught us that white people were not genetically evil or anything, they were just dumb, and when they learned something, they would be smarter about us...

Jeannie starts to do folk-dance steps in 3/4 time. Robbie joins in.

...and we could get together and change the world.

JEANNIE: Rosa Luxemburg had no patience for bourgeois women who didn't work. She called them—

ROBBIE: Co-consumptive.

JEANNIE: More parasitic than the parasites. She was a small, powerful woman.

ROBBIE: Zaftig.

JEANNIE: When she talked, people listened. I believe she would have marched with us.

ROBBIE AND JEANNIE *(They stop dancing)*: She was murdered by men who would later be Nazis.

ROBBIE *(Turning, kicking, squatting)*: Dancing in half circles. Trying to connect. She was internationalist—so far ahead of her time—we haven't begun to get there yet.

JEANNIE *(Overlap)*: —as opposed to nationalist.

ROBBIE *(Still dancing)*: In Pennsylvania a town with the Black Madonna and the little brown Jesus. A Polish town. In Eastern Europe way back...women more venerated...

JEANNIE: There's one in Texas too. I sent you the postcard. The shrine to Our Lady of Czestochowa.

ROBBIE: Not long ago in Poland a pilgrimage to her.

JEANNIE: But you've never explained why in Poland there'd be a black Madonna.

Pause.

ROBBIE: Socialism goes way back.

JEANNIE: But a burned statue or anything, there's no explanation for it?

ROBBIE: Way back, way back! Women gathered in groups to pick and hunt.

JEANNIE: Did they really hunt? That's unsubstantiated.

Pause.

ROBBIE *(Stops dancing)*: Of *course* they hunted. And of course it's unsubstantiated. And Africa.

JEANNIE: Old memories. Ancient stuff. We all come from one African woman. Dancing in circles, pushing walls. I was underneath him in the dirt too—he doesn't want to hear this, he thinks he civilized the world! I sold slaves when I worked at the Welfare Department. Did you put them on the ship?

Jeannie puts her hands on Robbie's hair. Pause. Robbie lifts them off.

4. Moment in the Chairs

They set up the two chairs. Light changes. One bright circle. Other areas dark. They sit in the light, face each other, hold hands and move their arms to and fro, as if giving and receiving dialogue.

They improvise on why they are angry with each other. The differences go deep. Jeannie thinks Robbie can see through her to something she can't admit. She thinks their idealism is similar. Robbie thinks admitting the differences in their histories is more important. Jeannie is concerned that she can't win. They try to reveal something to each other as if they are alone and honest about

their differences. The following is an example of the dialogue that
has resulted in performance.

JEANNIE: Your hands are like ice.

ROBBIE: What upsets me is language. I can't win in your language.

JEANNIE: You're going to win anyway. What upsets me is there's an underlying implication that you're gonna unmask me. That you're gonna get underneath something and pull it out. That you can see it and I can't.

ROBBIE: What do you think it is? I mean, it's better if you say it.

JEANNIE: Some kind of delusion, self-deception.

ROBBIE: About what? I mean, what's the content of it?

JEANNIE: About my idealism. I have some idea of . . . humanism, something that we share, more important than our differences. Of greater. . . . Of greater value.

ROBBIE: Let me see if I can use the language to say what I feel about your idealism. I think it covers over something in your history that makes your idealism still a whim. It angers me that even though your ancestors might have been slaves— because they did have white slaves . . . only made black slavery mandatory for economic reasons, so they could catch us when we ran away—that history has given you the ability to forget your shame about being oppressed by being ignorant, mean or idealistic . . . which makes it dangerous for me. *(Stands)*

JEANNIE: I have the same thing about education you were talking about. I mean I believed that through education, if I could change my thinking, that anything would be possible. And it just sounds so stupid.

Robbie may use this moment to say something more to Audience.
Jeannie takes chairs away, joins Robbie facing Audience. Beat.
They go stand in front of bench, pick up cups and drink tea.

5. Sally's Rape

ROBBIE:

Do you think Thomas
took his Sally to European tea rooms?

And what did she wear?

And what do you think Mrs. J. thought?

ROBBIE AND JEANNIE: That musta been some business, huh?

They take their cups to piano. Jeannie first sings with Robbie, then becomes Mrs. J. and does the dance of the frail white lady.

ROBBIE *(Plays piano and sings)*:
> Grandma Sally had two children
> by the master. One of 'em
> was my Grandma Alice, my mother's
> grandmother, where my mother got her name.

Robbie continues to play. Mrs. J. speaks, conscious of the music.

JEANNIE:
> In the woods . . .
> I immediately become Harriet
> in the woods.
> Swamps are my memory.

ROBBIE *(Coaching)*: Shoot.

JEANNIE:
> Shoot, how you gonna be scared of freedom?
> Some teachers don't know nothing.

ROBBIE: Once.

JEANNIE:
> Once somebody I almost married
> said I was too scared of dogs.
> I said I'm scared of slavery.
> I wanted to be . . . darker . . . deeper.
> These are dreams but the wounds remain
> and there are no meetings of ourselves
> at these crossroads.

Lights change. The Auction Block. Jeannie moves bench center to be the auction block, but then improvises with Robbie, deciding to move big table there instead. Jeannie takes bench down left. Robbie steps onto auction block, takes off her sack dress, drops it on

the block. She is naked. Jeannie starts to chant, "Bid 'em in,"
coaxing the Audience, taking time to thank them for joining in. It
should be a moment of communion.

ROBBIE:

On the auction block. With my socks rolled down,

I take off my sack dress. Mistress? Come on.

This is what they brought us here for.

On the auction block. They put their hands all down our
bodies

to sell you, for folks to measure you, smeltcha . . .

They say in Ecuador where 40% of the population is
African,

that Jesuits heaped us into huts by the hundreds

and listened while we bred.

JEANNIE: That's what they brought us here for.

Auction block light is blue. Jeannie circles down near Audience,
leading the chant, and back to dim light up right.

ROBBIE *(Still naked)*: Aunt Jessie said that's how they got their
manhood on the plantations. They'd come down to the quar-
ters and do it to us and the chickens.
A TIGHTNESS BETWEEN HER THIGHS. WHEN
IT LETS GO SHE SCREAMS WITH TERROR. AND
THEN TIGHTENS AGAIN. WHY DOES SHE KEEP
COMING TO ME IN THESE NIGHTMARES? THEY
SAY SALLY WAS TOUGH. BOUGHT A HOUSE AFTER
SLAVERY TIME. TAUGHT HER DAUGHTERS TO BE
LADIES. ASKED THE WHITE MAN, HOW MUCH
WAS THE HOUSE ON 23RD STREET. HE TOLD HER
AND LAUGHED. LIVING IN ONE OF THE RED
HOUSES, PAYING BY THE MONTH, TOOK IN WASH-
ING, CLEANED UP THEIR HOUSES FOR MONEY.
SHE ALWAYS SAID FOR MONEY. TOOK $750 TO
THE BANK, WHICH IS WHERE THE COLORED
HAD TO GO TO GET THE PAPER FOR PROPERTY.

SAID SHE DID ALL THAT AND NONE OF US EVER
HAD TO BE WHORES.

*Jeannie ends chant, signaling with her hands like a conductor.
Robbie asks the light board operator to bring up the lights as she
picks up the sack dress and holds it in front of her.*

(To Audience) I wanted to do this—stand naked in public on
the auction block. I thought somehow it could help free us
from *this*. *(Refers to her naked body)* Any old socialist knows,
one can't be free till all are free.

Lights back to auction-block blue. Robbie curls down onto block.

In the dream I. I am Sally being *(An involuntary sound of pain)*
b'ah. Bein' bein' I...I being bound down I didn't I didn't
wanna be in the dream, bound down in the dream I am I am
Sally being done it to I am down on the groundbeing done it to
bound down didn't wanna be bound down on the ground. In
the dream I am Sally down on the groundbeing done it to. In
the dream I am Sally being done it to bound down on the
ground.

*Jeannie moves auction block back, places chairs down right and
crosses past Robbie to bench. Robbie, carrying dress, goes to Jeannie's light.*

6. In a Rape Crisis Center

ROBBIE *(Putting on dress)*: Before they changed the Bill of Rights/
Constitution/Articles of Confederation—whatever it was for
white men before they changed it—it said they all had a right
to land, cattle, Negroes, and other livestock . . . pigs . . . dogs . . .
JEANNIE *(Curled up on bench)*:
    To be raped is not to scream
    but to whimper and lock and never to remember
    but feel the closing in the thighs

between the legs locking up everything
biting lips, the teeth bleed.

ROBBIE:

On the plantation you hafta stay tough and tight
no matter how many times they come down there.
Sally stayed down there with us in the quarters
and at night they pulled us out in the dirt.

Jeannie crosses to chairs, stands. Robbie crosses to bench, sits.

Wasn't nothing to it. You just stay tight till they finish. Sally
worked in the house, but she stayed down in the quarters with
us. He took Sally out on the ground.

JEANNIE: In a rape crisis center, your wounds are fresh. They can
put warm cloths on you, tell you it's not your fault.

ROBBIE:

Wadn't nuthin' to it. The others watched.
Sometimes they did it too.

Pause. She crosses and stands down left of Jeannie.

They say Sally had
dem chillun by the massa like it was supposed
to a been something. Shit, Thomas' Sally was just as
much a slave as our grandma and it was just as much a
rape.
One Sally's rape by the massa no gooder n'an n'othern.

JEANNIE: All anyone would have to do is keep you warm.

ROBBIE: After slaverytime, say Sally married Gilford, a black man,
and they had two boys. And nobody, not even them two chillun she had by the massa—which is what everybody called 'em
like that was supposed to a been something—nobody ever
blamed Sally for calling them two *boys* her real chillun.

JEANNIE: There's no reason to feel that cold all the time.

ROBBIE: COLD. VERY COLD. VERY VERY VERY COLD.

JEANNIE: Someone would give you a cup of tea. Hot chocolate.
Warm milk.

ROBBIE: These new ones with the alligators act like they wadn't born with no memory. I don't know what all went on underneath those houses of women and silent men.

JEANNIE: Herb tea.

ROBBIE: You . . . let the cabs roll by . . . let shit roll off your back . . . *stay* . . . ain't no rape crisis center on the plantation.

JEANNIE: Then what do you do about it?

7. Talking About Different Schools, and How to Do

Pause. Robbie crosses over to chairs. They both sit.

ROBBIE: My Ma Willie and my Aunt Jessie had a school. It was called—well, their school, I don't remember what it was called. But they had gone to Mr. Pierce's school. Now, Mr. Pierce's father or grandfather was—

JEANNIE: I think it was his grandfather.

ROBBIE: But Mr. Pierce himself had taught my grandmother and them, so it must have been his father who had been a slave and had worked in the big house and looked in and learned how the white folks do. So his son had a school called Mr. Pierce's School where the girls, and I reckon some of the boys, went to learn how to do. Now when my Ma Willie and Aunt Jessie opened their school it wasn't just for how to do. It was for reading, writing, and numbers, and Aunt—

JEANNIE: Tell them about the motto.

ROBBIE: Jeannie likes this. Back then they said, "Each one teach one." And that's how the learning was transmitted. My Aunt Jessie could name the capital and the river it was on of every state in the United States.

JEANNIE: Alphabetically.

ROBBIE: Alphabetically. One of the first words they learned was *garage*. It was a new word back then. Garage—a building in which you place an automobile.

JEANNIE: What about rhetoric?

ROBBIE: Oh yes, they learned rhetoric. My mother said rhetoric was learning to tell the truth over and over.

JEANNIE: You know we had classes in a garage too. But I think they were opposite. The whole idea was wild abandon. This was about a year before I invented the religion. But the whole thing was nature. My teacher had a long red ponytail and a drum under her arm, and we'd go running across the room. We were about six years old, all girls. Some forest...some beast...some storm...you know the whole thing—wild, free, running!

Robbie runs across the space and back.

Yeah, we were freer than that.

ROBBIE *(In her own world)*:

> What difference it a been, it a been by the master?
> They all come down there. They all do it to you.
> And do it to the chickens too.
> What difference it a been?

JEANNIE: What do you do about it? See, this section to me is where everything is clear. The difference in weight. I say the word "free," and what do you think of? A feather, or a butterfly. You say the word "free," it's totally different. It's light...substantial, flimsy...weighty...

ROBBIE: Come, let's do this.

Robbie and Jeannie get the auction block.

JEANNIE: I thought we weren't going to do this. It's so...art.

ROBBIE: Get up there. *(To light board operator)* Put the auction block lights on, please. *(To Jeannie)* Take off your dress. *(To Audience)* Let's do it for her, please....Bid 'em in. Bid 'em in.

Jeannie takes down one strap.

(To Jeannie) Do you have something to say? *(Jeannie shakes her head "no")* That's something right there.

Jeannie gets down and moves block back.

8. The Language Lesson

Robbie holds Jeannie by her shoulders from behind.

ROBBIE: Everybody know how on the day freedom come, we followed Uncle Buck up to the massa porch. And Uncle Buck said,

JEANNIE: Massa is we free?

ROBBIE: And that white man took out his shotgun, and said "Yeah, nigger, you free" and shot Uncle Buck dead.

JEANNIE: Massa is we free?

ROBBIE: Shot Uncle Buck dead.

JEANNIE: Massa is we free?

ROBBIE: Say it again.

JEANNIE: Is we free?

ROBBIE *(To Audience)*: They say Massa was mean and nasty. He was all dressed up, and the ladies too, and they all came back to the kitchen. And one of the uncles took the blame for stealing the bucket of fatback and greens that Sally was gon' bring down to the quarters for us. And they made him eat the whole bucket of fatback and greens, until he commenced to rolling on the floor and passing gas, and they laughed and laughed . . . and the ladies too.

JEANNIE: Is that it?

ROBBIE *(Aside)*: They say that day might not a been really rich white folks anyhow. *(To Audience)* On the day the really rich white folks came, they dressed up Sally and one of the uncles like staff, like house staff, so Massa and them would seem richer than they were and so we'd seem more profitable. They were figna sell us! Figna sell us further down south Georgia! If the war hadn't a come, no telling what woulda happened. *(Pause)* I reckon we'd a never been here to tell y'all this.

They call for Audience response. Robbie waves off dialogue. Jeannie sits on bench.

JEANNIE: But you were already in south Georgia. How much further down could you go?

ROBBIE *(Sits next to Jeannie)*: They say Sally had them children by the master to save us. How come they thought she had a choice? Survival is luck. Or unlucky.

They improvise. The following is an example of the dialogue that has resulted in performance.

You wanna try the language lesson?

JEANNIE: Okay. . . . They was from south o' Albany way down Seminole or Decatur.

ROBBIE: That's sort of—

JEANNIE: Jimmy Carter.

ROBBIE: Sort of a bad imitation of a white southerner.

JEANNIE: I'm not trying . . .

ROBBIE: As I've said before, try to know, like actors do, what you're talking about.

JEANNIE: Further south?

ROBBIE: Where slaves were sent, couldn't get back from, way away from their loved ones. It resonated dread. See it, know it, feel the dread when you say where that place was. *(Doing it)* They's from souf a Allbeny way down Semino o' De kaytuh.

JEANNIE: They's from south o' Al bany way down Semino o' Decatur.

ROBBIE: Better. When we learned the English language, we had to learn the English culture. I only learned later that iambic pentameter was street language . . . like rap . . . "To be or not to be, that is the question." Deep ambivalence. I could play Hamlet.

JEANNIE: If they let you.

ROBBIE: If I wanted to.

They sit quiet. Lights out. Applause.

Epilogue: Leaving the Audience Talking.

Lights up. Jeannie and Robbie get their cups of tea.

JEANNIE: There's a part we sort of want to do to involve the audience, but we get more involved . . .

ROBBIE: It has to do with talking to people, even if you already know 'em, and especially if you don't, how a lot of people in different cultures greet each other, I know some Native American cultures do: "Who are you and who are your people?" And where I come from, African-American folk be like, "Who children you?"

JEANNIE: So our idea was that you were going to turn to somebody else and find out something.

ROBBIE: Which you can do.

Robbie and Jeannie walk off.

GRANDMA SALLY

WORDS AND MUSIC BY ROBBIE McCAULEY

Grand - ma Sal - ly had two child-ren by the mas-ter.

One of 'em was my Grand-ma Alice, my mo-ther's grand-mo-ther,

where my mo ther got her name.

Copyright © 1993 by Robbie McCauley

THE DEATH OF THE LAST BLACK MAN IN THE WHOLE ENTIRE WORLD

SUZAN-LORI PARKS

One day I was taking a nap. Do you know how sometimes you dream something really hard, so when you wake up, you can see it? I had one of those waking dreams. When I woke up, I saw the title written on the wall. I said to myself, "You should write that down; you should write that down." So I went over to my desk and wrote it down.

The Writing Process

I try not to plan it too much. When I start writing a play, I usually start with a line. When I'm lucky, as with this play, I get the whole title. The title is the name of the thing so I know what to call it, how to call it; and it will come because I know its name. I float along, just writing, and then I get to a certain point where I need more underpinning. Have you ever seen them build a road, an overpass? They can go out really far and the road, with the concrete and the steel, is just hanging there. There's nothing supporting it underneath. It's the same way for me with the play. I can go out so far and then I have to support it somehow. So sometimes I need to plan a little bit, but I usually don't plan very much. I try to leave the page open to what comes. And I try to go with that.

Some people think that writing a play is about telling a story; maybe the playwright tells a story of her or his life; but for me, it's always about getting myself out of the way, letting the play come through. Of course, it has everything to do with me, but at the same time, it doesn't have anything to do with me. The question is, "Who am I/Who are we?" There isn't a simple answer. It's not the story of my life, but at the same time, it is.

Artistic Challenges and Discoveries

In *Last Black Man*, I allowed myself to go for sound over logical sense. Musicians do it all the time; they don't always follow the standard melody line. James Joyce did in *Finnegans Wake*.

Somebody can pick up a novel and put it down at their leisure, maybe talk with people in between readings. At a play, you sit down and you take it in. You also employ actors who are up there saying those words, who have been trained to understand plays in ways that might not help them perform your play. So when you're writing a play, it makes it that much more difficult to let go of sense and hold on to sound. But it's so important to do if theatre is going to keep going.

There are all these little sayings, like the phrase, "*That* rings true." So truth rings. Truth has a sound and a shape that might not explain or reveal itself logically to us, but will reveal itself through our other senses. In *Last Black Man*, it was so important to let the sound tell me where to go.

You read along and say, "Wow! What does that mean?" That question can be answered in the actual *digestion* of the line. We're not grappling with the words with only the front part of our brains; we're grappling with our whole digestive system. "Do in dip diddly did-did thuh drop/ Drop do it be dripted?/I say 'do.'" Eat it and see what happens, then you'll know.

It's a big challenge, a leap of faith for actors. We have a lot of fun. I am really grateful to all the great actors who agree to do my work. It just wouldn't happen without them.

The Aesthetic

I don't think about it. I have to be in it, so I can't be outside of it looking at it. All I know is that I work hard and I really push the form. I push the form because what I hear and see is so beautiful that I want to give black actors a chance to do some of the things that they don't often get invited to do. Don't get me wrong, there are a lot of great playwrights who are writing for black actors. I want more. I want them to have parts that really challenge their instrument; not just their emotional instrument, but their diction, their diaphragm.

There are only so many roles that really challenge the actor's entire instrument. I'm writing plays that challenge an actor's imagination and the imagination of an audience.

The mission of many plays is to tell a *known* history. But there are a lot of things that black people have done that haven't been written down— haven't been chronicled, are not remembered. There is a lot of history that has fallen through the gaps, the cracks; we read these events as having never happened. Those unchronicled events are what I'm interested in writing about.

The Power of the Word

Words are very old things. I love looking in the *Oxford English Dictionary*. The word "grammar" is etymologically connected to the word "charm." Most words have fabulous etymologies, thrilling histories. Because they're so old, they hold, they have that connection with what was. They're like charms—these old things in our mouths. Language is a physical act. It's something which happens in your entire body—not just in your head. Words are things that move our bodies, things we use onstage, and when we configure them in a slightly different way, it's magic—literally. People begin to appear who were never there. Like my character, And Bigger and Bigger and Bigger. Granted, he comes out of the novel *Native Son*, but through repeating, he gets even larger. Weird things begin to happen to that guy when I let him say his name over and over.

F/X of the Work

For directors and designers, I want them to be inspired to find new ways of working on their own work through working with me. That's what I get from them, so I want to give it back to them. I want to help them imagine the possibilities of theatre. Let's start digging and get our egos out of the way. This world is really incredible. Let's stop going over and over the same old ground and making the same old points.

For actors, I want them to really work hard—and they do—and have a good time. I want the same thing for the audience—to work hard and have fun; and on their way home, talk to whomever they came to see the show with and say, "Gee I didn't get it when that woman was walking across the stage. Was she dead?"/"Yeah, she was."/"Wow she was dead. Was the guy dead?"/"Yeah, they were all dead."/"Oh cool. I didn't get that." So I want everyone to feel and think and be inspired, have a good time and enjoy all the dumb jokes.

Definitions of Heroism

In *Last Black Man*, heroism is being there and seeing it through. I guess I have a greater understanding of the small gesture, or the great act that is also very small—like *being present*. He is present and trying to figure out what's wrong with him; she's present and trying to figure out what's wrong with him and what's wrong with her; and the spirit people come in to visit and their presence is helpful.

The Responsibility of the Theatre Artist

My sense of responsibility is not to the American theatre, it is to the figures who are in the play.

It is also important to give black actors work. When *Last Black Man* premiered at BACA Downtown in Brooklyn, it was a multiracial cast because I didn't have any feeling at that time that it needed to be an all-black cast. I didn't want people to jump to some easy political point about the play and sum it up in some quick statement. When Liz Diamond directed it at Yale Rep, she raised the question of an all-black cast and I agreed that we should give it a try. The play had received its first airing, so I thought that we should take another look at it from another point of view.

Since then I've really thought about what it means to have black people onstage. Just putting eleven black people onstage is in its own way moving and pushing the form of theatre. And eleven black people onstage whose conflict is something other than their conflict with white people is *very* avant-garde.

The Last Black Man's problem is that he is dead. His problem is not how he died or who killed him. It is: Am I dead? I think I'm dead. Who are you? Who am I? Who are these people who fill our house? What is this watermelon doing in my hand? Is this part of me? It doesn't look like my foot. Who are you again? It's the examination of a very small kind of question. Everybody asks those questions. It's not necessarily a race question, although it can be. I find that actors enjoy asking those questions because they are the questions that they ask in their daily lives.

Distinctions between Women's and Men's Writing

There is good writing and there is bad writing. Good writing is both very sexually rooted and not at the same time. When you're a good writer, you go beyond all your boundaries. That's part of what I mean by "getting out of the way."

The Darkness and the Light

As I've always understood it, we don't see light because it's moving so fast; we see what light illuminates. What I look at and look into is the place where light is not. I don't know if this is correct in the world of physics, but as a lay person very interested in physics, [I understand] there are places in space, like black holes, where there is no light. We sometimes think of vision as the light, or we're reaching toward the light, but actually I'm more interested in the things that are unseen. The darkness is what I look for, the unknown.

You could think of it in a couple of layers. I look into the darkness because that's where the people live who populate my plays. I bring them out, sometimes very much against their will. Maybe that's why it takes me so long to write a play. I can't physically pull them, drag them into this well-lit, clean place because they're much stronger than I am, they're much older. They have the gravitational pull of the black hole. I have to pull or invite the characters and at the same time not let them suck me into where they are because I don't live there. What I have to do is create a space in which they would like to be and convince them to come and live in my play; and so they come into the light, which in theatre of course is the stage. When a black actor walks into the light it's very much the same thing. You've created an environment in which that actor would like to be. I work like a dog to create an environment in which the character will visit long enough so that I can write it down.

I don't know if I'm moving toward the light. I think I'm moving deeper and deeper into that black hole. On opening night I'm moving toward the light. And when I'm in a play, really writing it, then there is light, but it's not sunlight or lamplight, it's light-weight. It's as if I could fly. Sometimes when I'm writing, I take a break and go for a walk or go to karate, and I feel if I just hopped off the curb a little bit too fast, I'd just fly off. In that sense, I'm definitely moving toward the *light*.

The tricky thing about the "light" and "dark" is the whole history of the way they've been used. We're taught that "dark" is the bad and "light" is the better one. I'm saying the darkness is basically where it's at. In the light is where we live—not greater, not better; it's just where we as humans exist. So I want the characters to come into where we exist so we can all experience them.

ABOUT THE AUTHOR

Suzan-Lori Parks is the author of *Imperceptible Mutabilities in the Third Kingdom*, produced by BACA Downtown in Brooklyn and awarded the 1990 Obie Award for Best Play. Her other plays include *Betting on the Dust Commander; The Sinner's Place; Fishes; Devotees in the Garden of Love*, premiered at Actors Theatre of Louisville's 1992 Humana Festival; *The America Play*, commissioned by Theatre for a New Audience, given workshop productions at Arena Stage and Dallas Theater Center in 1993, and to be presented by Yale Repertory Theatre in New Haven in January 1994 and at the Joseph Papp Public Theater as a co-production of the New York Shakespeare Festival, Yale Repertory and Theatre for a New Audience in February; and *Venus*, commissioned by the Women's Project and Productions. Parks is the recipient of two National Endowment for the Arts playwriting fellowships and has been awarded grants by the Rockefeller Foundation, the Ford Foundation, the New York State Council on the Arts and the New York Foundation for the Arts. She is an Associate Artist at the Yale School of Drama and a member of New Dramatists.

ABOUT THE WORK

The Death of the Last Black Man in the Whole Entire World was originally produced by BACA Downtown in Brooklyn in the fall of 1990, under the direction of Beth A. Schachter. It was subsequently presented as part of Yale Repertory Theatre's 1992 Winterfest in a production directed by Liz Diamond.

THE FIGURES

BLACK MAN WITH WATERMELON

BLACK WOMAN WITH FRIED DRUMSTICK

LOTS OF GREASE AND LOTS OF PORK

YES AND GREENS BLACK-EYED PEAS CORNBREAD

QUEEN-THEN-PHARAOH HATSHEPSUT

BEFORE COLUMBUS

OLD MAN RIVER JORDAN

HAM

AND BIGGER AND BIGGER AND BIGGER

PRUNES AND PRISMS

VOICE ON THUH TEE V

TIME

The present.

THE DEATH
OF THE LAST BLACK MAN
IN THE WHOLE ENTIRE WORLD

When I die,
I won't stay
Dead.

—BOB KAUFMAN

OVERTURE

BLACK MAN WITH WATERMELON: The black man moves his hands.

A bell sounds twice.

LOTS OF GREASE AND LOTS OF PORK: Lots of Grease and Lots of Pork.

QUEEN-THEN-PHARAOH HATSHEPSUT: Queen-then-Pharaoh Hatshepsut.

AND BIGGER AND BIGGER AND BIGGER: And Bigger and Bigger and Bigger.

PRUNES AND PRISMS: Prunes and Prisms.

HAM: Ham.

VOICE ON THUH TEE V: Voice on thuh Tee V.

OLD MAN RIVER JORDAN: Old Man River Jordan.

YES AND GREENS BLACK-EYED PEAS CORNBREAD: Yes and Greens Black-Eyed Peas Cornbread.

BEFORE COLUMBUS: Before Columbus.

A bell sounds once.

BLACK MAN WITH WATERMELON: The black man moves his hands.

QUEEN-THEN-PHARAOH HATSHEPSUT: Not yet. Let Queen-then-Pharaoh Hatshepsut tell you when.

LOTS OF GREASE AND LOTS OF PORK: This is the death of the last black man in the whole entire world.

A bell sounds three times.

BLACK WOMAN WITH FRIED DRUMSTICK: Yesterday today next summer tomorrow just uh moment uhgoh in 1317 dieded thuh last black man in thuh whole entire world. Uh! Oh. Dont be uhlarmed. Do not be afeared. It was painless. Uh painless passin. He falls twenty-three floors to his death. 23 floors from uh passin ship from space tuh splat on thuh pavement. He have uh head he been keepin under thuh Tee V. On his bottom pantry shelf. He have uh head that hurts. Dont fit right. Put it on tuh go tuh thuh store in it pinched him when he walks his thoughts dont got room. Why dieded he huh? Where he gonna go now that he done dieded? Where he gonna go tuh wash his hands?

YES AND GREENS BLACK-EYED PEAS CORNBREAD: You should write that down and you should hide it under a rock. This is the death of the last black man in the whole entire world.

LOTS OF GREASE AND LOTS OF PORK/PRUNES AND PRISMS: Not yet—

BLACK MAN WITH WATERMELON: The black man moves. His hands—

QUEEN-THEN-PHARAOH HATSHEPSUT: You are too young to move. Let me move it for you.

BLACK MAN WITH WATERMELON: The black man moves his hands. — He moves his hands round. Back. Back. Back tuh that.

LOTS OF GREASE AND LOTS OF PORK: (Not dat).

BLACK MAN WITH WATERMELON: When thuh worl usta be roun. Thuh worl usta be *roun.*

BLACK WOMAN WITH FRIED DRUMSTICK: Uh roun worl. Uh roun? Thuh worl? When was this.

QUEEN-THEN-PHARAOH HATSHEPSUT: Columbus. Before.

BEFORE COLUMBUS: Before. Columbus.

YES AND GREENS BLACK-EYED PEAS CORNBREAD: Before Columbus.

BLACK MAN WITH WATERMELON: HHH. HA!

QUEEN-THEN-PHARAOH HATSHEPSUT: Before Columbus thuh worl usta be *roun* they put uh /d/ on thuh end of roun makin roun*d*. Thusly they set in motion thuh end. Without that /d/ we coulda gone on spinnin forever. Thuh /d/ thing ended things ended.

YES AND GREENS BLACK-EYED PEAS CORNBREAD: Before Columbus.

A bell sounds twice.

BEFORE COLUMBUS: The popular thinking of the day back in them days was that the world was flat. They thought the world was flat. Back then when they thought the world was flat they were afeared and stayed at home. They wanted to go out back then when they thought the world was flat but the water had in it dragons of which meaning these dragons they were afeared back then when they thought the world was flat. They stayed at home. Them thinking the world was flat kept it roun. Them thinking the sun revolved around the earth kept them satellite-like. They figured out the truth and scurried out. Figuring out the truth put them in their place and they scurried out to put us in ours.

YES AND GREENS BLACK-EYED PEAS CORNBREAD: Mmmm. Yes. You should write this down. You should hide this under a rock.

LOTS OF GREASE AND LOTS OF PORK/PRUNES AND PRISMS: Not yet—

BLACK MAN WITH WATERMELON: The black man bursts into flames. The black man bursts into blames. Whose fault is it?

ALL: Aint mines.

BLACK MAN WITH WATERMELON: Whose fault is it?

ALL: Aint mines.

BLACK WOMAN WITH FRIED DRUMSTICK: I cant remember back that far.

QUEEN-THEN-PHARAOH HATSHEPSUT: And besides, I wasnt even there.

BLACK MAN WITH WATERMELON: Ha ha ha. The black man laughs out loud.

ALL *(Except Ham)*: HAM-BONE-HAM-BONE-WHERE-YOU-BEEN-ROUN-THUH-WORL-N-BACK-UH-*GAIN*.

YES AND GREENS BLACK-EYED PEAS CORNBREAD: Whatcha seen hambone girl?

BLACK WOMAN WITH FRIED DRUMSTICK: Didnt see you. I saw thuh worl.

QUEEN-THEN-PHARAOH HATSHEPSUT: I was there.

LOTS OF GREASE AND LOTS OF PORK: Didnt see you.

BLACK WOMAN WITH FRIED DRUMSTICK: I was there.

BLACK MAN WITH WATERMELON: Didnt see you. The black man moves his hands.

QUEEN-THEN-PHARAOH HATSHEPSUT: We are too young to see. Let them see it for you. We are too young to rule. Let them rule it for you. We are too young to have. Let them have it for you. You are too young to write. Let them—let them. Do it. Before you.

BLACK MAN WITH WATERMELON: The black man moves his hands.

YES AND GREENS BLACK-EYED PEAS CORNBREAD: You should write it down because if you dont write it down then they will come along and tell the future that we did not exist. You should write it down and you should hide it under a rock. You should write down the past and you should write down the present and in what in the future you should write it down. It will be of us but you should mention them from time to time so that in the future when they come along and know that they exist. You should hide it all under a rock so that in the future when they come along they will say that the rock did not exist.

BLACK WOMAN WITH FRIED DRUMSTICK: We getting somewheres. We getting down. Down down down down down down down down—

QUEEN-THEN-PHARAOH HATSHEPSUT: I saw Columbus comin./I saw Columbus comin goin over tuh visit you. "To borrow a cup of sugar," so he said. I waved my hands in warnin. You waved back. I aint seen you since.

LOTS OF GREASE AND LOTS OF PORK: In the future when they came along I meeting them. On thuh coast. Uh! Thuh Coast! I—was—so—polite. But in thuh dirt, I wrote: "Ha. Ha. Ha."

ALL: Ha. Ha. Ha. Ha. Ha. Ha. Ha. Ha. Ha. Ha. Ha. Ha. Ha. Ha. Ha. Ha. HHHHHHHHHHHHHHHH.

BLACK MAN WITH WATERMELON: Thuh black man he move. He move he hans.

A bell sounds once.

PANEL I: THUH HOLY GHOST

BLACK MAN WITH WATERMELON: Saint mines. Saint mines. Iduhnt it Nope: iduhnt. Saint mines cause everythin I calls mines got uh print uh me someway on it in it dont got uh print uh me someway on it so saint mines. Duhduhnt so saint: huh.

BLACK WOMAN WITH FRIED DRUMSTICK: Hen.

BLACK MAN WITH WATERMELON: Huh. Huh?

BLACK WOMAN WITH FRIED DRUMSTICK: Hen. Hen?

BLACK MAN WITH WATERMELON: Who give birth tuh this I wonder. Who gived birth tuh this. I wonder.

BLACK WOMAN WITH FRIED DRUMSTICK: You comed back. Comin backs somethin in itself. You comed back.

BLACK MAN WITH WATERMELON: This does not belong tuh me. Somebody planted this on me. On me in my hands.

BLACK WOMAN WITH FRIED DRUMSTICK: Cold compress. Cold compress then some hen. Lean back. You comed back. Lean back.

BLACK MAN WITH WATERMELON: Who gived birth tuh this I wonder who.

BLACK WOMAN WITH FRIED DRUMSTICK: Comin for you. Came for you: that they done did. Comin for tuh take you. Told me tuh pack up your clothes. Told me tuh cut my bed in 2 from double tuh single. Cut off thuh bed-foot where your feets had rested. Told me tuh do that too. Burry your ring in his hidin spot under thuh porch! That they told me too to do. Didnt have uh ring so I didnt do diddly. They told and told and told: proper instructions for thuh burial proper attire for thuh mournin. They told and told and told: I didnt do squat. Awe on that. You comed back. You got uhway. Knew you would. Hen?

BLACK MAN WITH WATERMELON: Who gived birth tuh this I wonder. Who? Not me. Saint mines.

BLACK WOMAN WITH FRIED DRUMSTICK: Killed every hen on thuh block. You comed back. Knew you would. Knew you would came back. Knew you will wanted uh good big hen dinner in waitin. Every hen on the block.

BLACK MAN WITH WATERMELON: Saint mines.

BLACK WOMAN WITH FRIED DRUMSTICK: Strutted down on up thuh road with my axe. By-my-self-with-my-axe. Got tuh thuh street top 93 dyin hen din hand. Dropped thuh axe. Tooked tuh stranglin. 93 dyin hen din hand with no heads let em loose tuh run down tuh towards home infront of me. Flipped thuh necks of thuh next 23 more odd. Slinged um over my shoulders. Hens of thuh neighbors now in my pots. Feathers of thuh hens of thuh neighbors stucked in our mattress. They told and told and told. On me. Huh. Awe on that. Hen? You got uhway. Knew you would.

BLACK MAN WITH WATERMELON: Who gived birth tuh me I wonder.

BLACK WOMAN WITH FRIED DRUMSTICK: They dont speak tuh us no more. They pass by our porch but they dont nod. You been comed back goin on 9 years not even heard from thuh neighbors uh congratulation. Uh alienationed dum. Uh guess. Huh. Hen? *WE AINT GOT NO FRIENDS,*—sweetheart.

BLACK MAN WITH WATERMELON: *SWEET-HEART.*

BLACK WOMAN WITH FRIED DRUMSTICK: Hen!!

BLACK MAN WITH WATERMELON: Aint hungry.

BLACK WOMAN WITH FRIED DRUMSTICK: Hen.

BLACK MAN WITH WATERMELON: Aint eaten in years.

BLACK WOMAN WITH FRIED DRUMSTICK: Hen?

BLACK MAN WITH WATERMELON: Last meal I had was my last-mans-meal.

BLACK WOMAN WITH FRIED DRUMSTICK: You got uhway. Knew you would.

BLACK MAN WITH WATERMELON: This thing dont look like me!

BLACK WOMAN WITH FRIED DRUMSTICK: It dont. Do it. Should it? Hen: eat it.

BLACK MAN WITH WATERMELON: I kin tell whats mines by whats gots my looks. Ssmymethod. Try it by testin it and it turns out true. Every time. Fool proofly. Look down at my foot and wonder if its mine. Foot mine? I kin ask it and foot answers back with uh "yes Sir"—not like you and me say "yes Sir" but uh "yes Sir" peculiar tuh thuh foot. Foot mine? I kin ask it and through uh look that looks like my looks thuh foot gives me back uh "yes Sir." Ssmymethod. Try by thuh test tuh pass for true. Move on tuh thuh uther foot. Foot mine? And uh nother "yes Sir" so feets mine is understood. Got uh forearm thats up for question check myself out teeth by tooth. Melon mine? —. Dont look like me.

BLACK WOMAN WITH FRIED DRUMSTICK: Hen mine? Gobble it up and it will be. You got uhway. Fixed uh good big hen dinner for you. Get yourself uh mouthful afore it rots.

BLACK MAN WITH WATERMELON: Was we green and stripe-dly when we first comed out?

BLACK WOMAN WITH FRIED DRUMSTICK: Uh huhn. Thuh features comes later. Later comes after now.

BLACK MAN WITH WATERMELON: Oh. Later comes now: melon mine?

BLACK WOMAN WITH FRIED DRUMSTICK: They comed for you and tooked you. That was yesterday. Today you sit in your chair where you sat yesterday and thuh day afore yesterday afore they comed and tooked you. Things today is just as they are yesterday cept nothin is familiar cause it was such uh long time uhgoh.

BLACK MAN WITH WATERMELON: Later oughta be now by now huh?: melon mine?

BLACK WOMAN WITH FRIED DRUMSTICK: Thuh chair was portable. They take it from county tuh county. Only got one. Can only eliminate one at uh time. Woulda fried you right here on thuh front porch but we dont got enough electric. No onessgot enough electric. Not on our block. Dont believe in havin

enough. Put thuh Chair in thuh middle of thuh City. Outdoors. In thuh square. Folks come tuh watch with picnic baskets. — Hen?

BLACK MAN WITH WATERMELON: Sweetheart?

BLACK WOMAN WITH FRIED DRUMSTICK: They juiced you some,
huh?

BLACK MAN WITH WATERMELON: Just a squirt. Sweetheart.

BLACK WOMAN WITH FRIED DRUMSTICK: Humpty Dumpty.

BLACK MAN WITH WATERMELON: Melon mines?

BLACK WOMAN WITH FRIED DRUMSTICK: Humpty damn Dumpty
actin like thuh Holy Ghost. You got uhway. Thuh lights
dimmed but you got uhway. Knew you would.

BLACK MAN WITH WATERMELON: They juiced me some.

BLACK WOMAN WITH FRIED DRUMSTICK: Just a squirt.

BLACK MAN WITH WATERMELON: They had theirselves uh extender chord. Fry uh man in thuh town square needs uh extender tuh reach em thuh electric Hook up thuh chair tuh
thuh power. Extender: 49 foot in length. Closer tuh thuh
power I never been. Flip on up thuh go switch. Huh! Juice begins its course.

BLACK WOMAN WITH FRIED DRUMSTICK: Humpty damn Dumpty.

BLACK MAN WITH WATERMELON: Thuh straps they have on me
are leathern. See thuh cord waggin full with uh jump-juice try
me tuh wiggle from thuh waggin but belt leathern straps:
width thickly. One round each forearm. Forearm mines? 2
cross thuh chest. Chest is mines: and it explodin. One for my
left hand fingers left strapted too. Right was done thuh same.
Jump-juice meets me-mine juices I do uh slow softshoe like on
water. Town crier cries uh moan. Felt my nappy head go frizzly. Town follows thuh crier in uh sorta sing-uhlong-song.

BLACK WOMAN WITH FRIED DRUMSTICK: Then you got uhway.
Got uhway in comed back.

BLACK MAN WITH WATERMELON: Uh extender chord 49 foot in
length. Turned on thuh up switch in I started runnin. First 49
foot I was runnin they was still juicin.

BLACK WOMAN WITH FRIED DRUMSTICK: And they chase-ted you.

BLACK MAN WITH WATERMELON: —Melon mines?

BLACK WOMAN WITH FRIED DRUMSTICK: When you broked tuh
seek your freedom they followed after, huh?

BLACK MAN WITH WATERMELON: Later oughta be now by now, huh?

BLACK WOMAN WITH FRIED DRUMSTICK: You comed back.

BLACK MAN WITH WATERMELON: —Not exactly.

BLACK WOMAN WITH FRIED DRUMSTICK: They comed for you tuh take you. Tooked you uhway: that they done did. You got uhway. Thuh lights dimmed. Had us uh brownout. You got past that. You comed back.

BLACK MAN WITH WATERMELON: Turned on thuh juice on me in me in I started runnin. First just runnin then runnin towards home. Couldnt find us. Think I got lost. Saw us on up uhhead but I flew over thuh yard. Couldnt stop. Think I overshot.

BLACK WOMAN WITH FRIED DRUMSTICK: Killed every hen on thuh block. Made you uh—

BLACK MAN WITH WATERMELON: Make me uh space 6 feet by 6 feet by 6. Make it big and mark it so as I wont miss it. If you would please, sweetness, uh mass grave-site. Theres company comin soonish. I would like tuh get up and go. I would like tuh move my hands.

BLACK WOMAN WITH FRIED DRUMSTICK: You comed back.

BLACK MAN WITH WATERMELON: Overshot. Overshot. I would like tuh move my hands.

BLACK WOMAN WITH FRIED DRUMSTICK: Cold compress?

BLACK MAN WITH WATERMELON: Sweetheart.

BLACK WOMAN WITH FRIED DRUMSTICK: How uhbout uh hen leg?

BLACK MAN WITH WATERMELON: Nothanks. Justate.

BLACK WOMAN WITH FRIED DRUMSTICK: Just ate?

BLACK MAN WITH WATERMELON: Justate. Thatsright. 6 by 6 by 6. Thatsright.

BLACK WOMAN WITH FRIED DRUMSTICK: Oh. —. They eat their own yuh know.

BLACK MAN WITH WATERMELON: HooDoo.

BLACK WOMAN WITH FRIED DRUMSTICK: Hen do. Saw it on thuh Tee V.

BLACK MAN WITH WATERMELON: Aint that nice.

A bell sounds once.

PANEL II: FIRST CHORUS

BLACK MAN WITH WATERMELON: 6 by 6 by 6.

ALL: THATS RIGHT.

BLACK WOMAN WITH FRIED DRUMSTICK: Oh. They eat their own you know.

ALL: HOODOO.

BLACK WOMAN WITH FRIED DRUMSTICK: Hen do. Saw it on thuh Tee V.

ALL: Aint that nice.

AND BIGGER AND BIGGER AND BIGGER: WILL SOMEBODY TAKE THESE STRAPS OFF UH ME PLEASE? I WOULD LIKE TUH MOVE MY HANDS.

PRUNES AND PRISMS: Prunes and prisms will begin: prunes and prisms prunes and prisms prunes and prisms and prunes and prisms: 23.

VOICE ON THUH TEE V: Good evening. I'm Broad Caster. Headlining tonight: the news: is Gamble Major, the absolutely last living Negro man in the whole entire known world—is dead. Major Gamble, born a slave, taught himself the rudiments of education to become a spearhead in the Civil Rights Movement. He was 38 years old. News of Major's death sparked controlled displays of jubilation in all corners of the world.

PRUNES AND PRISMS: Oh no no: world is roun.

AND BIGGER AND BIGGER AND BIGGER: WILL SOMEBODY TAKE THESE STRAPS OFF UH ME PLEASE? I WOULD LIKE TUH MOVE MY HANDS.

A bell sounds four times.

LOTS OF GREASE AND LOTS OF PORK: This is the death of the last black man in the whole entire world.

PRUNES AND PRISMS: Not yet—

VOICE ON THUH TEE V: Good evening. Broad Caster. Headline tonight: Gamble Major, the absolutely last living Negro man in the whole known entire world is dead. Gamble Major born a slave rose to become a spearhead in the Civil Rights Movement. He was 38 years old. The Civil Rights Movement. He was 38 years old.

AND BIGGER AND BIGGER AND BIGGER: WILL SOMEBODY TAKE THESE STRAPS OFF UH ME PLEASE? I WOULD LIKE TUH MOVE MY HANDS.

LOTS OF GREASE AND LOTS OF PORK: This is the death of the last black man in the whole entire world.

A bell sounds three times.

PRUNES AND PRISMS: Prunes and prisms prunes and prisms prunes and prisms prunes and prisms.

QUEEN-THEN-PHARAOH HATSHEPSUT: Yesterday tuhday next summer tuhmorrow just uh moment uhgoh in 1317 dieded thuh last black man in thuh whole entire world. Uh! Oh. Dont be uhlarmed. Do not be afeared. It was painless. Uh painless passin. He falls 23 floors to his death.

PRUNES AND PRISMS: No.

QUEEN-THEN-PHARAOH HATSHEPSUT: 23 floors from uh passin ship from space tuh splat on thuh pavement.

PRUNES AND PRISMS: No.

QUEEN-THEN-PHARAOH HATSHEPSUT: He have uh head he been keepin under thuh Tee V. On his bottom pantry shelf.

PRUNES AND PRISMS: No.

QUEEN-THEN-PHARAOH HATSHEPSUT: He have uh head that hurts. Dont fit right. Put it on tuh go tuh thuh store in it pinched him when he walks his thoughts dont got room. Why dieded he huh?

PRUNES AND PRISMS: No.

QUEEN-THEN-PHARAOH HATSHEPSUT: Where he gonna go now that he done dieded?

PRUNES AND PRISMS: No.

BLACK WOMAN WITH FRIED DRUMSTICK: Where he gonna go tuh wash his hands?

ALL: You should write that down. You should write that down and you should hide it under uh rock.

VOICE ON THUH TEE V: Good evening. Broad Caster. Headlinin tonight: thuh news:

OLD MAN RIVER JORDAN: Tell you of uh news. Last news. Last news of thuh last man. Last man had last words say hearin it.

He spoked uh speech spoked hisself uh chatter-tooth babble "ya-oh-may/chuh-naw" dribblin down his lips tuh puddle in his lap. Dribblin by droppletts. Drop by drop. Last news. News flashes then drops. Thuh last drop was uh all uhlone drop. Singular. Thuh last drop started it off it all. Started off with uh drop. Started off with uh jungle. Started sproutin in his spittle growin leaves off of his mines and thuh vines say drippin doin it. Last news leads tuh thuh first news. He is dead he crosses thuh river. He jumps in thuh puddle have his clothing: ON. On thuh other side thuh mountin yo he dripply wet with soppin. Do drop be dripted? I say "yes."

BLACK MAN WITH WATERMELON: Dont leave me hear. Dont leave me. Hear?

QUEEN-THEN-PHARAOH HATSHEPSUT: Where he gonna go tuh wash his dribblin hands?

PRUNES AND PRISMS: Where he gonna go tuh dry his dripplin clothes?

YES AND GREENS BLACK-EYED PEAS CORNBREAD: Did you write it down? On uh little slip uh paper stick thuh slip in thuh river afore you slip in that way you keep your clothes dry, man.

PRUNES AND PRISMS: Aintcha heard uh that trick?

BEFORE COLUMBUS: That tricks thuh method.

QUEEN-THEN-PHARAOH HATSHEPSUT: They used it on uhlong uhgoh still works every time.

OLD MAN RIVER JORDAN: He jumped in thuh water without uh word for partin come out dripply wet with soppin. Do drop be dripted? I say "do."

BLACK MAN WITH WATERMELON: In you all theres kin. You all kin. Kin gave thuh first permission kin be givin it now still. Some things is all thuh ways gonna be uh continuin sort of uh some thing. Some things go on and on till they dont stop. I am soppin wet. I left my scent behind in uh bundle of old clothing that was not thrown out. Left thuh scent in thuh clothin in thuh clothin on uh rooftop. Dogs surround my house and laugh. They are mockin thuh scent that I left behind. I jumped in thuh water without uh word. I jumped in thuh water without uh smell. I am in thuh river and in my skin is soppin wet. I would like tuh stay afloat now. I would like tuh move my hands.

AND BIGGER AND BIGGER AND BIGGER: Would somebody take these straps off uh me please? I would like tuh move my hands.

BLACK MAN WITH WATERMELON: Now kin kin I move my hands?

QUEEN-THEN-PHARAOH HATSHEPSUT: My black man my subject man my man uh all mens my my my no no not yes no not yes thuh hands. Let Queen-then-Pharaoh Hatshepsut tell you when. She is I am. An I am she passing by with her train. Pulling it behind her on uh plastic chain. Ooooh who! Ooooooh who! Where you gonna go now, now that you done dieded?

ALL: Ha ha ha.

PRUNES AND PRISMS: Say "prunes and prisms" 40 times each day and youll cure your big lips. Prunes and prisms prunes and prisms prunes and prisms: 19.

QUEEN-THEN-PHARAOH HATSHEPSUT: An I am Sheba-like she be me am passin on by she with her train. Pullin it behind/he on uh plastic chain. Oooh who! Oooh who! Come uhlong. Come uhlong.

BLACK WOMAN WITH FRIED DRUMSTICK: Say he was waitin on thuh right time.

AND BIGGER AND BIGGER AND BIGGER: Say he was waitin in thuh wrong line.

BLACK MAN WITH WATERMELON: I jumped in thuh river without uh word. My kin are soppin wet.

QUEEN-THEN-PHARAOH HATSHEPSUT: Come uhlong. Come uhlong.

PRUNES AND PRISMS: Prunes and prisms prunes and prisms.

LOTS OF GREASE AND LOTS OF PORK: This is the death of the last black man in the whole entire world.

PRUNES AND PRISMS: Not yet.

LOTS OF GREASE AND LOTS OF PORK: Back tuh when thuh worl usta be roun.

QUEEN-THEN-PHARAOH HATSHEPSUT: Come uhlong come uhlong get on board come uhlong.

OLD MAN RIVER JORDAN: Back tuh that. Yes.

YES AND GREENS BLACK-EYED PEAS CORNBREAD: Back tuh when thuh worl usta be roun.

OLD MAN RIVER JORDAN: Uhcross thuh river in back tuh that. Yes. Do in diddly dip didded thuh drop. Out to thuh river uhlong to thuh sea. Long thuh long coast. Skirtin. Yes. Skirtin back tuh that. Come up back flip take uhway like thuh waves do. Far uhway. Uhway tuh where they dont speak thuh language and where they dont want tuh. Huh. Go on back tuh that.

YES AND GREENS BLACK-EYED PEAS CORNBREAD: Awe on uh interior before uh demarcation made it mapped. Awe on uh interior with out uh road-word called macadam. Awe onin uh interior that was uh whole was once. Awe on uh whole roun worl uh roun worl with uh river.

OLD MAN RIVER JORDAN: In thuh interior was uh river. Huh. Back tuh that.

ALL: Thuh river was roun as thuh worl was. Roun.

OLD MAN RIVER JORDAN: He hacks his way through thuh tall grass. Tall grass scratch. Width: thickly. Grasses thickly comin from all angles at im. He runs along thuh path worn out by uh 9 million paddin bare footed feet. Uh path overgrown cause it aint as all as happened as of yet. Tuh be extracted from thuh jungle first he gotta go in hide.

BLACK MAN WITH WATERMELON: Chase-ted me outa thuh trees now they tree me. Thuh dogs come out from their hidin spots under thuh porch and give me uhway. Thuh hidin spot was under thuh porch of uh house that werent there as of yet. Thuh dogs give me uhway by uh laugh aimed at my scent.

AND BIGGER AND BIGGER AND BIGGER: HA HA HA. Thats how thuh laugh sorta like be wentin.

PRUNES AND PRISMS: Where he gonna go now now that he done dieded?

QUEEN-THEN-PHARAOH HATSHEPSUT: Where he gonna go tuh move his hands?

BLACK MAN WITH WATERMELON: I. I. I would like tuh move my hands.

YES AND GREENS BLACK-EYED PEAS CORNBREAD: Back tuh when thuh worl usta be roun.

LOTS OF GREASE AND LOTS OF PORK: Uh roun. Thuh worl? Uh roun worl? When was this?

OLD MAN RIVER JORDAN: Columbus. Before.

PRUNES AND PRISMS: Before Columbus?

AND BIGGER AND BIGGER AND BIGGER: Ha!

QUEEN-THEN-PHARAOH HATSHEPSUT: Before Columbus thuh worl usta be roun. They put uh /d/ on thuh end of roun makin roun*d*. Thusly they set in motion thuh enduh. Without that /d/ we could uh gone on spinnin forever. Thuh /d/ thing endiduh things endiduh.

BEFORE COLUMBUS: Before Columbus:

A bell sounds once.

Thuh popular thinkin kin of thuh day back then in them days was that thuh worl was flat. They thought thuh worl was flat. Back then kin in them days when they thought thuh worl was flat they were afeared and stayed at home. They wanted tuh go out back then when they thought thuh worl was flat but thuh water had in it dragons.

AND BIGGER AND BIGGER AND BIGGER: Not lurkin in thuh sea but lurkin in thuh street, see? Sir name Tom-us and Bigger be my christian name. Rise up out of uh made-up story in grown Bigger and Bigger. Too big for my own name. Nostrils: flarin. Width: thickly. Breath: fire-laden and smellin badly.

BLACK WOMAN WITH FRIED DRUMSTICK: Huh. Whiffit.

BEFORE COLUMBUS: Dragons, of which meanin these dragons they were afeared back then. When they thought thuh worl was flat. They stayed at home. Them thinkin thuh worl was flat kept it roun. Them thinkin thuh sun revolved uhroun thuh earth kin kept them satellite-like. They figured out thuh truth and scurried out. Figurin out thuh truth kin put them in their place and they scurried out tuh put us in ours.

YES AND GREENS BLACK-EYED PEAS CORNBREAD: Mmmmm. Yes. You should write that down. You should write that down and you should hide it under uh rock.

BEFORE COLUMBUS: Thuh earthsgettin level with thuh land land HO and thuh lands gettin level with thuh sea.

PRUNES AND PRISMS: Not yet—

QUEEN-THEN-PHARAOH HATSHEPSUT: An I am Sheba she be me. Youll mutter thuh words and part thuh waves and come uhlong come uhlong.

AND BIGGER AND BIGGER AND BIGGER: I would like tuh fit in

back in thuh storybook from which I camed.

BLACK MAN WITH WATERMELON: My text was writ in water. I would like tuh drink it down.

QUEEN-THEN-PHARAOH HATSHEPSUT: Down tuh float drown tuh float down. My son erased his mothers mark.

AND BIGGER AND BIGGER AND BIGGER: I am grown too big for thuh word thats me.

PRUNES AND PRISMS: Prunes and prisms prunes and prisms prunes and prisms: 14.

QUEEN-THEN-PHARAOH HATSHEPSUT: An I am Sheba me am (She be doo be wah waaaah doo wah). Come uhlong come on uhlong on.

BEFORE COLUMBUS: Before Columbus directs thuh traffic: left right left right.

PRUNES AND PRISMS: Prunes and prisms prunes and prisms.

QUEEN-THEN-PHARAOH HATSHEPSUT: I left my mark on all I made. My son erase his mothers mark.

BLACK WOMAN WITH FRIED DRUMSTICK: Where you gonna go now now that you done dieded?

AND BIGGER AND BIGGER AND BIGGER: Would somebody take these straps offuh me please? Gaw*. I would like tuh drink in drown—

BEFORE COLUMBUS: There is uh tiny land mass just above my reach.

LOTS OF GREASE AND LOTS OF PORK: There is uh tiny land mass just outside of my vocabulary.

OLD MAN RIVER JORDAN: Do in dip diddly did-did thuh drop? Drop do it be dripted? Uh huh.

BEFORE COLUMBUS: Land:

AND BIGGER AND BIGGER AND BIGGER: HO!

QUEEN-THEN-PHARAOH HATSHEPSUT: I saw Columbus comin Before Columbus comin/goin over tuh meet you—

BEFORE COLUMBUS: Thuh first time I saw it. It was huge. Thuh green sea becomes uh hillside. Uh hillside populated with some peoples I will name. Thuh first time I saw it it was uh

---

*A glottal stop and choking sound.

was-huge once one. Huh. It has been gettin smaller ever since.

QUEEN-THEN-PHARAOH HATSHEPSUT: Land:

BLACK MAN WITH WATERMELON: HO!

A bell sounds once.

PANEL III: THUH LONESOME 3SOME

BLACK MAN WITH WATERMELON: It must have rained. Gaw. Must-uh-rained-on-down-us-why. Aint that somethin. Must uh rained! Gaw. Our crops have prospered. Must uh rained why aint that somethin why aint that somethin-somethin gaw somethin: nice.

BLACK WOMAN WITH FRIED DRUMSTICK: Funny.

BLACK MAN WITH WATERMELON: Gaw. Callin on it spose we did: gaw—thuh uhrainin gaw huh? Gaw gaw. Lookie look-see gaw: where there were riv-lets now there are some. Gaw. Cement tuh mudment accomplished with uh gaw uh flick of my wrist gaw. Huh. Look here now there is uh gaw uh wormlett. Came out tuhday. In my stools gaw gaw gaw gaw they all out tuhday. Come out tuh breathe gaw dontcha? Sure ya dontcha sure gaw ya dontcha sure ya dontcha do yall gaw. Gaw. Our one melon has given intuh 3. Callin what it gived birth callin it gaw. 3 August hams out uh my hands now surroundin me an is all of um mines? GAW. Uh huhn. Gaw gaw. Cant breathe.

BLACK WOMAN WITH FRIED DRUMSTICK: Funny how they break when I dropped em. Though they was past that. Huh. 3 broke in uh row. Guess mmm on uh roll uh some sort, huh. Hell. Huh. Whiffit.

BLACK MAN WITH WATERMELON: Gaw. Gaw. Cant breathe.

BLACK WOMAN WITH FRIED DRUMSTICK: Some things still hold. Huh. Uh old layed eggull break after droppin most likely. Huh. 4 in uh row. Awe on that.

BLACK MAN WITH WATERMELON: Gaw. Cant breathe you.

BLACK WOMAN WITH FRIED DRUMSTICK: You dont need to. No need for breathin for you no more, huh? 5. 6. Mm makin uh history. 7-hhh 8-hhh mm makin uh mess. Huh. Whiffit.

BLACK MAN WITH WATERMELON: Gaw. Gaw loosen my collar. No air in here.

BLACK WOMAN WITH FRIED DRUMSTICK: 7ssgot uh red dot. Awe on that.

BLACK MAN WITH WATERMELON: Sweetheart—. SWEET-HEART?!

BLACK WOMAN WITH FRIED DRUMSTICK: 9. Chuh. Funny. Funny. Somethin still holdin on. Let me loosen your collar for you you comed home after uh hard days work. Your suit: tied. Days work was runnin from them we know aint chase-ted you. You comed back home after uh hard days work such uh hard days work that now you cant breath you. Now.

BLACK MAN WITH WATERMELON: Dont take it off just loosen it. Dont move thuh tree branch let thuh tree branch be.

BLACK WOMAN WITH FRIED DRUMSTICK: Your days work aint like any others day work: you bring your tree branch home. Let me loosen thuh tie let me loosen thuh neck-lace let me loosen up thuh noose that stringed him up let me leave thuh tree branch be. Let me rub your wrists.

BLACK MAN WITH WATERMELON: Gaw. Gaw.

BLACK WOMAN WITH FRIED DRUMSTICK: Some things still hold. Wrung thuh necks of them hens and they still give eggs. Huh: Like you. Still sproutin feathers even after they fried. Huh: like you too. 10. Chuh. Eggs still break. Thuh mess makes uh stain. Thuh stain makes uh mark. Whiffit. Whiffit.

BLACK MAN WITH WATERMELON: Put me on uh platform tuh wait for uh train. Uh who who uh who who uh where ya gonna go now—. Platform hitched with horses/steeds. Steeds runned off in left me there swingin. It had begun tuh rain. Hands behind my back. This time tied. I had heard of uh word called scaffold and thought that perhaps they just might build me one of um but uh uhn naw just outa my vocabulary but uh uhn naw trees come cheaply.

BLACK WOMAN WITH FRIED DRUMSTICK: 8. 9. I aint hungry. 9. 10. You dont eat. Dont need to.

BLACK MAN WITH WATERMELON: Swingin from front tuh back uhgain. Back tuh—back tuh that was how I be wentin. Chin on my chest hangin down in restin eyes each on eyein my 2 feets. Left on thuh right one right one on thuh left. Crossed eyin. It was difficult tuh breathe. Toes uncrossin then crossin for luck. With my eyes. Gaw. It had begun tuh rain. Oh. Gaw. Ever so lightly. Blood came on up. You know: tough. Like riggamartins-stifly only—isolated. They some of em pointed they summoned uh laughed they some looked quick in an then they looked uhway. It had begun tuh rain. I hung on out tuh dry. They puttin uhway their picnic baskets. Ever so lightly gaw gaw it had begun tuh rain. They pullin out their umbrellas in hidedid up their eyes. Oh.

BLACK WOMAN WITH FRIED DRUMSTICK: I aint hungry you dont eat 12 13 and thuh floor will shine. Look: there we are. You in me. Reflectin. Hello! Dont move—.

BLACK MAN WITH WATERMELON: It had begun tuh rain. Now: huh. Sky flew open and thuh light went ZAP. Tree bowed over till thuh branch said BROKE. Uhround my necklace my neck uhround my neck my tree branch. In full bloom. It had begun tuh rain. Feet hit thuh ground in I started runnin. I was wet right through intuh through. I was uh wet that dont get dry. Draggin on my tree branch on back tuh home.

BLACK WOMAN WITH FRIED DRUMSTICK: On back tuh that.

BLACK MAN WITH WATERMELON: Gaw. What was that?

BLACK WOMAN WITH FRIED DRUMSTICK: "On back tuh that"? Huh. Somethin I figured. Huh. Chuh. Lord. Who! Whiffit.

BLACK MAN WITH WATERMELON: When I dieded they cut me down. Didnt have no need for me no more. They let me go.

BLACK WOMAN WITH FRIED DRUMSTICK: Thuh lights dimmed in thats what saved you. Lightnin comed down zappin trees from thuh sky. You got uhway.

BLACK MAN WITH WATERMELON: Not exactly.

BLACK WOMAN WITH FRIED DRUMSTICK: Oh. I see.

BLACK MAN WITH WATERMELON: They tired of me. Pulled me out of thuh trees then treed me then tired of me. Thats how it has gone. Thats how it be wentin.

BLACK WOMAN WITH FRIED DRUMSTICK: Oh. I see. Youve been dismissed. But-where-to? Must be somewhere else tuh go aside from just go gone. Huh. Whiffit: huh. You smell.

BLACK MAN WITH WATERMELON: Maybe I should bathe.

BLACK WOMAN WITH FRIED DRUMSTICK: I call those 3 thuh lonesome 3some. Maybe we should pray.

BLACK MAN WITH WATERMELON: Thuh lonesome 3some. Spose they'll do.

A bell sounds twice.

PANEL IV: SECOND CHORUS

OLD MAN RIVER JORDAN: Come in look tuh look-see.

VOICE ON THUH TEE V: Good evening this is thuh news. A small sliver of uh tree branch has been found in *The Death of the Last Black Man.* Upon careful examination thuh small sliver of thuh treed branch what was found has been found tuh be uh fossilized bone fragment. With this finding authorities claim they are hot on his tail.

PRUNES AND PRISMS: Uh small sliver of uh treed branch growed from-tuh uh bone.

AND BIGGER AND BIGGER AND BIGGER: WILL SOMEBODY WILL THIS ROPE FROM ROUND MY NECK GOD DAMN I WOULD LIKE TUH TAKE MY BREATH BY RIGHTS GAW GAW.

LOTS OF GREASE AND LOTS OF PORK: This is the death of the last black man in the whole entire world.

A bell sounds slowly twice.

BLACK MAN WITH WATERMELON: I had heard of uh word called scaffold and had hopes they just might maybe build me one but uh uh naw gaw—

HAM: There was uh tree with your name on it.

BLACK MAN WITH WATERMELON: Jumpin out of uh tree they chase me tree me back tuh thuh tree. Thats where I be came from. Thats where I be wentin.

YES AND GREENS BLACK-EYED PEAS CORNBREAD: Someone ought tuh. Write that down.

LOTS OF GREASE AND LOTS OF PORK: There is a page dog-eared at "Histree" hidin just outside my word hoard. Wheres he gonna come to now that he done gone from.

QUEEN-THEN-PHARAOH HATSHEPSUT: Wheres he gonna go come to now that he gonna go gone on?

OLD MAN RIVER JORDAN: For that you must ask Ham.

BLACK WOMAN WITH FRIED DRUMSTICK: Hen?

LOTS OF GREASE AND LOTS OF PORK: HAM.

QUEEN-THEN-PHARAOH HATSHEPSUT: Ham.

PRUNES AND PRISMS: Hmmmm.

A bell sounds twice.

HAM: Ham's Begotten Tree (catchin up to um *in medias res* that is we takin off from where we stopped up last time). Huh. NOW: She goned begotten One who in turn begotten Ours. Ours laughed one day uhloud in from thuh sound hittin thuh air smakity sprung up I, you, n He, She, It. They turned in engaged in simple multiplication thus tuh spawn of theirselves one We one You and one called They (They in certain conversation known as "Them" and in other certain conversation a.k.a. "Us"). Now very simply: Wassername she finally gave intuh It and tugether they broughted forth uh wildish one called simply Yo. Yo gone be wentin much too long without hisself uh comb in from thuh frizzly that resulted comed one called You (polite form). You (polite) birthed herself Mister, Miss, Maam and Sir who in his later years with That brought forth Yuh Fathuh. Thuh fact that That was uh mother tuh Yuh Fathuh didnt stop them 2 relations from havin relations. Those strange relations between That thuh mother and Yuh Fathuh thuh son brought forth uh odd lot: called: Yes Massuh, Yes Missy, Yes Maam n Yes Suh Mistuh Suh which goes tuh show that relations with your relations produces complications. Thuh children of That and Yuh Fathuh aside from being plain peculiar was all crosseyed. This defect enhanced their multiplicative possibilities, for example. Yes Suh Mistuh Suh breeded with hisself n gived us Wassername (thuh 2nd), and Wassernickname (2 twins in birth joindid at thuh lip). Thuh 2 twins lived next door tuh one called Uhnother bringin forth Themuhns, She (thuh 2nd), Auntie, Cousin, and Bro who makeshifted continuous compensations for his loud and oderiferous bodily emissions by all thuh time saying excuse me n through his graciousness brought forth They (polite) who had mixed feelins with She (thuh 2nd) thus bringin forth Ussin who then went on tuh have MeMines.

YES AND GREENS BLACK-EYED PEAS CORNBREAD: Thuh list goes on in on.

HAM: MeMines gived out 2 offspring one she called Mines after herself thuh uther she called Themuhns named after all them who comed before. Themuhns married outside thuh tribe joinin herself with uh man they called WhoDat. Themuhns in WhoDat brought forth only one child called WhoDatDere. Mines joined up with Wasshisname and from that union come AllYall.

BEFORE COLUMBUS: All us?

HAM: No. AllYall.

LOTS OF GREASE AND LOTS OF PORK: This list goes on in on.

HAM: Ah yes: Yo suddenly if by majic again became productive in after uh lapse of some great time came back intuh circulation to wiggled uhbout with Yes Missy (one of thuh crosseyed daughters of That and Yuh Fathuh). Yo in Yes Missy begottin ThissunRightHere, Us, ThatOne, She (thuh 3rd) and one called Uncle (who from birth was gifted with great singin and dancin capabilities which helped him make his way in life but tended tuh bring shame on his family).

BEFORE COLUMBUS/BLACK MAN WITH WATERMELON: Shame on his family.

LOTS OF GREASE AND LOTS OF PORK/BLACK MAN WITH WATER-MELON: Shame on his family.

AND BIGGER AND BIGGER AND BIGGER/BLACK MAN WITH WA-TERMELON: Shamed on his family gaw.

YES AND GREENS BLACK-EYED PEAS CORNBREAD: Write that down.

OLD MAN RIVER JORDAN: (Ham seed his daddy Noah neckked. From that seed, comed Allyall.)

A bell sounds twice.

AND BIGGER AND BIGGER AND BIGGER: (Will somebody please will this rope—)

VOICE ON THUH TEE V: Good evening. This is thuh news: Whose fault is it?

BLACK MAN WITH WATERMELON: Saint mines.

VOICE ON THUH TEE V: Whose fault iszit??!

ALL: Saint mines!

OLD MAN RIVER JORDAN: I cant re-member back that far. (Ham can—but uh uh naw gaw—Ham wuduhnt there, huh).

ALL: HAM BONE HAM BONE WHERE YOU BEEN ROUN THUH WORL N BACK A-GAIN.

QUEEN-THEN-PHARAOH HATSHEPSUT: Whatcha seen. Hambone girl?

BLACK WOMAN WITH FRIED DRUMSTICK: Didnt see you. I saw thuh worl.

HAM: I was there.

PRUNES AND PRISMS: Didnt see you.

HAM: I WAS THERE.

VOICE ON THUH TEE V: Didnt see you.

BLACK MAN WITH WATERMELON/AND BIGGER AND BIGGER AND BIGGER: THUH BLACK MAN. HE MOOOVE.

ALL: HAM BONE HAM BONE WHATCHA DO? GOT UH CHANCE N FAIRLY FLEW.

BLACK WOMAN WITH FRIED DRUMSTICK: Over thuh front yard.

BLACK MAN WITH WATERMELON: Overshot.

ALL: 6 BY 6 BY 6.

BLACK MAN WITH WATERMELON: Thats right.

AND BIGGER AND BIGGER AND BIGGER: WILL SOMEBODY WILL THIS ROPE—

ALL: Good evening. This is the news.

VOICE ON THUH TEE V: Whose fault is it?

ALL: Saint mines!

VOICE ON THUH TEE V: Whose fault iszit?!!

HAM: SAINT MINES!

A bell rings twice.

—Ham. Is. Not. Tuh. BLAME! WhoDatDere joinded with one called Sir 9th generation of thuh first Sir son or You (polite) thuh first daughter of You WhoDatDere with thuh 9th Sir begettin forth Him—

BLACK MAN WITH WATERMELON: Ham?!

ALL *(Except Ham)*: HIM!

BLACK WOMAN WITH FRIED DRUMSTICK: Sold.

HAM: SOLD! allyall[9] not tuh be confused w/allus[12] joinded w/allthem[3] in from that union comed forth wasshisname[21] SOLD wassername[19] still by thuh reputation uh thistree one uh thuh 2 twins loses her sight through fiddlin n falls w/ugly old yuhfathuh[4] given she[8] S O L D whodat[33] pairs w/you[23] (still polite.) of which nothinmuch comes nothinmuch now nothinmuch[6] pairs with yessuhmistuhsuh[17] tuh drop one called yo now yo[9-0] still who gone be wentin now w/elle gived us el S O L D let us not forget ye[1-2-5] w/thee[3] givin us thou[9-2] who w/thuh they who switches their designation in certain conversation yes they[10] broughted forth onemore[2] at thuh same time in thuh same row right next door we have datone[12] w/disone[14] droppin off duhutherone[2-2] S O L D let us not forget du and sie let us not forget yessuhmassuhsuh[38] w/thou[8] who gived up memines[3-0] S O L D we are now rollin through thuh long division gimmie uh gimmie uh gimmie uh squared-off route round it off round it off n round it out w/sistuh[4-3] who lives with one called saintmines[9] givin forth one uh year how it got there callin it jessgrew callin it saintmines callin it whatdat whatdat whatdat S O L D

BLACK MAN WITH WATERMELON: Thuh list goes on and on. Dont it.

ALL: Ham Bone Ham Bone Ham Bone Ham Bone.

BEFORE COLUMBUS: Left right left right.

QUEEN-THEN-PHARAOH HATSHEPSUT: Left left left whose left...?

A bell sounds twice.

LOTS OF GREASE AND LOTS OF PORK: This is the death of the last black man in the whole entire world.

PANEL V: IN THUH GARDEN OF HOODOO IT

BLACK WOMAN WITH FRIED DRUMSTICK: Somethins turnin. Huh. Whatizit. — Mercy. Mercy. Huh. Chew on this. Ssuh feather. Sswhatchashud be eatin now ya no. Ssuhfeather: stuffin. Chew on it. Huh. Feathers sprouted from thuh fried hens—dont ask me how. Somethins out uh whack. Somethins out uh rights. Your arms still on your elbows. I'm still here. Whensit gonna end. Soon. Huh. Mercy. Thuh Tree. Springtime. And harvest. Huh. Somethins turnin. So many melons. Huh. From one tuh 3 tuh many. Must be nature. Gnaw on this. Gnaw on this, huh? Gnaw on this awe on that.

BLACK MAN WITH WATERMELON: Aint eatable.

BLACK WOMAN WITH FRIED DRUMSTICK: I know.

BLACK MAN WITH WATERMELON: Aint eatable aint it. Nope. Nope.

BLACK WOMAN WITH FRIED DRUMSTICK: Somethins turnin. Huh. Whatizit.

BLACK MAN WITH WATERMELON: Aint eatable so I out in out ought not aint be eatin it aint that right. Yep. Nope. Yep. Uh huhn.

BLACK WOMAN WITH FRIED DRUMSTICK: Huh. Whatizit.

BLACK MAN WITH WATERMELON: I remember what I like. I remember what my likes tuh eat when I be in thuh eatin mode.

BLACK WOMAN WITH FRIED DRUMSTICK: Chew on this.

BLACK MAN WITH WATERMELON: When I be in thuh eatin mode.

BLACK WOMAN WITH FRIED DRUMSTICK: Swallow it down. I know. Gimme your pit. Needs bathin.

BLACK MAN WITH WATERMELON: Choice between peas and corns —my feets—. Choice: peas. Choice between peas and greens choice: greens. Choice between greens and potatoes choice: potatoes. Yams. Boiled or mashed choice: mashed. Aaah. Mmm. My likenesses.

BLACK WOMAN WITH FRIED DRUMSTICK: Mercy. Turns—

BLACK MAN WITH WATERMELON: My likenesses! My feets! Aaah! SWEET-HEART. Aaah! SPRING-TIME!

BLACK WOMAN WITH FRIED DRUMSTICK: Spring-time.

BLACK MAN WITH WATERMELON: SPRING-TIME!

BLACK WOMAN WITH FRIED DRUMSTICK: Mercy. Turns—

BLACK MAN WITH WATERMELON: I remembers what I likes. I remembers what I likes tuh eat when I bein in had been in thuh eatin mode. Bein in had been: now in then. I be eatin hen. Hen.

BLACK WOMAN WITH FRIED DRUMSTICK: Huh?

BLACK MAN WITH WATERMELON: HEN!

BLACK WOMAN WITH FRIED DRUMSTICK: Hen?

BLACK MAN WITH WATERMELON: Hen. Huh. My meals. Aaaah: my meals. *BRACH-A-LEE.*

BLACK WOMAN WITH FRIED DRUMSTICK: Whatizit. Huh. — GNAW ON THIS! Good. Uhther pit?

BLACK MAN WITH WATERMELON: We sittin on this porch right now aint we. Uh huhn. Aaah. Yes. Sittin right here right now on it in it ainthuh first time either iduhnt it. Yep. Nope. Once we was here once wuhduhnt we. Yep. Yep. Once we being here. Uh huhn. Huh. There is uh Now and there is uh Then. Ssall there is. (I bein in uh Now: uh Now bein in uh Then: I bein, in Now in Then, in I will be. I was be too but thats uh Then thats past. That me that was be is uh me-has-been. Thuh Then that was be is uh has-been-Then too. Thuh me-has-been sits in thuh be-me: we sit on this porch. Same porch. Same me. Thuh Then thats been somehow sits in thuh Then that will be: same Thens. I swing from uh tree. You cut me down and bring me back. Home. Here. I fly over thuh yard. I fly over thuh yard in all over. Them thens stays fixed. Fixed Thens. Thuh Thems stays fixed too. Thuh Thems that come and take me and thuh Thems that greet me and then them Thems that send me back here. Home. Stays fixed, Them do.)

BLACK WOMAN WITH FRIED DRUMSTICK: Your feets.

BLACK MAN WITH WATERMELON: I: be. You: is. It: be. He, She: thats us. (Thats it.) We: thats he in she: you aroun me: us be here. You: still is. They: be. Melon. Melon. Melon: mines. I remember all my lookuhlikes. You. You. Remember me.

BLACK WOMAN WITH FRIED DRUMSTICK: Gnaw on this then swallow it down. Youll have your fill then we'll put you in your suit coat.

BLACK MAN WITH WATERMELON: Thuh suit coat I picked out? Thuh stripely one? HA! Peas. Choice: *BRACH*-A-LEE.

BLACK WOMAN WITH FRIED DRUMSTICK: Chew and swallow please.

BLACK MAN WITH WATERMELON: Thuh stripely one with thuh fancy patch pockets!

BLACK WOMAN WITH FRIED DRUMSTICK: Sweetheart.

BLACK MAN WITH WATERMELON: SPRING-TIME.

BLACK WOMAN WITH FRIED DRUMSTICK: Sweetheart.

BLACK MAN WITH WATERMELON: SPRING-TIME.

BLACK WOMAN WITH FRIED DRUMSTICK: This could go on forever.

BLACK MAN WITH WATERMELON: Lets. Hope. Not.

BLACK WOMAN WITH FRIED DRUMSTICK: —Sweetheart.

BLACK MAN WITH WATERMELON: SPRING-TIME.

BLACK WOMAN WITH FRIED DRUMSTICK: Sweetheart.

BLACK MAN WITH WATERMELON: SPRING-TIME.

BLACK WOMAN WITH FRIED DRUMSTICK: This could go on forever.

BLACK MAN WITH WATERMELON: Lets. Hope. Not.

BLACK WOMAN WITH FRIED DRUMSTICK: Must be somewhere else tuh go aside from just go gone.

BLACK MAN WITH WATERMELON: 6 by 6 by 6.

BLACK WOMAN WITH FRIED DRUMSTICK: Thats right.

BLACK MAN WITH WATERMELON: Rock reads "HooDoo."

BLACK WOMAN WITH FRIED DRUMSTICK: Now you know. Know now dontcha. Somethins turnin—.

BLACK MAN WITH WATERMELON: Who do? Them do. Aint that nice. Huh. Miss me. Remember me. Missmemissmewhatsmyname.

BLACK WOMAN WITH FRIED DRUMSTICK: Aaaaah?

BLACK MAN WITH WATERMELON: Remember me. AAAH.

BLACK WOMAN WITH FRIED DRUMSTICK: Thats it. Open wide. Here it comes. Stuffin.

BLACK MAN WITH WATERMELON: Yeeeech.

BLACK WOMAN WITH FRIED DRUMSTICK: Eat uhnother. Hear. I eat one. You eat one more.

BLACK MAN WITH WATERMELON: Stuffed. Time tuh go.

BLACK WOMAN WITH FRIED DRUMSTICK: Not yet!

BLACK MAN WITH WATERMELON: I got uhway?

BLACK WOMAN WITH FRIED DRUMSTICK: Huh?

BLACK MAN WITH WATERMELON: I got uhway?

BLACK WOMAN WITH FRIED DRUMSTICK: Nope. Yep. Nope. Nope.

BLACK MAN WITH WATERMELON: Miss me.

BLACK WOMAN WITH FRIED DRUMSTICK: Miss me.

BLACK MAN WITH WATERMELON: Re-member me.

BLACK WOMAN WITH FRIED DRUMSTICK: Re-member me.

BLACK MAN WITH WATERMELON: My hands are on my wrists. Arms on elbows. Looks: old-fashioned. Nothin fancy there. Toes curl up not down. My feets-now clean. Still got all my teeth. Re-member me.

BLACK WOMAN WITH FRIED DRUMSTICK: Re-member me.

BLACK MAN WITH WATERMELON: Call on me sometime.

BLACK WOMAN WITH FRIED DRUMSTICK: Call on me sometime. Hear? Hear? Thuh dirt itself turns itself. So many melons. From one tuh 3 tuh many. Look at um all. Ssuh garden. Awe on that. Winter pro-cessin back tuh back with spring-time. They roll on by us that way. Uh whole line gone roun. Chuh. Thuh worl be roun. Moves that way so they say. You comed back. Yep. Nope. Well. Build uh well.

A bell sounds twice.

FINAL CHORUS

ALL: "Yes. Oh, me? Chuh, no—"

VOICE ON THUH TEE V: Good morning. This is thuh news:

BLACK WOMAN WITH FRIED DRUMSTICK: Somethins turnin. Thuh page.

A bell sounds twice.

LOTS OF GREASE AND LOTS OF PORK: This is the death of the last black man in the whole entire worl.

PRUNES AND PRISMS: 19.

OLD MAN RIVER JORDAN: Uh blank page turnin with thuh sound of it. Thuh sound of movin hands.

BLACK WOMAN WITH FRIED DRUMSTICK: Yesterday today next summer tomorrow just uh moment uhgoh in 1317 dieded thuh last black man in thuh whole entire world. Uh! Oh. Dont be uhlarmed. Do not be afeared. It was painless. Uh painless passin. He falls twenty-three floors to his death.

ALL: Yes.

BLACK WOMAN WITH FRIED DRUMSTICK: 23 floors from uh passin ship from space tuh splat on thuh pavement.

ALL: Yes.

BLACK WOMAN WITH FRIED DRUMSTICK: He have uh head he been keepin under thuh Tee V.

ALL: Yes.

BLACK WOMAN WITH FRIED DRUMSTICK: On his bottom pantry shelf.

ALL: Yes.

BLACK WOMAN WITH FRIED DRUMSTICK: He have uh head that hurts. Dont fit right. Put it on tuh go tuh thuh store in it pinched him when he walks his thoughts dont got room. He diediduh he did, huh.

ALL: Yes.

BLACK WOMAN WITH FRIED DRUMSTICK: Where he gonna go now now now now now that he done diediduh?

ALL: Yes.

BLACK WOMAN WITH FRIED DRUMSTICK: Where he gonna go tuh. WASH.

PRUNES AND PRISMS: Somethins turnin. Thuh page.

AND BIGGER AND BIGGER AND BIGGER: Somethins burnin. Thuh tongue.

BLACK MAN WITH WATERMELON: Thuh tongue itself burns.

OLD MAN RIVER JORDAN: He jumps in thuh river. These words for partin.

YES AND GREENS BLACK-EYED PEAS CORNBREAD: And you will write them down.

A bell sounds three times.

BEFORE COLUMBUS: All these boats passed by my coast.

PRUNES AND PRISMS: Somethins turnin. Thuh page.

QUEEN-THEN-PHARAOH HATSHEPSUT: I saw Columbus comin/I saw Columbus comin goin—

QUEEN-THEN-PHARAOH HATSHEPSUT/BEFORE COLUMBUS: Left left left whose left . . . ?

AND BIGGER AND BIGGER AND BIGGER/BLACK MAN WITH WATERMELON: Somethins burnin. Thuh page.

BEFORE COLUMBUS: All those boats passed by me. My coast fell in-to-the-sea. All thuh boats. They stopped for me.

OLD MAN RIVER JORDAN: Land: HO!

QUEEN-THEN-PHARAOH HATSHEPSUT: I waved my hands in warnin. You waved back.

BLACK WOMAN WITH FRIED DRUMSTICK: Somethins burnin. Thuh page.

QUEEN-THEN-PHARAOH HATSHEPSUT: I have-not seen you since.

ALL: Oh!

LOTS OF GREASE AND LOTS OF PORK: This is the death of the last black man in the whole entire worl.

OLD MAN RIVER JORDAN: Do in diddley dip die-die thuh drop. Do drop be dripted? Why, of course.

AND BIGGER AND BIGGER AND BIGGER: Somethins burnin. Thuh tongue.

BLACK MAN WITH WATERMELON: Thuh tongue itself burns itself.

HAM: . . . And from that seed comed All Us.

BLACK WOMAN WITH FRIED DRUMSTICK: Thuh page.

ALL: 6 BY 6 BY 6.

BLACK WOMAN WITH FRIED DRUMSTICK: Thats right.

A bell sounds twice.

BEFORE COLUMBUS: LAND: HO!

YES AND GREENS BLACK-EYED PEAS CORNBREAD: You will write it down because if you dont write it down then we will come along and tell the future that we did not exist. You will write it down and you will carve it out of a rock.

(Pause)

You will write down thuh past and you will write down thuh

present and in what in thuh future. You will write it down.

(Pause)

It will be of us but you will mention them from time to time so that in the future when they come along theyll know how they exist.

(Pause)

It will be for us but you will mention them from time to time so that in the future when they come along theyll know why they exist.

(Pause)

You will carve it all out of a rock so that in the future when they come along we will know that the rock did yes exist.

BLACK WOMAN WITH FRIED DRUMSTICK: Down down down down down down down down—

LOTS OF GREASE AND LOTS OF PORK: This is the death of the last black man in the whole entire worl.

PRUNES AND PRISMS: Somethins turnin. Thuh page.

OLD MAN RIVER JORDAN: Thuh last news of thuh last man:

VOICE ON THUH TEE V: Good morning. This is thuh last news:

BLACK MAN WITH WATERMELON: Miss me.

BLACK WOMAN WITH FRIED DRUMSTICK: Miss me.

BLACK MAN WITH WATERMELON: Re-member me.

BLACK WOMAN WITH FRIED DRUMSTICK: Re-member me. Call on me sometime. Call on me sometime. Hear? Hear?

HAM: In thuh future when they came along I meeting them. On thuh coast. Uuuuhh! My coast! I—was—so—po-lite! But.˒ In thuh rock. I wrote: ha ha ha.

ALL: Ha. Ha. Ha. Ha. Ha. Ha. Ha. Ha. Ha. Ha. Ha. Ha. Ha. Ha. HHHHHHHHHHHHH. HA!

BLACK WOMAN WITH FRIED DRUMSTICK: Thuh black man he move. He move. He hans.

A bell sounds once.

ALL: Hold it. Hold it. Hold it. Hold it. Hold it. Hold it. Hold it.

THE
MOJO
AND THE
SAYSO

AISHAH
RAHMAN

In the early seventies, I was pregnant with my daughter, Yoruba, at the time of the infamous killing of Clifford Glover. He was a ten-year-old boy who, while walking with his father, was fatally shot by a policeman in a case of mistaken identity in Queens, New York. When a woman decides to bring a new life into the world she looks at the world and says, "What am I doing? What kind of world awaits this child within me?" I couldn't help but put myself in Mrs. Glover's place.

When I heard it, I was so profoundly affected that I wanted to run out and do something, but the only thing that I could do was to sit down and write. I didn't start writing the play right then, but it always stuck in the back of my mind. I followed the case and it was the same old thing; they let the officer off. A couple of years later, I read in the *Amsterdam News* that his mother was complaining that her minister had swindled her out of her check that she received for his wrongful death. It was at that time that I knew I would have to write something about the story. After I investigated and did some research, I knew that the family were people who were voiceless. And I had to give voice to them.

The Aesthetic

Clifford Glover and his family haunted me. I wanted to go behind the scenes and follow the family after the headlines. My biggest question was: How does a family survive this? How, because so many black families do survive this and have to go on. I was trying to dramatize the unconscious or emotional levels of character. And that's why I find that I always have to make some kind of leap that might be described in some Eurocentric term like "absurdist." But I don't think of it that way.

My work is in the tradition of what I call the "jazz aesthetic," which acknowledges the characters' various levels of reality. They have a triple-consciousness: of the unborn, the living and the dead. Jazz may be discussed primarily as an articulation which has a specifically African-American historical framework from which it flows. The jazz aesthetic in drama expresses multiple ideas and experiences through language, movement, visual art and spirituality simultaneously. The jazz aesthetic is found in art, poetry, drama and fiction and is not contingent upon jazz music to be.

Definitions of Heroism
To be heroic is to be able to love in spite of all the soul-crushing experiences that define black life in America.

Distinctions between Women's and Men's Writing
Women's writing. Men's writing. Gay and lesbian writing. Black writing. Such categories are only literary apartheid that marginalizes specific groups of writers. They are false commercial distinctions that have nothing to do with the quality of writing. There are only two kinds of writing. Good and bad.

The Responsibility of the Theatre Artist
The writer's responsibility is to keep theatre alive. When I say, "theatre alive," I don't mean the kind of theatre that is going on now. The responsibility is to try to keep an idealistic view of theatre in a capitalistic and anti-art environment. We must try to keep the ideal of theatre belonging to the people; of theatre as an artform instead of only a business form. As writers, we must think of ourselves—I think of us—as priests and priestesses of the word with a holy mission to be responsible to people.

The Darkness and the Light
Life and art is a journey. When you're young, you think that you're in this thing for fame and fortune, and that motivates you. I realized that art—and in my case, writing—is a lifetime process. It's a journey. The darkness of the journey is when you stop sometimes, and look around you and say, "What am I writing this for? Nobody will read it." The darkness is the business side of it, the not getting paid, not getting the recognition; not getting the opportunity that any artist needs to be able to see their work.

The light is doing the work. It's the creative process of pulling a story out of nothingness. It's also the times that you're appreciated. What's happened to me is that there's a whole new generation that appreciates my work. You may not have had a production for one or two years, and yet a whole bunch of college students know your work and write theses about it. The light is the actual joy of writing and leaving a legacy on paper.

The Mojo and the Sayso is certainly a story of dark and light. It is a story of the darkest dark there is—the loss of life of a loved one. And the light that came out of that is the light in the African-American experience: to be able to continue to love (in spite of everything). It is the darkness and the light of our lives here in America. And to take it a step further, that is the darkness and light of all people in the same circumstances. It's the darkness and the light of the human spirit.

ABOUT THE AUTHOR

Aishah Rahman is a native New Yorker. In addition to *The Mojo and the Sayso*, for which she won the Doris Abramson Playwriting Award, Rahman's works include *Lady Day: A Musical Tragedy; Unfinished Women Cry in No Man's Land While a Bird Dies in a Gilded Cage; Transcendental Blues; The Lady and the Tramp;* a musical biography of Zora Neale Hurston, *The Tale of Madame Zora;* and the libretto, *Opera Marie Laveau.* Her latest play is *Only in America.*

Rahman was the recipient of 1988 fellowships from the Rockefeller Foundation and the New York Foundation for the Arts. She co-founded Blackberry Production Company and teaches in Brown University's graduate creative writing program.

ABOUT THE WORK

The Mojo and the Sayso was originally produced by Crossroads Theatre Company in New Brunswick, NJ, under the direction of George Ferencz. The play was part of TCG's *Plays in Process* series in 1989. The acting edition is published by Broadway Play Publishing Inc.

CHARACTERS

AWILDA

ACTS

BLOOD

PASTOR

TIME

Now. Sunday.

PLACE

The living room of the Benjamins' home.

AUTHOR'S NOTE

The Mojo and the Sayso is a story of a family: vulnerable human beings who sustain pain and love, hatreds, fears, joys, sorrows and degradation, and finally triumph.

The production style should serve and illuminate the absurdity, fantasy and magic mayhem that are intrinsic in this script.

THE MOJO AND THE SAYSO

[*for Clifford Glover and all the others . . .*]

O deliver not the soul of thy turtle-dove
unto the multitude of the wicked . . .
PSALM 74:19

ACT ONE

Morning. Lights up on the Benjamins' living room. Stage left is a mantelpiece with a collection of various colored candles on it. Center stage, on a slightly raised platform, is a half-built car. Hubcaps, tires, fenders, etc. are scattered around. The rest of the room is neat; it is only the platform area that is disordered. Awilda, dressed entirely in white, is frantically searching for something among the mechanical automotive parts. Her voice is heard over the whir of an acetylene torch which Acts, inside the car frame, is using.

AWILDA *(Searching frantically for something very important)*: Ball joints, tires, shock absorbers, spark plugs, carburetors.
ACTS: The treasures and dreams that's buried in a junkyard!

Awilda stares at him unbelievingly for a second, then continues her search.

Damn near tore my paws off trying to get to this baby but I got it. Knowed it was only a few left in the world. Never thought I'd own one but I do now. A Lycomen engine. They used to put it in only the best of machines back in '47. Used to put it in a deluxe car they called the Auborn Cord. It had an electric shift, front-wheel drive same as you got today. Car was so advanced, so ahead of its time they took it off the market. Man this engine was so bad they used to put her in aeroplanes. Now I'm gonna put her right in, Jim!

AWILDA: Wrenches, hammers.

ACTS: Soon I'll be finished the dream car of my mind.

AWILDA *(Reacts to his last words by looking at him and shaking her head; she resumes her search)*: Batteries, mufflers, spark coils, piston rings, radiator caps, gaskets, fenders, exhaust pipes. White gloves? No white gloves.

ACTS: A chrome-plated masterpiece. Brown and gold-flecked with a classy body . . . built with my own hands.

AWILDA: I can't find them.

Acts' only response is to continue working.

I searched and looked and searched and still can't find them. I searched and looked and rummaged all through this mess and I still can't. . . . *(Going to the mantelpiece)* Let's see. Orange. A good color for concentration. *(She lights the candle and is immediately soothed)* There. I've lit the way to my white gloves. I'll have them in time to go to church.

Acts' only response is to bang with his hammer.

Pastor Delroy wants all us saints dressed in white. Pure white, from crown to toe.

ACTS: What a beautiful engine. They don't come any better.

AWILDA: Don't forget this Sunday is special.

ACTS: A priceless engine. Tossed away in the junkyard.

AWILDA: It happened three years ago today.

ACTS: Been looking for this engine for three years.

AWILDA: And Pastor is having a special memorial service today for Linus.

ACTS: And what do you know? Boom! This morning out of all the hundreds of other mornings. This is the morning I find him.

AWILDA: There's gonna be organ music.

ACTS: Must be some kind of special sign . . . finding this engine this morning.

AWILDA: And flowers. Gladiolas and carnations. Lovely church flowers.

ACTS: Now that I got the engine I want, I can finish him. Finish him today. Three years is a long time.

AWILDA: Our choir will sing "Sweet Lil' Jesus Boy."

ACTS: Soon he'll be purring like a kitten. Soon every nut and bolt will be in place.

AWILDA: And the congregation will bow their heads for a moment of silence. And think of Linus.

ACTS: Shut up! I see no need to draw attention to the unfortunate by-products of your womb!

AWILDA: Our children. What became of our children?

ACTS *(Getting up suddenly and leaving the room)*: We'll say no more about it. No more!

AWILDA *(Hurling these words at his exiting back)*: You never talk about anything! Especially not about Linus.

ACTS *(Returns, carrying a steering wheel)*: That's another thing. He's dead. Let the dead rest. I never mention the boy's name in this house since the funeral but just like a woman you just talk and talk and always call his name.

AWILDA: LINUS IS NOT DEAD. I remember him. Every part. I remember his scalp, his bones, his smooth flesh, the bright color of his blood, his white teeth, his boy smell. As long as I remember him, Linus is alive.

ACTS: Linus is dead. *(Taking her in his arms)* But I'm here.

AWILDA *(Pushing him away)*: If Linus could run as fast as you did, he could be here too.

Acts recoils from her as if she had slapped him.

AWILDA *(Horrified at what has slipped out of her mouth)*: "He that is cruel troubleth his own flesh." Book of Proverbs, 29th Chapter, 11th verse. I feel terrible. I hope you can forgive me.

ACTS *(Returning to his car)*: You know a junkyard is a funny place. Most of the cars are thrown in the scrap heap because of lots of wear and tear. Not because they are worthless. Not worthless at all.

AWILDA: Forgive me. It's just that we used to have two boys and now there's only one.

Acts' only response is the voice of his hammer.

And that one floats around with a bomb in his heart.

Acts continues to pound away.

While I dream of Linus every night.

Acts' hammer continues to be his only response.

I did it again last night.

Acts' hammering begins to accelerate.

The only way I can remember it is to tell it.

Acts continues to hammer away.

It's always the same dream. Linus is still ten years old but yet he is older than all of us. You and Linus and I are strolling down the avenue. Suddenly, Aretha's voice is all around us. We breathe it in with our bodies. It is like a feeding. When all of a sudden the music changes and the sound of Monk's piano jumps in front of us. The boy and I jump into the chords, leaving our bodies like old clothes.

Acts stops working on the car, looks at her as if this is the first time he has ever heard this.

A-n-d you . . . you steal our bodies and run!
ACTS: I do not! I DO NOT!
AWILDA: You run and run and run and run! *(In the voice of Linus)* "Daddy, Daddy. Please . . . don't . . . run."
ACTS *(Yelling and screaming)*: You are such a liar! Look at you with your face twisted like a peach pit. You are such a liar! If lies were brains you'd be smart. If lies were mountaintops you'd be way up. If I wasn't such a calm and gentle man I'd strangle

you till you admit that I don't run away. That I rush to your side. That I put your bodies in mine. I keep telling you that.

AWILDA: I know. Maybe I'll get it right tonight.

ACTS: If you could only go to sleep thinking, "He could never run away and leave us in danger."

AWILDA: But when I'm awake, I tell you that I believe you. Besides, what do you care what I think as long as God knows the truth. Isn't God enough for you?

ACTS: HELL NO! I need people. I need you. There are nights when I see myself all the way to my bones. Check out every corner of myself and feel strong about me. But come the morning...I look at you and the doubt I see in you makes me guilty.

AWILDA: "Heal me O Lord, my bones are vexed. My soul is sore vexed." Clean my thoughts and keep the Devil out of them. I want to believe you. I have to believe you but...but...just give me another chance. I'll dream it right. I promise. I'll wake myself up if I dream it wrong.

ACTS: All of us have a dream world. Get in, my lady.

Reluctantly, Awilda climbs in the frame of the car and sits. He continues in the manner of a king showing his queen the castle.

This is where the radio's gonna be. Soon you'll be able to flick the dial to your favorite music. Not none of them Jesus songs, honey. I mean give me a break. You should learn how to drive. Be good for you. Give you something else to think about. You comfortable? I'm gonna cover the seats with something soft. Mink maybe. Just for you. Gonna put a bar in the back. You can keep your ginger ale in there. If you want. Here we go sweetcakes. Past Jamaica Avenue. Mmmmmmm. Smell the air. Someone's barbecuing. On. Here we go. We're cruising up past Kissena Boulevard, down Sunset, past Jamaica Avenue. Mmmmmmmmmm. Smell the air. Someone's barbecuing. Look at those old wooden frame houses next to the tall apartment buildings. See the churches. See the ladies in they pinks and yellows and whites and blues. See the folks hanging out. See them turn they heads as we go riding by. Whew! Hot, isn't it? Let's get a couple of beers and drive out to the beach, take off our clothes and lay in the sun—

AWILDA (*Standing up, breaking the spell*): I'm late for church.

ACTS: Shh. Don't be scared. Don't be nervous. You with me now. Sit back down!

AWILDA (*Sitting down*): I can't help it.

ACTS: I know. I know. Just get it together. Listen, don't you hear what people are saying? They are saying, "There goes the wizard of the automobile world. Acts Benjamin and his wife. See that car he's driving? He only builds them for the leading citizens of the world." (*Sees Awilda getting up and tries to pull her back*) Hey, where are you going? We're almost there. I'll park the car and we can lay in the sun—

AWILDA: I want to get out. I need my white gloves! I'm late for church!

ACTS: It's folks like you that give religion a bad name.

AWILDA (*Escaping from the car*): Now you listen to me. I'd rather do what God tells me than listen to you. (*Resuming her search for gloves*) All you do is rummage through junkyards, bringing scrap that been thrown away right here, in our living room, working on the car, in our living room, every hour, day or night, winter or summer, snowstorm or heat wave, in our living room!

ACTS: That's just why I want it in the house—so that the weather don't matter.

AWILDA: All the time, whacking, banging, drilling on that . . . that . . .

ACTS: Car . . . it's a car. I've told you two hundred times before. Don't call my car out of its name. Please . . . don't . . . badmouth . . . my . . . car . . . !

AWILDA: All the time working on that car. Something I always wanted to ask you. Tell me. Just what do you get out of it? What do you see in it?

ACTS: Anything I want to.

AWILDA: Just tell me what.

ACTS: I'm glad you finally asked. When I look at this car I see lots of things.

AWILDA: What things?

ACTS: I see understanding. No worries. I see tittie-squeezing and pussy-teasing.

AWILDA: It's no wonder that I turned to Christ.

ACTS: No wonder.

AWILDA: Pastor says that you . . .

ACTS: If I didn't have firsthand personal knowledge that Jesus done locked your thighs and thrown the key away, that religion done stole your natural feelings, I'd be 'clined to think that you and that jackleg son of a bi—

AWILDA *(With religious fervor)*: Jealous. That's what you are. Just plain jealous. Imagine being jealous of God. That's why you bad-mouth the messengers of God's word every chance you get. I used to have a hard heart like you till Pastor saved me. One day I was listening to him preach, my breath grew short, my throat closed up and I couldn't breathe. It was Pastor Delroy I was looking at but Jesus that I was seeing. "Lord," I said. "Lord, I am in your hands."

Her fervor has aroused Acts. He goes towards her and seriously tries to possess her. Awilda struggles hard.

ACTS: I was once into that holiness bag and I know that trick. All them jackleg pastors and deacons and elders laughing at you and taking your money. All you women jumping up and down yelling, "Come sweet Jesus" need to stay home and say it to your husbands!

AWILDA: You ain't nothing but the Devil!

ACTS *(Suddenly disgusted, walks away from her, laughing harshly)*: Forget about the Devil. Forget about the sign of the Cross. It is the sign of power *(Holds up a dollar bill)* and the sign of the trick *(Holds up a pair of soiled white gloves in the other hand)* that counts.

AWILDA: You! You had them all the time.

ACTS *(Returning to work on his car)*: Maybe.

AWILDA *(Snatching up the white gloves)*: These white gloves are genuine brushed cotton. The other day I was downtown window-shopping, thinking about what I would wear in church today and suddenly I found myself in Bonwit's. I don't know how I got there. It was like my feet had grown a mind of they own. I wanted to turn around and run but something made me brazen it out. So I marched to the glove counter and stood there. Four detectives followed me. The salesgirl left the blue-haired, silver-foxed madame she was waiting on and rushed over to me. "Can I help you, Miss," she said. Imagine that. "Miss" to me though I am a married woman and had— at one time—two children. Then I told her, "I'm not a Miss, I'm a Mrs., and I'd like a pair of white gloves." "They start at fifty dollars, Miss," she snapped. And then I took my time and made her show me lace gloves, net gloves, nylon gloves, leather gloves, and I didn't like any of them until she showed me these. The most expensive ones and I said, "Oh, aren't they lovely. I'll take them." And so after all that aggravation I don't see why you would hide them from me unless you wanted to make me late for church and keep me here with you.

ACTS *(Working on the car)*: I'm getting kinda hungry, woman.

AWILDA: Sure. What would you like. Spark plugs? Machine oil? Gasoline? *(Acts ignores her)* I really think sometimes that you are turning into that car.

ACTS: Honk honk!

AWILDA: You could come with me if you wanted to. You could get dressed and come with me to church.

ACTS: Don't get started on that again. Please.

AWILDA *(Going toward the windows)*: I'm opening up all the windows.

ACTS *(Preoccupied)*: Yeah, yeah, yeah, yeah.

AWILDA: Every night I lay out your striped blue suit and your Van Heusen shirt with the rolled collar and your diamond stickpin and your patent-leather wing tips and your ribbed silk socks and your monogrammed hand-embroidered linen pocket handkerchief hoping that you will come to church with me.

ACTS: Me? I keep telling you. I don't go for that bull. Besides, your beloved Pastor is there. You don't need me.

AWILDA: Need? I need you to talk to me. What happened that night. . . . Tell me that. That's what I need.

Silence. Acts works on the car.

See that? All the trouble we went through was for God but all you think about is that car. You can build me a Rolls Royce and say it's mine but it ain't. It's God's car.

The sound of Acts working is his only response.

Mr. Benjamin. I'm a God-fearing woman and I'm opening all these windows wide so that He can come in here and fill your heart.

ACTS *(Looking up from his car)*: Stay away from the windows.

AWILDA *(Running around, opening up windows)*: Get him God. Get him God. Come in. Come in. Stab his soul. Pierce his stubborn heart!

ACTS *(Enraged, runs around slamming windows)*: Shutupshutup-shutup. Goddammit! *(He smashes all the windows with a tool)*

AWILDA *(Singing at the top of her voice)*:

> I knit my world
> With strong church yarn
> With stitches even and unbroken
> For God is my true husband
> Who keeps me from harm
> He is my only one.

As Acts finishes breaking the windows, they gaze at each other silently. The maniacal peal of church bells rushes through the broken windows. Awilda goes over to the mantelpiece, fighting tears, tries to light a candle but the wind from the broken windows keeps extinguishing it.

AWILDA: Blue is for peace.

Acts stands there gazing at the broken glass.

I...we...need a blue candle.

ACTS *(Looking at the broken windows and glass)*: I'll clean it up later. I'm going to finish that car tonight. *(Returns to car)*

AWILDA: We've got to take care of one another. Keep healthy. There's no one else to look after us. *(Begins a frantic search for something)* Where is it? I know I put it here.

ACTS: Where is what? You got the white gloves, don't you?

AWILDA: YOU KNOW what I'm looking for.

ACTS: I don't have anything to do with it. Ever since it come in the mail yesterday, I give it to you.

AWILDA: I couldn't look at it. But I remember. I put it right here.

ACTS: Then that's where it should be.

AWILDA: It's not.

ACTS: It should be right where you put it.

AWILDA: It isn't.

ACTS: Look. If it can't walk, if it ain't got legs of it own, then it's gotta be where you put it.

AWILDA *(Discovering a check)*: Aha! Here it is. And I didn't put it there. Why do you keep doing that?

ACTS: What? Doing what?

AWILDA: The check. Putting it near my candles. This is the second time I've moved it away from here.

ACTS: I don't. I didn't.

AWILDA: Then how did it get here next to my candles?

ACTS: Don't ask me.

AWILDA *(Gingerly taking up check and looking at it)*: UGH. I hate to touch it. It feels...funny. It's got an awful smell too. It must be the paper they use nowadays to print these things. "Payment for Wrongful Death." Big digits. Now we got lots of money. Lots of money for the life of our boy. How do they figger? How do they know? How do they add up what a ten-year-old boy's life is worth to his parents? Maybe they have a chart or something. Probably feed it into a computer. Bzzzz. "One scrawny brown working-class boy. Enter. No wealthy relatives. Size 4 shoe. A chance of becoming rich in his lifetime if he plays Lotto regularly." How many dollars? How many cents? Do they know about the time I found out I was pregnant with him? My absolute joy that God has sent me this child. True, I already had Walter but that was before you. But you loved us anyhow and soon Linus was growing inside of me because we were in love. Yes, there was never enough money and we were always struggling but that's just the way life is. We knew we were supposed to have this baby. You took me to your mother and father and sisters and all your sisters, brothers, aunts and uncles. Your whole tribe. You told them, "This is my woman and she's going to have our child." They all hugged and kissed me. Do they know about the way you would put your head on my stomach and listen? Did they figger in the way you held my hand with tears in your eyes when I was in labor? When he was born the grandparents, aunts, uncles, neighbors and friends brought presents, ate and drank and danced and sang. Do they know about those moments? Did they add them in here? And what about Linus himself? He would make me throw out all my mean, petty, selfish parts and give him the best person I could be. Remember when he was good? Remember when he was bad? The times he was like us yet someone brand-new? And...what...about...what...he... might...have...been? How do they figger? How do they know?

ACTS: Evil. Blood money. Payoff. Hush money....Do what you want with it and don't tell me.

AWILDA: No one could fault you if you put it in the bank or started your own something with it. Every worldly person has got some fantasy.

Acts glares angrily at her but doesn't answer.

I understand. If you would only talk about that night. Tell someone what really happened. Somebody. Anybody. Especially me. *(Acts continues to remain silent)* One thing for sure. It ain't ordinary money and I won't buy a car or a house or store up riches like a vain, greedy sinner.

ACTS *(Barely audible)*: I tried to protect him.

AWILDA *(Does not hear Acts and continues)*: I thought Walter would have taken over after Linus. Look after everything. Look after us....After "the accident" I put all my hopes on Walter. He was always making something. He was smart! He was kind! He was tender! You remember?

Acts holds her.

Now he's got a grenade for a soul. Guns. Knives. Before the "accident" there wasn't a mean bone in his body. He loved everybody. Everybody loved him. He used to sing and dance and laugh all the time. You remember?

ACTS: Go to church. I think a storm is coming.

AWILDA *(Holding her arms as if cradling a child, singing a lullaby)*:

> Go to sleep my little son.
> Snow is falling on the sun.
> Trees run blood and sidewalks grow
> Guns besides a dead boy child!

(Suddenly walking away from Acts) Don't worry about a storm. The sun will light my path all the way to church. When I get there I will just pay attention to the songs and sermons, the music and words, voices, faces and feelings that keep me going. I guess I just believe in spiritual things. Spiritual things is all.

ACTS: Better go. It's getting late.

AWILDA *(Whirling around dervishlike in her agony)*: Then you stop time. I want you to stop it. Stop...time...now. Turn time back in its track. Make time go back to when Linus was alive. Make time go back to when Walter was tender. He was gentle. He wouldn't hurt anybody. Turn back time! Stop! Time! Stop!

During Awilda's monologue, Blood has stuck his face through one of the broken windows. While she is still speaking, he surreptitiously climbs through the window, registering fear and confusion.

BLOOD *(At first in the voice of a terrified little child)*: Mommy? Daddy? What's wrong? What happened? You aren't hurt are you? O GOD! MA? POPS? *(Guns drawn, searching for imagined invaders)* ALL RIGHT. WHOEVER YOU ARE I KNOW YOU ARE HIDING IN THIS HOUSE. I KNOW YOU ARE HERE SOMEWHERE IN HERE. THROW OUT YOUR WEAPONS. GIVE YOURSELF UP. 'CAUSE I CAN BOMB YOU, SHOOT YOU OR CUT

YOU. I DONE WARNED I AIN'T NO PUNK YOU
DEALING WITH. THIS IS ME. BLOOD! *(He stalks
around the room, searching for enemies)* Come on out. YA
STUPID PUNK BASTIDS. I GOT YA COVERED
FROM EVERY ANGLE. I WANT YOU ALIVE BUT I
HAVE ENUF TO BLAST YA OUT! BETTER COME
ON OUT NOW 'CAUSE YOU FOOLING WITH A MAN
WHO IS NOT AFRAID OF DEATH!

ACTS: FUCK YOU! This is our home. Put that gun down!

AWILDA: This is our home!

BLOOD *(Continuing his search)*: I'LL BREAK YOUR NECKS.
I'LL SMASH YOUR HEADS! I'LL BREAK YOUR
BACKS!

AWILDA: Walter! *(To Acts)* Look at him! Imagine being afraid of
my own son!

BLOOD: It's okay Ma. Don't be afraid. COME ON OUT, GUYS.
YOU DON'T HAVE A CHANCE!

ACTS: Give . . . me . . . the . . . gun, Walter.

BLOOD: GIVE IT UP! COME ON OUT! IT'S ALL OVER.
I'LL BUST YOUR HEADS!

AWILDA: A killer ain't a pretty sight.

BLOOD: SHOW YOURSELVES NOW. HOW MANY OF
THEM DID YOU SAY THERE ARE, POPS?

ACTS: There's nobody in the house but us, punk, so . . . give . . .
me . . . the gun!

BLOOD: I'LL BLOW UP EVERY CORNER OF THIS
HOUSE TILL THEY COME OUT WITH THEIR
HANDS UP!

*Acts has sneaked behind Blood. He knocks him down and gets the
gun.*

ACTS *(Pressing the gun right to Blood's head)*: You want to play
crazy? I'll show you how! This is the lowdownest trick you've
pulled yet. This tops all!

BLOOD: You just can't sneak up from behind, knock me on the
floor and take my piece.

ACTS: I can't?

BLOOD: You'd better give it back to me before I get mad.

ACTS: You will?

AWILDA (To Blood, in a soft, terrified voice; she keeps on repeating the words underneath the following dialogue): Don't run don't shoot don't run don't shoot don't run don't shoot.

ACTS (Touches Awilda to reassure her): Will snookums get soooo maddy mad and doo-doo all over hims diapers? SHITFACE. YA FUCKING DUMB-ASS KID.

BLOOD: I'M NOT A KID. I'M A MAN.

ACTS: Didn't I tell you to keep your behind parts away from here till you could stop acting like a hysterical female. Like a lady on the ra—

BLOOD: I'M NO LADY, MISTER. I'M A MAN!

ACTS (Keeping the gun aimed at his head): Then stand up... M-A-N.

BLOOD: Why you putting that pistol at me? I'm your son.

ACTS: Get up!

BLOOD (Getting up): Listen to me. Quit pointing it at me. It's loaded. You never listen.

ACTS: You busted into my house with a loaded gun and you want me to listen. Go ahead. Talk!

BLOOD: I...I...just came to say goodbye.

ACTS (Pressing the gun right up against Blood's temple): Damn right you gonna say "goodbye."

BLOOD: Easy. It's loaded. Let me explain.

ACTS: Speak, liar.

BLOOD: When I opened my eyes this morning I got that old feeling again. As I lay in my room, on my bed, I could see Linus's blood on every street. The chalk outline of his body on every corner. I could see his brown leather jacket and his baseball cap tipped to the side. Once again this city was getting to me. I had to split. As I was coming down the street, walking to this house, I practiced saying goodbye. I knew you would be working on the car and when I told you I was leaving again you would grunt but not look at me. Mom would light a candle for me and look at me, accusing me, but not saying anything. As I come near the house I sense something isn't right. I creep up on the porch, afraid of my own eyes. Windows are busted. I hear Mom's voice. What's she saying? Sounds like crying. You are standing. Just standing in a river of broken glass. Staring. Staring out a busted window. What am I supposed to think? I stare in, thinking, "Don't worry Pops. Your son's here. I'll protect you."

ACTS: Well, well, well. You protect me? What we have here is mighty Robin Hood. All you need is your pointed, upturned ballet slippers and your green tights!

BLOOD: It's the truth.

ACTS: You're a liar and this *(Indicating gun)* is a lie.

Blood just shakes his head from side to side.

Never play with guns. Even if they aren't loaded. Didn't I always teach you that?

BLOOD: You wanna kill me Pops? It's loaded.

ACTS: Liar!

BLOOD: Believe me. It is.

Acts pulls the trigger. It clicks empty. He looks at Blood with disgust and throws the empty gun at his feet.

ACTS: Get that thing away from around me!

BLOOD *(Pleadingly)*: So it wasn't loaded. Aren't you the one that always says, "Attitude is everything, Son"?

ACTS: A bellowing bull never gets fat.

BLOOD *(Walking and talking like a tough-guy gangster type)*: You gotta be hard. Tough. Cold. Ice. Steel. Woof or be woofed at. Take no shit. Play with death. Learn to gamble. Learn to win. Learn to kill.

AWILDA: Your brother wouldn't like to see you act this way. Especially today. Have some respect. I thought you were going to kill us.

BLOOD: You afraid of me? O my God, Mom. I could never hurt you.

AWILDA *(Begins to sweep the broken glass)*: I mean there's all kinds of other ways to enter a house. You could have knocked on the door. Rang the bell . . . come through the front door. . . . A lot of other ways.

BLOOD: I'm sorry.

AWILDA: I remember the time you smashed the blue Mercury into the plate-glass window of Mr. Johnny's barbershop. Your father straightened out the motor bed, plugged the holes in the radiator, hammered out some of the dents and folds in the fender and taped a new light onto its front. It was one of the few times you helped him. Linus was always working on cars with him but you hardly did. You were different.

BLOOD *(Taking broom from Awilda)*: You shouldn't do that. I'll do it.

AWILDA *(Exiting)*: Pastor's waiting for me. I'm late for church.

BLOOD *(Goes over to Acts)*: Isn't there anything you can do?

ACTS *(Working on the car)*: Do? About what?

BLOOD: Can't you get her away from that holy hustler? Can't you stop her from always going crosstown to his so-called "church"?

ACTS: I tried, Walter.

BLOOD: I keep telling you the name is "Blood."

> *Almost unconsciously, without being told, Blood begins to hand Acts tools that he needs. They pass the tools between them like a surgical team during the following monologue.*

ACTS: I know why you doing all this. I know. I know why you so set to hurt me. It's your doubt about that night. Something you can never bring yourself to tell me. But the thought is always in you. I see it. I catch you looking at me wondering . . . and then turning away when I look at you. You think what people say about that night is true. I knew that soon as you went and changed your name. That wasn't right. You and I was real tight. Closer than father and son. We was Ace Boon Coons. 'Member the time I made a deluxe racer for you out of a rusty bicycle frame I found in the yard? We had a lot of nice years together before. . . . Why you wanna go and call yourself "Blood" when you got a perfectly good name like Walter Acts Benjamin the Second? There's a lot that goes into a name and you shouldn't just go and call yourself something else. A name belongs in a family. It was passed down to me and I take it and give it to you even though you ain't my flesh and blood directly. And you take it and throw it away. You shouldn't do that. I remember the first time I heard how good things were in New York. I decided to see for myself. I wasn't used to the cold and almost went back home but after a while I decided to stay. The first job I had in the city was driving a cab. Then I carted coal for a couple of years. After that I worked as a long-shoreman when I could. Then I went to work for a man named Quinn at the wrecking yard on Springfield Boulevard. And I worked many years as a garage handyman hoping one day to achieve the title of mechanic. I went near crazy from being alone until I met you and your ma. I first saw her in a little restaurant on South Road. The Silver Fly. I had to have her. We stayed up late talking and laughing. Soon we got married because after all that aloneness I been through she was having a kid for me. A baby with my eyes, my nose, my mouth and my name. Now I'm telling you straight, boy, what happened to your brother is done. I can't change it. Your mother can't change it and God won't. You ain't no different from any other person that something terrible has happened to. Don't let what happened to Linus madden or cheapen you. I bear a lot of pain but I bear it with expression. Just who in the hell do you think you are?

BLOOD *(Walks away from him)*: Who am I? I want to be a righteous gunman like George Jackson. Or his brother, Jonathan. I would have liked to walk in the courtroom where they acquitted the cop that shot my brother in the back with my guns drawn and announce, "All right, gentlemen, I'm taking over." Just like Jonathan did. Alone and armed. Righteous and tough. Beyond fear. He knew his fate and did not hesitate. A man evolved to the highest level. Now they mighta shot some bullets into Jonathan Jackson's brain that day but he ain't dead. I got to be him 'cause I sure ain't me. I should be the kind of man that pours down hot revenge on his enemies because I had a brother, once. A kid brother. Sometimes he used to pee in the bed. A scrawny, ash-brown kid, ninety-four pounds, about this high. He was always beating up on little girls 'cause he liked them. Used to be afraid of being weak and afraid. We used to arm-wrestle all the time and I'd let him win and then show him how I could beat him anytime I wanted to. He looked up to me and I liked that.

ACTS: Tell you what, "Blood" or whatever you call yourself. We got some money now. Plenty of it with that "wrongful death" check from the city that come yesterday. Ask your mother for some. You'd be able to go anyplace.

BLOOD: I don't want any of that money. I can get all kinds of bread.

ACTS: Yeah?

BLOOD: Yeah.

ACTS: You called me on the phone and asked me for money, I remember.

BLOOD: That was a long time ago.

ACTS: When you gonna pay me back?

BLOOD: Soon.

ACTS: You need money. Ask your mother.

BLOOD: You think I want to stand here and argue with you about that filthy blood money? I know the price we've all paid for it.

ACTS: You sure you don't want to come sneaking up on us and knife us in the back?

BLOOD: That's not funny, Pops. I hate that money much as you. It's no treasure. It's no pot of gold after the rainbow.

Awilda starts to enter and stops. Audience sees her standing and listening. Blood and Acts are unaware of her presence.

ACTS: Money, money, money. It's the story of our lives. "Learn how to make you a dollar, boy. Earn some spending change and keep you some folding money and don't let anybody take your money from you," I used to preach to Linus. So he would get up every Saturday and go to the yard with me before dawn. That's when they shot him. Right before daybreak. And though everybody knew the truth, they said Police Officer Rhea was only doing his duty.

BLOOD: In school he would tear up his work in a rage if he got a bad mark. At home, he was our mother's favorite child and I knew it. When he discovered he had a joint he used to go around touching it, looking at it, airing it out, seeing how far he could pee with it. What a little brat!

AWILDA (*Entering the room, concentrating on her white-gloved hands*): Pastor said Linus would have turned out to be somebody. Somebody big. You know what Pastor says. Pastor says we should give Linus a special memorial. Something unusual and unselfish. That's what Pastor says.

Lights start to dim as Awilda continues to turn her hands inside out, stretching her arms toward the sky as if she were dancing.

Ever notice how when you wash white gloves just one time all the life seems to go out of them? Suddenly they are old. Like faded bits of sunlight. Can you tell these are not fresh, pure, unwashed white gloves that I'm wearing to church this morning?

ACT TWO
Scene One

Evening. New windowpanes. Everything has been cleaned. Blood is repairing the last window. Acts is underneath his car, working.

BLOOD (*Talk-singing to himself as he hammers a nail in place and plays an imagined guitar*):
    And I said to myself
    'Cause I'm always talking to me,
    "Self," said I,
    "We all must die
    And darkness will soon surround us."

    "Ohhhhhhhh NO!" self hollered,
    "I don't want to be dead,
    Me, I ain't never gonna die
    Gonna buy a car,
    Gonna drive it far,
    Gonna drive away from me, myself and I."
    (*Steps back and surveys his work*) Shall I paint them, stain them or what?
ACTS (*Preoccupied*): Mmmmm. Yeah. Okay...

BLOOD: Which one?

ACTS: Whatever. Valves are slightly worn but that's light stuff.

BLOOD *(Angrily)*: How would you like the windows done up in red? Red paint?

ACTS: Wrist pins and connecting rod bearings are in good condition.

BLOOD: It must be hard on Mom.

ACTS: She'll be glad you fixed them. Low oil consumption. This baby is practically brand-new.

BLOOD: I'm not talking 'bout the windows. I mean her. My mother and your wife.

ACTS: What about her? The flywheel is okay too. Hotdammit! It's gonna be something else when I finish.

BLOOD: Nothing else matters to you. That's gotta be hard on her.

ACTS: S'no difference between a car and a woman. Cool 'em. Ignite 'em. Give 'em plenty of lubrication. Keep their engine in good condition.

BLOOD *(As he speaks he writes red graffiti on the new windowpanes)*: I had a woman once. She worked at the express counter in the supermarket. I used to make seven, eight shopping trips a day just to walk through her line. Every time she saw me she smiled and I was sure she really loved me. Whenever she asked me if I wanted a single or double bag I knew she was really pledging her love. And all those times I replied, "Single bag, thank you" I was really asking her to let me drink her bathwater.

Although I never knew her name, we were very happy. All over the city I drew red hearts for her. No clean space went unmarked. I even added some of my blood to the red paint. When I pricked all my fingers and toes I started on my knuckles and ankles. It hurt like hell!

One time I stayed up all night making hearts for her. Next morning I ran to our supermarket and got on her line. Some man was with her making her laugh. She didn't even know that I was there. I just stood there looking at her. I screamed at her silently, "You love him and not me. You want his low voice, his strong chest and his big thighs. Why can't you want me?" I was very angry.

ACTS (*Surveying the windowpanes without ever stopping his work*): I know what you trying to do but it won't work. You striving to prevent me from getting my work done. You hate this car. You trying to keep it from being born. Now you can act a fool if you want but just don't get in my way.

BLOOD (*Resignedly looking over the car*): It's state-of-the-art all right.

ACTS: Damn straight.

BLOOD: You sure ain't no "pliers-and-screwdriver" mechanic.

ACTS: Never was. Never will be.

Blood takes out a gleaming knife with a feather stuck in its handle and plays with it.

What . . . is . . . that?

BLOOD: It's a knife, man.

ACTS: For what?

Blood slowly takes out an orange and begins slowly to peel it as he looks at the car.

BLOOD: For peeling things. I like to peel things. Just like to see if with one slow continuous steady movement I can take the skin off anything in one, long, thin, graceful, piece.

ACTS: Hope you can handle a knife better than you can a gun.

BLOOD: I can do a lot of things. (*Holding up the entire orange peel in one piece*)

ACTS: What about important things? You remember the first time I put you underneath a car?

BLOOD: No. I don't remember.

ACTS: You need to kneel down beside me again and take another look. Give you a different perspective when you laying on your back flat out, looking up inside the belly of a car.

BLOOD: No thanks. All you do is wake up thinking about your car and sleep dreaming about it. No thank you. What about me? You never really talk to me. And when you talk you never really say anything.

ACTS: Okay, you been after me all this time so I'm gonna talk. Gonna tell you something. So listen real good.

As Acts speaks, Blood keeps peeling, letting the peelings and fruit pile up on the floor. Every once in a while he seems to nick himself accidentally.

In this world, in order to survive, you gotta have a little gris-gris to depend on. It could be anything. A prayer, a saying, a rabbit foot, a horseshoe, a song. A way of looking at life, a way of doing things, a way of understanding the world you find yourself in. Something that will never fail to pull you through the hard times. Now I see you got no formula for survival, no magic, no juju, so let me give you a very important piece of mojo right now. Always remember that the secret of a car is its engine. The engine is the car's heart. Treat it right and you can trust it. The trick is you gotta take your time and learn it. Study it inside out. Most folks abuse the engine by racing it when it's cold. How would you like to be waked up in the morning by someone shouting and screaming at you while you're still yawning and under the covers? You couldn't respond even if you wanted to. It takes time to fully warm up. And you gotta give it good fuel. Then you gotta inspire it. Set it on fire. Ignite the bad boy. Then he's gotta be stroked and lubricated real good. Now don't forget there's plenty of fire and heat inside so you gotta cool him off, too. Learn the engine, boy. Understand the heart. It's the secret of life.

BLOOD: Is that all you can talk about? Cars? Is that all?

ACTS: Fool! Is that all you think I'm talking about? *(He grimaces in sudden pain)*

BLOOD: What is it . . . what's wrong?

ACTS *(A gesture of weariness)*: Nothing. I ache all over.

BLOOD: What do you expect, hunched over that car all day and night? A good massage will fix you up. *(He begins to massage Acts' shoulders, gently at first and then with increasing violence)*

ACTS: Ahhhhhh. That feels good. Ouch. Not so rough.

A look passes between Blood and Acts which establishes the element of distrust between them.

BLOOD *(Continuing the massage)*: Is this where the pain is? *(Gives him a powerful whack on his shoulders)*

ACTS (*Trying unsuccessfully to move away from him*): No! Get away from me.

BLOOD (*Trying to continue massage*): Be still.

ACTS: Kinda rough there, aren't you, "Blood"?

BLOOD (*Poking Acts*): Is the pain here? Or there?

ACTS: Let me go! Ouch! Ow!

Another look passes between them.

BLOOD: Oh, I'm sorry, man.

ACTS: Walter, don't you know when you're hurting someone?

BLOOD: I'm not sure what you want, Dad.

ACTS: I want you to stop, Son.

BLOOD (*Gives Acts a final, painful shoulder jab*): There! Doesn't that feel better?

ACTS: Holy shit. What the hell is going on here?

BLOOD: Every movement, every touch means something. (*Suddenly releasing Acts and running toward the car*)

ACTS: Get back. Don't touch it. Keep away.

BLOOD: It's a beautiful car. Just beautiful. (*He begins to disarrange various parts of the car*)

ACTS: That's not it! That's not it at all! Get away from the damn thing. Stand back. (*Pushing Blood away from the car*) Just look at it and don't touch a damn thing!

Blood stands for several beats, looking at the car. He holds his hands together as if in prayer. Then he suddenly begins to pick up the peelings and fruit from the floor and carries them to Awilda's candles on the mantelpiece, where he spreads them while mumbling in a strange language. Acts watches him, fascinated.

BLOOD: It's a ritual.

ACTS: Ritual?

BLOOD: Yes. For your forgiveness.

ACTS: Mine?

BLOOD: Yes.

ACTS: Why?

BLOOD (*Searching*): Because...because...you broke the windows!
WHY DID YOU BREAK THEM?

ACTS: That was because your mother started on me about her "Pastor." I went off. The ground parted. Quick flashes of lightning stabbed at my head. My blood boiled.

BLOOD: I know the feeling.

ACTS: Be careful. It's in our blood.

BLOOD: What's it called?

ACTS: It ain't a disease. It's a condition. A condition I tell you. All of us are thinking about one thing. A boy brought up in the city and killed by wild dogs. *(Returning to his car)* But when I am working on this car I don't feel a thing. I feel clean. I feel strong. I feel free.

BLOOD: I feel like shit!

ACTS: Get away from your mother's candles.

BLOOD: My mother! What do you care about her?

ACTS: I do. A lot. But she's with her "Pastor" now.

BLOOD *(Exploding, violently blowing out candles)* Shit on her Pastor! *(Blows out more candles)* To hell with his so-called church! *(Blows out some more candles)* I hate Sunday con men! *(Blows out the last candles)* And their wicked trickerations!

ACTS: Don't do that! What gives you the right?

BLOOD: Pops, let's leave here. Let's not stay here. We should just take that money and run. You and me and Mom should get outta this place. Make a new start.

ACTS: Oh yeah? Where, for instance?

BLOOD: Let's go to Mexico.

ACTS: Mexico? What they got down there for me besides refried beans and the worthless peso?

BLOOD: You could get land cheap down there. In less than ten years it's worth three times what you paid. You could build cars down there. I know a special spot down there. A city in the mountains.

ACTS: That's your world. My world is right here. A world where all the cars that my mind can conjure up is brought to life.

BLOOD: Forget it man.

ACTS: So . . . you liked it down in Mexico.

BLOOD: I didn't get in trouble with the police if that's what you mean.

ACTS: Then why did you come back this time?

BLOOD: We're family. We're chained together.

ACTS: Then why are you leaving?

BLOOD: I can't stay here. Do you know what it means to be the surviving brother? You never talk about the morning that Linus was killed. You were with him when he got killed but you don't tell what really happened.

ACTS: You know Walter, you'll be okay once you get yourself together. Take care of your own self. You need to get a mojo and don't worry about me none. The right mojo will give you the sayso. Put you in the driver's seat. The right mojo will take you over those moments of terror, doubt or even surprise. Nothing surprises me no more. I'm ready to take it all on.

At this moment we hear the singing, talking and laughing voices of Awilda and Pastor Delroy offstage. Blackout.

Scene Two

The stage slowly lights up as Awilda and Pastor Delroy enter the room, still singing. Awilda, radiant and nervous as a young girl on a date, is carrying a bouquet of multicolored gladioli. The Pastor wears a clerical collar, robe and white gloves.

AWILDA: Mr. Benjamin! Walter! You two, we have special company. Oh Pastor, what a voice you have. Deep and rich and full like a . . . a . . . man! You could have been a singer with millions of fans instead of a man of God. In church I can hear your voice over all the others. *(To Walter and Acts)* What a lovely service. You two should have been there. Going to church is like going to a garden where beautiful music grows. And the beautiful carnations and gladiolas on the altar. I brought some home because church flowers are special.

PASTOR: Brothers Benjamin, senior and junior. Peace and love. Our lovely sister Awilda asked me to stop by.

ACTS: Oh yeah?

PASTOR: I see you are still working on your car? Imagine that. Looks like you'll even be finished soon. *(Makes a gesture to touch the car)*

ACTS *(Ferociously)*: Don't touch him.

PASTOR *(Backing away, frightened)*: Brother Acts. I've always felt that you fear me. There is no need to. Don't you know that "He that feareth is not made perfect in love"?

ACTS: Don't you know that he that fucketh around with my car will be made perfect in death?

PASTOR: Brother Benjamin, you can't mean that I'm not welcome here?

ACTS: You never had any trouble feeling comfortable before. The wife seems to fry chicken just the way you like it.

PASTOR: You don't expect me to refuse the gracious invitations of the lovely saints of my congregation, do you?

ACTS: I have a line in my mind that divides the killer beast from the gentle man. Be careful. You are stepping awfully near the edge.

AWILDA: There's something wrong in here. I felt it as soon as I walked in. New windows? All written over in red paint, AND WHAT IS THIS SHIT AROUND MY CANDLES? Who blew them out? What the Devil is going on around here now?

BLOOD *(Going toward her, trying to calm her)*: Easy Ma, let me explain.

AWILDA *(Shrinking back from him)*: That's all right. I should have known. Every time you're around I never know what is going to happen.

BLOOD: I'll . . . I'll scrub the paint off . . . before I split.

AWILDA: No! Don't leave. Today is Linus's anniversary.

BLOOD: LINUS IS DEAD!

Awilda is lighting all the candles as if to revive him.

PASTOR: Sister, do not despair. Linus is near us, though unseen. His spirit depends on us to remember him in special ways.

ACTS: Back off, Delroy! You are stepping on my line.

PASTOR: I feel Linus nearer and nearer. Sometimes I can see him.

I can see him standing large as life in front of me. He never looks at me. He's just there.

BLOOD *(To Awilda)*: Can't you see it's just an act?

PASTOR: I tell you sister, there is no death. "The stars go down to rise upon some fairer shore. And bright in heaven's jeweled crown they shine, forevermore!"

ACTS *(Grabbing him)*: You have just crossed the equator. Get the hell out!

AWILDA: Pastor should be here.

BLOOD: I'm sorry about the windows. I was only trying to communicate with my father.

AWILDA: I wanted Pastor here when I told you about the money.

PASTOR: Amen.

ACTS: What . . . about . . . the . . . money?

AWILDA: Linus is getting a memorial.

PASTOR: Praise Him!

BLOOD: It's a damn shame.

AWILDA: What are you saying?

BLOOD: It's a damn shame that I'm alive and Linus isn't.

PASTOR: I tell you all that Linus is alive and we must remember him.

ACTS: We need to be alone right now, Delroy.

AWILDA: No.

PASTOR *(Seductively)*: Awilda.

ACTS: Awilda, Awilda, now you listen. I been thinking. This car is gonna be finished soon. Then we gonna leave. All of us. We gonna slip out easy like a soft wind. When folks catch on that ain't nobody in this house anymore you know what they gonna do? They gonna break in and I leave everything to all of them. My rubber galoshes, my old brown leather longshoremen's jacket with the lamb's-wool lining, my checkerboard, my dreambooks, my fishing poles—I'll get new ones—my Gene Ammons' seventy-eights and my tools. Let them take my acetylene torch, cutters, dollies and hammers, my balancers and hydraulic pressers, my reamers, hones and wrenchers, my gauges and gappers, and place them in the middle of Springfield Boulevard and burn them! Any second, this car will be finished and we'll all get in. I want you to put on the blue dress you was wearing at the Silver Fly that day I first seen you. And Walter's gonna wear his Mexican shirt. The car radio's gonna be on. The dial will be set. Chuck Berry, Ivory Joe Hunter and Nat King Cole will be bluesing around. Little Esther is wanting a "Sunday Kind of Love." Jimmy Garrison is on bass. Max is on drums. Monk is on piano. The Orioles. The Moonglows. Little Willie John and Aretha. All the sounds of all the ages coming together in my car.

AWILDA: I remember how I used to love driving with you, listening to music, feeling the wind against my cheeks.

PASTOR: Seek ye not the vain pleasures of this world, sister. Remember Linus.

AWILDA: Ever since the money came I been thinking. We need something money can't buy. That's why I...I...

PASTOR: You want me to hold your hand while you tell them?

AWILDA: No.

PASTOR: You want me to tell them for you?

AWILDA: No.

PASTOR: All right, then tell them!

AWILDA: I'm giving the money to Pastor's church in Linus's name.

PASTOR: Amen.

Acts begins a slow, dangerous laugh.

There is no greater memorial.

Acts lunges at Pastor and narrowly misses him.

(Remaining calm as he sidesteps Acts and speaks in a soft, sanctimonious voice, full of righteous piety) "He delivereth me from my enemies. Yea, from those that rise up against me. Verily I say unto you, 'He delivereth me from the violent man.'" My poor, sinful brethren. You are consumed with hypocrisy and greed. "And the greedy man shall retch up his desire for it is an unclean thing." And the hypocrites shall burn! burn! in the lower depths. Rise! Cleanse yourselves and admit that you want that money. You don't want God to have it. You lust after

each dollar and have silent plans how to spend every cent.

Remember, beloved, "Lying lips are an abomination and the liars shall all be stripped of their foul pretense." Why do you denounce my church? Why do you rail against my religion? Why do you attack all that is upright and righteous in this ungodly world full of evil fornicators? Why do you attack me?

My only concern is Linus and his immortality. Do not let the world forget him. He who was crushed by the forces of wickedness! He who was the fairest among boys. He who was snatched from us before the soft down of manhood kissed his cheeks. His loins yet girded with innocence. A bright-eyed, graceful manchild. O! Countless are the splendors of this world but none more splendiferous than was that fine, tender young boy!

BLOOD (*Taking out his knife*): You weren't counting on murder, were you?

PASTOR: Perhaps you're right. I'll just come back some other time.

Pastor tries to leave; Blood stops him with the knife.

AWILDA: Walter, stop it. I've been so afraid that you would hurt someone.

ACTS (*Moving toward Awilda*): Walter, put the knife away. I keep telling you, it's not a mojo.

BLOOD: I have got to find a way to make you all listen to me. (*Everyone is frozen*) I've got to find a way to make you all LISTEN TO ME!

Down in Mexico, in spots where I've been, some natives have a ritual for this kind of man. They believe in releasing the lies from his flesh. They just skin the poor devil alive. I've seen it done and it's just like skinning a fruit. Now listen up, your righteousness. I'm a-going to take my knife and slowly cut you from your larynx to your rectum. Then I'm going to flop you on your belly and peel away your lying skin in one piece just like a new suit of clothes. Just like an orange peel. (*Everyone is terrified as he keeps talking. He menaces Pastor with the knife*) First, I'll work the skin over your skull and cut it with care so that it all comes off in one piece. Don't worry. I'll be careful when I cut around your eyes.

Pastor emits a terrified howl.

I'll make an incision in your throat to a point midway in the calf of your leg.

ACTS: Walter.

BLOOD: I'll grab your scrotum. Or is it scrotii?

PASTOR: Oh Jesus!

BLOOD: And make an incision in each.

PASTOR *(Doubling over in imagined pain, protecting his groin)*: Ohhhhhhhhhhhhhhh.

BLOOD *(To Pastor)*: STRIP!

Pastor blinks frantically, not believing his ears.

AWILDA: Walter!

BLOOD: Look at him. I want you to look. You won't look at me and you can't see through him. *(To Pastor)* I . . . said . . . off . . . with . . . the . . . clothes, holiness.

Pastor slowly begins to remove his clerical collar, his white gloves and his robe. Around his neck is gleaming gold jewelry; he is dressed in a silk suit and other items of luxury. He has revealed himself as a "dandy man." When he takes off his white gloves he reveals the talons of a bird of prey with gleaming rings around them. Acts, Blood and Awilda are amazed at first and then Acts and Blood double over, convulsed with laughter.

AWILDA: Pastor? Pastor?

BLOOD *(Ridiculing him in a singsong chant)*: "He took Ms. Johnson's money, poor old Miss Baker's Social Security, and made her throw in those diamonds he's wearing for an extra blessing."

ACTS: Wife? Is this who you trust over me?

AWILDA *(In a daze):* No.

BLOOD: Off with your clothes, reverent reverend.

Pastor continues to undress. He is wearing a jeweled G-string, S&M boots and other suggestive clothing.

BLOOD: "Jeanie Taylor, Diane Williams and little Dickie Hill were disgraced by his sexual conduct. But his congregation forgave him."

AWILDA *(Gets nearer to Pastor and inspects every inch of him)*: Take it all off. Down to the bone. I want to see it all.

Pastor hesitates; Blood menaces him.

BLOOD: All off. You heard the lady, holy father.

As Pastor strips, he begins to take on the movements and rhythms of a vulture. He reveals a feathered body, a hook nose and webbed, claw feet. He makes vulture noises as he begins to execute broad, swooping circles around Awilda, as if stalking his prey.

AWILDA *(Beating back the Pastor/vulture as if exorcising something within her)*: Scavenger! Bird of Prey! Vulture!

They both turn around in circles, he stalking her, she beating him off.

He has sharp eyes and a keen sense of smell. He can see dead animals from a great distance.

She tosses him her church flowers and white gloves, which he gobbles up, eating and retching at the same time.

He eats carrion, dead animals, dead things. He often vomits when feeding.

Pastor/vulture begins to stalk her once more.

Drive back the unclean scavenger with living flesh. He only thrives on decay. Drive him out with living thoughts and a living heart. He only feeds on the dead. Only the living live in here. Out! Out! Out!

Pastor/vulture is driven out through the window. Exhausted, Awilda collapses in the arms of Acts and Blood.

ACTS: Awilda.
AWILDA: Tell me what happened that night. Please
BLOOD: Go ahead, Pops. Tell her.
ACTS: You are right, Son, I ran. I ran away.
BLOOD: What!?
ACTS: We both ran. The boy and I both ran.

Acts holds the check, inspecting the look, feel of it as he talks to it. Lights dim, candle flames grow higher as Acts continues. Awilda and Blood listen intently, for this is the first time they have ever heard the story.

ACTS: It's funny how it always comes back to money. It's funny how money is supposed to explain everything and make anything all right. It was a Saturday, right before dawn, and as you know, the boy and I were on our way to the yard. Fooling around with cars is in my bones so I figure since Linus takes after me in so many ways he could learn it real good and earn a little change too. So when he turned ten, he started coming with me on Saturday mornings 'cause the rest of the week he's in school like he's supposed to be. He was a nice boy. Very respectful. Very intelligent. He would have been a good mechanic some day.

I remember it was early spring but the dew made it cold. The sky was that light purplish gray you get right before dawn. We was both walking, not saying too much. I guess it was just too early to be doing a lot of talking. We walked down New York Boulevard through the vacant lot littered with broken glass, past the trees that rise right out of the trash and grow fifty feet tall. Suddenly two guys with plain clothes pull up in a plain car and yell at us, "Stop." Their car screams to a halt. I didn't even recognize them as humans so how should I know they was cops, creeping toward us, hissing, "Stop, you sons of bitches," laughing and drinking as they cursed us. Said in the papers they was looking for two grown burglars. My little son and I wasn't no burglars.

My wallet was bulging on my hip. I had just gotten paid. I had it all figured out. These drunken jokers are ordinary crooks trying to rob me. I figure the way they are drinking I can outrun both of them and you remember how Linus could outrun a chicken. "Run," I command and we take off. Linus shoots out in front of me and I was right behind.

They didn't even chase us. A flat loud sound ripped the air and Linus fell and instantly became a red pool, his eyes a bright, white blank. They shot Linus in the back. They killed him! They shot my boy!

Always, always, in my head, "Should I have stood my ground and fought them? Was I trying to protect my money more than Linus?" Ain't no way I could run away and leave Linus alone, is there? LINUS RAN AHEAD OF ME AND LEFT ME! I know that's the way it happened. But sometimes a man can get confused and the way something awful happens isn't always the way you remember it. I play it back all the time in my head and my only thought that night was to protect Linus. At least that's the way I remember it.

He slowly tears the check to shreds. Suddenly the car headlights are blinking, the motor is running, the horn is honking and the radio is playing.

AWILDA *(Coyly)*: Mr. Benjamin, my blue dress is ready.

ACTS: Blue dress?

AWILDA: You know, the one I was wearing that day we first met. *(She removes her church clothes and reveals her blue dress)*

BLOOD *(Dancing around and singing in a Spanish accent while revealing his Mexican shirt)*: No more pain, no more blood, no more pain, no more blood.

ACTS *(Taking off his mechanic's clothes, reveals his striped blue suit, rolled-collar shirt, diamond stickpin, leather wing tips, etc.)*: I did it just like I said I would. It's crashproof, with an automatic fire extinguisher, electric shift and front-wheel drive, and rear seats that rise through the sunroof. A pretty machine nine hundred times as powerful as human man. It ain't even a machine. It's a force of nature, that's what it is. The Mojo 9. Built by a man who walked through iron times and is still kicking.

See, look. My eyes are clear. My skin is tight and my body well-tuned for any situation. You all should trust me. Come with me. Mojo can take us anyplace. Mojo will get you through. I'll show you how to build an engine, boy, and you won't have to worry your head about nothing. Come on. What are you two standing there for? Get in. What are you waiting for?

Acts, Awilda and Blood all climb in the car and the Mojo is driven straight through the door.

FROM

THE

RESURRECTION

OF THE

DAUGHTER:

LILIANE

NTOZAKE

SHANGE

I want to create a character, a woman of color whom we could experience from different points of view. The way that I experience myself is not my whole life; or the way that I experience my daughter is not her whole life. I was interested in these ideas: What do other people think of us? And when they take us to heart, how do they integrate us into their lives? I wanted to give Lili's version of herself and people she cared about, along with their versions of her. It's important to  know what other people think of us even if we don't like it. At least that way we know if we're being effective or not.

One of the reasons I like writing about adolescent girls and young women is because we know so little about ourselves; in a literary sense, there are so few of us. And one of the reasons I try to investigate girls from different backgrounds and girls with different senses of success is because I want to make sure that we all know that none of our desires are illegitimate.

The Psychoanalytical Narrative

The narrative, or throughline, is based in the "shrink sessions" [excerpted here]. Other characters [elsewhere in the novel] tell us things about Liliane that she either denies or never mentions, so the only way we can really understand her is in her sessions with her analyst. In the outside world [of the novel], there are crazy things going on that we experience as elements of Liliane's source material through which she becomes this woman who has integrity by the end [of the book].

In the preface to *Playing In the Dark*, Toni Morrison discusses a book by Marie Cardinal, *The Words to Say It*, which I had also read a few years ago. In introducing Marie Cardinal's remarkable dissection of her own psychoanalysis, Toni Morrison says, "The narrative into which light seems to cast itself surfaces most forcefully in certain kinds of psychoanalysis. . . ." This is important to me because as black people we exist metaphorically and literally as the underside, the underclass. We are the unconscious of the entire Western world. If this is in fact true, then where do we go? Where are our dreams? Where is our pain? Where do we heal? And part of the reason I created Lili is to give us the space to do that. I'm trying to give all of us, through Lili's vulnerability and audacity, the right to discover whatever it is we are, without having to deal with what the world thinks we are. We know that we have always been the outsider. We know that from any study of African art; e.g., the de Menil collection which traces the African presence in European art back to the 1200s. We know that, because in a way we could say, after *Invisible Man* and poor little Bigger [in *Native Son*], that we should all just put our pens back and go back to bed. But I don't think we need to do that because we still have living, breathing black people out here, and we need to be able to talk about ourselves in language with the dignity of poetry.

In psychoanalysis, you can't do anything but talk. The limitations imposed by that form allowed me to investigate parts of Liliane as a character and certain kinds of language that I would be unable to do in another setting. I have a character whose voice leads me and her to a broader sense of what being alive is—a kind of being alive that, as she approaches it, allows her to experience more things as opposed to fewer things. Her sensibility can become more refined and more acute as she discovers all these things that are herself as she speaks them.

All my life, my big villains have been violent men and violent white people; and then opacity in language or thought. Psychoanalysis penetrates that opacity by allowing our beings to take from the words what we want them to mean. "Rooms in the Dark" is a sparse section [of the novel] because we have to dance through the words so we can really make them take root in us. As Liliane clarifies things, they take root in her, not as chaos or something scary, but in something she can breathe with, relax in and own. She has to own it so that it doesn't terrify her and therefore she can be stronger.

Rites of Passage

The Greek and Arabic roots of the name Liliane mean "new beginnings." This girl is reinventing herself. She goes to Africa, Asia, North America—places where we were colonized. And by reconstituting colonized people and figuring out the historical antecedents for the events in her life, she figures out who she is, and who she (we) can be.

Definitions of Heroism

For Lili, heroism is the willingness to know your mother and not be ashamed. None of our mothers are who we want them to be, but I really adore mine. To know and accept one's mother is, for women, our biggest challenge and gift. It's a gift to us to know what they did and how they did it, all the mistakes they made, but it's still Mommy.

On Psychoanalysis and People of Color
People of color have always been acted on by social service agencies and experiments like Tuskegee or sterilization of women in Puerto Rico, so we have real reason to be suspicious of professions that want to know all our business because they don't always use it to our advantage. In specific circumstances, when you're at a specific point in your life and you voluntarily seek out a method of introspection, it's very revealing. There is a trust that evolves between a good psychoanalyst and the analysand that heightens the ability to discern reality which prepares us to be more efficient and deliberate in every other aspect of our lives. We need any tool that helps us become a more productive people. Exquisite experiences in psychoanalysis prepare us to feel more than we ever imagined, not less.

Distinctions between Women's and Men's Writing
I have been remarkably fortunate to have studied in a formal manner literature of people of color from all over the world; sometimes in translation, most of the time not. This allowed me to escape what I really feel to be one of our primary prisons, which is the English language. Even though I enthusiastically submitted myself to years of scholarly pursuit of dreams and similes of the great Western literature, I always knew that for the most part I did not exist. Therefore when you ask me about the differences between women's literature and men's literature, I have to respond that there is a patriarchal literature to which we all submit—even when we look at advertisements for Coca-Cola—but that is not all there is. Men of color, be they Chinese or Korean or Panamanian or Haitian or from Detroit, those men submit to that same patriarchy just like women do. So there's a subcategory that we are, as always in the last days of imperialism, that has to do with liberating people who don't exist. In that category, a whole new crop of young male writers—Edward Said, Kenan, Simon Ortiz, Alurista, Reggie McKnight, Gavin Moses—is responding as violently as I do to the humiliations and inequities imposed upon us by a Western patriarchy. In that sense, there is no difference.

It becomes different when we become very specific and when women's lives are not shuffled about like so many cards, where one deck can be exchanged for another—that fifty-two women for another fifty-two women. As women we can't afford that, whereas it's really not terribly dangerous to men to do that. As far as I can tell at this point, the new crop of women writers—such as Suzanna Cartier, new writing from Toi Derricotte, Jordan Keith and my sister Ifa Bayeza—they are even more daring than we are because they are willing to tackle the world in terms of women's needs and desires: the world I tackle in stuff I write is already limited by our inability to do things. So the younger women go into areas where I wouldn't know how to; I have no idea how to write about a woman in corporate America. They're not quite as battle-weary as we are, so they are capable of seeing more.

The Darkness and the Light
My darknesses are my dreams and my memories; and they are very scary. My light is always female. I believe this from my grandmother, my great-aunt Effie and my mother. They survived death, disease, war, white people and plain old hatred with dignity and style. I just want to approach what they did; not even be it, just get near there. They were fabulous women.

ABOUT THE AUTHOR

Ntozake Shange is the author of *for colored girls who have considered suicide/when the rainbow is enuf*, *Spell #7* and *A Photograph: Lovers-in-Motion*. In collaboration with Emily Mann and Baikida Carroll she wrote a musical adaptation of her novel *Betsey Brown*, produced by the McCarter Center for the Performing Arts in 1991. *The Love Space Demands: A Continuing Saga* was part of the Crossroads Theatre Company's Genesis Project in 1992. Her other works include the volumes of poetry *Nappy Edges*, *A Daughter's Geography*, *Ridin' the Moon in Texas* and *From Okra to Greens*, and the novel *Sassafras, Cypress and Indigo*. Shange has worked and performed with numerous artists and groups, including Dianne McIntyre's Sounds in Motion, Raymond Sawyer's Afro-Asian Dance Company, Ed Mock's West Coast Dance Works, the Stanze Peterson Dance Company, and the musicians David Murray, Fred Hopkins, Oliver Lake, Henry Threadgill, Billy Bang and the late Steve McCall. Shange is the recipient of two Obie awards (one for her adaptation of Brecht's *Mother Courage and Her Children*); and of fellowships from Chubb & Son Inc., the Guggenheim Foundation, the National Endowment for the Arts and the Mac-Dowell Colony. Among her many awards are the Medal of Excellence from Columbia University, the Los Angeles Times Book Review Prize for Poetry, two Audelco Awards, the Houston International Festival Prize for Literature, a poetry grant from the New York State Council on the Arts and the Lila Wallace Reader's Digest Writer's Award.

ABOUT THE WORK

The Resurrection of the Daughter: Liliane, a new novel by Ntozake Shange (forthcoming from St. Martin's Press), chronicles the journey of a visual artist from adolescence to womanhood. The prismatic composition of the novel is derived from two narrative lines (one from childhood and one from adult life); the Psalms, which are from her journal; and a series of dramatic scenes between Liliane and her psychoanalyst, entitled "Rooms in the Dark," of which dialogues II, IV, V, VI and VII are included here. The novel is also being adapted for the stage.

CHARACTERS

LILIANE

ANALYST

from THE RESURRECTION OF THE DAUGHTER: LILIANE

Rooms in the Dark

II

Very long pause.

LILIANE: Maybe it's not the silences. *(Long pause)* Not the silences that bother me. *(Long pause)* It's just the noise like a roar inside my head takes over when it's silent. *(Long pause)* It's not quiet that I avoid. I never really talk out loud, *en pleine aire,* when I walk and I walk everywhere I can. I prefer men who like to walk 'cause then we can talk with our eyes or our bodies or some strange sign'll bring us together. No it's not quiet that I avoid. I'm quiet when I can hear music.

ANALYST: What music?

LILIANE: Oh, Bartok and B. B. King, Celia Cruz or Gloria Lynne. I don't like listenin' to ex-lovers very much, but I won't turn them off. Down maybe, but not off.

ANALYST: Are ex-lovers part of the noise in your head? *(Long pause)* Or more in the silence?

LILIANE: You are interfering with my paradigm here. The music was part of a quiet that's quite appropriate and tangible, some pleasing part of my own body, my smile, my breath.

ANALYST: But you turn ex-lovers down.

LILIANE: Yes, down, not off. If I turned them off, they'd be part of the silence and then I wouldn't be able to hear anything palpable. It's like going to the moon.

ANALYST: The moon?

LILIANE: *Si, la luna, la lune,* the moon in quiet with Machito or Turrentine is a sultry wanton giggle in my eye, but in silence the moon is just another dry cracking surface like talkin' to white people all the time makes me choke. I can't breathe in silence.

ANALYST: Why is that?

LILIANE: 'Cause it presses down on me like a man who doesn't know his own weight can fuck me to death 'cause literally he's also blocking my esophagus, or like a wrong turn in the middle of the night in South Boston can take my breath away. What difference does it make? It's quiet. It's silent. So what? You know, that's not my biggest problem, right?

ANALYST: What is your biggest problem?

LILIANE: Damn it. I told you, Jesus Christ, I musta told you a thousand times, I can't breathe.

ANALYST: When it's silent?

LILIANE: Yes.

ANALYST: That's why my silences, here with you, are troubling, then?

LILIANE: Oh... (*Long pause*) How're you gonna help me in silence?

ANALYST: Well, then we can get to hear the noises in your head that are choking you.

LILIANE: It wasn't always true. (*Long pause*) Uhmn. I didn't always need to hear anything or not hear anything. I have never had asthma, but now when somebody, even a soap starlet's voice, isn't audible, if there's no music or chatter, or the phone's not ringing, I mean, not answered, I start gaspin' and next thing I know I'm holdin' my throat like my hands are healin' hands and I can't find any air. I forget where I am. My feet aren't really on the ground. Oh hell, I don't know where my feet are when there's that kinda force, my God, all I can imagine is being caught inside a roll of thunder—. Now, could you get aholda yourself in a roll of thunder?

ANALYST: Why not lightning?

LILIANE: 'Cause I'm not burnin' up, I'm chokin' to death. (*Long pause*) I told you I can't take this. I cannot survive in silence.

ANALYST: It's not really the silence you believe you can't survive. It's the noise in your head that you only hear in silence.

LILIANE: I've only mastered Quiet Time, how's that?

ANALYST: A start.

Very long pause.

LILIANE: When it's really silent, I can't feel anything. I mean, I start to lose where the floor is. Why a flower is different from a rug—you know, to feel—or even that walls don't curve under themselves like cats. I just know that I've gotta go to sleep right now or get outta here. I've gotta find somebody to talk to me, somebody who knows me.

ANALYST: Somebody who loves you.

LILIANE: No.

ANALYST: *No?*

LILIANE: Doesn't matter 'long as he won't hurt me.

ANALYST: "Me"?

LILIANE: Oh. Don't put on so.... You know, the bastard tried to choke me right at Sheridan Square the night my show opened. He spit on the sidewalk, turned round, and wrapped his fingers 'bout my neck like I was a magnum of Perrier & Jouet.

Long pause.

ANALYST: I thought—

Long pause.

LILIANE: We were lovers. *(Long pause)* We usedta walk all the time and hear the most beautiful music. *(Long pause)* Now, whenever a melody ends, I feel his fingers on my throat. Some of my hair, in the back, is caught in his fingers and he's shakin' me down from the Riviera as if nobody was around. People walked past, went across the street to the park. And nobody said anything. Did anything. The traffic kept comin', cars to New Jersey and cabs with medallions kept movin'. I heard the downtown IRT and all. Outta nowhere but he was right there. Outta nowhere I heard him screamin', "Who do you think you are?" and...I couldn't breathe. So I couldn't answer...I couldn't answer... "It's me, Lili...just me..."

Very long pause.

ANALYST: This is very important.

LILIANE: Yeah. How's that?

ANALYST: Well. You turn down ex-lovers in quiet.

LILIANE: Yeah, I'm not afraid in music.

ANALYST: Or language.

Long pause.

LILIANE: It's these silences.

ANALYST: Where lovers become assassins without warning.

LILIANE: It's the noise. A horrible throbbin' roar . . . and . . .

ANALYST: You can't hear yourself. *(Long pause)* Or protect yourself.

LILIANE: I can't even say my name. I can't breathe. *(Long pause)* But, why. Why would he hurt me like that?

ANALYST: Maybe he couldn't stand to hear the music in you.

LILIANE: Music? Oh God. He even shouted when he talked about music he loved, like a delicacy in the tone of his voice would actually impugn the virility of a note. . . . I like to caress sounds and images I care for with my fingers, my tongue, my lips. He was always shouting, shouting till my ears hurt.

ANALYST: Noise, again. A noise that hurts, yea?

LILIANE: Why am I lowering my eyes when you say that? "A noise that hurts."

ANALYST: A noise that. . . . It's the silence.

LILIANE: How can hurtin' be associated with shame? Lowering my eyes 'cause somebody's hurt me, then I'm guilty of . . . feeling? That's crazy. Maybe. Maybe not. Could be protecting yourself from the Gorgon or Medusa. So you don't turn to stone and stop feeling. *(Very long pause)* You're not helpin' me when you don't respond. *(Long pause)* I'm gettin' a knot in my throat. I'm frightened and my heart's beatin' up and out that window. *(Long pause)* Don't you hear me talkin' to you, dammit?

ANALYST: Yes, I'm here. You are doing impressive work, Liliane. *(Long pause)* We are starting to decipher the noise.

LILIANE: Oh, oh. My ears ache.

ANALYST: The noise.

LILIANE: Yes. Yes. He's screamin' and chucklin'. Please . . . I don't want to cry. I don't want to start cryin', talk to me, please.

ANALYST: He's always talking to you, even in the silence. Before I can really talk to you, we've got to hear what he is screaming at you. Then we can end this conversation with this man who can't caress words or images he cares about like you do.

LILIANE: There's a cave in my chest.

ANALYST: That's where his voice can boom and steal the air from you, so you can't breathe, Liliane.

LILIANE: Yes, I know.

ANALYST: Take those noises he makes of words and make them small enough for your mouth to say.

LILIANE: But, it's so mean. Why say such mean things?

ANALYST: That's how he makes the silence into such a racket. When there is nothing, he's still there screaming, he's right there making sure it hurts.

LILIANE: I can't take this.

ANALYST: Then he's pretty well succeeded.

LILIANE: I could just keep talkin'...I c'd...

ANALYST: Lili, you don't have to keep hearing him resounding when you are being still.

LILIANE: I do. I do, if there's no music. *(Long pause)* But, you said I had the music.

ANALYST: Yes.

LILIANE: You know it was such a lovely night we went walkin' in Noe Valley. All the harbor, two of those bridges that hang in the night, glowin', like magic. I was feelin' pretty good. I'd made those labia outta different kinds of soil, you know, fertile, infertile, sandy, black, clay. Was feelin' sorta sexy and stretched in a good way. We're goin' down this hill and lights are twinklin', ordinary houses glistened like FAO Schwarz, lovely, you know. I'm plannin' this party, you know, to show my labia boxes....He starts, starts laughin'.

Long pause.

ANALYST: What was so funny?

LILIANE: Well, he thought it was just hilarious that my artist friends, alla my artsy friends, had girlfriends who weren't black. Mingo's girl was Chinese. José-Alberto had Myo who was Vietnamese. Joe Scahenger had a white woman and, lemme see, I think maybe it was Adam was with a Chicana from East Oakland.

ANALYST: What was so funny about that?

LILIANE: Well...

ANALYST: Yes.

LILIANE: Uh. He thought it was so funny. For all the labia boxes I made it didn't look like there were many men sniffin' after a colored woman. Thought niggahs weren't so revved up 'bout white women no more, they sure weren't comin' home to get none. "Looks like don't nobody want you all, English-speakin' Negresses." He kept laughin'... and I am havin' trouble breathin', now. See, what you've done?

ANALYST: Yeah.

LILIANE: Well, what is that?

ANALYST: We broke the silence.

Long pause.

I V

LILIANE: So what do you want to do today?

ANALYST: We do what we usually do. You say what's on your mind. We go from there.

LILIANE: I don't want to talk about anything. I want to go home. That's what I want to do.

ANALYST: Okay. Let's go home then.

LILIANE: That's clever. That's very clever. You know and I know that we're not going anywhere. This is a room with shadow, light, a couch, a large soft chair, and a closed window.

ANALYST: Yes, that's true.

LILIANE: Well, then all this talk about going home is crazy. We're stuck in this room. *(Long pause)* I mean, I know I came here voluntarily. I wanted to come 'cause I'm coming out of my body. This is really odd. Parts of me, my feelings are streaming out of my hands and my thighs. I sense, when I am walking, that my thoughts are dripping down my calves from behind my knees. I am leaving puddles of myself underneath me and I can't pick myself back up, put myself back together.

ANALYST: Is that why you want to go home?

LILIANE: No, I left my house to come over here. Oh, this is really crazy.

ANALYST: You brought your crazy selves that were falling away from you here. Maybe this is their home. The slipping parts of you may need to be somewhere puddles of feelings aren't out of place.

LILIANE: This is a fuckin' mess.

ANALYST: I don't mind.

LILIANE: I do. I do. I do.

ANALYST: Why all this vehemence about a little messiness. People are messy creatures.

LILIANE: I just want to get myself together.

ANALYST: Like a puzzle?

LILIANE: What?

ANALYST: What parts are missing that keep you from being "to-gether"?

LILIANE: Missing. What's missing? I forgot to tell you I lost a baby. I got rid of a baby. (Long pause) I don't know. There was no way around it. Huh, I'm not the mother type, you know. I think they should come talkin' and potty-trained, you know. I just couldn't stand it, the idea that some child, somebody, would love me like nobody else on the earth and all I'd be able to say is I don't know how to do this and whoever your pop is doesn't care about me or you enough to pretend he cares. Oh, this is nuts . . .

ANALYST: Are the puddles of your selves mixed up with the lost baby?

LILIANE: I don't know. I just want to go home. Is it time to go yet?

ANALYST: No, we've more than fifteen minutes.

LILIANE: Fifteen minutes, oh. Where was I? . . . I know. I never did like to see women with babies. They looked so beat down, cov-ered with baby equipment, just mommy, not a woman with a name or feelings, like a pack animal or something. I don't have any place to put a baby.

ANALYST: Of course not. You're overflowing, coming out of your-self, in streams, and messes.

LILIANE: I thought for sure I would never tell him, you know. Why burden a flawless relationship with a mistake? God, whatta jackass I was. I say to myself, he's not like the rest. That's why I love him. I'm not in this relationship by myself. I can tell him what has happened to us. It's not just my responsibility. We can work this out together. If women keep taking responsibility for the relationship, men'll never be full partners, mature caregivers. What shit. He starts going back over the months, my last period, where we made love, like this is some kind of scientific interrogation. My body is going to reveal to him how this happened. Like I'm a body of evidence. Jesus. We fucked. The sperm got out and found a egg. It's as simple as that. I know how we got pregnant. I want to know what we're going to do now. Not, how did this happen. What kinda idiocy is that? Well, I covered my head with ostrich feathers and a red clay mask. Next thing I know I'm with child. Maybe, I should call the news: "Woman inseminated by Feather Fetish." Or better yet, I think I'll hire a skywriting plane and tell the world what I discovered: "Only the man you fuck doesn't know fuckin' makes you pregnant. Let's tell 'em." How's that?

ANALYST: Pretty expensive, those planes. Pretty dense feelings in those clouds where you're going to write the news.

LILIANE: I wanted to take the words back as soon as I said them. I wanted him to not know. He doesn't know. I couldn't stand him looking at me that way. I could not take it. How he looked at me.

ANALYST: What kind of look was it?

LILIANE: Like I had a disease or I was contaminated or stupid or clumsy.

ANALYST: You know you are none of those things.

LILIANE: I know. I know I can't stand to look at him now. Not anymore. It's not like he didn't do his share. He drove me, waited, paid his half of the doctor's bill, brought me dinner. But it was so fuckin' obligatory like I was his sick relative or something heroic he'd done. He did. Then, when I started bleeding, he got all hysterical. It wasn't much, just a little blood. I thought he was going to lose it. He says this is too much for him to take. He needs a break. I wished I'd had a gun, a brick, anything. It was too much for him. Was his body vacuumed, suc-

tioned out of his groin like so much dirt? Did the nurse raise
her eyes at him: too bad he doesn't love you all over her face.
They took the money from my hand like there was blood on
my check. I looked to see if there was blood on my check, but
it was on my leg. And he only saw a mess. Some complication
my body presented to his emotional structures that used to
cover me. They used to protect me, but now with the last rem-
nants of this baby coating my legs, he was disgusted. Well, I'm
glad. I'm glad I didn't have that baby 'cause if bloody messes
are too much for him then, goddammit, he didn't love either
one of us enough to be any itsy li'l muthafuckin' part of our
lives. He did not. He did not. Now . . . that's all.

ANALYST: That's quite a lot.

LILIANE: Yeah.

ANALYST: Now we know why you think parts of yourself are falling
out of you. You've got to pick up the baby and let her come
into your life. You've got to own her, accept her.

LILIANE: I know. I want to do something for her birthday. She's
three years old tomorrow. I figured it out. She's three tomorrow.

ANALYST: Liliane, it may be messy, but loving and grieving don't
cancel each other out.

LILIANE: I really want to go home now. I want to build a house for
her spirit to visit, somewhere close by me. Make her a home.

ANALYST: Somewhere you can visit, too. Well, it's time.

V

LILIANE: So what do you want to do today?

ANALYST: What do you want to do? We can do anything you like.

LILIANE: I should have known you'd say that. "We can do whatever you want." Don't you get tired of being caught up in a
bunch of neurotics' fantasies?

ANALYST: Is that what you think I do?

LILIANE: Well, how would I know actually? I mean, I can only
extrapolate generalities from my experience with you? You
know, move from the specific to the general, the universal

where we are as one with each other in our ability to defy wisdom and keep doing the same ridiculous things that make us come here.... Come here to get particularly out of our universal sufferings.

ANALYST: Are you suffering today?

LILIANE: Not significantly. I'd say not to any great extent. I'm pullin' my own heartstrings, I guess you can say that. I'm tuggin' my own heartstrings. "Broken-hearted melody. Sing a song of love . . ."

ANALYST: The last words are "Sing a song of love to me."

LILIANE: Oh really, is that what you'd like me to do, huh? Sing to you, croon a lyric of romance and passion?

ANALYST: If that's what you'd like to do.

LILIANE: But I can't do that. You're my analyst. How would it look for me to seduce my analyst? Then I'd be a real sickie, a raging nymphomaniac for real. I really need to do that. Get worse, so I can get better.

ANALYST: What might seem like, feel like getting worse, whatever that is, may actually be a sign of getting better.

LILIANE: Right.

ANALYST: No, I mean it. The more easily you move through feelings or memories that you find terribly disturbing, the less dangerous these feelings are to you, the less likely you are to . . .

LILIANE: Awright. I feel like sucking your toes.

ANALYST: Hum. I don't think anyone has ever wanted to do that before.

LILIANE: Oh, come on. You're sort of cute sometimes. I mean, some woman sometime must have wanted to suck your toes. You can't be that deprived.

ANALYST: What do you think?

LILIANE: What do you mean, "What do you think?" I told you what I think. It's impossible that somebody, man or woman, I don't mean to be presumptuous about your preference, but I know somebody must have sucked your toes, somebody must've. (Long pause) Well, aren't you going to defend yourself?

ANALYST: I didn't know I was under attack?

LILIANE: Jesus, here I am offering my highly refined sensual skills and you think you're under attack. God, men are weird.

ANALYST: I didn't reject your lovely proposition in any way, Liliane. You introduced the sparring here.

LILIANE: Well, I don't want to talk about this anyway.

ANALYST: Okay.

LILIANE: Well, don't you see this is dangerous. What I said to you is dangerous.

ANALYST: No. How is that?

LILIANE: You know, sometimes, I think you should pay me money. Shrinks and analysts, therapists, counselors, all you guys, can't let your patients, your clients, get personally involved. It's unethical.

ANALYST: Yes, unethical as well as criminal.

LILIANE: But, who'd believe a woman who was seeing a shrink in the first place who said her shrink attack—seduced her. That's nuts in the get-go.

ANALYST: No, what's nuts is the professional who'd violate those boundaries, take advantage of a trust when that vulnerability is essential for treatment.

LILIANE: But they do it. (Long pause) I know some who do it. Sleep with their clients. That's why I know I'm crazy. I gotta be crazy.

ANALYST: There's nothing crazy in what you just said. Nothing at all.

LILIANE: Well, say I had a lover who was a "counselor," I'm not going to say what kind, but say I was his lover and he confided in me that he had slept with his female patients, a few of them, sort of like he was doing them a favor. They were in great need, pain, some of them. So he fucked them.

ANALYST: How does that make you crazy?

LILIANE: 'Cause I was his lover. How could I be attracted to a man who had so little respect for another woman's confusion, her trust in him. He was supposed to help them, not fuck them. How did a dick get to be a cure for emotional problems? . . . No, wait. Freud's all up in here, shit. I didn't report him. You know, anonymously or anything. I didn't even stop seeing him for a while.

ANALYST: Is that why you are afraid now?

LILIANE: What the hell makes you say that?

ANALYST: Your legs are tucked up under you, your arms are clasped over your hips like you are protecting yourself from something, someone.

LILIANE: There's nothing going to hurt me in here. There's nobody else in this damn room but me and you.

ANALYST: Is that what's frightening?

LILIANE: What?

ANALYST: That only you and I are here?

LILIANE: What could you do to me? You just sit up in that chair and suspend silences when you don't ask stupid questions. "What are you going to do to me?" Ha. You wish you could do something.

ANALYST: I am not going to seduce or attack you. I am not going to jeopardize myself or you in any way. Do you understand, Liliane?

LILIANE: Yeah. *(Long pause)* Well, aren't you going to ask me do I understand, again.

ANALYST: No, I am virtually certain you believe I will not make any of that kind of overture.

LILIANE: Oh yeah. How do you know? I didn't say a thing.

ANALYST: No, but you're "whippin'" your legs in the air in a very sensual manner, and you're fondling your breast, to the right.

LILIANE: So what does that mean?

ANALYST: What do you think?

LILIANE: I guess it means, I guess it means if I want to say I feel like sucking your toes, I can go on and feel like that.

ANALYST: And we can talk about it.

LILIANE: Talk about how it feels to suck your toes.

ANALYST: And how you imagine that makes me feel.

LILIANE: Jesus. Don't you ever give up?

ANALYST: Nope, but it's time.

LILIANE: Thank God. *(Long pause)* I need to get out of here before I want to take your shirt off.

ANALYST: See you next week, Liliane. We'll talk about it.

LILIANE: Betcha. By golly. Wow. Ciao.

VI

LILIANE: I can't have therapy today.

ANALYST: That's the time we should work most intensely.

LILIANE: Listen. Stop fuckin' around. I can't have no goddamned therapy this morning. I'm tellin' you. I don't think I can do anything today.

ANALYST: You already have done something. You came here.

LILIANE: He killed her. She's dead.

ANALYST: Who's dead?

LILIANE: My friend, Roxie. She's dead. He killed her this morning. Really early this mornin'. It was on the news. "Woman found strangled in bedroom, while child looked on. . . ." I can't believe this. I just can't have therapy today. That's all.

ANALYST: I am very sorry to hear this, Liliane. I am. *(Long pause)* Would you like to lie down or sit over in the chair by the window, perhaps.

LILIANE: No, I don't want to lie down. Dead people lie down. Roxie was in her bed lying down. That bastard. That cocksuckin' bastard.

ANALYST: You saw Roxie recently didn't you, Lili?

LILIANE: Yes, of course. Our show opened two days ago. She had these wonderful jalapeña earrings on that lit up every ten seconds. The work was so strong, too. Roxie was so happy, so happy, but I knew it. I knew she had to get away from that jackass. I knew it. And now, he's gone and killed her. Strangled her, stabbed her. I knew it. I knew it. Oh God. Oh, I knew. I could feel it.

ANALYST: But did Roxie, know it?

LILIANE: Yes, we all told her. We told her over and over. This guy is not right, Roxie. Get him out of the house. We told her. . . . And Sierra saw this. This fool tied her mother's hands and feet with pantyhose, stabbed her and choked her. Oh God. Oh God. I feel like something's ripping me apart, tearing my soul up, tearin' me to pieces. . . . What can I do? Please, please, I don't know what to do.

ANALYST: Here's some tissues. . . . No need to rush or hurry, Liliane. Take time.

LILIANE: Time. Time. Take my time. I could've gone over there. I could have called to see if she was all right. I could have taken Sierra for the night. Oh, Jesus, what kind of friend am I? I knew something terrible was going to happen. I knew. I knew and I didn't do anything. I didn't do anything. Roxie's dead, murdered and I didn't do anything.

ANALYST: Liliane. First. Hear me out now. First of all, you did not kill Roxie. I know this hurts. She meant a great deal to you. You loved her very much, but you did not kill Roxie or help her to get killed. You were her friend. She was not a friend to herself.

LILIANE: Shut up. Shut up. You don't understand. That mutha-fuckah was everywhere; all the time tellin' her that she was weak, she couldn't draw a straight line. She couldn't cook. She couldn't balance a checkbook. She dressed like a slut. She was a tramp with good luck. She was a pitiful mother. She didn't deserve the grants she got, the reviews. He said she didn't de serve him. Can you imagine? Him? And that bastard killed her.

ANALYST: That's right, Liliane. He killed her, not you.

LILIANE: But we told her. We tried to tell her. She called me at my workshop, you know, where I teach. She called me. She was so *frightened*. She had the secretaries track me down in the cafe-teria. I jumped up and ran to a payphone to get back to her and she was whispering that she wanted to see somebody quickly. She thought Sierra was in danger. She wanted to get out of the house, but I was at work. I said: "Come pick up my keys. You both can stay with me." She said that he'd think of us first. That that wasn't a good idea. I said: "Okay, come and get some money and go to a hotel." Then, she had to go. She said: "I've got to go. I'll talk to you later. Awright." Like she wasn't scared anymore, like we were talking about a luncheon or something. I knew he must have come round. I knew, in my bones, he must have come round. *(Long pause)* Then, when I called her back that night, she said she was going out for din-ner by the bridge with that dog, Tony. She swore she'd call me later. . . . When she called, she said they were going to get mar-ried. I couldn't believe it. Why are you going to marry a man

who's jealous of your work, your friends, your child, even?
How could she marry somebody who made her so afraid?
She'd just start cryin', sometimes, for no reason at all. No reason at all. Just tremblin' so. I can see her now.

ANALYST: But did Roxie see anyone?

LILIANE: Well, she took your number. Then she said she didn't want to confide in a man.

ANALYST: Yes. I recall that.

LILIANE: She did go a couple of times to that woman you recommended, but she stopped going because Tony said anything they needed to work out they could do together or she obviously didn't trust him. And she fell for it. She believed that fool. Jesus.

ANALYST: And not her friends like you.

LILIANE: It doesn't matter. It doesn't matter, now.

ANALYST: Yes, it does. It matters immensely. You loved Roxie very much and Sierra. There's been a terrible tragedy that you will have to work through, realize you are not responsible for Roxie's death. Roxie is.

LILIANE: Fuck you. What in the hell are you talkin' about? Roxie didn't strangle herself. She didn't put sixteen knife wounds up and down her body. She didn't tell Sierra: "Come, darlin', watch Tony kill Mommy."

ANALYST: Didn't she?

Very long pause.

LILIANE: No. No. She didn't. She didn't. She did not.

ANALYST: Did she leave the house?

LILIANE: No.

ANALYST: Did she let Sierra stay with friends until she and Tony worked things out?

LILIANE: No. I told you, no.

ANALYST: Did she ask him to give her some time to herself for her to work things out for herself?

LILIANE: No. She couldn't ask him something like that.

ANALYST: Did she discontinue her counseling?

LILIANE: Yes, but you don't understand. You don't understand.

She was killed. He killed her. Said he heard "God." Said "the Lord" was displeased with her painting and her friends. Her art and her friends were smut, the Devil's handiwork. . . . That cocksucker no more heard God than I have a million dollars in the bank. The lyin' muthafuckah. Oh, my God. Roxie. Roxie. Why didn't you listen to me? Why didn't you listen to me? *(Long pause)* He told her she couldn't do anything right. Nothing. He even told her she couldn't paint. Told her she couldn't paint. It was only 'cause she was a woman that she got so many breaks. Breaks? Roxie. Roxie. Why didn't you run away from him like the antelopes you carved could run. . . . You know, Roxie had a piece from this last show. It's still hanging right now at the gallery. Her pieces are in the room next to mine. These antelopes are so delicate, two, three inches at the most, a fine misty-gray flat stone, she painted wild flowers all around them, glorious rose, yellows, and lavender flowers all around the antelopes. And over the antelopes boughs of magnolia trees carved just as finely. Roxie used to say these were southern antelopes, probably, resting near Lake Pontchartrain, lapping murky brown swamp water of French roast and chicory. It's sold already. Somebody bought it, going to take it home, look at it, see the beauty of it, the odd humor and sweetness of it. Roxie, why didn't you listen to me? Why didn't you listen . . .

ANALYST: Liliane, what's happening?

LILIANE: Sierra is crying that she wants to stay with Aunt Lili 'cause I wasn't ready to leave the opening yet. We'd only been there 'bout an hour. People were still comin', but the jackass, Tony, pulled his junked-up car out front, wouldn't stop honking for Roxie to come outside. He refused to come see the show, said a bunch of bitches weren't worth lookin' at 'less we were sucking his dick. Jesus. So Roxie smiled, and waved goodbye, but it wasn't right. It wasn't right. . . . Butch, Sierra's father, offered to keep her, but that seemed to terrify Roxie. She said that Tony wouldn't like that. He thought Sierra should only see her father on the days arranged as always, no exceptions. Butch got furious. He was the father. He'd see Sierra when he wanted. Then Roxie pleaded with him not to make so much of it. Then she ran outside with Sierra. Butch went after them. Tony jumped out of the car. They had words. Butch came back in, real subdued. Butch told me there was nothing we could do but let her go.

ANALYST: He was right, you know.

LILIANE: Butch didn't want Roxie to die. God. He's Sierra's father. He didn't want the mother of his child to die. They were friends.

ANALYST: But even Roxie's friends couldn't stop her, Liliane.

LILIANE: Not her, *Tony*. Tony killed her. Why can't you accept that?

ANALYST: I'm not denying that Tony did this heinous crime, Liliane. I'm simply trying to help you accept that Roxie left herself and Sierra in very dangerous hands after repeated warnings from you and Butch, you see?

LILIANE: I was right in the first place. I told you I can't have therapy today. I just can't.

ANALYST: What do you want to do?

LILIANE: I want to shoot Tony. I want to kill him. I want to hurt him like he hurt Roxie and Sierra.

ANALYST: And you as well. Tony has hurt you, too.

LILIANE: I want to see him dead.

ANALYST: Well, is he in custody?

LILIANE: Yes, of course, but he's pretending to be crazy. Son-of-a-bitch.

ANALYST: Still, there'll be an arraignment, a trial.

LILIANE: Yes.

ANALYST: That's how things are done in this country, right?

LILIANE: Stop asking me questions. I'm not on trial here. He doesn't deserve a trial. He needs his eyes pulled from their sockets. I want to beat his skull with a baseball bat until there's nothing left but a pile of his filthy mean demented brain that long-haul trucks run over again and again so we can't even tell he was human.

ANALYST: Tony is human, Liliane.

LILIANE: No. No, he isn't. He's an animal and he's alive, and, and . . .

ANALYST: Roxie is dead.

LILIANE: I have to go home now. I have a lot of things to do. A memorial service, an inventory of paintings and sculptures, bank accounts. Roxie didn't have any family, except Sierra, Butch, and me. That is all she had.

ANALYST: You all loved her very much. Liliane. That's a lot.

LILIANE: I'll call to reschedule. I'm not good at handling . . . death, you see.

ANALYST: Liliane, are you all right?

LILIANE: No. I'm not awright. I have to go home.

ANALYST: But, Liliane, you're walking toward the window, not the door.

Very long pause.

LILIANE: Mommy. Mommy, don't leave me like this. Don't go. Don't go. Daddy, stop her. Please, Daddy, make her come home. Why are you standin' here like that? Mommy, Mommy come back. Come back to me. Come back, Mommy. Don't leave. Don't leave me, Mommy.

ANALYST: Where is your mother going, Liliane?

LILIANE: She's going to hell, he said. She's dead. She's dead, now, he said. She's going to hell.

ANALYST: Liliane, dead people don't walk outside windows for us to see.

LILIANE: Can't see her now. She's dead. She's going to hell.

ANALYST: How did your mother die, Liliane?

LILIANE: She walked out the front door. She walked out the front door and went past the weeping willow tree, the azaleas, the roses and Japanese ivy and died.

ANALYST: But how, Liliane?

LILIANE: My father said she was dead, that's how. If she set foot out the door, she was dead as far as he was concerned.

ANALYST: And you? What about you?

LILIANE: Daddy said she died in a boating accident. No body. That's why there was no body at the service, just flowers. No body. Everybody was very sad. They had food and told stories. Patted my head 'cause she was dead. She was going to heaven they said. Daddy said we'd be all right. We'd be fine.

ANALYST: And your mother?

LILIANE: I don't know. . . . She had to go, I know she had to go. She could've taken me with her. Daddy said she had to go and to forget she'd ever had a daughter. Forget she had me or he'd see her rot in jail. Unfit. Slut. Tramp. Whore. Rot in jail. She's going to hell. Mommy, Mommy, why didn't you take me. Mommy, Mommy, come get me, Mommy. Daddy says she's dead; she's dead. Better. Sluts can't raise children. Sluts run off with their lovers and die. They die and they can't take their children. I can't go with Mommy. She's dead. He said she was dead.

ANALYST: Is she, Liliane? Is your mother dead?

LILIANE: No. I don't think so. I don't know. She said not to worry. She said I'd understand, someday, I'd understand; she couldn't live with my father anymore. She said she'd die if she stayed. If she stayed, she'd die. She went out the door and died anyway. . . . Oh, Jesus, you must really think I'm crazy now, huh?

ANALYST: No. You are making a lot of sense. If Roxie had done what your mother did, she might be alive now, like your mother.

LILIANE: My mother's been dead for years.

ANALYST: No. She's very much alive in you. She's helping you, even now.

LILIANE: Helping me? How's she helping me?

ANALYST: By reminding you of the window.

LILIANE: The window?

ANALYST: Yes. The window that opens to a world, worlds of beautiful trees and flowers and sunlight. A world full of life, Liliane.

LILIANE: But I'm not a part of it.

ANALYST: I beg to differ, Liliane. You are very much a part of it. If you need to call me for an emergency or just to chat, you know the number.

LILIANE: Could you, I know this is irregular, but do you think you could find the time to go see Roxie's show? It's the last of her we've got.

ANALYST: I think we should definitely talk some more about that, Liliane. Call, if you need me.

LILIANE: Yeah. I think I'll try the door this time. See you.

VII

LILIANE: Well, I guess I finally started to straighten some of this mess out.

ANALYST: I didn't know things were crooked.

LILIANE: Awright, let's lighten up on the "cute" factor here. Okay?

ANALYST: It's your session, Liliane. But "cute" or "ugly" is of little significance.

LILIANE: See. You just don't know how to leave things alone.

ANALYST: What would you have me leave alone?

LILIANE: This is hard enough as it is, without having to mull over my every single word and pause. I'll forget what I wanted to say and where I was going with it.

ANALYST: So, now you are composing your sessions before you even see me?

LILIANE: No, this is what I'm talking about. You're confusing me.

ANALYST: What seems confusing may, in fact, be the beginning of understanding.

LILIANE: Jesus. All I wanted to tell you was that I called Daddy.

ANALYST: Yes.

LILIANE: I called Daddy. I asked him right out where my mother was.

ANALYST: Yes.

LILIANE: I said, "Daddy, I know Mommy didn't die. Where did she go? And how could you do this to me? How could you?"

ANALYST: That was very brave, Liliane.

LILIANE: You're as crazy as he is. How can it be brave to live with the truth, when the lie was so much worse.

ANALYST: Not everyone is able to do that.

LILIANE: Not able to do what?

ANALYST: Not everyone is able to see the heinous in "lies" that support what is their truth, or truths. It's easier sometimes to imagine that lies are true, so we can avoid having to question ourselves, what our truths are.

LILIANE: His beliefs or truths are the last goddam things on my mind. How could a grown man just change my whole life, leave me feeling like an orphan, telling people for years that my mama was dead, I didn't have a mama, when he knew the whole time that she was no more dead than me or you? Every time I think about this my breathing is so heavy. I can't get enough air. I can't move. I feel all this pressure on my chest and my legs like I was deep-sea diving, but I haven't gone anywhere. I haven't gone anywhere at all.

ANALYST: Are you so sure, Liliane?

LILIANE: Am I so sure what? That I haven't gone anywhere? Yes. I'm right here where I always am.

ANALYST: But where you are is very different now than it was before our last time together? Your mother isn't dead. Your father lied to you for so many years that the truth is now suspect and tenuous. You are not a little girl whose mother is at the bottom of the sea somewhere.

LILIANE: Stop it. Stop it. I can't take this. I don't understand what's happened to me. I lose my best friend. My mother's not dead. I mean, I don't have a mother, don't know where the hell she is, if she's not dead now, and all that bastard could tell me was he thought he did the best thing at the time. "I did what I thought best at the time, my dear" like this is some reasonable response to why did you tell me my mama was dead when I know you sent her away. What could she have done that was so terrible? Who gave you the right to take my mama from me? He did what he thought best. Jesus, every time I look around white folks are fuckin' with me. No matter what I do or how I feel, I've gotta deal with these goddam white people.

ANALYST: Liliane, I'm sorry, but I'm afraid I don't understand what white people have to do with your mother's death or disappearance.

LILIANE: Of course not. Nobody understands what white folks have to do with anything except the Enlightenment. Shit. Don't you get it?

ANALYST: No, I don't. Would you help me "get it"?

LILIANE: Shit. Here we go again. I pay you money, but I'm going to help you get it.

ANALYST: Liliane, you don't have to help me do anything. You choose what and how we proceed with your treatment. You know that.

LILIANE: Hey, we just established that I hardly "know" anything these days, and you want to know why? Do you want to know why or not? Fuck it. I'm going to tell you whether you want to know or not. White folks got us so tangled up and wound round ourselves we can't live without them or the idea of them where we can touch it. If we live like white folks don't exist, like they don't matter. They kill us. Bang. You dead: Nigger. If we act decent, they treat us like fools. If we spend our lives hating them, we look as foolish and psychotic as they do to the rest of the world. Well, shit, that may not be true 'cause they've got the rest of the world kissin' their behinds, too.

ANALYST: What did the white people do to you, Liliane?

LILIANE: Now, you're really quick. How about slavery? How do you like that for a start?

ANALYST: Humm. I thought there might be something more current weighing on your mind, but perhaps I was wrong.

LILIANE: Oh, I can move it right on up to date for you, sir. What you think about us being defined as chattel or being valuable or valueless in relation to white folks? That's not too far off from slavery, is it? A white man owns you or he doesn't. We are free or slave, right? Seems pretty clear to me. Easy, even a child could understand.

ANALYST: Lili...here's some tissue....Maybe you're crying because, as a child, you didn't understand what you see as so easy, so simple.

LILIANE: I just never thought....It never crossed my mind that my mama'd run off with a white man.

ANALYST: Is this something your father told you?

LILIANE: Said: "Once she told me she'd always love him, I had no choice. I told her, Liliane, I told her, she'd lose you and everything we'd worked for. I couldn't let you go with her, don't you see?" "Darling Liliane," he called me, "Darlin' Liliane." I don't want to talk about this anymore.

ANALYST: Liliane, you don't have to talk.

LILIANE: But if I don't talk, how can I get better or anything? How can I be doing my therapy if I don't talk to you?

ANALYST: Sometimes our work is talking. Sometimes our work is simply being, experiencing feelings and thoughts we'd put so far away we have no words for them. Then, the silence and our breathing allow these feelings to find the shapes and sounds of the words *we need.*

LILIANE: The white people made my father kill off my mother, take my mother away from me. It was such an affront to his "manhood," his "dignity" that he wouldn't allow my mother to live in the house with a white man in her heart, can you believe that? Didn't matter if it was a some other kind of man, a Sikh or a Tamil, a Brazilian, anybody, but not a white man. And poor mama, all she did was fall in love and 'cause she fell in love with a "white" man she got "disappeared" like this is Argentina? I can't move my arms. Everything is very heavy and slow. I can't move, I'm tellin' you.

ANALYST: Why do you want to move, Liliane?

LILIANE: Oh, God, I don't know, but I've got to do something.

ANALYST: Why do you have to do "something," Liliane?

LILIANE: Because everybody else is crazy, that's why.

ANALYST: What would happen if you didn't do "something"? What if you were still? Then what?

LILIANE: You know, I've spent all these years seeing after Daddy, making sure that I didn't upset him too much, going to all the honor and society affairs on his calendar whenever I could and he banished my mother because she was going with a white boy.... I just can't believe it, but I wished I had told him about Zoom now. Now I wish I had moving pictures of that cracker's hard pink dick going in and out of my body, and me screaming with pleasure, wet, calling him "my sweet daddy" or some shit like that.

ANALYST: Then what would you do?

LILIANE: Then I'd watch him have a heart attack and die. He'd turn red in the face, be so mad his jaws'd quiver. Then his eyes would get that look like a laser beam designed by colored people so it cuts quick. I'd start laughing, and he'd die right in front of me. Just like that.

ANALYST: And then?

LILIANE: Then I'd be the girl who shamed her father to death on purpose and whose mother ran off with a white boy, leaving her family and the race to fend for themselves.

ANALYST: Is that what happened, Liliane?

LILIANE: No, shit. Can't you see, I don't know what happened. I mean, I know what happened to me, but none of it makes any sense. It doesn't make any sense to me, I mean. Daddy's always been just like he is: if I knew not to bring a white boy home, surely Mama knew it. And Daddy knew my mother was not likely to feel fulfilled in the throes of club meetings, auxiliaries, and narrow ideologies. What in the fuck were they doing together in the first place? Just doesn't add up. Well, shit, it added up to make me, didn't it?

ANALYST: Yes.

LILIANE: Maybe you're right. . . . You know about clearing things up. Now, I understand why Daddy thought he had to watch me so carefully, intimidate boys I knew. He thought I was like my mother, and I'd run off on him. Isn't that funny?

ANALYST: Why is it funny?

LILIANE: I had no intentions or thoughts about ever leaving Daddy's house until I realized I really had to.

ANALYST: Why was that?

LILIANE: You know, doctor, kinship taboos.

ANALYST: Oh really?

LILIANE: Yeah.

ANALYST: Tell me some more about this.

LILIANE: What's to tell: a girl can't marry her father.

ANALYST: But you were just going to "kill off" your father. Nothing very romantic there.

LILIANE: No, but it might just be the kind of affection he understands.

ANALYST: Uh. Liliane, looks like we're at that time.

LILIANE: Huh, shit. I really don't want to leave right now.

ANALYST: Just remember, you don't have to do anything, just be and feel.

LILIANE: If I feel any more things, I'll lose my mind.

ANALYST: Worse things could happen.

LILIANE: I know. At least I know that.

FROM

FIRES

IN THE

MIRROR

ANNA

DEAVERE

SMITH

The interview of Mr. Cato brought me full circle in my own *On the Road* project. In the early days, eight years ago, when I began this project, I was using three questions in every interview to help me learn how to listen: Have you ever come close to death? Have you ever been accused of something that you did not do? Do you remember the circumstances of your birth? Those were questions a linguist had given me; she told me they would most certainly get people to speak in an original manner.

I asked those questions for only one of the *On the Road*s and then I never did anymore. Mr. Cato answered all of those questions without me asking them. He speaks in such an unusual manner; he crosses the boundaries of his own consciousness three times, very quickly—more quickly than most people. He was a perfect example of what I'd been seeking, which is what I call "speaking in character"—this unique type of speaking that is close to what dramatic speech wants to be.

That was magical, that that happened eight years later. It gave me a lot of faith in the Crown Heights material. When I went to Crown Heights, I didn't really know what I was going to do. I actually met [Mr. Cato] quite late in the rehearsal process. Meeting him made me think that it was meant to be, that I should be there.

The other big thing that happened in Crown Heights was meeting the Lubavitchers, who are very passionate speakers, even though I am clearly someone outside of their community. They speak also in a way that is custom-made for my project—they speak from the heart. In relationship to the way most people talk, they speak a different kind of truth because they haven't been polluted, though they may not tell me the *truth* about the secrets of their society. And I make no mistake; I don't think the Lubavitchers who were willing to talk to me are necessarily at the center of their community. They are a very insular community and they choose certain people who walk on the border, who deign to speak to us in the general population.

Relatively speaking, most of the people I meet in daily life, and certainly in our business, are not people who are speaking honestly. Most people speak with their ambitions and their careers cloaking the truth.

And so, to quote Eudora Welty, when I met the Lubavitchers, "My ears opened up like morning glories." It's the difference between Wonder Bread and real grain. It was very important to go back to something more natural. Also, I've been interviewing a lot of academics, and that speech, too, is a beautiful kind of speaking, but it's cloaked speech. It's not from the heart.

Definitions of Heroism

I don't believe in the single hero, so there we have a problem. It's probably why I don't write traditional plays right now. It's hard for me to believe in those kinds of things. I don't believe in any authority. If I have to divide the world into "the us's" and "the thems," I find that I have less and less in common with people who grew up believing in one person, such as their father, as a hero. Even if they become disillusioned with their [hero's] behavior and it becomes a love/hate relationship, if their behavior is based around this belief in one person, I have less and less that I can communicate with them. A lot of my students have been like that in the past. I think it's very normal, very organic, to actually have that feeling. Certainly, for the Lubavitchers—my God, the Rebbi, he is that [hero]. I don't feel that there was a single hero in Crown Heights. There are re-markable people who do remarkable things that they don't have to do to survive, and I'm interested in that.

I don't know what makes people do something for the social good. I met a kid, Henry Rice, who talks about being on the street corner talking to a group of little kids about the power of the vote. What does that come from? That's amazing to me! And yet he was somebody who also didn't want to have anything to do with the politicians. He thought they were "Uncle Toms." When he talks about Richard Green encouraging him to get in his van, Henry says,

> *he said,*
> *"Henry, I need you in this van.*
> *Drive around with me.*
> *Let's keep some of these kids off the street tonight."*
> *I said, "Okay."*
> *He said,*
> *"The blood*
> *of Black men are on your hands tonight!"*
> *I said, "Okay."*

Even though Richard Green is speaking in this very dramatic manner, "the *blood* of *Black men* are on your *hands* tonight," the kid's response is, "Okay. Okay." And he does it. I don't know what that's about. He became a very important person in community relations in the course of the year after that happened to him.

When the L.A. uprising happened, my first performance of *Fires in the Mirror* got cancelled, so I went up to the demonstration in Times Square. Richard Green was walking around with a megaphone the way you and I would carry a purse, or the way somebody else would carry a gun. And I said, "What are you doing with this megaphone? Are you going to make a speech?" He said, "Oh no, I always carry it in the street because a lot of times you see trouble, and a lot of times if you just talk to them they'll calm down." Where does that come from?

I have this problem [of the single hero] with *Twilight.* Many people ask me, "Wasn't there anybody who brought it all together? Didn't you find any hero?" My answer is "No," because first of all, there isn't anybody who brought it together. Most people spoke about their own people. A hero would have to be somebody who could see beyond the boundaries of their own experience and their own ethnicity in this day. We need somebody who can negotiate difference, but there's very little in education, in art or in culture in the last twenty years that encourages that. And that's for good reason. It's very important that we had what we had in the last twenty years, which was theatre of identity—crucial. It was a survival technique and I'm very glad it happened. And I think it has to still happen.

What I talk about now is the need to get just a few people—because not everybody is inclined to do this—who can get in these little boats, like rowboats, canoes, not great big things...no steamships or yachts. It's not something you could get a grant for or that you should; it's just a little thing that you can build out of wood, and people who are inclined to do that—go behind, between these fortresses of thought.

It's wishful thinking. It's dishonest to expect heroes if we have not emotionally invested in this. But if we expect a hero in the next twenty years, then those of us who can are going to have to encourage people to cross the line and be homeless.

The Darkness and the Light

Certainly, I'm attracted to darkness. In my own personal life, I don't like conflict. And in the business side of my professional life, I hate conflict. But my subject matter is all dark, except now I'm doing something that is actually the opposite. I'm making a piece with Judith Jamison which is all about light and beauty, about Alvin Ailey and the dancers and their incredible beauty. And yet the story of the Ailey company is also a story of beauty and pain. It's about people who work very, very hard to be perfect.

Alvin Ailey was doing work which was a spectacle about the beauty of black people, but it was also political and social because the fact is, and I'm quoting him, "You can't have a company primarily of black dancers and have it not be political and social." The Ailey company is thirty-five years old now. In its roots, it defies an incredible gravity when you think of what it means to take control of the image of the black body, of the nearly nude black body, and put it on the stage for the world to watch. It certainly defies the stereotypes of how the black body has been portrayed before—scrunched and misshapen into these ugly forms that lacked dignity. He did not escape being pulled to the darkness of how that beauty was mis-handled in the past. So even there, when I think that I'm dealing with pure beauty, I don't escape the fact that the subject itself was attracted to darkness.

I'm pulled to our problems in America, and that has to do with why the human spirit finds itself rolling in the grime and the disease of hatred and unfairness and meanspiritedness. I'm interested in how people speak about this and how the act of speech helps them to arrange the elements of the grime in such a way that they can see beams of light. Those beams of light are the understanding of how and why this came to be. This [un-derstanding] gives us the feeling of more control over it.

In *Fires in the Mirror*, Conrad Mohammed deals with this. He uses words like "outrageous" or

> But the most significant crime—
> because we could have recovered from all of that—
> but the fact that they cut off all knowledge from us,
> told us that we were animals,
> told us that we were subhuman,
> took from us our names,
> gave us names like
> Smith
> and Jones
> and today we wear those names
> with dignity
> and pride,
> yet these were the names given to us in one of the greatest crimes
> ever committed on the face of the earth.

Particularly now, everything points to the disaster in public education, and at the same time much points to the likelihood of highly technical ways of giving information to people even in disadvantaged atmospheres through the use of computers and media for education.

The light becomes the inevitability that character will, I believe, al-ways be a part of the human spirit. That is what is going to reveal itself to us in our darkest, darkest hours; that is what will uplift us from our poverty on the one hand and our tendency to be excessive—our greediness—on the other. I do believe in the human spirit as it takes form in character. Character is the unusualness of certain human beings—unpredictable, like Henry on the corner. That lives. And as dramatists we have the opportunity to make it into a more solid form which people can recognize and therefore expect; we can make it appear onstage and people can expect to find it in their lives around them, and then that means they help create it among themselves.

Thoughts on Women in Theatre

The business—what I see of it so far—is not nice. Even when we are valued, we don't have access to the kinds of bonds that men have—not just with men, but with women. It's more likely that men—white men and men of color—find people who want to do their work, and not only because it means money in their pocket, success for their institutions and grants. All of the people in [this anthology] could mean that to an institution—money, grants, prestige—but I don't know how likely it is that these same men and women in these institutions would fall in love with us. I think it goes back to this deep, deep thing that is in every society. There are societies where people will abort and kill their children if it's going to be a woman. In most families, the son is loved in a way by his mother, his father and his siblings that a woman is not; a father is loved and hated in a way that a mother is not.

We are all strange orphans, black women in this world of theatre and media. There are people who care about us and there are people who respect us, but we are forced to wrap ourselves, adorn ourselves. That wrapping is incredible evidence of our creativity—however we decide to wrap ourselves, whether it's with scarves or jewelry or Donna Karan, it's wrapping that says, "I take control of this image." It's a coat of protection and it is to make ourselves seen in the world. But vulnerability is what is ultimately so important. I wonder how free we feel to be absolutely vulnerable. How many of us really allow that vulnerability, and on every level? It's all well and good if an artistic director says, "I want you to come work here," but it's much bigger than that. It's back to this thing: Are there any *homes* for black women? I wonder how much of our work is evidence of our comfort, or our discomfort, of our having people around us in our professional lives who feel pulled to invest in more than money and interest—real care? I don't know.

I might be naive, and maybe I'm only speaking from a very "self" perspective, but I feel that there's a way in which we are nomadic. If we are nomadic, why is it that we are walking and walking and walking and not finding a place to rest? Is it that the houses that we enter are warm instead of hot? It makes me really sad, to tell you the truth.

ABOUT THE AUTHOR

Actor, playwright and performance artist Anna Deavere Smith has acted Off Broadway, in resident theatres and in film and television. She premiered her latest one-woman performance play, *Twilight*, at the Mark Taper Forum in June 1993, with subsequent performances scheduled for the McCarter Theatre Center and the New York Shakespeare Festival.

Fires in the Mirror and *Twilight* are part of a series of works written and performed by Smith entitled *On the Road: A Search for American Character*. Also included in the series are pieces she created for the Eureka Theatre of San Francisco *(From the Outside Looking In: San Francisco, 1990)*; The Rockefeller Conference Center, Bellagio, Italy *(Fragments: On Intercultural Performance)*; Crossroads Theatre Company *(Black Identity and Black Theatre)*; Princeton University *(Gender Bending)*; the National Conference of Women and the Law, and others.

In addition to her many awards for *Fires in the Mirror*, Smith received a Drama-Logue Award for her play *Piano*, which was circulated by TCG's *Plays in Process* program in 1989. Her film and television appearances include *The Arsenio Hall Show*, *Dave* and Jonathan Demme's *Philadelphia*.

Smith has taught at many of the major U.S. theatre-training schools, including the American Conservatory Theatre, Carnegie-Mellon University, New York University and Yale University. She is currently an associate professor of drama at Stanford University.

ABOUT THE WORK

Winner of Obie, Drama Desk and Lucille Lortel awards and the Joseph Kesselring Prize, and runner-up for the Pulitzer Prize in Drama, *Fires in the Mirror* premiered at the New York Shakespeare Festival in May 1992. Smith toured the piece extensively, including performances at the Royal Court Theatre in London, the Brooklyn Academy of Music, the American Repertory Theatre in Cambridge, Mass. and the McCarter Theatre Center in Princeton, New Jersey. In April 1993, the *American Playhouse* version, directed by George C. Wolfe, aired on PBS stations nationwide.

from FIRES IN THE MIRROR

from IDENTITY

Ntozake Shange
The Desert

This interview was done on the phone at about four PM Philadel-
phia time. The only cue Ntozake gave about her physical appear-
ance was that she took one earring off to talk on the phone. On
stage we placed her upstage center in an armchair, smoking.
Then we placed her standing, downstage.

Hummmm.
Identity—
it, is, uh . . . in a way it's, um . . . it's sort of, it's uh . . .
it's a psychic sense of place
it's a way of knowing I'm not a rock or that tree?
I'm this other living creature over here?
And it's a way of knowing that no matter where I put myself
that I am not necessarily
what's around me.
I am part of my surroundings
and I become separate from them
and it's being able to make those differentiations clearly
that lets us have an identity
and what's inside our identity
is everything that's ever happened to us.
Everything that's ever happened
to us as well as our responses to it
'cause we might be alone in a trance state,
someplace like the desert
and we begin to feel as though
we are part of the desert—
which we are right at that minute—
but we are not the desert,
uh . . .

we are part of the desert,
and when we go home
we take with us that part of the desert that the desert gave us,
but we're still not the desert.
It's an important differentiation to make because you don't
    know
what you're giving if you don't know what you have and you
    don't
know what you're taking if you don't know what's yours and
    what's
somebody else's.

George C. Wolfe
101 Dalmations

The Mondrian Hotel in Los Angeles. Morning. Sunny. A very nice room. George is wearing denim jeans, a light blue denim shirt and white leather tennis shoes. His hair is in a ponytail. He wears tortoise/wire spectacles. He is drinking tea with milk. The tea is served on a tray, the cups and teapot are delicate porcelain. George is sitting on a sofa, with his feet up on the coffee table.

I mean I grew up on a Black—
a one-block street—
that was Black.
My grandmother lived on that street
my cousins lived around the corner.
I went to this
Black—Black—
private Black grade school
where
I was extraordinary.
Everybody there was extraordinary.
You were told you were extraordinary.
It was very clear
that I could not go to see *101 Dalmations* at the Capital
    Theatre

because it was segregated.
And at the same time
I was treated like I was the most extraordinary creature that
    had
been born.
So I'm on my street in my house,
at my school—
and I was very spoiled too—
so I was treated like I was this special special creature.
And then I would go beyond a certain point
I was treated like I was insignificant.
Nobody was
hosing me down or calling me nigger.
It was just that I was insignificant.
(Slight pause)
You know what I mean?
So it was very clear
(Strikes teacup on saucer twice on "very clear")
where my extraordinariness lived.
You know what I mean.
That I was extraordinary as long as I was Black.
But I am—not—going—to place myself
(Pause)
in relationship to your whiteness.
I will talk about your whiteness if we want to talk about that.
But I,
but what,
that which,
what I—
what am I saying?
My blackness does not resis— ex— re—
exist in relationship to your whiteness.
(Pause)
You know *(Not really a question, more like a "hmm")*
(Slight pause)
it does not exist in relationship *to*—
it *exists*
it exists.

I come—
you know what I mean—
like I said, I, I, I,
I come from—
it's a very com*plex*,
con*fused*,
neu-rotic,
at times destructive
reality, but it is completely
and totally a reality
contained and, and,
and full unto itself.
It's complex.
It's demonic.
It's ridiculous.
It's absurd.
It's evolved.
It's all the stuff.
That's the way I grew up.
(Slight pause)
So that *therefore*—
and then you're White—
(Quick beat)
And then there's a point when,
and then these two things come into contact.

MIRRORS

Aaron M. Bernstein
Mirrors and Distortions

Evening. Cambridge, Massachusetts. Fall. He is a man in his fifties, wearing a sweater and a shirt with a pen guard. He is seated at a round wooden table with a low-hanging lamp.

Okay, so a mirror is something that reflects light.
It's the simplest instrument to understand,
okay?

So a simple mirror is just a flat
reflecting
substance, like,
for example,
it's a piece of glass which is silvered on the back,
okay?
Now the notion of distortion also goes back into literature,
okay?
I'm trying to remember from art—
You probably know better than I.
You know you have a pretty young woman and she looks in a
    mirror
and she's a witch
(He laughs)
because she's evil on the inside.
Thats not a real mirror,
as everyone knows—
where
you see the inner thing.
Now that really goes back in literature.
So everyone understood that mirrors don't distort,
so that was a play
not on words
but on a concept.
But physicists do
talk about distortion.
It's a big
subject, distortions.
I'll give you an example—
if you wanna see the
stars
you make a big
reflecting mirror—
that's one of the ways—
you make a big telescope
so you can gather in a lot of light
and then it focuses at a point
and then there's always something called the circle of
    confusion.

So if ya don't make the thing perfectly spherical or perfectly
parabolic
then,
then, uh, if there are errors in the construction
which you can see, it's easy, if it's huge,
then you're gonna have a circle of confusion,
you see?
So that's the reason for making the
telescope as large as you can,
because you want that circle
to seem smaller,
and you want to easily see errors in the construction.
So, you see, in physics it's very practical—
if you wanna look up in the heavens
and see the stars as well as you can
without distortion.
If you're counting stars, for example,
and two look like one,
you've blown it.

R H Y T H M

Monique "Big Mo" Matthews
Rhythm and Poetry

*In reality this interview was done on an afternoon in the spring of
1989, while I was in residence at the University of California, Los
Angeles, as a fellow at the Center for Afro-American Studies. Mo
was a student of mine. We were sitting in my office, which was a
narrow office, with sunlight. I performed Mo in many shows, and
in the course of performing her, I changed the setting to a performance setting, with microphone. I was inspired by a performance
that I saw of Queen Latifah in San Francisco and by Mo's behavior in my class, which was performance behavior, to change the
setting to one that was more theatrical, since Mo's everyday
speech was as theatrical as Latifah's performance speech.*

Speaking directly to the audience, pacing the stage.

And she say, "This is for the fellas,"
and she took off all her clothes and she had on a leotard
that had all cuts and stuff in it,
and she started doin' it on the floor.
They were like
"Go, girl!"
People like, "That look really stink."
But that's what a lot of female rappers do—
like to try to get off,
they sell they body or pimp they body
to, um, get play.
And you have people like Latifah who doesn't, you know,
she talks intelligent.
You have Lyte who's just hard and people are scared by her
hardness,
her strength of her words.
She encompasses that whole, New York-street sound.
It's like, you know, she'll like . . .
what's a line?
What's a line
like "Paper Thin,"
"IN ONE EAR AND RIGHT OUT THE OTHUH."
It's like,
"I don't care what you have to say,
I'm gittin' done what's gotta be done.
Man can't come across me.
A female she can't stand against me.
I'm just the toughest, I'm just the hardest/You just can't come
    up
against me/if you do you get waxed!"
It's like a lot of my songs,
I don't know if I'm gonna get blacklisted for it.
The image that I want is a strong strong African strong Black
    woman
and I'm not down with what's going on, like Big Daddy Kane
    had a song
out called "Pimpin' Ain't Easy," and he sat there and he talk
    for the

whole song, and I sit there I wanna slap him, I wanna slap him
    so
hard, and he talks about, it's one point he goes, yeah
um,
"Puerto Rican girls Puerto Rican girls call me Papi and
White girls say
even White girls say I'm a hunk!"
I'm like,
"What you mean 'even'?
Oh! Black girls ain't good enough for you huh?"
And one of my songs has a line that's like
**"PIMPIN' AIN'T EASY BUT WHORIN' AIN'T
    PROPER. RESPECT AND
CHERISH THE ORIGINAL MOTHER."**
And a couple of my friends were like,
"Aww, Mo, you good but I can't listen to you 'cause you be
    Men
bashin'."
I say,
"It ain't men bashin', it's female assertin'."
Shit.
I'm tired of it.
I'm tired of my friends just acceptin'
that they just considered to be a ho.
You got a song,
"Everybody's a Hotty."
A "hotty" means you a freak, you a ho,
and it's like Too Short
gets up there and he goes,
"B I AYYYYYYYYYYYE."
Like he stretches "bitch" out for as long as possible,
like you just a ho and you can't be saved,
and 2 Live Crew . . . "we want some pussy," and the girls! "La
    le la le la le la,"
it's like my friends say,
"Mo, if you so bad how come you don't never say nothin'
    about 2

Live Crew?"
When I talk about rap,
and I talk about people demeaning rap,
I don't even mention them
because they don't understand the fundamentals of rap.
Rap, rap
is basically
broken down
Rhythm
and Poetry.
And poetry is expression.
It's just like poetry; you release so much through poetry.
Poetry is like
intelligence.
You just release it all and if you don't have a complex rhyme
it's like,
"I'm goin' to the store."
What rhymes with store?
More, store, for, more, bore,
"I'm goin' to the store I hope I don't get bored,"
it's like,
"WHAT YOU SAYIN', MAN? WHO CARES?"
You have to have something that flows.
You have to be def,
D-E-F.
I guess I have to think of something for you that ain't slang.
Def is dope, def is live
when you say somethin's dope
it means it is the epitome of the experience
and you have to be def by your very presence
because you have to make people happy.
And we are living in a society where people are not happy with
their everyday lives.

from SEVEN VERSES

Letty Cottin Pogrebin
Near Enough to Reach

Evening. The day before Thanksgiving, 1991. On the phone. Direct, passionate, confident, lots of volume. She is in a study with a roll-top desk and a lot of books.

I think it's about rank frustration and the old story
that you pick a scapegoat
that's much more, I mean Jews and Blacks,
that's manageable,
because we're near,
we're still near enough to each other to reach!
I mean, what can you do about the people who voted for David
     Duke?
Are Blacks going to go there and deal with that?
No, it's much easier to deal with Jews who are also panicky.
We're the only ones that pay any attention
(Her voice makes an upward inflection)
Well, Jeffries did speak about the Mafia being, um,
Mafia,
and the Jews in Hollywood.
I didn't see
this tremendous outpouring of Italian
reaction.
Only *Jews* listen,
only *Jews* take Blacks seriously,
only *Jews* view Blacks as full human beings that you
should *address*
in their rage
and, um,
people don't seem to notice that.
But Blacks, it's like a little child kicking up against Arnold
Schwarzenegger
when they,
when they have anything to say about the dominant culture

nobody listens! Nobody reacts!
To get a headline,
to get on the evening news,
you have to attack a Jew.
Otherwise you're ignored.
And it's a shame.
We all play into it.

from CROWN HEIGHTS, BROOKLYN

Michael S. Miller
"Heil Hitler"

A large airy office in Manhattan on Lexington in the 50s. Mr. Miller sits behind a big desk in a high-backed swivel chair drinking coffee. He's wearing a yarmulke. Plays with the swizzle stick throughout. There is an intercom in the office, so that when the receptionist calls him, you can hear it, and when she calls others in other offices, you can hear it like a page in a public place, faintly.

I was at Gavin Cato's funeral,
at nearly every public event
that was conducted by the Lubavitcher community and the
     Jewish
community as a whole
words of comfort
were offered to the family of Gavin Cato.
I can show you a letter that we sent
to the Cato family expressing, uh,
our sorrow over the loss,
unnecessary loss, of their son.
I am not aware of a word
that was spoken at that funeral.
I am not aware of a—
and I was taking notes—
of a word that was uttered

of comfort to the family of Yankele Rosenbaum.
Frankly this was a political rally rather than a funeral.
The individuals you mentioned—
and again,
I am not going to participate in verbal acrimony,
not only
were there cries of, "Kill the Jews"
or,
"Kill the Jew,"
there were cries of, "Heil Hitler."
There were cries of, "Hitler didn't finish the job."
There were cries of,
"Throw them back into the ovens again."
To hear in *Crown Heights*—
and Hitler was no lover of Blacks—
"Heil Hitler"?
"Hitler didn't finish the job"?
"We should heat up the ovens"?
From *Blacks*?
Is more inexplicable
or unexplainable
or any other word that I cannot fathom.
The hatred is so
deep-seated
and the hatred
knows no boundaries.
There is no boundary
to anti-Judaism.
The anti-*Judaism*—
if people don't want me
to use,
hear me use the word anti-Semitism.
And I'll be damned if,
if preferential treatment is gonna
be the excuse
for every bottle,
rock,
or pellet that's, uh, directed

toward a Jew
or the window of a Jewish home
or a Jewish store.
And, frankly,
I think the response of the Lubavitcher community was
    relatively
passive.

Norman Rosenbaum
My Brother's Blood

A Sunday afternoon. Spring. Crisp, clear and windy. Across from City Hall in New York City. Crowds of people, predominantly Lubavitcher, with placards. A rally that was organized by Lubavitcher women. All of the speakers are men, but the women stand close to the stage. Mr. Rosenbaum, an Australian, with a beard, hat and wearing a pinstripe suit, speaks passionately and loudly from the microphone on a stage with a podium. Behind him is a man in an Australian bush hat with a very large Australian flag which blows dramatically in the wind. It is so windy that Mr. Rosenbaum has to hold his hat to keep it on his head.

Al do lay achee so achee aylay alo dalmo
My brother's blood cries out from the ground.
Let me make it clear
why I'm here, and why you're here.
In August of 1991,
as you all have heard before today,
my brother was killed in the streets of Crown Heights
for no other reason
than that he was a Jew!
The only miracle was
that my brother was the only victim
who paid for being a Jew with his life.
When my brother was surrounded,
each and every American was surrounded.
When my brother was stabbed four times,

each and every American was stabbed four times
and as my brother bled to death in this city,
while the medicos stood by
and let him bleed
to death, it was the gravest of indictments against this country.
One person out of twenty gutless individuals
who attacked my brother has been arrested.
I for one am not convinced that it is beyond the ability of the
    New York police
to arrest others.
Let me tell you, Mayor Dinkins,
let me tell you, Commissioner Brown:
I'm here,
I'm not going home,
until there is justice.

Richard Green
Rage

*Two PM in a big red van. Green is in the front. He has a driver. I
am in the back. Green wears a large knit hat with reggae colors
over long dreadlocks. Driving from Crown Heights to Brooklyn
College. He turns sideways to face me in the back and bends
down, talking with his elbow on his knee.*

Sharpton, Carson, and Reverend Herbert Daughtry
didn't have any power out there really.
The media gave them that power.
But they weren't turning those youfs on and off.
Nobody knew who controlled the switch out there.
Those young people had rage like an oil-well fire
that has to burn out.
All they were doin' was sort of orchestratin' it.
Uh, they were not really the ones that were saying, "Well
stop, go, don't go, stop, turn around, go up."
It wasn't like that.
Those young people had rage out there,

that didn't matter who was in control of that—
that rage had to get out
and that rage
has been building up.
When all those guys have come and gone,
that rage is still out here.
I can show you that rage every day
right up and down this avenue.
We see, sometimes in one month, we see three bodies
in one month. That's rage,
and that's something that nobody has control of.
And I don't know who told you that it was preferential treat-
        ment for
Blacks that the Mayor kept the cops back . . .
If the Mayor had turned those cops on?
We would still be in a middle of a battle.
And
I pray on both sides of the fence,
and I tell the people in the Jewish community the same thing,
"This is not something that force will hold."
Those youfs were running on cops without nothing in their
        hands,
seven- and eight- and nine- and ten-year-old boys were
        running at
those cops
with nothing,
just running at 'em.
That's rage.
Those young people out there are angry
and that anger has to be vented,
it has to be negotiated.
And they're not angry at the Lubavitcher community
they're just as angry at you and me,
if it comes to that.
They have no
role models,
no guidance
so they're just out there growin' up on their own,

their peers are their role models,
their peers is who teach them how to move
what to do, what to say
so when they see the Lubavitchers
they don't know the difference between "Heil Hitler"
and, uh, and uh, whatever else.
They don't know the difference.
When you ask 'em to say who Hitler was they wouldn't even
        be able
to tell you.
Half of them don't even know.
Three-quarters of them don't even know.
(Mobile phone rings; he picks it up)
"Richard Green, can I help?
Aw, man I tol' you I want some color
up on that wall. Give me some colors.
Look, I'm in the middle of somethin'."
(He returns to the conversation)
Just as much as they don't know who Frederick Douglass was.
They know Malcolm
because Malcolm has been played up to such an extent now
that they know Malcolm.
But ask who Nat Turner was or Mary McCleod Bethune or
        Booker T.
Because the system has given 'em
Malcolm is convenient and
Spike is goin' to give 'em Malcolm even more.
It's convenient.

Carmel Cato
Lingering

Seven PM. The corner where the accident occurred in Crown Heights. An altar to Gavin is against the wall where the car crashed. Many pieces of cloth are draped. Some writing in color is on the wall. Candle wax is everywhere. There is a rope around the area. Cato is wearing a trench coat, pulled around him. He stands

very close to me. Dark outside. Reggae music is in the back-
ground. Lights come from stores on each corner. Busy intersection.
Sounds from outside. Traffic. Stores open. People in and out of
shops. Sounds from inside apartments, televisions, voices, cook-
ing, etc. He speaks in a pronounced West Indian accent.

In the meanwhile
it was two.
Angela was on the ground
but she was trying to move. Gavin was still.
They was trying to pound him.
I was the father.
I was 'it, chucked, and pushed,
and a lot of
sarcastic words were passed towards me
from the police
while I was trying to explain: It was my kid!
These are my children.
The child was hit you know.
I saw everything, everything,
the guy radiator burst
all the hoses,
the steam,
all the garbage buckets goin' along the building.
And it was very loud,
everything burst.
It's like an atomic bomb.
That's why all these people
comin' round
wanna know what's happening.
Oh it was very outrageous.
Numerous numbers.
All the time the police sayin'
you can't get in,
you can't pass,
and the children laying on the ground.
He was hit at exactly eight-thirty.
Why?

I was standing over there.
There was a little child—
a friend of mine
came up with a little child—
and I lift the child up
and she look at her watch at the same time
and she say it was eight-thirty.
I gave the child back to her.
And then it happen.
Umh, Umh, *(Sharp utterances)*
My child, these are the things I never dream about.
I take care of my children.
You know it's a funny thing,
if a child get sick and he dies
it won't hurt me so bad,
or if a child run out into the street and get hit down,
it wouldn't hurt me.
That's what's hurtin' me.
The whole week
before Gavin died
my body was changing,
I was having different feelings.
I stop eating,
I didn't et
nothin',
only drink water,
for two weeks;
and I was very touchy—
any least thing that drop
or any song I hear
it would affect me.
Every time I try to do something
I would have to stop.
I was
lingering, lingering, lingering, lingering,
all the time.
But I can do things,
I can see things,

I know that for a fact.
I was telling myself,
"Something is wrong somewhere,"
but I didn't want to see,
I didn't want to accept,
and it was inside of me,
and even when I go home I tell my friends,
"Something coming I could feel it
but I didn't want to see,"
and all the time I just deny deny deny,
and I never thought it was Gavin,
but I didn't have a clue.
I thought it was one of the other children—
the bigger boys
or the girl,
because she worry me,
she won't et—
but Gavin 'ee was 'ealtee,
and he don't cause no trouble.
That's what's devastating me even until now.
Sometime it make me feel like it's no justice,
like, uh,
the Jewish people,
they are very high up,
it's a very big thing,
they runnin' the whole show
from the judge right down.
And something I don't understand:
The Jewish people, they told me
there are certain people I cannot be seen with
and certain things I cannot say
and certain people I cannot talk to.
They made that very clear to me—the Jewish people—
they can throw the case out
unless
I go to them with pity.
I don't know what they talkin' about.
So I don't know what kind of crap is that.

And make me say things I don't wanna say
and make me do things I don't wanna do.
I am a special person.
I was born different.
I'm a man born by my foot.
I born by my foot.
Anytime a baby comin' by the foot
they either cut the mother
or the baby dies.
But I was born with my foot.
I'm one of the special.
There's no way they can overpower me.
No there's nothing to hide,
you can repeat every word I say.

LIVE

AND IN

COLOR!

DANITRA

VANCE

I didn't intend to be a performer. I was intending to do something more traditionally smart, like be an anthropologist, but I went away to drama school in London (the Weber-Douglas Academy of Dramatic Art) to study classical acting. All the American students there wanted to come back and be on Broadway in a musical comedy. Comedy was the last thing that I wanted to do in life; as a classically trained actress, you understand that we did not want to do comedy because that's so  traditional and historically supported. No, no, no, I wanted to do the classics only. But I started doing comedy because I wanted people to listen to the things that I thought were important, to understand my point of view or be willing to look at things from my perspective.

According to my sister, whatever you are doing when you are seven years old is what you're going to be doing for the rest of your life. The only thing that I can see is that in second grade I used to sit in the back of the class with all the bad girls and make them laugh. Because I was the good girl at the table with all the bad girls, the teacher would say, "Now will you all shut up. I know it's not Danitra." (I'm rewriting my history to fit my sister's theory.) I always used humor to make my point because I found that it worked for me. If I had to tell my mother something that I thought she wouldn't like or something that would make her think I didn't like her, I would couch it in such a way that everybody would get it but they would be laughing. I never told jokes and I still don't tell jokes because I can't remember the lines. When I was at that table in second grade, they laughed because of the way I looked at things.

When I came to New York, I found out that someone who writes and performs their own stuff is a performance artist. I thought performance art was something that someone did that no one could understand. And I didn't think it could be funny.

I used to go to comedy clubs. In that tradition, you try to adjust yourself to your audience because basically you want them to laugh. So you go out there with your set jokes and if they don't respond a certain way, you say "Don't go that way because they're not gonna like it. Well what about this? Oh, they're really silly or really stupid, so just pretend you're a helicopter and they'll be happy and laugh." But I thought, "No, I'm saying what I have to say. If they don't like it, that's too bad."

It's not that it's easy to get up on the stage, start talking and say to hell with the audience. You do think about what they think, but I'm not doing it to let them be who they were when they came in anyway. Let me be who I am and see what that effect is.

The Responsibility of the Theatre Artist

The artist's responsibility is to tell the truth and not keep perpetuating a big lie on top of another big lie. In the paintings of Romare Bearden, there is a truth that you recognize and relate to; it touches you or makes you feel something; it's undeniable. If you say you're an entertainer, then you don't have a responsibility. You can just go out there and do an imitation of a butterfly and it will be funny and that's enough because you didn't say that you were an artist. And I'm not even saying that I'm an artist, because I can get up as whatever I want to. And my truth is not everybody's truth.

Selection of Characters

Certain people have stories that need to be told. One of the first characters that I had in this piece was Cabrini Green Harlem Watts Jackson. She's in the tenth grade, she's a Libra, her favorite sport is running, she's a cheerleader, she's fifteen years old and she has two children. People always see her and think she's young, she's pregnant, oh she has no future, no dreams. Well, *no*, you don't know who she is. She's just like whoever you think you are with hopes, dreams, ideals and ideas. It's not the worst thing that ever happened to her. I wanted to tell her story in a funny way because I know those girls.

A few years ago, I taught at an alternative high school where there were a lot of young women who had children. Their stories were so real and touching, but they're not really blended into Cabrini Green because I don't go for that touching stuff too much, because it's not that funny. Some reporters came to the school to do a news story on them. The headline said "Unwed Mothers . . . " And the girls said, "Miss Vance, who's a unwed mother?" I said, "You are." "What's wed have to do with it?" See, they would say, "Uh, Miss Vance, you got any kids?" No. "You married?" It was always in that order. That was how they saw it. You didn't have to be married to have a baby. It's true, isn't it?

These stories must be told in order to get to the truth of why these things happen. They need to have their story told truthfully just as much as an astronaut or athletes or singers. I bring the same intelligence to a crack-addicted homeless person as I would to somebody who is a positive role model.

Point of View and the Comedic Form

If white is the highest on the totem pole, I'm not that. If male is the highest, I'm not that. I am a black woman, which is supposedly the bottom. To me, the bottom is the most powerful position to be in because you can see the sun. If everybody else is so busy looking down at you, they're missing out on what's going on in the whole rest of the world, while we're looking up and seeing everything there is to see. Even if they're blocking your view, it is better to be able to see all the things that are over you than to be looking down on the ground.

My comedy comes out of looking up from the bottom. You take the thing that you see and you always tend to think that you're looking down on it. In the fall, there are all these leaves that get a bit wet on the bottom. They look like one thing on the top, but if you pick it up and turn it over, it's a whole different leaf on the other side. I try to flip things over, show that other side, turn things inside out and even upside down. I take each character's life in that way and say, if this was me, what's the truth of that?

When I was a little girl, I used to think "I'm everything that there is in the whole world so I should be able to understand everything there is to understand because everything is me." In my shows (but not this one), I usually say, "I think of myself as Everywoman and some men." Most shows that I do have a lot to do with gender identification, transexuality, but this show is more about race.

Artistic Challenges and Discoveries

There's something about the American culture that is expressed so perfectly in the television talk-show format. It's become a way of healing people through the TV. It's very odd that people are so willing to open up their wounds to strangers, especially thousands of people they don't even see. In this show, I play different channels, talk-show hosts, guests and even people off-camera. It was a challenge for me as an actor, and I thought it would be fun to play a lot of different characters and have them interact and communicate. The biggest challenge with this show is to get the audience to ask questions.

I believe in keeping everything to a minimum. This show had a technical thing that I would ordinarily stay away from, but it had a theme or concept—which is another thing that I don't particularly care for—I was exploring my fascination with the talk-show format. I've learned that it's better for me to stay away from any kind of high-concept; but this show was a low-tech high-concept—or a low-concept high-tech—show.

Distinctions between Women's and Men's Writing
When you say women, you say we.

You know how people say that there are two kinds of people in the world? I tend to think there are probably more than two kinds, but if we want to say that there are only two kinds, what are they? I used to say that there were men and women. Now I say there are artists and non-artists. I keep changing it all the time. You find your own family and relate to people who are of like mind whether they're male or female or whatever they may be. Any group that I say I like will always show out, as my grandmother would say. I love my black people because that's my family and it's me, but you can't say "Elect a black president and everything's gonna be fine," because we are conservative and we are crazy and we're everything everybody else is. You can't like a group, you can only like individuals. So when you think about male and female and breaking it down that way, it's like—"Oh excuse me, but put her over there with them. Okay, bring him over here with us."

Definitions of Heroism
Me, of course! I'm always the hero of all my dreams. Heroism is just me being me out there doing it. I used to think that some force or some institution could stop you from doing what you wanted to do. Well actually no one can stop you. You may not be able to do it on HBO or in prime time, but if you have something you want to say or do, you can do it. I think of myself as a hero because I'm the one out there jumping around, saying all these things. People can like me or not like me or laugh at me or hiss at me. Once you're out there on the edge, there's no place to go except over the edge.

The Cultivation of the Craft
Acting school can be bad because it makes you focus so much on how to act. Then you go to see plays and try to figure out how to act the way somebody else acts. Good actors act like people, not other actors. It's so important not to spend a lot of time going to drama school because you have to be able to read the paper, look at other people, see whatever is real in the world and then bring that onstage with you. You have to have something to say.

My grandfather used to say that class, especially in the black community, doesn't have anything to do with how much money you have. You all live in the same neighborhood, you're all black, and you can have different classes within the same family because it's really about awareness. You have to open your eyes and be aware of all the things that are going on around you, filtering them through whatever it is that is you in order to know yourself. That life is the truth that you're trying to bring onstage, even though it's all an illusion. You're creating the illusion of life.

The Darkness and the Light

Einstein kept trying to figure out what keeps the world together. Every time he got closer to figuring out what the thing was, it would disappear and the theory wouldn't work. He finally decided that whatever keeps the world together, that's what God is. If the halo of blackness around the Milky Way is what allows us to see it, then God is a black thing—which is why I ain't no African American. I'm black, with the same mysterious halo. It's not an African-American halo; it's a black halo. See?

The light and the dark influence the work that you have to do, and that makes it more interesting than trying to choose one. Sometimes something seems bright that isn't. Sometimes something seems dark, but within that darkness is a certain something wonderful that you can't see with your eyes.

ABOUT THE AUTHOR

After graduating with honors from Roosevelt University, Danitra Vance performed in clubs in Chicago and at the American Folk Theatre and other venues in New York City, where she formed her own company, Women in Comedy Lab, with Bronwyn Rucker. Her performance-art career was launched at La MaMa E.T.C., which presented her and the Mell-O White Boys (Steve Canale, Rob Yampolsky and Ron Stach—alternates Geoff Allnut and Jones Miller). Her performance piece *D' Vance & D' Boys* was premiered on the West Coast by Life on the Water in San Francisco. Producer Lorne Michaels subsequently recruited Vance for the eleventh season of NBC's *Saturday Night Live*. She appeared in the New York Shakespeare Festival's production of George C. Wolfe's *The Colored Museum* and in *Spunk*, his adaptation of three stories by Zora Neale Hurston, at Crossroads Theatre Company and the New York Shakespeare Festival as well as in Los Angeles and London. Her recent films include *Sticky Fingers, Limit Up, Little Man Tate* and *Jumpin' at the Boneyard* (which won her a nomination as best supporting actress in the 1993 Independent Spirit Awards). She is the recipient of an NAACP Image Award and a Drama-Logue Award for her performance in *The*

Colored Museum, and Obie and Drama-Logue awards for *Spunk.* She has published essays in *Genesis Journal, Women of Power* and the anthology *The Choices We Made* (Random House, 1990).

ABOUT THE WORK

Live and In Color!, a one-woman show, was presented as part of Crossroads Theatre Company's 1991 Genesis Festival of New Plays. Shelby Jiggetts served as dramaturg/director. Some of the material has also been seen in the context of Danitra Vance's performances with the Mell-O White Boys at La MaMa E.T.C., the New York Shakespeare Festival, Carnegie Hall, Life on the Water, the New Museum of Contemporary Art, the Mark Taper Forum and the Royal Court Theatre, among other venues.

LIVE AND IN COLOR!

PART ONE

*A full-size foam mattress on the floor is made up like a bed. Pa-
pers, notebooks, a bottle of water, a phone are all around the bed.
The covers and pillows are arranged so that it looks as if there
were someone in the bed. Maybe there are also some costumes under the covers. On a platform closer to center is the Talk Show set.
There are four chairs: three for the guests and one for the host.
There is a television with a remote control. The television also
serves as a monitor for the audience. In the audience, there are
two microphones and a video camera that picks up Danitra and
the audience as indicated.*

*We hear a scream in the dark. Lights up on Danitra in the bed.
She pulls the covers down from over her head and continues
screaming.*

DANITRA:

Sometimes I wake up screaming.

Sometimes I believe I'm clinically depressed.

Maybe my show is on. *(She turns on TV using the remote control)* Naaaa. *(She turns off TV with remote. She picks up the Singleton Maxwell Notebook and reads)*

[SINGLETON MAXWELL M.D./MIDOL JUNKIE]

SINGLETON MAXWELL M.D.: This message is for women only because men really don't have a clue, do they. Adam was not a
rough draft, Adam was a doodle. Ladies I am Singleton Maxwell M.D., the woman gynecologist that designed the O.B.
Method. I am currently on a lecture tour, with a presentation
entitled WARNING: THE DANGER OF BEING A WOMAN.
I have spoken before many prestigious groups including most
recently a joint meeting of the League of Women Intellectuals
and the Sluts Against Smut.

I became a gynecologist because of my gynecological mysteries. Our combined gynecological mysteries prompted me to write a pamphlet *(Shows cover) Between Your Legs and You.* You can pick it up almost anywhere. In the book I postulate, "Is there a Capitalist plot against women?" I mean to say.... Why is it that whenever I have monthly pain the first thing I think of is give me strength, give me antiprostaglandins, give me antispasmodics, give me drugs.

She puts on her sunglasses. Traditional blues music underscores the following monologue.

SINGLETON MAXWELL M.D./MIDOL JUNKIE *(Singing)*:
> In the kitchen barefoot expecting my eighth child
> I must take my Midol, so I don't go wild
> I'm a Midol junkie and I don't know why
> Keeps me feeling funky so I take it all the time
> It helps before, during and after
> Gives me laughter through my tears
> I've been on it for years
> It helps my lower back pain
> Takes away the strain of being a Woman Woman Woman
> WOMAN, WO-O-O-M-A-A-A-N
>
> Yes I'm a Woman W-O . . . W-O *(Forgets lyrics)*
> Yes I'm a Woman W-O *(Still can't remember)*

(Spoken) Baby you don't know me. I killed my first husband. It wasn't really my fault though. It all happened the night before my period was supposed to start and I am sure it was the hormonal imbalance that led me to commit murder. "Did I have to kill him?" "Did I have to kill him?" "Did I have to kill him?" Yes, I had to kill him. He hit me, and I always told myself I would never stay with anybody who hit me. While I packed the scenario unfolded. I leave him, he finds me, he looks pitiful and boyish, I forgive him, we spend six blissful months together. He hits me again, harder, then he says "I'm sorry baby, I love you more than life itself, doesn't six months

of bliss mean anything to you?" He cries, I cry, a year of happiness until he loses his job, bam bam bam, he buys me a puppy, a cute little black springer spaniel, he kicks the dog. . . . I'm living the life of the battered wife. I watch Oprah and Phil and Sally and Shirley and Jane and Wilma and Betty and Veronica. . . . I started to wonder who would play me in the made-for-TV version of my life. My lawyer said for me to plead insanity and I said I thought that was just for men. I went to prison.

(Singing)
> W-O . . . W-O. . . . Oh you know,
> Oh you know, o. u. know, all of you know.
> I may not be able to spell my name
> but Midol keeps me tame
> when I'm feeling evil.

(Spoken) Take only as directed.

Danitra goes back to bed. Chitchats. She picks up the Clair Voyant Notebook.

[CLAIR VOYANT—RAH RAH RAH]

CLAIR VOYANT: We are in the house of worship. In this house of worship, they don't believe in God or Allah or Yahweh. They believe in the powers-that-be. And when they get the feeling, when they want to be a witness, when they have a comment about something, they don't say amen or shalom or Abslum I slinkum, they say Rah Rah Rah. Can you say that? Say it again. Rah Rah Rah. Yea. So when you feel it, say Rah Rah Rah.

Welcome to the Temple of the Chanting Guru Jesus Allah Mode. Where we have combined the religions of the East and the beliefs of the West and created what we consider to be the very best. We call it insanity. Yes friends, you too can be a lunatic. For those of you who are here for the very first time, I am your high priestess, *(Marching)* the drum majorette for the downhearted, the pom-pom girl *(Gestures)* for people with pent-up frustrations, the cheerleader for the cheerless. Rah Rah Rah. I am a pyromaniac here to light up your life. My name is Clair Voyant and I know what you're thinking. You are thinking, "Who, in the name of the father, in the name of the son, in the name of the holy ghost and Mrs. Muir, is she?"

Well let me tell you a little bit about me. I am a psychotherapist, a psychodramatist, a spiritual reader, a faith healer and a part-time country/western singer. *(High-pitched scream)* I get the feeling, I get the feeling, I get the feeling that some of you are wondering, "What can she do for me?" Well, I say unto you—you tired, you poor, you huddled masses yearning to breathe free—ask not what Clair Voyant can do for you; ask what you can do for Clair Voyant. For the powers-that-be help me help thee. When you're weary, feeling small, when tears are in your eyes, I will dry them all. I'm on your side when times are tough and pain is all around, like a bridge over troubled water, like a bridge over troubled water, like a, like a, like a bridge over troubled water, I will lay me down. Oh yes, walk on my legs, kneel on my back, sit on my face. You can't hurt me—I'm a bridge. You can't hurt me, you can only help yourself. Help yourself out of the usual into the unusual, out of the ordinary into the extra-ordinary, out of the normal into the abnormal.

Are you a normal person? Most people are. But we here at the Temple of the Chanting Guru Jesus Allah Mode believe even people who have been normal their entire lives can be cured. I mean, why be a plain box of popcorn or why be a plain box of caramel corn when you can be a box of Crackerjacks, a surprise in every pack? Oh yes. You, you *(Points out someone in audience)* might be a teeny-tiny riddle book. You, you *(Chooses someone else)* might be a plastic pinky ring. Or you, *(Chooses someone else)* you might be a lick-on tattoo.

But there is something special in each & every one of you here tonight. Come, come, come into my arms, let me know the wonder of all of you all of you baby I love you. Now, whoa whoa whoa, now, whoa whoa whoa, now & hold on fast, could this be the magic at last? Free at last, free at last, thank the powers-that-be, you too may soon be free. For if you're tired, lonely, brokenhearted or ugly; if you're sad, bitter, twisted or afraid; if you have a headache, sore feet or iron-poor blood— you don't need a doctor. You don't need a doctor. *(Stomps foot)* No! You don't need a doctor. *(Does the happy hallelujah dance)* You don't need a doctor, no, you don't. *(Stoops then leaps into the air)* YOU DON'T NEEEEEED a doctor. What you need is a mechanic for your mind. *(High-pitched scream)*

I get the feeling, I get the feeling, I get the feeling that we have a few nonbelievers with us here tonight. And for you nonbelievers, I have one simple question: Are you a hardtop or a convertible? This is a very important question, because we here at the Temple believe the human mind is a lot like an automobile. Yet very few of us care for our minds as carefully as we care for our cars. Is your mind new or used? When was the last time you had your points & plugs checked? Had your wheels rotated? How long have you had your present mind? These are all very important questions, children. And I am reminded of our topic for tonight which is why—I ask you why—I say unto you, why are women depressed? *(Pause)* Who cares?

Then I was thumbing through a book the other day, *Unfinished Business* by sister Maggie Scarf, $14.95 Doubleday Press, and she said women are depressed because they care. Men care more about their jobs and women care more about people. Men can't understand that because as baby boys, men could not distinguish between a line drawing and a picture of a human face. Later I was leafin' through the paper and I came across this article. *(Raises gigantic Xerox over her head)* "My God It's Difficult to Be a Woman" it say "My God It's Difficult to Be a Woman" oh, yes "MY GOD IT'S DIFFICULT TO BE A WOMAN," and I just had to read it because it was written by a man. *(Reads from the article)* In conclusion, Andrew M. Greeley tells us, "What we need is a reorientation of our social values, so that emotions are considered at least as important as achievement; then there would be no need for these painful bouts of depression." This man is a lunatic. And you too can be a lunatic. All you have to do is heal yourselves. I can't touch every one of you, although I might like to. You have to heal yourself.

Now, a car has a horn to honk, and we have mouths with which to scream. So simply watch this all-the-way live demonstration & then do as I do. When I say heal, I want you to honk your horns like this. "Heal." *(She slaps the palm of her hand to her forehead and screams as long and as loud as she can)* All of you can do this. Heal! *(She and audience scream)* Pitiful. It don't cost you nothing. Heal! *(She and audience scream)* You know you can do better. Heal! *(Everyone Really Screaming)* Now don't you feel better? You have just taken your first step out of the ordinary into the extra-ordinary.

Danitra goes back to bed, turns on TV with remote control.

DANITRA: Nope. *(She cuts the TV off. Picks up the Aquanetta Feinstein Notebook)*

[AQUANETTA FEINSTEIN—COLOR ME AQUANETTA]

AQUANETTA: When I was in high school in Chicago, they had me in the retarded class. Now that I'm living in New York City, I'm what you call a avant-garde rap artist.

I have three ablums, one is "Aquanetta Feinstein and the Automatic Drips Good to the Last Drip" and I have a solo ablum of which I am very proud. It's called "Color Me Aquanetta."

The reason I am so popular is because I have a philosophy of art...I think art should be about the artist. Art should be about the person making the art. Art should be what you call "autobiological."

This is called "Rainbow Coalition."

Working
in a popular, trendy department store
behind the slipper bar,
a man looks at the shoes and remarks, " '(&-%$)."
I say, "What."

He says, "'(*-$#&'#)."
I say, "What."
He says, "Did you hear what I said,
I said faggot shoes.
No I'm just kidding."
And I scream.
We are all faggots.
You remind me of Joan Crawford,
except for the eyebrows.
Sometimes
I believe
I am Linda Evans.

Visiting SoHo,
arty, farty, lap-of-luxury lofts
a woman in size three-and-a-half, triple "E" shoes
        mumbles
"He's a wretch." "He's such a wretch."
On my way to the little girls' room I scream.
WE ARE ALL WRETCHES.
WE ARE ALL WAXED LIPS.
WE ARE ALL SANDALS LIKE WHAT JESUS WORE.

Eastside Upper Westside all around the town
a cavalier California girl depresses me with a tale of a
suicidal paraplegic with brain damage, before she can
describe the wedding night, I leave.
On my way to the "A" train,
no longer the Duke Ellington train I scream...
We are all suicidal.
We are all overwound watches.
We are ALL SPINACH AND BRUSSEL SPROUT
        ON CRUTCHES.

WHO DO YOU THINK YOU ARE—YOUR NAME
MALCOLM X
a dead hero—dead
but not dead like Jimi Hendrix

Lizzie Borden
the perfect murderess
not like Jean Harris the diet-doctor killer
Frances Farmer and Billie Holiday
WE ARE ALL ENDANGERED SPECIES.

We are all earth
and air
and fire
and water
even if we don't believe in Shirley MacLaine.

I am somebody
I am somebody else
Y'all too

I am the Pulitzer Prize
I am the Nobel Prize
I am the prize inside Captain Crunch
Silly rabbit, Trix are for kids
We are all kids
We are all bunnies dressed up like waitresses.

We are all cousins
This is my country, land that I love
We are all foreigners
WE ARE ALL RAISINS
AND RAISINETTES
AND JU-JU-BEES.

PART TWO

Danitra picks up remote from bed. Crosses to Talk Show set.

DANITRA: Maybe I watch too much television. Na! I only watch talk shows.

She clicks on TV with remote. She sits in the host chair, facing the audience. Video camera picks her up; she is on the monitor. As she becomes each character, she moves to a different chair.

HOST: For those of you just joining us, my guest is noted dance therapist Tracy Dance Donaldson. In your book, you ask the question: "Are white people really rhythmically retarded?"

TRACY: I speak of neighborhood after neighborhood, area upon area, where children and parents alike, having not been exposed to rhythm or blues, or even as much as an Aretha Franklin album to call their own. This rhythmic deprivation inevitably leads to rhythmic retardation.

HOST: Well, that's very controversial. And I'm sure the audience wants to get in on this. So let's bring the house lights up, and you in the audience can just step up to the mike.

House lights up. Camera pans studio audience, rests on microphone. The Host encourages the audience to ask questions. Host and guest improvise responses to audience.

Tracy, have you finally proved why white people can't dance?

Camera back to Host. House lights down.

TRACY: Yes. From my first study, those were my findings. But I have recently reinterpreted my research and come to the conclusion that Euro-Americans actually refuse to learn to dance.

HOST: Why the new slant?

TRACY: New Kids on the Block. All those little noncolored-colorless-non-African-American girls had New Edition all over their bedroom walls. I know their Eurocentric parents did not like seeing the handsome black boys in their little girls' rooms. So, what I call the New Elvis syndrome sets in and poof! New Kids. Poof, they can dance after hours and hours of practice and promises of fame and fortune. They learned to dance all the popular dances because they were motivated. Motivated by the almighty dollar. When white people smell

green, they can be any color. Or at least, imitate any color...
Miss Saigon, Westside Story—Pinky!

HOST: You seem so angry. When you were here before you were so
serene.

TRACY: I didn't want to lower myself to the level of the white bigots
who claim we are inferior. I am not prejudiced. I have been
explaining them to them for so long. I have been trying to
prove they are not inferior to illustrate a point. But maybe it's
too much. Michael McDonald records. Too much Hall and
Oates. Maybe I heard Michael Bolton's version of "Georgia on
My Mind" too many times. Then again, *(Near tears)* I think
Vanilla Ice pushed me over the edge. And the white rap group
called Young Black Teenagers... it's too much!

TV channel changes. On camera: full body shot of Robin the Reluctant Transsexual.

ROBIN: I had only been a man for a couple of years when I recorded "I'm a Man, I Can Do Anything." I was still excited.
All the possibilities of masculinity lay before me. I had suits
from Brooks Brothers, vocabulary from Brooklyn Navy Yard. I
had a job and a future.

I tried dating. Then I lost my job. Then, I joined a men's
rights group and discovered I was more oppressed now, as a
man, than I ever was as a woman.

I get these animalistic urges. I belong to the most violent,
unreasonable, viperous, bearish aspect of the human race.

My next hit was "I've Got a Ding Dong...I Call Him
Goofy." *(Stands and gyrates hips)*

> I've got a ding dong...I call him Goofy
> The things he does are unpredictable to—to me
> Think Thang, Thing Thang, My Thang, Ding Dong

When I was a woman, I used to think too much. Now I don't
think at all. This thing down here is such a nuisance. I'll be on
the subway and I don't know why I have to sit like this. *(Sits*

with legs spread wide apart) Then, some chick will get on and try to squeeze in between me and another guy sittin' the same way. One says somethin' like, "Judging from your shoes and fingers, your dick is not so big you can't put your legs together. And if your schlong is so long you can't put your legs together, maybe you better stand up and let that pregnant woman sit down." Then the white guy next to me stood up. The pregnant lady sat down and there's me squeezed up next to the rail like this. *(Demonstrates)*

Danitra becomes Nefertiti Ali-Baba.

ALI-BABA: That's what I'm talkin' 'bout. The Black woman has no respect for the Black man.

ROBIN: She was a white chick.

ALI-BABA: Thank you for correctin' me, brother.

HOST: Joining us in our discussion is Nefertiti Ali-Baba.

ALI-BABA: Y'all know me as the author of the big-sellin' book, *The Brothers' Road Map to Understanding Sisters (And I Use the Word Loosely)*. I have recently completed a new book, a better book. Probably the book I should have written first, *The Black Man's Guide to Understanding the White Woman*. Because you know the problem with the Black woman is that she tries too much to be like the White woman and if the Black man can understand the White woman, he can surely understand the Black woman. The majority of whom are just inexpensive imitations of White women.

HOST: Let me make sure I understand what you are saying, Miss Ali-Baba. You, a Black woman, you are sitting here on my nationally televised talk show and you are saying the Black woman is only a cheap imitation of the White woman?

ALI-BABA: There's connotation and denotation and if I have to tell you the difference between cheap and inexpensive, maybe I shouldn't even try to talk to you. I should have a pow-wow with my brother here and leave you the hell out of it.

Host bristles.

ROBIN: There's no need to be disrespectful to the hostess there, Miss Ali-Baba.

ALI-BABA: I'm sorry, my brother. And if I step out of line again, feel free to give me an open-handed slap across the mouth.

Channel changes.

WOMAN GUEST: When I got to LAX, there was no one there to meet me, so I took the shuttle. By the time I got off at Phil and Chris's, a guy there told me Chris had to go to the emergency room and when they came home, Chris went to bed. Phil told me that Chris had AIDS and that he, Phil, was HIV positive.

I thought to myself, it's a good thing I am who I am or this could be . . . not too cute. I didn't know a lot about AIDS. I shook hands with a person with AIDS before I knew what it was. What I'm saying is I never lived with someone with AIDS. I never lived with someone HIV positive and I was afraid. I was afraid I'd turn stupid.

Part of me thought I might throw up my hands and run screaming from the house. I mean part of me wanted to want to do that. This was a few years ago and AIDS was in the paper and on the news every day and everyone seemed to be a little hysterical.

I guess I'm not a hysterical person.

HOST: You say you're not a hysterical person. If there was a time for hysteria, it would have been then. Had you seen something or read something that—

WOMAN GUEST: I had seen you on your talk show.

HOST: You know, I always like to think this show performs a public service, that it enlightens and educates—

WOMAN GUEST: No. You had a PWA on your show and the entire audience hated him. And you never touched him. You didn't shake his hand. You even sat a chair or two away from him and stretched your microphone over to him. You could have taught this country how to be humane but you seemed to side with ignorance. Even your expert doctor said he couldn't guarantee these were the only ways to get the virus. I knew I didn't want to be like you.

HOST: You seem to. . . . You've given us so much. . . . Let's go to a commercial right now.

Camera is turned off.

I don't know who you think you are, but this is my show. How dare you get up on national television and humiliate *me*!

WOMAN GUEST: How dare you get up on national television and dehumanize every person with AIDS. Where was all that compassion and intelligence you talk-show hosts are supposed to have?

HOST: Let me tell you something, Miss Holier Than Me, I am famous for my compassion, my sympathy, my empathy, my Ph.D. *People* magazine named me one of this year's "Most Fabulous People" because of my warmth and compassion.

WOMAN GUEST: I used to feel the same way until I saw that show.

HOST: We're coming back from commercial in about one minute and I want you to tell the viewing audience you saw that on someone else's show. Tell them I didn't do that.

WOMAN GUEST: Honey, when you come back from commercial, you won't have a guest to talk to. I didn't come here for this.

HOST: Oh! Believe me, I can run this show without you or any other guest. But let's see how you run the show without me. *(Walks off the set)*

WOMAN GUEST *(To audience)*: How many of you saw that show? It was a few years ago. *(No response)* If the host doesn't come back, will some of you go to the microphones and ask me questions about living with someone who has AIDS or—

VOICE OF THE DIRECTOR: We're back!

Woman Guest looks blank, clueless, lonely. She looks toward the wings for the Host. She looks toward the audience. "Help" is written in her eyes. If an audience member gets up, we'll take the question. If not . . .

You're turning stupid.

WOMAN GUEST: I didn't want to turn stupid. I gave Phil a big real hug. Not a cheek-to-cheek, hand-on-the-shoulders hug, a *real* hug. And I hugged Chris the same way. But stupidity always lurked somewhere. *(Screams)* The toilet seat! I always put tissue on the seat. That's how my grandmother raised me. Maybe I should sit on the bare seat to prove I wasn't afraid of AIDS. Prove to who? *(Screams)* The shower! I can't get it from taking a shower. EEK! The razors! I don't use other people's razors anyway. Dishes! Couldn't I be the first, the very first person to contract AIDS in some odd, unusual way? I mean, doctors and nurses in hospitals wear gloves and masks and stuff. Yes! No! Maybe. Yes! No! Stop it!

I wasn't having sex with them. I had never had a blood transfusion. I was not an IV drug user. If there was some other way for me to get AIDS, some other way no one knew about, then okay. I would be an innocent victim just like Phil and Chris and everyone else fighting this syndrome or that disease or any other malady.

Not long after that, I found a lump in my breast. I had a mastectomy. Then I started this book. All proceeds go to the National Fund for Sick People. *Funny Things People Say to People That Are Sick:*

"I thought you were dead."

"Why don't you have the other one removed?"

"How are you?"

You can ask me questions now.

Questions from audience. Pause.

Oh, okay, nobody wants to talk to me. I see some of you are wearing red ribbons. Big deal! What difference does that make? Go hold a crack baby. Go hold an AIDS baby. You want a medal for that? If that ribbon was made out of ten pounds of steel that you had to sling over your shoulder, that might say something. "Count me, too. I'm struggling, too." Fifty thousand women die every year of breast cancer. Wear a ten-pound ribbon for them and one for lupus and one for diabetes and every other life-threatening, life-altering—. Since this is a talk show, and since this is *my* talk show. That's all I have to say.

Camera holds on Woman Guest for uncomfortable moments, then pans the audience. Blackout.

EPILOGUE

Lights up on Danitra in the bed. She picks up The Complete Works of Shakespeare.

[FLOTILDA WILLIAMS AS JULIET]

FLOTILDA: I'm Flotilda Williams. I'm a classical actress. Right now I am in a production downtown with a group called Shakespeare in the Slums. We are doing a play by Mister William Shakespeares call *Romeo and Juliet*. And me, I'm Juliet, okay. Now what I want to do for y'all is to extrapolate and explainate on what be going on in the show. The show starts and a lot of things happen but really we just gonna skip all that and get to the good part, where I come in.

I'm at this party, a lot of fancy people there and I'm there and I'm there with my Mama and the Nurse. Even so I manage to meet this guy. A very good-lookin' guy, makes me laugh with his funny funny jokes, probably got some money. So I like him. His name is Romeo. I have thus extrapolated the title—Romeo and me, Juliet, okay.

Anyway the party is not even half over when my Mama and the Nurse say, "Juliet it's time to go." And I say, "Okay, I'll be right with you." So she find Romeo and they say goodbye by touching fingertips like this, *(Gesture)* completely missing the point.

After that I go home and I'm trying to be asleep but I can't sleep 'cause I'm thinkin' 'bout this guy. How much I want to see him again. How much I want to talk to him again. How much I want to do things with him I've never done before.

Now in the meantime the guy, Romeo, is down in the alleyway lookin' up in my window. Now he not lookin' up in my window because he a freak or nothin' like that, he lookin' up in my window because he like me, okay. Then he start to talk to hisself. Now, he not talkin' to hisself 'cause he crazy or nothin', he talk to hisself 'cause it's a play, okay. People in plays talk to theyselves a lot.

And he say, he say,
"But soft! what light throo yonder windo' break?"
That's when I break through the window.

It's nighttime and I'm on my back porch and I'm in a really bad mood because of this whole situation. And I say my first line, stomp my foot and say,
"Ay me!
O, Romeo, Romeo! wherefore art thou Romeo?"
Wherefore mean why. She sayin' why why why you gots to be Romeo? Wherefore art thou Romeo!!!

"Deny thy father and refuse thy name;
Or, if thou wilt not, be but sworn my love
And I'll no longer be a Capsulet"
And she thinking,
"'Tis but thy name that is my enemy
Thou art thyself, though not a Montagoo."

What's a Montagoo?

"It is nor hand, nor foot,
Nor arm nor face, nor any other part
Belonging to a man."

You know what she talking about. So she say,
"Romeo, doff thy name,
And for that name which is no part of thee
Take all myself."

Juliet was hip, you dig. She had it going on and she was down. So anyway, you know their families had a kinda Family Feud-type thing going on. Juliet family, maybe like the Crypts and Romeo people could be like the Bloods, you know what I'm

saying. And Romeo is not like Michael Jackson, he's a lover
and a fighter, okay. Then she see him down in the alleyway
and they talk and talk all lovey-dovey lovey-dovey—back and
forth back and forth, beat beat, beat beat. They got a passionate blood flow going back and forth. I got really good reviews
on this part. Spend some money, get some culture.

Then she say to him,
"My bounty is as boundless as the sea,
My love as deep; the more I give to thee,
The more I have, for both are infinite.
(Hears noise)
I hear some noise within, dear love, adieu."
That mean 'bye.
"Anon, good nurse!"
That mean I'll be right with you, nurse.
"Sweet Montagoo, be true.
Stay but a little, I will come again."

Then she gone. Then she come right back but she has to be
really quiet 'cause her Mama n Daddy can't stand his Mama n
Daddy n his Mama n Daddy can't stand her Mama n Daddy.
So they have to be really really quiet 'cause if they catch them
together, they'll kill him n her too. So she say, she say,
"Three words dear Romeo, and goodnight indeed.
If that thy bent of love be honorable,
Thy purpose marriage, send me word tomorrow,
By one that I'll procure to come to thee,
Where and at what time thou wilt perform the rite."
That mean marry me, marry me,
I'm not giving up nothin' till you marry me.
"And all my fortunes at thy foot I'll lay
And follow thee, my lord, throughout the world.
(Hears noise)
I come anon.—But if thou mean'st not well
I do beseech thee
(Noise)
By and by, I come—

To cease thy suit and leave me to my grief."
That mean if you not gonna marry me, don't mess with my mind. I can find somebody else.
"A thousand times goodnight."

Then she gone again. This time she gone a little bit longer because she had to talk to her Mama n the Nurse. I don't know why she had to talk to the Nurse 'cause you know she not sick.

She back as soon as she can but she can't see Romeo. But she know he gotta be out there somewhere 'cause they got that passionate blood flow going back and forth back and forth and she can feel him out there beatin' in the night. What she want to do is holler "Yo, Romeo, where you at?" But she can't do that because Juliet is a very dignified girl, and hollerin' off the back porch is a very iginant thing to do. So she say, she say,
"Romeo, hist, Romeo."
Then she see him.
"'Tis almost morning. I would have thee gone
And yet no further than a wanton's bird
Who lets it hop a little from her hand
Like a poor prisoner in his twisted gyves
And with a silk thread plucks it back again
So loving-jealous of his liberty."
I don't know what that part mean.
Then she say,
"Good night. Good night! parting is such sweet sorrow
That I shall say goodnight till it be morrow."

(Exits)

This page serves as a continuation of the copyright page.

Inquiries regarding individual plays should be addressed to the following:
Cage Rhythm *copyright © 1993, 1994 by Kia Corthron. All inquiries regarding rights should be addressed to John B. Santoianni, The Tantleff Office, 375 Greenwich Street, Suite 700, New York, NY 10013, (212) 941-3939.*
The Death of the Last Black Man in the Whole Entire World *copyright © 1989, 1992 by Suzan-Lori Parks. All inquiries regarding rights should be addressed to Brad Kalos, ICM, 40 West 57th Street, New York, NY 10019, (212) 556-5600.*
The Dramatic Circle *copyright © 1992 by Adrienne Kennedy. All inquiries regarding rights should be addressed to Bridgett Aschenberg, ICM, 40 West 57th Street, New York, NY 10019, (212) 556-5600.*
Fires in the Mirror *copyright © 1992, 1993 by Anna Deavere Smith.*
For live stage amateur and stock performances contact Dramatists Play Service, 440 Park Ave. South, New York, NY 10016, (212) 683-8960. For all other rights contact Suzanne Gluck, ICM, 40 West 57th Street, New York, NY 10019, (212) 556-5600.
Live and In Color! *copyright © 1991, 1994 by Danitra Vance. All inquiries regarding rights should be addressed to Frank Frattaroli, William Morris Agency, 1350 Ave. of the Americas, New York, NY 10019, (212) 586-5100.*
The Mojo and the Sayso *copyright © 1989 by Aishah Rahman. All inquiries regarding rights should be addressed to Broadway Play Publishing Inc., 357 West 20th St., New York, NY 10011, (212) 627-1055.*
The Resurrection of the Daughter: Liliane *copyright © 1993, 1994 by Ntozake Shange. All inquiries regarding rights should be addressed to David Guc, The Gersh Agency, 130 West 42nd St., New York, NY 10036, (212) 997-1818.*
Sally's Rape *copyright © 1991 by Robbie McCauley. All inquiries regarding rights should be addressed to Harold Schmidt Literary Agency, 668 Greenwich Street, Suite 1005, New York, NY 10014, (212) 727-7473.*
White Chocolate for My Father *copyright © 1992 by Laurie Carlos. All inquiries regarding rights should be addressed to Harold Schmidt Literary Agency, 668 Greenwich Street, Suite 1005, New York, NY 10014, (212) 727-7473.*
WOMBmanWARs *copyright © 1991 by Judith Alexa Jackson.*
All inquiries regarding rights should be addressed to Judith Alexa Jackson, 214-216 Avenue A, New York, NY 10009.
X *copyright © 1986 by Thulani Davis. All inquiries regarding rights should be addressed to Faith Childs Literary Agency, 275 West 96th St., New York, NY 10025, (212) 662-1232.*